THE UNIVERSITY
LOOKS ABROAD:

Approaches to World Affairs at
Six American Universities

Education and World Affairs

Established in 1962 as a private, nonprofit educational organization, Education and World Affairs is concerned chiefly with the activities of American colleges and universities in international relations. Its principal purpose is to study, analyze and make recommendations about those activities. Its priorities and approaches are determined by its Board of Trustees and are based on continuous consultations with American universities and colleges and many other private groups as well as with United States governmental agencies. EWA draws its basic support from grants of the Ford Foundation and the Carnegie Corporation of New York made when the organization was launched in 1962.

The views expressed in its publications are those of Education and World Affairs itself, its study committees, or individual authors, as the case may be. They are not necessarily the views of the foundations and other donors whose funds support the organization's work.

Board of Trustees

THE UNIVERSITY
LOOKS ABROAD:

*Approaches to World Affairs at
Six American Universities*

A report from Education and World Affairs

WALKER AND COMPANY / *New York*

CONTENTS

MICHIGAN STATE   47

TULANE   99

INDIANA   **219**

THE UNIVERSITY IN WORLD AFFAIRS:

AN INTRODUCTION

by William W. Marvel, President, Education and World Affairs

No one has yet fully tabulated the many roles universities play in twentieth century society—and it is unlikely that anyone ever will. There are too many; the roster grows too rapidly; and, perhaps above all, variations from one country to another greatly complicate the task. But even a full catalog would reveal little we do not already know; it would simply support our recognition of the university as one of the most adaptable and evolutionary institutions of man's invention. There is pure fascination in the thought that a modern complexity such as Berkeley can trace its lineage back almost a thousand years to the medieval establishments at Bologna and Salamanca. And there is even greater fascination in contemplating the growth which this extended family system will experience, in every corner of the world, in the remaining years of this century.

Small wonder, therefore, that the university is the object of such world-wide attention, curiosity and affection. It has become a first necessity of every newly independent country, frequently ranking ahead of a national airline as a prestige symbol. In many parts of Latin America, the perception of the university is changing: the old complacency with an assemblage of faculties of medicine, pharmacy and law—the ancient mechanisms whereby society's elites perpetuated themselves—is giving way to the search for modernity, quality and inclusiveness. Rebounding from the scourges of Nazism, Fascism and war, the universities of Western Europe have shown remarkable recuperative power. No longer content with the ivory tower, high abstraction and all that the classical tradition implied, they are increasingly concerned with empiricism, the social sciences and a linking up with contemporary problems.

Who can doubt that in the Soviet Union the universities have been major change agents in the maturation of that country as a great power, or in the "mellowing" of its role in world politics? Indeed, the first moves in the post-Stalin era to open up more normal intercourse with the West were in the field of educational and scientific exchanges, and therefore focused on the universities. The United Kingdom in the last few years has been going through an experience that in its case is unique: an intensive re-examination of the relevance and adequacy of its higher educational system. That country is now adding new universities and modifying its traditional approach in ways that would have been unimaginable a decade ago. The list could be expanded: in Japan, Australia, Egypt, India and certainly not least Communist China (about which we in the United States know so little) universities have come to bulk large in the calculations of national leadership.

Thus, the concerted attention we in the United States have given our colleges and universities in the last fifteen or twenty years is not a peculiarly American phenomenon. The growth and change of our higher educational system, the extent to which our universities have become the object of inquiry, review and commentary, and the democratization of access to higher education—in all these things the differences that mark American developments are those of degree. We are part of a great world-wide effort of reshaping the university and strengthening its bonds with society—a movement largely stimulated by developments in the United States.

One tendency to be seen in this simultaneous, universal concern with education and especially with institutions of higher learning is the evolution of universities toward more common patterns. They are becoming increasingly similar, one to another, around the world. The point should not be exaggerated: there is little danger that universities are moving so fast in this direction that soon we shall have carbon-copy institutions around the earth. National, historical and cultural traditions, fortunately, will never cease to exert their shaping influence, to impart a certain personality and idiosyncrasy to the institutions of a particular country or region. We can be thankful for the strength of those traditions, for who would welcome a world of homogenized universities, lacking the color and flavor that diversity and variation assure?

But the trend is present. In many Latin American countries, for example, major efforts are being made to staff higher education with full-time teaching scholars, tending to bring those universities into line with the prevailing pattern in the United States and Western Europe. The increasingly prominent role of our own federal government in financing higher education makes our system more nearly comparable to the relationship of government to higher education found in other parts of the world.

Then there is the closing of the gap between science and non-science within higher education. This is far from being a massive trend, but on the other hand there can scarcely be a university leader who is not concerned about making scientists more humanistic, and assuring that humanists, social scientists and others are conversant with the purposes and methods of science. So the scientific and technological institutions will become more like general universities, while attention to science and engineering will be an increasingly strong requirement for any general university that aspires to first rank.

Even in the service role of the university, which is so distinctive a part of the American pattern, we observe a gradual involvement of European institutions of higher learning. There is no headlong rush, but there is a trend toward adding service to the traditional European university purposes of research and teaching.

It is probably inevitable that the world's universities should be moving down different but converging roads in matters of purpose, orientation, structure and staffing. They are, after all, being acted on by roughly the same constellation of forces: mounting costs of education, hence the need for huge financial investment; spiraling demands for university services, imposed by national societies in all stages of development; recognition of high-talent manpower (the "product" of universities) as a country's most precious and critical resource; the race to keep up with the advancing frontiers of scientific knowledge; and the sharp upward trend in the numbers of those seeking admission to universities, as the commitment to equality of educational opportunity becomes a nearly universal phenomenon. When an African vice-chancellor, a Latin American rector and a United States university president meet, it is obvious why they so quickly find themselves on the same wave length!

From the standpoint of the pages that follow, it is the *result* of this process that interests us. One meaning of this growing alikeness of universities, rooted as they are in distinct cultural traditions and separated by thousands of miles of ocean and desert, is the strengthening of the *international intellectual community*. Essentially, that community exists among men of learning, who seek after new knowledge, who are at home in the realm of ideas—and who feel the responsibility to transmit their learning, knowledge and ideas to their own contemporaries and to the generations that follow. It is to be found among men who are drawn together by bonds of common interest and pursuit, who communicate across national boundaries and language barriers.

In theory, such a community might exist without universities, but the possibility is remote. The university is in fact the institutional form of this intellectual community. It is in the university itself, and in the things that university people do, that one senses and feels the existence of this community. Therefore, the more agreement that exists among universities around the world on fundamental matters of purpose, role, structure and functioning, the more readily can scholars move about in the world of universities and the more easily are their ideas disseminated. Thus is the international intellectual community translated from concept to reality.

In the widest sense, it is with the membership of American colleges and universities in the intellectual community of the world that the present volume is concerned. In putting it this way, we include virtually every institution of higher learning in the United States, for surely this is not a case where some are members and others are not. Participation is a matter of degree; simply to *be* a college or university makes some extent of membership almost unavoidable. Even the most modest institution will have courses in European history, world literature and a few foreign languages. To move from there to the massive involvement in the outer world found at the universities examined in the following pages is to travel far. But there is no predetermined point on the journey where the threshold is crossed and the candidate suddenly becomes eligible for membership in the world intellectual community. That membership, one might say, is inherent in the fact of being an institution of higher learning.

If this great intellectual community has therefore been present to some degree for as long as we have had universities in the world, it follows that most of the things now being done by U.S. institutions in the area of international affairs are not basically new activities. There are new forms, more sophisticated rationales, more elaborate machinery and an enormous increase in the scale of activity, but the fundamental processes are the same. It all still has to do with learning and teaching and exchanging ideas across national boundaries. It is essential to keep this in mind when considering the proud chapter in the history of higher education now being written by American universities as they assume growing responsibilities in world affairs. To forget this thread of continuity with the past is to see present efforts as a vast disruptive and diversionary influence. To remember it is to recognize in what we are now doing the very essence of the university tradition.

In our approach to the international involvement of universities, we crossed an important watershed in the United States about 1960. Behind us were two decades of growing activity by American higher education on the world affairs front. Early in 1940's our universities were drawn into support of the national war effort, mounting a vast array of training programs to produce the kind of quickly trained manpower demanded by the worst conflagration the world had ever seen. But the beginnings of what a decade later would become a massive development in American higher education occurred during the peacetime years of the late 1940's. We had learned a bitter lesson during the war concerning our national ignorance of peoples, cultures and languages outside the Western European tradition. Taking that lesson to heart, leaders in some of the universities and the foundations collaborated on the first area study programs, which focused on the Soviet Union and Asia.

Before 1950, therefore, the seeds of many of the important developments of the next fifteen years had been sown in the terrain of American academia. The fifties were a period of sprouting and growth on many different sectors of the front. This was the decade of the Fulbright program and the start of university contracts for institution-building abroad on the part of the foreign aid agency (first the Foreign Operations Administration and then the International Cooperation Administration). Area and language centers expanded in number and grew in strength on the campuses of the nation. Concerted research efforts in many aspects of international affairs were undertaken at the larger universities. The comparative study of political systems underwent refurbishing and reinvigoration, largely through the impetus of the group of dedicated scholars who made up the Comparative Politics Committee of the Social Science Research Council.

This was also the decade of the foreign student, as men and women came to the colleges and universities of America in ever-growing numbers, and as our own young people at both the graduate and undergraduate levels went abroad to pursue their studies as "foreigners" in the universities of other lands. During the latter half of that decade the Iron Curtain was first breached by a new program of academic and scholarly exchanges with the Soviet Union.

It was a period of experimentation and innovation in many distinct parts of the world affairs front of higher education. Programs were launched in several key universities for the development of materials and the training of teachers looking toward the growth of international and non-Western studies among undergraduates, as a part of liberal arts education. Attempts to correct America's weaknesses in foreign languages, especially in the little-studied or "exotic" languages, got well under way in the fifties. The Council on Higher Education in the American Republics (CHEAR) was founded as a new arrangement for regular exchanges on common problems of higher education among North American and Latin American university leaders. The ferment and new approaches of the 1950's were a fitting prelude to the even more significant changes that were to occur in the early 1960's.

The fact that the United States entered a new period of development about 1960 is revealed by several new trends that set in as the decade opened. For the first time *the whole university* came into focus as the major actor on the stage of international education. Up until then, although nearly everything that went on in that field was obviously related to the universities and colleges, we were not yet at the point of considering these diverse activities within the context of the university as a total, integral institution. One reason for tying this new conception to the year 1960 is the publication by the Ford Foundation in the last month of that year of the report of the Committee on the University and World Affairs, usually referred to as the Morrill Committee report. On the committee were assembled a distinguished group of men from universities, foundations, business and government. Their report was a systematic attempt to clarify the international role of American universities and to suggest ways that our institutions of higher learning might perform more effectively in the realm of world affairs. The Morrill Committee report has other significances, but the point here is that it took *the university as its focal point,* relating to it such constituent parts of the full picture as foreign students, language studies, education for technical assistance, and world affairs in liberal education.

The 1960's were to see two kinds of developments closely related to this focus on the whole university. First, there emerged a new concern as to how universities should approach the problem of integrating and relating in a meaningful fashion their far-ranging international interests. On one campus after another, faculty and administration began to question how the institution should organize itself internally in order to carry its growing responsibilities on the international front and to derive from those activities the maximum possible educational benefit. Secondly, a strong trend developed toward new arrangements for interinstitutional cooperation, the working out of various patterns among colleges and universities that would permit greater division of labor, economy of effort, and maximization of results. Major moves were made by some of the largest universities, for example, Illinois, Indiana, Wisconsin and Michigan State in the Midwest Universities Consortium for International Activities; and nine major American institutions in a consortium to assist the development of a new technological university in Kanpur, India. At the same time, some of the smaller colleges were coming together into new associations so as to achieve through common action a level of participation in world affairs that would be far beyond the reach of a single small institution acting on its own. The Associated Colleges of the Midwest, the Great Lakes Colleges Association and the Regional Council for International Education based on the University of Pittsburgh—all were formed at least partly with an eye to the possibilities of educational enrichment that would stem from an active role on the international front.

The other reason for thinking of 1960 as a watershed was the shifts that occurred in the pattern of financial support for college and university programs in world affairs. The United States government came prominently into the picture under Title VI of the National Defense Education Act, which, although adopted earlier, did not become a major influence in the academic world until the early 1960's. So the responsibilities that had been largely borne by the private foundations during the forties and fifties were to be shared, on an increasing scale, by the federal government. And at about the same time, the Ford Foundation, the major private source of support for university activities in the international area, adopted a new approach. Ford began a series of grants that provided to selected institutions large-scale, long term, all-university wide support for their international programs. Based on careful planning and the development of an integrated approach by the institution itself, these new grants further emphasized the total university as the framework for the participation of American higher education in world affairs.

Finally, 1960 represents a time of transition because our basic interpretation of foreign aid, and especially our understanding of the role of educational assistance within it, took on a new sophistication with the passage of the International Development and Security Act of 1961. Contracting with universities for the conduct of programs abroad began, of course, during the 1950's. But it was only after the opening of the new decade that the role of education and manpower planning in national development came to be generally appreciated within the foreign aid agency, then renamed the Agency for International Development (AID). Although this new understanding was not translated into action as rapidly as many observers wished, it gradually brought significant changes—in the formulation of programs, in the evaluation of accomplishments, in the relationship of research to other aspects of foreign assistance, and in the felt need within AID for a closer partnership with the university community.

We are now five years past the watershed of 1960. The major, almost glacial resistances to constructive university involvements in world affairs have receded. These last five years have been a time of inquiry and searching for new answers, of continuing efforts to make our national performance more effective. One needs no crystal ball to foresee that further progress and further refinements in our approach lie ahead in the second half of this decade. We are still in an era of re-thinking, re-assessment and re-formulation, within the government, within the foundations, and within the universities themselves. The Office of Education has recently been reorganized, among other reasons, to enable it more effectively to discharge its proper responsibilities in the area of world affairs. The McGovern Bill now pending in Congress would close one of the significant gaps in federal support, by providing funds for universities to strengthen their resources for the training of young people to work abroad in the technical assistance field. AID continues to reach out in search of better answers to the perennial problem of how it can more effectively foster the development process among the less advanced peoples of the world. New institutional arrangements, perhaps better suited to the needs and conditions of the mid-1960's—such as the proposed National Institute of Educational and Technical Cooperation proposed in John Gardner's report, *AID and the Universities*—are being more actively discussed. And as the role of the federal government in this area grows larger and more pervasive, the more urgent it becomes for the private foundations to re-evaluate their own approaches and programs.

Within the higher educational community itself, the universities long-committed and long-engaged on the world affairs front continue active, reviewing their institutional arrangements, refining their techniques and often extending their involvement. And with every passing month, they are joined by new universities seeking paths into this intriguing, frustrating, yet promising and enriching area of international activity. On every sector of the front one finds portents of new developments in store for the years ahead. If hopes are realized they will strengthen the work of American colleges and universities in world affairs, but in any event, they are bound to affect it deeply.

This is the background against which Education and World Affairs undertook the present review of approaches to world affairs at six American universities. Twenty years of substantial accomplishment had brought us to the point where there were a number of lessons to be learned. The experience of universities that had pioneered in this field would be useful, it seemed to us at EWA, for guiding other institutions that would travel the same route.

To seek out this kind of story and present it as a service to American higher education is the very essence of EWA's purpose. Originating in a proposal of the Morrill Committee, EWA is itself a product of the times —of the concerted attention to the role of universities in world affairs that developed about 1960. It stemmed from a belief in university and foundation circles that, given the new scale of international effort by American higher education, there should be at least one organization devoting itself full time to the review, analysis and assessment of the directions in which we were moving.

As EWA got under way during 1963, and as it consulted with a widening circle of university and college people, the idea of the present study became an ever-recurring theme. To begin its direct communication with leaders of higher education, EWA organized during 1963 and 1964 six conferences in different parts of the United States. On each of these occasions participants expressed their own urgent need for deeper insights into the experience in world affairs already accumulated by the leading universities. Early in its life EWA began to get requests for campus visits and other forms of consultation, aimed at interpreting and transmitting the techniques and best practices already developed within the university community.

It thus became clear that some form of stocktaking of where we had come by the mid-1960's was in order. Rather than embark at this time on a long and elaborate national survey, it seemed more relevant from the standpoint of present needs to sight in on the specific lines of development on particular campuses—to seek the big picture of "where we are" in 1965 by bringing certain leading universities successively before the camera lens.

No magic formula was available for the selection of the particular institutions to be studied. It was a matter for discussion and deliberation within the framework of several criteria that inevitably applied. First, in the nature of the study, the universities would have to be those with substantial, longstanding involvement in world affairs. Secondly, they would obviously have to be willing to participate and cooperate in the effort, and to encourage their administration and faculty to work intensively with members of the EWA staff. And finally, among the universities identified for such study, there should be a reasonable diversity in the types of institution, size, geographical location and character and stage of development in the international field. As a result of juxtaposing and balancing these criteria, the six universities whose world affairs stories are told in the following pages were selected.

The actual conduct of the study, as is so often the case, turned out to be more complex and time-consuming than was at first expected. It was not that EWA began in the comfortable belief that it would be a job easily and simply done. We recognized that the wide diversity that characterizes American higher education has its own mirror reflection within every complex university. Clearly we were not dealing with universities that could be viewed as homogenous entities. The task of probing within to find the springs of action, the sources of innovation, and the resistances to change we realized to be extraordinarily difficult. The process, furthermore, poses special problems for the outsider. In an attempt to act in concert with the individual university and to arrive at balanced and responsible judgments, EWA sought to develop the closest possible cooperation with the faculties and administrations of the selected institutions.

The procedure was approximately the same at each of the universities. A member of the faculty or administration became EWA's chief "correspondent" and point of contact. In preparation for the intensive visit of several days, the members of the EWA staff who would later go to the institution did their homework. Everything available in printed or written form was assembled in the EWA office in New York for study by those who would make the visit. Careful and comprehensive schedules of appointments, with individuals and groups throughout the institution, were arranged beforehand by EWA's "correspondent" on the campus.

These visits were the principal information-gathering technique and in each case were conducted by three or four members of the EWA staff. This use of small teams for the campus visit had several advantages: it provided mutual reinforcement and the ability to coroborate points made when several of the men were together; and of even greater importance, it enabled the EWA visiting group to cover more ground and to gain a more comprehensive feel for the institution in the limited time available. Following the visit, each member of the team was responsible for writing a given segment of the story.

From that time forward, the main responsibility for the final product fell on Allan A. Michie, EWA's Director of Information and Publications. He visited each university, did the first draft chapters and undertook the painstaking process of checking back with the universities to assure factual correctness and reasonable agreement in interpretation. Only after full discussion and consultation had occurred with the university people (including further campus visits in a few instances) did Mr. Michie write the final text of this volume.

The following Education and World Affairs staff members, in addition to Allan A. Michie, participated in the visits to the universities: Peter N. Gillingham, Sheldon Pollack, Howard A. Reed, Henry G. Russell and Roger Sheldon. In the stages of planning and shaping this report, it has greatly benefited from the comments and suggestions of Ralph H. Smuckler, formerly Vice President of Education and World Affairs, and Maurice Harari, presently Vice President. The education acquired by all of us on the EWA staff in the course of this study is in itself invaluable.

A special word of appreciation should be extended to each of the six universities—Cornell, Indiana, Michigan State, Stanford, Tulane and Wisconsin—and to the individuals at those institutions who gave so generously of their time and energy in the effort to make this presentation accurate and meaningful. We at EWA are grateful to the universities for their willingness to open their doors for this kind of review, and for their splendid cooperation throughout the study. We hope that there will be few judgments or conclusions that our friends on the several campuses will find uncongenial—and none that they will deem unreasonable. To analyze and comment publicly upon the situation in individual universities is always a delicate business, and EWA has tried to proceed in the spirit of that realization. It has sought verification or correction of its conclusions in consultation with a number of specialists outside the six universities. Therefore, although the final responsibility clearly rests with EWA, we have been fortunate to enjoy a wide network of assistance in the carrying out of this study.

For those who consult this volume in search of clues for the future development of their own institutions, a final point should be made. As we approached this study, we realized that our investigation would reveal the wide diversity of form and practice in American higher education. The distinct traditions, personality and milieu of each of the universities were certain to be reflected in their several approaches to world affairs. We were not disappointed in this expectation. Although any institution that is serious about its commitments in the international realm must undertake conscious self-analysis of is own strengths and limitations, and must plan rationally the extension of its commitments, nevertheless on any particular campus the results of this process will reflect all the factors that contribute to that institution's individuality. Leadership at or near the top of the university is an indispensable ingredient, but to move a whole institution forward on the world affairs front is a formidable task, one that can scarcely succeed unless the strategy is worked out in close harmony with the traditions of the campus. Some centralized direction and control are inevitable, but the technique will vary from place to place.

So there are no quick answers, no general formulas, no easy "school solutions" to the problems that institutions face as they move toward progressively wider involvement in the area of world affairs. Imbedded in the experience of universities that have moved well down that road of involvement are important lessons to be learned. These lessons must be ferreted out and interpreted by those who seek guidance. In the last analysis, the challenge to American universities—as they so well know—is not simply to *adopt* what they find, but to *adapt* to their unique circumstances the practices and techniques of the more experienced institutions.

STANFORD

I

Perched on the skyline of the rolling foothills that form a theatrical backdrop to Stanford University is a spectacular 70-ton, 150-foot-diameter, fully steerable steel-and-aluminum parabola antenna, third largest in the world, designed and built by Stanford space scientists to explore the sun, planets, and interplanetary gases by means of radar beams. The "Big Dish," as it is known to Stanford students on the campus below, is something of a status indicator for American universities in the space age, but in Stanford's case it is also highly symbolic and appropriate.

Almost from the moment of the university's opening for instruction in 1891 as The Leland Stanford Junior University—to give it its rather ponderous full title—it has been a wide-ranging, outward-looking educational institution, anxious to shed its Western confines and involve itself in the world around it. The register for Stanford's second academic year shows that its 764 students already included representatives from fourteen foreign countries (with Canada first in number, Japan second). The first course in Far Eastern history to be offered anywhere in the United States was given there in 1906, and ever since Stanford has placed a major emphasis on Asian and Far Eastern studies.

To become a world university in a little more than seven decades is a considerable achievement, and, as American universities go, Stanford is still considered young, scarcely more than two generations old. Its youth is illustrated by the fact that members of its first classes are still alive.

In the course of its lifetime of seventy-odd years Stanford has grown from a student body of fewer than 600 to 10,775 today, of whom 5,700 are undergraduates. Some 830 of its students come from no fewer than seventy-three foreign nations or overseas possessions. Its professional faculty numbers 811, five of them Nobel Prize winners.

No longer a "gentleman's C school," as it was in the between-wars years, Stanford claims that practically all its entering freshmen are among the top 5 per cent of the nation's high school graduates. It attracts more National Merit Scholars than any other university except Harvard and M.I.T., and is second only to Harvard as the undergraduate choice of Presidential scholars. For two years in a row Stanford ranked first nationally as a study center for National Science Foundation science faculty fellowship winners. In a 1965 listing of the institutional quality of leading graduate schools, undertaken by Albert H. Bowker, Chancellor of the City University of New York, in his capacity as President of the American Statistical Association, Stanford was ranked in the top ten in the social sciences, in the humanities, and in science.

Early Internationalism

Each university or college develops its own idiom—growing out of its geographical location, its history, its financial condition, and so on.

Located in the Santa Clara Valley, adjacent to the city of Palo Alto (Stanford has its own post office) and in fairly close proximity to San Francisco, Stanford spreads over some 8,800 acres on the original site of Senator Stanford's Palo Alto stock farm. It is private, independent, non-denominational, coeducational, and residential.

The university consists of seven schools—Humanities and Sciences, Engineering, Education, Business, Earth Sciences, Law, and Medicine.

Some of these characteristics Stanford shares with other institutions of its size. What has provided the Stanford idiom, and shaped it from a provincial campus to a university with worldwide involvements, has been a serie ` of fortuitous developments, going back to its very founding.

Leland and Jane Stanford, cofounders of the university, were pioneers in the development of the West, and especially of California. A lawyer and then a successful merchant, Leland Stanford became a leader in California business and politics, played a major part in the construction of the first transcontinental railroad, and was elected Governor of California and later United States Senator. One of the founders of the new Republican party in his state, he was a firm follower of Lincoln and is credited with keeping California in the Union while he was Governor during the Civil War years.

During a European tour with his parents, Leland Junior, their only son, died of typhoid fever in Italy, two months before his sixteenth birthday. Stricken by their loss, the Stanfords decided to devote their wealth to a memorial to their son, and they chose to found an educational institution— "a university of high degree"—in his name. Their Palo Alto estate, on which the Senator bred and trained world champion trotting and pacing horses, was chosen as the site.

While the massive stone buildings, built of buff sandstone quarried nearby and topped with red tile roofs, were slowly rising on the new campus, Senator and Mrs. Stanford sought a president. They aimed high. One of the first they tried to lure to Stanford was Andrew Dickson White, who had been president of Cornell since its opening in 1868.

"Go to the University of Indiana; there you will find the president, an old student of mine, David Starr Jordan, one of the leading scientific men of the country, possessed of a most charming power of literary expression, with a remarkable ability in organization, and blessed with good sound sense. Call him." This was the advice White reportedly gave to the Stanfords, and they headed their private railway car for Bloomington, Indiana, that same evening.

Jordan, like White at Cornell, was an educator in the international mold. Then forty, he had been at Indiana—first as professor of natural sciences, then as president—for twelve years, but the prospect of building a new university in a pioneer state—Jordan later said—was "so challenging to one of my temperament that I could not decline." He accepted the offer the same afternoon, and remained at Stanford as its president for twenty-one years.

In June, 1893, a little less than two years from the time 465 eager young students gathered for opening day at Stanford, Leland Stanford passed away. As the surviving founder, Mrs. Stanford took over and for several parlous years, while the estate was ensnarled in litigation, she and Dr. Jordan kept the university going on a hand-to-mouth financial basis. In 1903 she relinquished her control over university affairs and two years later she died.

Another factor contributing to Stanford's early internationalism was its choice of presidents, each of whom in his own way has been a practicing internationalist. Jordan, whom one of his students characterized as "the last completely educated man," was an ichthyologist—but it was as a pacifist that he gained worldwide renown (and later, during World War I, some notoriety in the United States). A dedicated antimilitarist, he became in 1910 the chief director of the World Peace Foundation and lectured tirelessly on its behalf in Europe, Japan, Australia, and his own country. John C. Branner, a Cornell classmate of Jordan's, who served as interim president from 1913 to 1915, had been a consulting geologist in Brazil and wrote a classic work on Brazilian grammar. Ray Lyman Wilbur, who succeeded Branner and served twenty-six years in the presidency, had been university physician during Stanford's typhoid epidemic of 1906, and then Dean of the Medical School: on leave from Stanford he served in Herbert Hoover's Cabinet as Secretary of the Interior. Donald B. Tresidder, president from 1943 to 1948, had taken a medical degree, served as president of Stanford's Board of Trustees, and was the widely traveled head of the Yosemite Park and Curry Corporation when named to the Stanford post.

The present president, J. E. Wallace Sterling, who followed Tresidder in office, is a Canadian by birth and an American by education. After doing graduate work in British Commonwealth studies at Stanford's Hoover Institution he received his Ph.D. from the university in 1938 and served as professor of history at the California Institute of Technology—"introducing the engineers to the humanities," says one of his friends—before coming back to Stanford as its president in 1949.

A third factor influencing Stanford's outward look in its early days was the presence on its faculty of distinguished internationalists, professors who influenced generations of students by their teaching and example. One such was Graham Stuart, a political scientist and Latin American specialist, who was influential in directing students into the foreign service: another was Percy Martin, a specialist on Brazil who spent years editing a *Who's Who in Latin America*. Stanford was strong in history from its founding. In 1906 Payson Treat was appointed professor of Japanese history, and in

1908 a Japanese professor, Yamato Ichihashi, the first Japanese professor to teach the history and government of his native country at a United States university, was added to the staff. Together they served as catalysts to interest class after class in the Far East.

From War to War

World War I and its aftermath marked another watershed in Stanford's international dimension. It brought about a sharp shift in student interests. Despite Dr. Jordan's pacifism, student volunteers left the campus, and when the United States entered the conflict Stanford was depleted of students and faculty alike.

In the years after that war, when the rest of the nation was turning inward, three events moved Stanford even more toward being an institution with worldwide concerns. One was the appointment of President Wilbur as the first chairman of the Institute of Pacific Relations, which created a new area of interest that was to reach and affect many phases of the university's life; the second was the establishment of the Hoover War Library; and the third was the creation of the Food Research Institute.

In the three decades leading up to World War II these institutions and programs and the ferment they created throughout the university were reflected in broadened curricula, in important faculty appointments from abroad, and in new attempts to give international perspective to problems of traditionally domestic focus.

Both the Hoover Library and the Food Research Institute owe their presence to Herbert Hoover, Stanford's most famous alumnus (class of '95). During World War I, when Hoover, already a Stanford trustee, headed the Commission for Relief in Belgium, he made frequent trips from England to the Continent. On one of his crossings he read a statement by Cornell's Andrew White lamenting the fact that historians were hampered in their interpretation because no effort was made to collect and preserve contemporary accounts and documentation of events when they were happening. Mr. Hoover suddenly realized that his relief work—which was later in the war to extend to other parts of Europe and to continue well after the armistice—placed him in a unique position to document the World War, as it was then known. Almost as soon as his ship docked he had begun sorting and storing documents, and soon he was shipping crates of material to his alma mater. At the end of the war—aided by funds Hoover provided—teams of Stanford historians, supplemented by historians from other institutions, scoured Europe, baling and bundling documents in great batches and sending them back to Stanford. The Hoover reputation helped open government and military archives throughout Europe, and many of the secret documents were given with injunctions "not to be opened until 1970," "to be held for twenty-five years," and so on. Committed to

Hoover's care, some still remain, holding facts that may alter history until the date comes for their release.

Stanford already possessed, through Hoover's foresight, a large collection of documentary material relating to the food problems and other economic aspects of the World War. This led him to suggest to the Carnegie Corporation of New York—which was then looking to establish an institute "for the study of the problems of production, distribution, and consumption of foodstuffs"—that such a research center be located at his alma mater. In 1920 the foundation and the university signed a ten-year agreement, by which the Carnegie Corporation would provide the money for a Food Research Institute, a nonprofit organization belonging with but not to the university, a center where experts and scholars could engage in basic research on economic aspects of food.

In two ways the Institute set a new direction of major significance in the pattern of Stanford's activities in international studies: it was the first agency of the university assigned to conduct worldwide studies, and it was the first to be foundation-funded.

The years of World War II and then the immediate post-war years, bringing a flood of returned veterans under the terms of the G. I. Bill, brought to Stanford—as they did to many educational institutions across the nation—a new surge of interest and concern with the problems of the world. Shaped by their war experiences, the returning veterans—impatient to get their delayed education—had no time for campus provincialism. The difference between Stanford and many universities and colleges that failed in good part to capitalize on the stimulus of returning G. I.s is that Stanford had ready the mold in which this new interest could flourish—a growing heritage of international involvement and a receptive faculty and administration. The impact made by that immediate post-war generation of students is still measurable on the Stanford campus today.

II

"Stanford might have been a somewhat westernized, regional university prior to the Second World War," concedes Robert J. Wert, Vice Provost and Dean for Undergraduate Education, "but now we are as internationally minded as any in the United States." Certainly as far as the student body is concerned, involvement in international affairs is very visible at Stanford. Among major American universities Stanford ranks first in the number of Peace Corps volunteers per capita (in June, 1964, seventy-five Stanford seniors enrolled in the Peace Corps). The university ranks among the top ten institutions nationally in Rhodes scholarship winners, and it ranks third nationally (behind Harvard and Princeton) in the number of undergraduates winning Marshall scholarships.

The director of the university news bureau estimates that 20 per cent of

Stanford's students are involved in international activities—a minority, but a far larger percentage than at most American campuses. And at Stanford it is an active minority.

The depth of Stanford's student immersion in international affairs shows in at least four ways: the place international studies now occupy in the curriculum; the student-organized and student-run Institute of International Relations, now the largest and most comprehensive in any American university; the presence on the campus of more than 800 students from other lands; and the system of Stanford campuses abroad.

Changes in the Curriculum

At the undergraduate level, courses with a substantial international content are found throughout Stanford's wide range of course offerings. In fact, so widespread are they that the university is now preparing a special supplemental booklet to describe the more than a dozen international programs and list international-content courses as an aid to those students wishing to include them in their study programs and as a reminder to the faculty and student body of the university's global interests. Dean Wert remarked that so great was student interest in international courses that students often pressed for courses the administration was not yet able to provide.

The political science department permits emphasis on international relations within its B.A. program to give special training to students interested in the whole field of international relations; and second, to give professional preparation to students expecting to enter one of the fields of work in international relations.

Under the General Studies Program two senior colloquia are required of all seniors who are B.A. candidates, with a few exceptions (such as those going into Law or Medicine at the end of their third year, and those in honors programs in the humanities). The colloquia, limited to fifteen students each, and conducted by a faculty member, consist of analysis and discussion sessions supposedly built around subjects or issues of continuing importance, many of them involving world affairs. Unfortunately the sessions are uneven—some professors are offhand in their preparations, and students are assigned to the colloquia alphabetically—and, as a result, few students respect or value the program.

An unsolicited gift of $50,000 from the Garrett Corporation, a Los Angeles aerospace firm, enabled Stanford to introduce in 1964-65 an optional, sophomore-junior level course in East Asian civilizations. Its six sections of twenty-five students each were quickly filled, and nine sections are planned for 1965-66.

Student Internationalism

Stanford's Institute of International Relations is the only student group ever to win the Freedoms Foundation Medal: it has also had three consecutive awards from the Association of International Relations Clubs as the best international relations group in the United States.

The origins of the IIR go back to Stanford's postwar students. In 1946 twenty veterans organized the Stanford International Relief Organization and began collecting old clothing for the relief of their counterparts in war-torn European universities. In time they were sending shipments to no fewer than twenty-two different institutions abroad.

Encouraged by this, a few other international groups sprouted on campus. One of these was the SOIS—Stanford Overseas Information Service—formed to provide information for students wishing to go overseas. Late in 1947 those who were interested—most of them veterans—decided to group the various small bodies into one student organization, the IIR.

Technically all Stanford students are members of IIR through their membership fee in the Associated Students of Stanford University, which in turn provides funds for the IIR, but in fact only about 400 students—undergraduate and graduate students—are the "actives." Of these students about fifty consider themselves "the elite," and run the organization, including the election of officers. The "actives" are brought in on specific projects throughout the year.

The 1964-65 president, Gary Messinger, believed that about half the present student body had some overseas experience, either at a Stanford overseas campus, a Peace Corps or People-to-People assignment, Operation Crossroads in Africa, Project Concern, the medical relief agency in Hong Kong, or an organizational or private visit abroad. This estimate may be high, but it accounts for a considerable student participation in international activities. Many students return from an experience abroad, said Messinger, and then come in and volunteer to work for IIR.

Aside from its regular programs—speeches, publications, scholarships, dances, foreign travel, films, TV programs and so on—the IIR is closely affiliated with the I-Club, the campus club for foreign students, and the president of the I-Club, always a foreign student, is automatically a member of the IIR board. The IIR maintains its own library and operates a Stanford Overseas Information Service to assist Stanford students planning vacations, study, or careers abroad. The student organization also provides more than 200 California high schools with programs and materials on international problems, and publishes a bimonthly newsletter.

The IIR each year stages a mock United Nations, in which some 300 students participate. It also sends one to four delegates annually to the Collegiate Council for the United Nations in New York, where students representing more than 250 schools around the world see the U. N. in action and meet the men who run it. The conference division also sponsors an annual Foreign Policy Institute with distinguished speakers, seminars, and extensive background preparations, in which both town and gown participate.

Messinger contended that in certain instances student interest has been ahead of faculty. "Perhaps 50 per cent of the visitors we have speaking on campus would not come to Stanford were it not for student initiative and interest," said the IIR's president. Speakers at the Foreign Policy Institutes in the past have included Ralph Bunche and Christian Herter. Meanwhile the Political Union—which devotes itself to domestic issues—has brought in for campus talks such leading figures as the late John F. Kennedy and Richard M. Nixon.

In fact so rich is the diet of public affairs that Stanford is beginning to experience an unexpected problem, one the IIR refers to as "speaker affluence." When Bunche spoke on campus for the IIR in 1961 there was no need to turn out a crowd: his appearance was a major event and he had an overflow audience. However, by 1964 so many prominent speakers had competed for campus attention that Peace Corps head Sargent Shriver couldn't quite fill Memorial Auditorium.

Other projects of the IIR include the Winter Hostel program, a series of six one-day retreats in January and February at which at least one prominent Stanford faculty member and fifteen to twenty students spend an entire day in informal give-and-take discussion of current world topics. Subjects covered last year ranged from "Modern Germany" to "Pacifism: Prospects and Problems." A Peace Corps "desk" at IIR headquarters (upstairs in the Student Union) provides an ongoing source of information about the Peace Corps and sees that Corps representatives appear on campus as often as possible—which undoubtedly helps account for Stanford's high rate of P. C. enrollment. Student initiative was also responsible for a series of foreign student exchanges. In 1961 the IIR established a relationship with Makerere University College in Uganda, enabling a Stanford student to go to East Africa each year. This was followed by a program in which a dozen or so students from Japan spent a quarter at Stanford auditing classes, living in dormitories and fraternities, and traveling in California.

Foreign Students

Foreign students have always been part of the Stanford campus, particularly students from Western Europe, Canada and—because of Stanford's Pacific location—the Far East. For some years there were two houses, operated much like fraternities, where Japanese and Chinese students clustered: they remained active until World War II. Similarly at the campus eating clubs various ethnic tables—the Spanish table, the German table and so on—came together, survived for a few years, died out, and were reassembled as new generations of foreign students came on campus.

This easy adjustment to the presence of foreign students ended with the vast influx of foreigners over the past few years, and the care and education of its foreign student population is now highly organized. Currently there are about 830 foreign students at the university, 88 per cent of them in graduate studies, which puts Stanford in nineteenth place among American educational institutions for total foreign student enrollment. There is a turnover of 250 to 350 foreign students a year. The 1964-65 figure, by the way, represents a 20 per cent increase over 1963, which in turn represented a 20 per cent increase over 1962. If this rate of increase were to continue, Stanford would have about 2,300 foreign students by the end of the decade.

In addition to the 800 or so regularly enrolled foreign students, about 200 "senior foreign scholars" are on campus, temporarily connected with Stanford as teachers, research workers, and the like. The exact number is uncertain—the 1963-64 annual report of the Foreign Student Adviser notes that "because of the extreme difficulty in securing data on scholars from departments and individual faculty members, the above figures must be considered tentative"—but it is estimated that their number has at least doubled within the past two or three years. This rapid increase led to the establishment of an Office for Foreign Scholars within the new International Center.

Until the autumn of 1964 Stanford operated with a Foreign Student Adviser, who reported to the Dean of Students, but last year a new and senior post was created, that of Assistant Graduate Dean for International Students; the holder reports to the Dean of the Graduate Division. This change reflected the great increase in the proportion of the university's foreign students at the graduate level. Also, the title of "assistant dean" carried more prestige than "foreign student adviser."

Stanford's graduate admission procedures are decentralized in the various schools and departments, and the supervisor of the Office of Foreign Graduate Admissions has a largely facilitative role. Inquiries and applications for admission to the graduate schools are routed and processed through this office, but are sent on to the respective schools or departments for acceptance or rejection.

In 1963-64 this office received 1,400 applications and an "infinite number" of inquiries. Of the 1,400, 669 were admitted, and of these 251 showed up for registration. (These figures are exclusive of the Master of Business Administration program. In the MBA program in the same year there were 155 foreign applicants, of whom 48 were admitted and 24 arrived.)

Stanford does not operate a double standard for foreign students. In fact, it insists on a course in remedial English, if necessary, and demands that graduate applicants fill in any gaps in their undergraduate education before full admission to the Stanford graduate program. Its English-for-foreign-students course is widely used, even by foreign graduate and post-doctoral students. Unlike some other American institutions, Stanford has had no difficulty persuading foreign students deficient in English to take the remedial work: in fact, so popular is the course that some administration sources want to charge extra for it! Two points of view are contending. One argues that Stanford is demeaning itself by offering English as a "foreign language." Those involved in international studies and the care of foreign students insist that the course must be continued.

The campus focal point for foreign student activity is the new Bechtel International Student Center (named for its main donor, international construction man Stephen D. Bechtel). This is open to all Stanford students, visitors from overseas, faculty, staff, and the local community, but it is mainly used by the foreign students, some of the students back from the overseas campuses, and campus student groups concerned with international affairs. Open daily, it puts on a variety of cultural and recreational activities and an almost ceaseless round of social affairs designed to mix foreign students, American students and the local community. The Center also serves as a home base for the I-Club of foreign students, and houses the offices of the Assistant Graduate Dean for International Students, the Foreign Student Adviser, the Coordinator for Foreign Visitors, and the Community Committee for International Students. The Center also publishes its own monthly newsletter.

Complementing the efforts of the International Center is the Community Committee for International Students, a group of men and women from the Stanford campus and nearby communities who, since 1953, have worked to promote a person-to-person relationship with foreign students. More than 1,200 families are signed up to extend hospitality to foreign students, and the dedicated members of the CCIS are indefatigable in arranging welcomes and home-stays with local families, explaining customs, conducting tours, dispelling homesickness, and taking care of a variety of foreign student needs as they arise. The CCIS also publishes a quarterly newsletter appropriately called *Communiqué*. In 1964-65 the organization began an "English in Action" program to pair foreign students and volunteers for conversational practice.

Although there has been no systematic study of the interaction between foreign students and the community—a study that might prove useful nationally—there is no doubt, as evidenced by the fact that Stanford's CCIS has no trouble lining up a continual supply of community volunteers, that foreign students have influenced the Stanford community, both academic and off campus.

Stanford Overseas

Air travel has made possible a geographical extension of Stanford not contemplated when Leland Stanford and his wife determined to build a university in California. Stanford now operates no fewer than five European "campuses" and two advanced study centers abroad. During the six years after 1958, when the first overseas campus was opened, more than 2,300 undergraduates had attended the three main overseas campus centers in Germany, France, and Italy.

An overseas study center had long been a dream of Dr. Friedrich W. Strothmann, head of the European languages department at Stanford. Almost single-handedly he located a site in Germany—a remodeled sanitarium known as Landgut Burg, on a 30-acre estate 12 miles east of Stuttgart—worked out a program, and gained a $15,000 grant from the Fund for the Advancement of Education. He had the Stanford administration's blessing.

"Our motivation was that this country is going to need more young people interested in foreign affairs and proficient in foreign languages," said President Sterling. "What could Stanford do about it? The overseas study center is our answer."

The Stuttgart campus was launched in June, 1958, and the operational pattern developed for Stanford-in-Germany was repeated when similar campuses were opened in France and Italy in 1960. The French center is located at Tours, in the heart of the chateau country. The Italian center is a villa in the hills above Florence, significant in Stanford history as the city in which young Leland Stanford died. The Stuttgart campus has room for seventy-three students; the Florence and Tours centers take eighty each.

The overseas program is geared entirely to the Stanford academic year and to the general studies program, and uses the summer quarter as well. The undergraduate at an overseas campus loses no time, and no credits, in his academic career. Tuition and room and board fees are the same as on the home campus, and the amount also includes transportation costs to Europe. The only fixed additional cost to the student is his return travel, and air charter flights bring this down. Scholarships remain in force and travel grants and loans are available.

Language prerequisites are kept at a moderate, easily met level, so that it is possible for students in virtually all academic fields to attend. Once overseas they receive two hours a day of intensive language instruction from nationals. This, coupled with the necessity of using the foreign tongue, increases proficiency: also, the stimulus of living in a foreign culture is expected to encourage the students to understand the life around them. Classes overseas are compressed into a four-day week, allowing three-day weekends for travel in Europe, where distances to other foreign countries are not great.

In higher education circles the Stanford plan for overseas campuses has been singled out for criticism on the ground that it encourages little "American ghettos" abroad with close-knit groups of students keeping to themselves. Some students who have participated complain that the somewhat isolated campus colonies abroad make it more difficult to break through local barriers. The Stanford administration rejects this criticism, and in fact contends that the Stanford-abroad concept has several advantages over the conventional junior-year-abroad program of many other educational institutions. Most European universities will not admit American students on a visiting basis without two years of college work, but the Stanford program is open to sophomores as well as to juniors and seniors. In fact, most of the participants attend in their sophomore year, and about a third of the class is chosen each year. The result of this is that for the first time on any large scale the opportunity for study abroad has been made available to undergraduates working toward careers in the sciences, engineering, law, medicine, and other professions, who must ordinarily follow a fairly rigid sequence of courses, especially in their junior and senior years.

Undergraduates spend two quarters (six months) on the overseas campus and then return to Stanford. This means that the overseas campuses can accommodate annually (they are fully used on a twelve-month basis to make ends meet) twice their capacity, or 466 students, a major consideration when the home campus facilities are taxed to the utmost.

Selection for an overseas campus is based primarily on academic standing (applicants must be in the top half of their class), personal characteristics and language competence. Close contact with Stanford-at-home is maintained (a few years ago undergraduates from Stanford-in-Florence startled Italians during the football season by draping a "Beat Cal" banner from the top of the Leaning Tower of Pisa), and two members of the regular Stanford faculty offer courses at each center, in addition to the staffs of professionally qualified nationals who teach the intensive language courses.

One thing Stanford faculty members and the administration agree on: they are satisfied that the academic dividends from the system of overseas campuses have been considerable, and the impact in the international field is real and visible. "The overseas campuses have jazzed up more interest in international affairs at Stanford than any other single activity," remarked President Sterling. The phraseology may not be presidential, but the enthusiasm is partly paternal: two of the President's children have attended overseas campuses.

Although no systematic study has been made of the feedback from the overseas campuses—an area in which Stanford has been remiss and on which it has a wealth of student comment—Sterling has his own rough measurements of their impact. These include an increase in the number of history students (Stanford has long been strong in this discipline, but there are now some 600 majors in history, many of them in European history, which is viewed in good part as an outgrowth of the overseas campuses); a similar increase in enrollment in foreign languages, art, and art history courses; the expanded activities of the IIR, reinforced by returning students; and the interest in the Political Union, an organization Sterling encouraged on the model of the Oxford Union. Professor Richard Lyman, Associate Dean of Humanities and Sciences, asserts that the overseas campuses not only help stimulate interest in international affairs but also seem to awaken new student interest in the United States and in domestic public affairs.

Some of the influences of the overseas campuses have been unexpected. Having lived with their faculty members at the overseas centers, returning students have expressed interest in extending this to the Stanford campus, and arrangements are being made for faculty members to live with the students in the dormitories to achieve a closer student-teacher relationship. Other ideas nurtured through living on the campuses abroad have not been so easy to accommodate. The heady experience of living in mixed quarters in the small communities of Stanford abroad encourages returning students to agitate hopefully for coed housing on the Stanford campus (a prospect the trustees are considering for construction in 1966). Likewise, the fact that wine is served with meals (if the student pays for it!) to conform to the European custom at the campuses abroad encourages the worldly student returnees to press for a relaxation of the no-liquor restrictions on the home campus!

An interesting outgrowth of the overseas campus system is that each overseas unit maintains its social identity back on the home campus, and the daily calendar of student activities in the student newspaper, *The Stanford Daily,* carries such announcements as: "Italy Group VII Reunion," "Italy Group VIII Coffee Hour," "Italy V: *L'ultima reunione!*" There is an Overseas Campus Board of representatives who have attended the European centers, and occasionally one group will publish a brochure describing life on the overseas campus for the groups that will follow.

The apparent satisfaction with the overseas campuses led the Stanford administration late in 1964 to launch two new European campuses for the 1965-66 academic year. One will be in Britain, at Harlaxton Manor, a turreted old manor house in the heart of Lincolnshire, about 100 miles north of London. The other will be in part of an aging Austrian spa hotel at Semmering, 57 miles south of Vienna. Eighty Stanford men and women will attend each of the British and Austrian campuses for the usual six-month terms. "The addition of two more European campuses to the existing three will allow more than 50 percent of Stanford undergraduates to study in Europe before receiving their degree," says Dr. Robert A. Walker, director of the overseas campuses.

So far Stanford has decided against enlarging its overseas campus installations to accommodate students from other universities and colleges, partly because the course content is tied closely to the core courses taught at Stanford and would therefore not necessarily be suitable for other universities or colleges, and partly because the installations are small and expensive to operate.

Quite different from the European campuses are the two study centers Stanford has founded in Tokyo and Taipei. They are designed to provide intensive language training for both advanced undergraduates and graduates and to prepare specialists in Asian studies. Selected students spend at least a full year at one or the other of these centers, and many of the students who attend have gone earlier to a European campus.

Stanford opened its Tokyo center in 1961 and its Taipei center in 1962. It later received some financial assistance from the Carnegie Corporation, the Asia Foundation, and the Ford Foundation, but before the centers had been in operation very long the financial burden per student proved excessive for Stanford, and both centers were converted into interuniversity organizations—Taipei in 1963, Tokyo a year later—in which Stanford participates with other major institutions. The Interuniversity Program for Chinese Language Studies is located in its own building on the campus of National Taiwan University, and now involves nine American institutions —Columbia, Harvard, Cornell, Princeton, Yale, Michigan, Washington, Stanford, and the University of California (Berkeley)—and is administered by Stanford. Through 1964-65, seventeen Stanford graduate students, fifty-one other graduate students, and nine undergraduates from other institutions had studied there.

The Interuniversity Center for Japanese Studies is now located in its own quarters on the campus of International Christian University in Tokyo, and has become a cooperative effort of the sponsors in Taipei, plus the universities of Oregon and British Columbia. By the end of the 1963-64 school year, twenty Stanford undergraduates, twenty Stanford graduate students, twenty-one other undergraduates, and twenty-five other graduate students had attended the Tokyo center.

In addition, a wide variety of graduate fellowships for overseas study are available to Stanford students at the dissertation research level, for studies in Britain, France, Germany, and Italy. Students in Britain may enroll at University College, London. The programs in France, Germany, and Italy are supported by grants from those governments, supplemented by Stanford grants. Since 1963 a Stanford-Warsaw University Graduate Student Exchange Program has made possible a year of research for Stanford students in the humanities and the social sciences at the dissertation level, with emphasis on study of Slavic languages. Their Polish counterparts come mostly from the natural sciences. Funds are provided by the Department of State and Stanford, with foundation assistance.

For several years Stanford has provided overseas study opportunities to participants in Ford Foundation-supported three-year programs in German and classics, beginning with the students' junior year and leading to the M.A. in either of these fields. Participants in the German program spend the spring and summer quarters at the University of Hamburg, under a

Stanford resident professor; those in the classics program spend the summer quarter in Italy and Greece at various archaeological sites, under the direction of a Stanford professor.

Each summer since 1960 some eighty or more American teachers of German have been selected to study at Bad Boll's Evangelische Akademie near Stuttgart to brush up their language competence and learn new methods of teaching. This program is directed by Stanford's Modern European Languages department, with funds from the National Defense Education Act. Through 1964 a total of 416 high school teachers had participated.

Campus Internationalism

Reflecting campus interests, many of the nonacademic campus activities have a pronounced international tone.

The Stanford University Press, the only complete book plant among university presses in the United States, publishes some forty titles a year, and many of these are on international subjects, either historical or modern. Of ten books published in the latter part of 1964, no fewer than eight dealt with international subject matter.

The Stanford Daily devotes a substantial number of column inches each day to international news, relatively more than most small-town American newspapers, and to international campus activities. It produced a special international supplement on Southeast Asia when the IIR held its 1964 Foreign Policy Institute.

The *Stanford Calendar,* a bulletin published by the administration, lists each week the visitors from foreign lands who will be on the campus, and the dates of their visits. So many have descended on Stanford that a special Office for Foreign Visitors was set up in 1956-57 to arrange their tours, hospitality, and appointments. In that year there were some 200 foreign visitors, many of them drawn by the resources of the Hoover Library. In 1964 the office coped with 767 foreign visitors, nearly a fourfold increase, accounted for largely by Stanford's increasing and expanding international involvements. About half the foreign visitors come under the auspices of various federal agencies, and the rest through foundation contacts, foreign embassies and consulates, and faculty contacts. The only jarring note is that the hospitality extended costs Stanford about $50,000 per year.

As to be expected, with nearly 76,000 Stanford alumni, many of them scattered over the world, the loyal graduates of the institution are an active resource in the international field. Of more than sixty Stanford clubs organized by the 23,000-member Stanford Alumni Association, no fewer than twenty are located outside the United States, from Bangkok to Mexico. A highlight of Stanford alumni activity for more than thirty years has been the annual Stanford Conferences, held in key cities in the United States, at which faculty, students, and administration speakers join with alumni in provocative discussions of educational issues and ideas. In 1965, as a reflection of the university's overseas activities, faculty members from the European campuses met with local alumni in Paris to conduct the first Stanford Conference overseas.

III

The components of Stanford's international studies program are many. Some are outgrowths and expansions of earlier university involvements, such as the Hoover Library and the Food Research Institute, whereas others owe their impetus to new Stanford interests, academic fashions, and trends. Most of them involve activities at the graduate and professional levels of the university.

The Hoover Institution

Since its founding after World War I as as the Hoover Library, the research center—now known as the Hoover Institution on War, Revolution and Peace—has grown into a national and international depository for vast documentary collections of material on political, social, and economic change in the twentieth century. Thousands of students and scholars from the United States and abroad have used its resources and facilities.

The process of acquiring documents and background papers initiated by Hoover during World War I was continued in the 1920's, and by the end of that decade bales of documents overflowed the library's shelves and stacked up in the basements of the campus buildings. In 1941 the collection was gathered into its own building, a tall tower erected in the middle of the campus. The fourteen air-conditioned floors of the shaft contain millions of items—books, documents, posters, pamphlets, and photographs. There are well over 23,000 newspaper and periodical titles stored there. Each of its major area collections (Western Europe, Eastern Europe, Africa, East Asia, and the Middle East) is outstanding. The distinguishing feature of the Hoover Institution is that it houses under one roof for convenient study records of the major upheavals of the contemporary world. It is reputed to have more material on the growth and spread of Communism than can be found anywhere outside Russia. It has perhaps more pro- and anti-Mussolini data than can be found in Italy. It has probably the most complete record on Hitler and the Nazi movement extant. It is the place where scholars can document such important twentieth-century happenings as the story of Vichy France and the French Fifth Republic, the rise of the Chinese Communists, underground movements in Africa, Asia, and Latin America, the turbulent history of the Middle East, or the development of the Western alliance.

In time, the use of academic searchers to gather material became less and less essential. Donors knew the institution's reputation and sent in material as they found it. For instance, a German-born American soldier, who attended a Civil Affairs Training School at the Hoover Institution during the early part of World War II, remembered the library when he found bound volumes of the complete file of *Der Stürmer* on a visit to Julius Streicher's former country home soon after Germany's defeat. This vivid record of Nazi anti-Semitism is now part of the institution's extensive collection on the Hitler regime. The collapse of the regimes in Italy, Germany, and Japan at the war's end sent Hoover Institution agents scurrying to round up archives, and in Tokyo a special Hoover Institution office was opened with the permission of General MacArthur. This flow of material continued into the 1950's, and was curtailed only because of financial difficulties.

Funds to operate the institution come from three sources: voluntary contributions, income from an endowment of approximately $2 million, and an annual Stanford contribution of a minimum of $125,000. Well over half its present budgetary requirement (approximately $600,000 per year) is provided by voluntary contributions.

The institution has its own staff of scholars, and visiting scholars—as many as 400 a year—come from all over the world. Each is free to pursue his independent interests, but certain common aims pervade institution research. Because of the wide scope of its holdings, its approach is multi-disciplinary, and whenever possible research is placed in an international perspective. The staff of the institution represents some fifteen nationalities and speaks twenty-five languages.

The institution sponsors an extensive publication program of its own, and several important research and bibliographical projects have been initiated in the past few years. These include a history of the Communist International, studies of Communist activity in Africa, and a series of monographs on Communist China as an economic power. Other major studies being planned include a history of Chinese Communism, the role of the United States in Africa, a history of the Paris Peace Conference, and an analysis of the development and future of the Western alliance. For some time the institution published an *Africana Newsletter,* a compilation of research in the field; and in the spring of 1965 it took over the editing and publishing of the *African Studies Bulletin* for the African Studies Association.

Food Research Institute

Since its founding in 1921, jointly by the Carnegie Corporation and Stanford, the Food Research Institute has continued to operate under its original terms of reference for "research in the production, distribution and consumption of food." Now, however, its research activities extend over six continents.

Its funds come from endowment by the Carnegie Corporation and the

Rockefeller Foundation, which provide one-third of its expenditures; Stanford support, for somewhat less than 20 per cent of its budget; and research grants from government or private agencies, foundation grants, and gifts, for the rest.

The institute is engaged primarily in research, with some teaching responsibilities at the advanced level. The emphasis is generally on long-range research problems as they cross national boundaries. Generally, the institute has shied away from service contracts overseas, although these may be accepted if they tie in closely with the institute's own research interests.

Until World War II the institute concentrated on food grains throughout the world, but in the past decade its focus has widened to include food and agricultural and nutritional aspects of economic development. Some of the early studies dealt with famine and collectivization problems in the Soviet Union, reflecting Mr. Hoover's interests and concerns, but more recently studies have concentrated intensively on tropical Africa and Latin America.

The staff of the institute normally numbers eleven or twelve, most of professorial rank, with a supporting staff of the same size. The institute operates like a department of the university. Courses are given at the institute and can be counted as economics courses toward university credits. The institute rounds out its own program for a Ph.D. and uses regular economics department courses. However, its own courses are tied heavily to research. Thus the institute serves not only as a source of substantive knowledge but also as a center for training research workers in the economic and international aspects of food and agricultural problems, the training of American students planning careers in the technical assistance and development fields, and the training of students from newly developing nations who plan such careers. Three-fourths of the students admitted are on fellowships awarded to students trained abroad, with preference to applicants from the underdeveloped world; the rest are students who have done their undergraduate training in the United States.

The institute issues a periodical, *Food Research Institute Studies,* a compilation of research reports published three times a year.

Comparative Education Center

Investment in education is accepted as a fundamental factor in the forward thrust of nations, particularly the underdeveloped of the world. But there is a scarcity of research to demonstrate what educational means and ends may be best suited to certain national and cultural conditions.

Stanford's Comparative Overseas Education Center, part of the School of Education, has engaged in a variety of research activities to help fill this research gap. A concept of Paul R. Hanna, an educator with wide-ranging concerns who has served from the outset as its director, the center was established in 1954 and has been financed by the Ford Foundation and Stanford, with research grants from the U.S. Office of Education, the Agricultural Development Council, the Peace Corps, and similar sources. Its three-year doctoral program prepares educators to enhance the human resources of underdeveloped countries. Some of its graduates now hold high-level positions as specialists in comparative education with AID, OECD, the Special Fund of the UN, UNESCO, and universities in the United States and abroad.

Admission to this doctoral program requires a master's degree in a substantive discipline and at least two years of successful employment in education in the United States or overseas. Each year a small group of highly selected doctoral candidates is admitted to undertake three years of advanced training and research: 60 percent of these are United States citizens, 40 percent from other nations. The first two years are devoted to advanced courses and seminars in the social sciences, language, and education. The third is spent on a research project overseas. Such research has dealt with rural education in India, industrial education in the Philippines, a survey of French education in France's former African colonies, and education in Japan, Taiwan, the Congo, and the Middle East. In overview, this research program is coordinated to achieve a global view of the problems associated with human resource development and the development of countries under different conditions. Comparative studies thus try to extract from the research generalizations and action principles hitherto untested or unobserved, from which better educational strategies may be devised.

Studies in Economic Growth

Economics as an academic discipline has gained the reputation of being slow to internationalize. This oversimplifies a complex professional attitude. Economics is a universal subject, to begin with, and some economists argue that they need neither international service, experience, nor commitments to be good economists. Others assign different priorities to their interests: some rank work in econometrics ahead of the international problems of the underdeveloped nations. By and large, good economists—in contrast to most of the other social scientists—do not like to become regional or area or country specialists: their interests are defined by fields of specialization, not by geography.

Stanford's economics department has long harbored a few men who are declared internationalists and who have found their professional satisfaction in working with the developing areas of the world. One such was Hollis Chenery, now at Harvard, who went to the planning staff of AID after teaching at Stanford. While at Stanford, Professor Chenery often spent as much time afield as he did on campus, and his enthusiasms encouraged several individual economics professors to hold workshops and conduct research and training activities on international economic problems. In 1960, with the aid of a Ford Foundation grant, these activities were consolidated into a Research Center in Economic Growth, intended to facilitate research and the training of graduate students in economic development and comparative studies. In 1961, when Emile Despres, a development economist on the faculty at Williams, was brought to the Stanford campus, he was named director of the center.

The center now concentrates on three types of research: (1) comparative studies of individual aspects of the economic structure; (2) studies of economic development in selected countries; (3) analyses of the formulation, execution, and effectiveness of various development policies. It has established contacts with kindred institutions overseas and participates in an international exchange of scholars and graduate students.

Communication Research

Stanford's Institute for Communication Research, a division of the department of communication (training in journalism, broadcasting and film), is far out front in its special field—research on how best to use the media and scientific knowledge of communication to accelerate economic and social development in the emerging nations.

That this is so is largely due to its director, Wilbur Schramm, a pioneer in the communications field and a prolific contributor to the written word himself. His latest book, *Mass Media and National Development,* eloquently makes the point that radio, television, films, newspapers, and all the other techniques of modern communication are the most effective instruments available for speeding up economic growth in the underdeveloped areas of the world.

The institute came into being at Stanford in 1955 when Schramm came there from the University of Illinois. His interest in the obvious correlation between economic development and the existence of modern communications media was whetted by a session in India in 1962, when he advised the Indian government on establishing a communications institute. In 1964 he headed a team studying, on behalf of UNESCO, the mass media training needs of the East and Central African nations.

The institute offers a Ph.D. in mass communication research, and Schramm admits that it is "rough." It includes courses in such areas as statistics, psychology, advanced mathematics, sociology, and computers before the students even get to mass communications! With its heavy emphasis on research, the institute has a small staff—four communications experts, including Schramm—and the students number only four or five postdoctoral plus some thirty research associates and assistants, candidates for advanced degrees. Schramm gets about seventy-five applications for admission each year, a good many of them from abroad, but the institute can accept only about five.

Current studies include several on India—communication in Indian villages, urbanization, literacy, and mass media—and one on the tactics and techniques the Castro regime has used in Cuba "to restructure the socialization processes with the intention of creating the type of citizenry needed to run the 'new Cuba.' " The institute also has one service contract, this one with the Peace Corps, to study the effectiveness of the television-taught classes the Peace Corps has introduced in Colombia.

Political Studies

The political science department at Stanford is third largest in the university in number of undergraduates, but in the between-wars years it was overshadowed by the international giants on campus, the Hoover Institution and the Food Research Institute. In those days it was thought to be reluctant to wade into international waters, but the department has been drastically changed over the past decade or so with the gradual infusion of faculty members with international experience or interests, until its turnover has been almost complete.

Beginning about 1957 individual department members, paced at the outset by Robert C. North, an expert on Soviet and Chinese affairs, began to meet informally each week at the grass roots level. Out of these meetings has grown Stanford's Institute of Political Studies. Established in the autumn of 1963, and located in two converted old residences on the edge of the campus, it is a loose arrangement of research groups in political science, each of which has an identity of its own and is autonomous in administration and research funds. The director is Gabriel Almond, a distinguished political scientist who came to Stanford in 1963 and is chairman of the political science department.

There are seven major research programs in various stages of development at the institute, three concerned with international politics, four with national and local government.

The earliest outgrowth of the informal meetings held in 1957 and 1958 is now a unit of the institute with the somewhat jargonized name of Stanford Studies in International Conflict and Integration. Discussion in those years centered on the possibilities of applying systems analysis techniques to research and teaching in international relations. Interest focused on past crises to see why wars break out and why small wars escalate into big ones. In 1960 the Ford Foundation backed this approach with a five-year grant of $250,000, and the Conflict Study Project was launched. The search for methods to make content analysis of documentary materials led project members to harness the electronic computer to a sizable portion of the routine clerical tasks involved in the processing, retrieval, and analysis of large flows of information. Based on the belief that a computer can be programmed to analyze levels of international tensions on a/ day-to-day basis, they have investigated such crises as the Bosnian crisis of 1908-9, the last weeks prior to the outbreak of World War I, selected periods in the Arab-Israeli conflict, and the Japanese decision to attack Pearl Harbor.

The director of the Stanford Studies in International Conflict and Integration is Professor North, and the associate director is Jan F. Triska, who also heads the more recently launched Stanford Studies in Communism, also under the Institute's umbrella. Triska's group intends to use some of the same research techniques being used in conflict-integration analysis to describe the composition of the Communist system, its subsystems, and their patterns of interaction in order better to understand changes in Communist tactics and goals. Recent studies deal with the decision-making elite in Communist-controlled countries; comparative strategy and behavior in relationships among the satellite Communist nations and those with politico-economic affinities to Communist countries; and the Sino-Soviet schism. This research unit benefits particularly from its ready access to the library and resource facilities of the Hoover Institution.

In the summer of 1964, fifteen leading political scientists from Japan, India, Nigeria, Latin America, and the United States met at the Institute under Almond's direction to plan a unique worldwide collaborative study of political attitudes in the emerging nations. The project was later refined into a "four nation study," a comparative analysis of change in India, Japan, Nigeria, and Mexico, each of which is in a different stage of development, and awarded a $250,000 Ford Foundation grant in 1965. The factors being examined are changes in the pattern of government ideology; the measure of participation in government and public life; and the use of public leaders as transmission belts of political ideas, upward and downward, by the elite. One unusual aspect of this U.S.-originated research project is that the work in each country will be done under the supervision of indigenous social scientists.

ICAME

In 1961 the Ford Foundation approached the deans of several major business schools throughout the United States, many of which were already involved in international programs, with a proposal to have American graduate schools of business help their counterparts in developing countries by upgrading the staff already teaching in these nations. Stanford's School of Business was awarded a $3,500,000 grant over a seven-year period.

Six other American business schools—Harvard, Columbia, Indiana, Michigan State, M.I.T., and the University of California (Los Angeles)—cooperate with Stanford, and their deans sit with Stanford's Ernest C. Arbuckle, Dean of the Graduate School of Business Administration, on the advisory board of the International Center for the Advancement of Management Education (ICAME), as the project is named. Initially fifty educational institutions overseas were included as participating schools, but this list has now been cut to thirty-eight. Each foreign institution nominates its faculty candidates for enrollment at ICAME, but Stanford Business School representatives personally interview applicants and make the final selection.

The program lasts a full academic year, and consists of a core curriculum at ICAME, on the Stanford campus. The students can also take other courses in the Business School or elsewhere in the university if these fit in with their own teaching and research interests. Faculty members are in part drawn from Stanford, in part brought in from other universities for this program.

A significant feature of ICAME is its use of the case study method to build up information on business or management problems in the underdeveloped nations, information that was hitherto nonexistent as far as American business schools were concerned. Each professor-student coming to ICAME is asked to submit, before his arrival, material about an industry or management problem in his own nation that poses a significant problem. Further documentation is brought with him when he comes to Stanford. Meanwhile an ICAME research assistant travels abroad to the business or industry to "check out" the case. The case study is used for ICAME teaching purposes and is added to its worldwide files.

Each year ICAME, with thirty-five to forty students in each group, concentrates on one subject. The first year—1962-63—focused on financial management and control, the second on marketing management and distribution, the third on production problems. The 1965-66 field is to be human relations—personnel management and employment relationships.

ICAME has not been without its headaches. One major problem is that many of the participants are mature adults who think of themselves as scholars, although their grasp of modern business practices may be short of American standards, and who therefore resist being treated as "students" in an academic course. They find it hard to mix with the more junior participants, for whom the normal academic practices of assigned papers, examinations, and grades are more acceptable spurs to learning.

The program does not make a great contribution to the university— apart from the permanent director, faculty members are brought into the program only for short periods—but it is regarded as a service program. Encouraged by Dean Arbuckle, the faculty of the Business School has agreed to continue the program as a major commitment in international activities.

Stanford Research Institute

The Stanford administration has not encouraged the growth of campus institutes and centers—although it has not been able to run counter to the trend—on the grounds that institutes tend to become independent and because decentralization makes for untidy administration.

If a reminder of this is necessary, it is visible at any time from the top of the Hoover Tower on the Stanford campus: four miles away, in Menlo Park, stand the headquarters and principal laboratories of the Stanford Research Institute (SRI), a nonprofit organization performing contract research for industry, government, and foundations in the fields of the physical and life sciences, engineering (principally electronics), economics and management sciences, agriculture, and international development. About 75 per cent of SRI's present contracts are for government work, and about 15 per cent of its total projects are in the international field. Its contract research volume during 1965 will run to about $43 million.

The SRI was formed in 1946 by a group of West Coast industrialists, in cooperation with the Stanford University trustees, who hoped to provide a West Coast diversified research center that would profit from the postwar boom expected from the expansion of the aircraft and related defense industries in California. Ever since, the relations between SRI and the university have not been as close as the founders had hoped. Physically SRI is separate from Stanford and operates independently of it: it has its own research facilities and equipment and, except for a half dozen or so scientists who hold joint SRI-Stanford faculty appointments, its own full-time staff.

The early years were touch and go for SRI. Tided over by a loan from Stanford University, it was saved by the flood of defense contracts that followed the outbreak of the Korean War. Now it has some of the attributes of a university: a division for Economic Development, an Agricultural Research Center, offices in Washington and New York, and overseas representation in Zurich, Milan, Tokyo, Bangkok, Lima, and Toronto. "In some parts of the world," boast SRI executives, "SRI's name is better known than Stanford's."

There are advantages, however, to retaining the Stanford name: it often helps in recruiting staff members, some of whom are interested in joint appointments or in teaching at the university. Most prominent of these is Dr. Eugene Staley, internationally known expert in the economics of developing nations and director of SRI's International Development Center, who held a joint appointment as professor of education at Stanford in 1965-66, enabling him to serve in the School of Education's Comparative Education Center.

In turn, SRI claims that it offers certain advantages to Stanford. It provides a handy consulting arrangment for Stanford faculty members (although SRI is not at all limited to calling on them); it offers job opportunities for Stanford graduate students; and at times the combined research facilities and knowledge of the two institutions can be brought to bear on a problem.

The SRI is eager to expand its overseas activities. One idea that has been discussed over the past few years is the suggestion that SRI take on the administrative-management functions of an overseas service contract, leaving Stanford professors—who, like professors anywhere, do not take kindly to administrative chores—to supply the academic-research components of a project. This sharing of functions would save Stanford from having to set up its own service machinery for overseas operations, and might deter SRI from striving to become a quasi-academic institution. The Stanford administration admits that in theory such a relationship might be feasible, but in view of the history of Stanford-SRI relations it is not one the university wants to start on a major scale.

An opportunity to determine how such teamwork would hold up in practice presented itself late in 1964 when Professor William O. Jones, director of Stanford's Food Research Institute, designed a proposal for research on farm marketing facilities and practices in tropical Africa, an investigation into the movement of staple foodstuffs from farm to consumer in various African countries. The proposal called for a study of farm marketing practices in three locations in Africa to be conducted by small teams of American farm marketing specialists, drawn from land-grant universities with AID contracts in Africa, accompanied by African agricultural economists.

Unwilling to assume the logistical problems of managing teams in the field over a period of some thirty months required for the study, Professor Jones approached SRI with his proposal. Institute's Economic Development division prepared a contract submission to AID under which SRI would act as the prime contractor, assuming overall program management, leaving Jones to formulate research plans and design the study as chairman of a coordinating committee. Reluctant to limit its role to straight housekeeping on the contract, SRI intends to assign one of its senior economists to the study staff. At the end of May, 1965, AID signed a contract, giving the new SRI-Food Research Institute team the go-ahead. The results will be closely watched by the faculty and administration of the university.

Asian Studies

Stanford was one of the first American universities to commit itself to Asian studies. In 1906, the year Stanford began offering a course in Far Eastern history, the first in the United States, William James delivered the Founder's Day address and charted a role for the university as "mediating between America and Asia, helping the more intellectual men of both continents to understand each other better!" President Wilbur was a founder of the Institute of Pacific Relations, and the Hoover Library has long been collecting materials on the Far East. Thus it was not surprising that Stanford's first area studies program was that on East Asia, initiated with a Ford Foundation grant of $225,000 in 1957, to coordinate and strengthen faculty teaching and research in this area.

High points of the first five years of this program include the establishment of a National Defense Education Act Chinese-Japanese Language and Area Center that ranks among the highest in the number of National

Defense Foreign Language Fellowship holders; an increase in the faculty of the department of Asian languages from four in 1957 to thirteen by 1961; and the establishment of overseas centers in Tokyo and Taipei for graduate and undergraduate instruction in language and area study.

A five-member East Asian Studies Committee took over from the original East Asian Research Committee in the autumn of 1963; it acts as an executive committee for the program. It includes professors of history, economics, political science, and Asian languages as well as the associate dean of the graduate division, and has primary responsibility for the direction of East Asian Studies. A larger committee, which includes all faculty members with some interest in Asian studies, meets occasionally, primarily for discussions of general policy and topics of mutual interest. The Asian Studies Committee coordinates the various offerings in Asian studies, but it does not offer a degree. As a policy the university encourages primary emphasis on a discipline rather than an area.

The range of undergraduate courses in East Asian studies covers art, history, anthropology, political science, language, literature, economics, and philosophy. In the Asian languages and literature departments there are currently fourteen undergraduates and graduate students working toward an M.A. or Ph.D.

In 1962 the East Asian Studies program was allocated $600,000 over a five-year period from the overall Ford Foundation grant for international studies.

Latin American Studies

For more than half a century Stanford has maintained some institutional commitment to Latin American studies. John C. Branner, who became President in 1913, was a geologist who knew the language and culture of Brazil as well as its terrain. Between the wars the teaching and scholarship of Percy Martin, Graham Stuart, and others influenced a generation of future teachers and government personnel. The Food Research Institute has studied Latin American nutrients since its founding. Geologists, petrologists, and others in the School of Earth Sciences have done field work in South and Central America for decades.

In most universities—as in the United States itself—interest in Latin America waned during and after World War II owing to the greater attractions of new and emerging nations in Asia and Africa, and Stanford was no exception. Nevertheless a nucleus of scholars remained, men oriented toward Latin America, and Latin American students continued to come to Stanford in numbers: in 1962-63 there were seventy-eight students from fifteen countries in Latin America and the Caribbean, representing 12 percent of the total foreign student population. Stanford's problem, however, was a fragmentation of faculty and campus involvement with Latin America, a condition that has plagued the university for a score of years.

Before World War II ended John W. Dodds, then Dean of the newly founded School of Humanities, farsightedly laid the base for a series of interdepartmental area programs. Ronald Hilton, an academic entrepreneur who had joined the Stanford staff in 1942 to teach Spanish, was made responsible for a Hispanic American areas studies program, and as the years went by he established around himself the university's most conspicuous effort in the field of Latin American studies. In 1961 the program was given institute status and a name—the Institute of Hispanic American and Luso-Brazilian Studies.

Hilton, English-born and Oxford-educated, was a French linguist who witnessed the fall of the Spanish monarchy in 1931 and was caught in the siege of Madrid during the Spanish Civil War, on which he reported for London newspapers. It occurred to him then—as it had to Herbert Hoover in an earlier war—that someone should be collecting the contemporary documents of the conflict. Years later, established at Stanford, he determined to do something about collecting documentary materials on Spain and Latin America.

The Institute, as Hilton conceived it, was to be conducted as a teaching and research organization concerned primarily with the study of contemporary developments in Latin America, Spain, and Portugal (the ancient Lusitania, hence Luso-Brazilian). Language was the basic tool—but not the traditional Iberian literature: instead work at the Institute was based on the vivid, living Spanish of the daily newspapers of Spain, Portugal, and Latin America, on periodicals, political tracts, and documents, on correspondence and interviews with politicians, diplomats, and businessmen involved in South American affairs. The focus of the program was politics, the predominant and current interest of Latin America, Spain, and Portugal.

In 1948 Hilton began publishing a monthly journal, the *Hispanic American Report,* and in due time this became accepted as an authority on events in Spain, Portugal, and Latin America—at a time when no one else was doing anything comparable to keep abreast of political, social, and economic developments in those areas. Edited for specialists—at its peak the circulation never went above 2,500 copies monthly—the *Hispanic American Report* filled a useful background role, and at times, such as during Castro's takeover in Cuba, its comments rated national attention.

Such attention made the Stanford administration uneasy about the *Report.* Edited by Hilton, who was responsible to no one for its contents or comments, it was not beholden to Stanford—and yet it carried the Stanford reputation behind it. Furthermore, it was produced entirely by students at the Institute. A compulsive clipper and filer himself, Hilton organized the monthly production with IBM precision: students clipped, filed, and discussed events in their assigned areas, then wrote reports to a prescribed word length to cover developments in the respective countries. Hilton contended that the work on the *Report* was the "cement" that held his students to the Institute: his critics among the administration and faculty alleged that he was "exploiting student labor" at the expense of scholarly training.

Over the years the university tried various means to widen the field of Hispanic-American and Luso-Brazilian studies, to bridge departmental lines, improve the training of graduate students, and bring together scholars with mutual interests in the context of the curriculum, but these efforts were thwarted by personality conflicts and internecine departmental struggles. Not attached to any discipline, the Institute and the *Report* lacked disciplinary support in the academic power struggle, and Hilton himself, firm in his opinions and free in expressing them, was not an academic team player.

In January, 1963, the administration appointed—on the recommendation of the Committee on International Studies—a Committee on Latin American Studies, representative of the entire university and including Professor Hilton as one of its members. Professor Spaeth, chairman of the full International Studies Committee, served as chairman.

The new committee was charged with planning Stanford's future development in the Latin American field, a long-range assignment made more urgent by the fact the Ford Foundation had requested Stanford, along with several other major American universities, to submit a statement of its overall development plans for Latin American studies (the foundation's grant to Stanford in late 1962 to support its international programs had excluded Latin America, pending a study the foundation was making on how best to strengthen Latin American studies throughout the United States).

High on the committee's agenda was the future of the *Hispanic American Report*. The first proposal was the creation of two boards to supervise the production of the *Report*—a faculty board to review the monthly contents, help formulate editorial policy, and discuss the issues growing from university sponsorship; and a national board to review annually the balance and accuracy of the periodical. Consideration of the effectiveness of advisory bodies in the past led the committee to realize that the problem lay not so much in the content of the *Report* as in the relation of the *Report* and its method of preparation to the curriculum of the Institute and its academic standing. A review by the School of Humanities and Sciences determined that the doctoral program being offered by the Institute was not academically sound. It was recommended that henceforth the Institute operate wholly at the M.A. level and that its activities be confined solely to the production of the *Report*. A request for funds for added staff for the *Report* was therefore included in the submission Stanford made to the Ford Foundation in September, 1963, for a grant to assist the expansion of the university's Latin American efforts.

In November, 1964, the long-simmering problem spilled over. At the direction of the Dean of Graduate Studies, all Ph.D. candidates were removed from the Institute and Professor Hilton was informed that the Institute would concentrate on giving practical instruction at the M.A. level. Hilton's answer was to resign as director of the Institute and editor of the *Report*. Although he intended it as a tactical maneuver, his resignation was accepted by the administration. The *Report* was suspended. Hilton was later persuaded to remain at Stanford in his capacity as professor of romance languages.

In November, 1964, the Ford Foundation announced it had granted Stanford $550,000 to support its Latin American program.

After a period of reorganization Stanford, in the autumn of 1965, embarked on a new and expanded program of graduate work in Latin American studies. The Institute went out of existence, and in its place the university offered a new interdisciplinary program leading to the M.A. degree in Latin American studies. Under a new Committee on Latin American Studies, headed by an anthropologist, A. Kimball Romney, the program includes courses in anthropology, economics, geography, history, modern European languages, political science, and sociology, and courses in the Food Research Institute and several of the professional schools as well. The program is designed primarily for graduates of colleges and professional schools who wish to specialize in Latin American affairs, and for prospective doctoral candidates who wish first to acquire an understanding of Latin American language and culture. Students at the M.A. level who then intend to seek admission to doctoral candidacy in a discipline may enter this program for regional specialization or may choose courses relating to Latin America while working toward the M.A. in a discipline. Stanford does not offer a Ph.D. degree in Latin American studies, but a qualified candidate may be helped to form a cross-disciplinary doctoral program focused on that region.

Another innovation for the autumn of 1965 was the establishment of an NDEA Language and Area Center for Latin America.

Unsuccessful efforts were made by the university to persuade other universities and organizations to take over publication of the *Hispanic American Report,* but it remains in limbo, with its archives temporarily stored in the Hoover Institution.

African Studies

Stanford has long had a nucleus of scholars interested in Africa, and the research facilities for such scholarship, but until recently the potential of these was not fully developed. The course offerings have until recently been more limited than the interest in African affairs on campus would indicate.

Somewhat paradoxically, Stanford's strengths in this area imposed their own limitations, in that studies of Africa took their coloration from the Food Research Institute and the Hoover Institution. Individual members of the Food Research Institute were studying economic aspects of African food and agriculture in the 1930's, but it was not until 1953 that the Institute began aggressively collecting materials on African economics, agriculture, and nutrition and began devoting sustained attention to Africa. Similarly the Hoover Library collection on Africa up to 1952 was acquired partly by accident and usually unsystematically, with heavy emphasis on European Africa. In 1952 the library appointed its first Curator of the African Collection, which has steadily improved since. The weakest part of the Stanford African collection, in anthropology and ethnology, is now being actively built up by the department of anthropology. More recently attention has been given to the politics of Africa, and active research is presently going on in history, sociology, communications, education, and mathematics.

The prior interest of the Food Research Institute in Africa was recognized when an allocation of $100,000 was made available—out of the $2,500,000 Ford Foundation grant given Stanford in 1962—to organize African studies at the university. A Subcommittee for African Studies was set up under the chairmanship of Professor William O. Jones, director of the Food Research Institute, who served until September, 1965, as director of the program. The seven-member subcommittee includes representation from the Hoover Institution and the departments of history, anthropology, biology, and political science. Some thirty faculty members who have demonstrated interest in Africa attend the general meetings of the African Studies Committee.

Ever since the subcommittee was formed Jones has pressed for a wider base in African studies. Only a few courses were given by the Food Research Institute, which offered a program of study leading to the M.A. and Ph.D. degrees in the general field of agricultural economics relating to Africa. With this specialized approach Stanford could not compete with the first-rank African studies centers in the United States.

In the spring of 1965 Jones achieved a breakthrough with the appointment of four regular faculty members, African specialists in history, political science, anthropology, and a joint appointment in education and political science. In addition, the Food Research Institute is seeking to add staff with an African interest and, hopefully, an interest in food research as well. These new appointments will permit Stanford to add at least half a dozen new courses on Africa beginning in the 1965-66 academic year. Joseph Greenberg, a specialist in African linguistics, will serve as chairman of the African studies program, replacing Jones.

Some consideration has apparently been given by the Africanists on campus to establishing a formal Institute of African Affairs, but the sentiment of the administration and the African specialists is that such a campus-wide effort would require a much greater expansion of African studies than Stanford now considers desirable. Professor Jones believes efforts should be made to add experts in African arts and African agricultural development, but he does not favor expanding to cover the almost endless range of African languages. A possible factor entering into the consideration not to create a major African center is that there already exists in the area one African study center with international status, at the University of California (Los Angeles), as well as an African studies program at the University of California (Berkeley).

Western European Studies

Since World War II the tendency in American colleges and universities has been to take Western European studies for granted and instead to pursue more exotic studies or to concentrate resources on areas previously neglected. At Stanford the period of neglect was less conspicuous because the university has long been strong in Western European history and modern European studies.

In 1963 an allocation of $168,000 for five years was made from Ford Foundation funds to establish a faculty seminar in Western European Studies. The fund is operated by the history department, but its impact is interdisciplinary. The largest part of the grant is used to cover salaries for visiting scholars, but there are fellowships for graudate students to study abroad and funds for faculty travel for research. The visiting scholar program each year invites to Stanford someone who is completing a manuscript, specifying that he present it for discussion at seminars composed of Western European specialists from Stanford and neighboring universities, and that he give a graduate or undergraduate course or both in the history department.

Library Resources

The Stanford libraries—consisting of the Main Library, forty departmental units and six special libraries (Hoover Institution, Food Research Institute, Jackson Business, Lane Medical, Law, and Linear Accelerator Center)—have labored under the double strain of an expanding student body and spreading international commitments. The Main Library—which is to be supplemented in the university's building expansion program—was built when the student body was less than 3,000. Despite the fact that funds for acquisitions doubled in the five years after 1959-60, it is deficient in space, number of volumes per student, and ability to meet the demands of new scholastic requirements and new teaching methods. A new undergraduate library is under construction.

The total university library system has respectable collections in most international areas. However, as with most university libraries, the increased emphasis on international studies has created special problems. The concentration on graduate studies, for instance, has placed a great load on the library, not only for space and funds, but for trained assistants to handle the specialized materials. The library has had to hire and train its own staff of specialized bibliographers. Also, to get the materials needed to develop area programs requires a mechanism for acquisitions abroad. There is no such mechanism, and individual buying trips are costly and time-consuming. Worse, competitive buying among American and other universities in an area such as Africa merely drives prices upward and often ends in fragmenting and splitting collections. Stanford therefore cooperates with U.C.L.A. and the Berkeley campus in buying and lending documents, manuscripts, and materials.

In the early days of area specialization universities tended to overlook the increasing strain on library resources. Thus, in Stanford's 1962 grant from the Ford Foundation, up to $500,000 was to be spent on strengthening the Hoover Institution as part of the university's total library system, but nothing was allocated for the main library. In the 1963 presentation to the Ford Foundation for a special grant for Latin American studies, funds were requested for both acquisitions and staff needs for the central university library.

The main library and the Hoover library have traditionally had spheres of influence. The Hoover is, in general, responsible for material concerning revolutionary movements, especially those of the left, political parties, and military affairs, and has a general emphasis on contemporary historical, political, economic, and social affairs. The main library concentrates on *belles-lettres,* linquistics, archaeology, anthropology, pre-twentieth-century history, fine arts, and a general humanities and social science emphasis. The division of focus, recognition of a situation that has gradually evolved over the years, is coodinated through a subcommittee on libraries of the Committee on International Studies. In the past few years the percentage of Stanford student users of the Hoover library has greatly increased, with more than 50 percent of the users being undergraduates. In 1963-64, 70 percent of the Hoover library's users were Stanford students and faculty.

Professional Schools

"When I came to Stanford in 1955," recalled Wilbur Schramm, director of the Institute of Communication Research, "the international wing of the political science department was *the* international element on campus. Now it has rippled out all over the campus, into most disciplines. It is admittedly not an even spread, but there is *some* interest in *all* departments, in *all* areas of the academic community, even in the professional schools."

Despite this widening interest, participation in the economic and social development of the less developed nations of the world—more particularly, through technical assistance contracts with AID and other agencies—has never been high on Stanford's list. Those responsible for the university's internationalism contend that this is because of the drain on the resources of a university that such programs represent. Stanford, they feel, may have perhaps been more insistent than some universities in demanding that any overseas technical contract embarked upon should have solid teaching and research relationships to the university, a requirement that ruled out a good many contracts for service abroad. In any event, experience with AID contracts to date has not been encouraging for Stanford, and its present commitments are limited to a five-year AID contract for the Graduate School of Business to design and launch a graduate business school at Lima, Peru, and a few smaller undertakings.

There is, however, an ongoing discussion among faculty and administration as to why, how, and under what conditions university personnel might undertake contracts to carry out services abroad for AID, the Department of State, and other government agencies and certain American foundations. Robert Rosenzweig, Associate Dean of the Graduate Division, who has responsibility for review and approval of any AID or outside contracts at Stanford, reports that "the rising competence in international studies at Stanford is producing greater faculty interest in such activities and a growing recognition by government agencies of the contribution which this university can make to the achievement of their objectives. Thus, it is reasonable to expect increasing pressure from both sides—faculty and government—for the university to engage in overseas (contractual) projects."

Dean Rosenzweig, a political scientist who has had several years' experience with the U.S. Office of Education, takes what might be called a hard-nosed academic approach to such outside contracts. He is not against them *per se,* but believes any such undertakings should be measured against two basic questions: (1) What in today's world is Stanford's educational role? (2) Would AID contracts help or hinder Stanford in performing its role? He feels that a great deal of hard thinking needs to be done on these and related questions by the Stanford faculty and administration before the university commits itself to too many overseas service contracts.

This attitude is mirrored on a smaller scale in some of the professional schools. The School of Earth Sciences, for instance, no longer engages in AID contracts. Its former dean, Charles Park, found them too difficult to administer, too much involved in red tape, and too limiting in research and publication opportunities. A factor contributing to this attitude may be that the faculty of the School of Earth Sciences appears able to find numerous other means of working overseas, primarily for private extracting concerns. In some cases contracts between Stanford and a number of private corporations go back many years: there appears to be no limit to the number of offers faculty members receive, and they are obviously financially advantageous. A majority of the faculty have at some time been on assignments in Latin America. In addition, the School has an informal cooperative arrangement with the University of Bahia, Brazil. Faculty members returning from these foreign assignments frequently serve as guest lecturers in the social science departments concerned with the areas where the technical work has been done. To assist in filling temporarily vacant positions, the School encourages retired professors of similar departments in other universities to live in the vicinity, and then offers them "associate status," which includes library facilities, so they are available when short-term absences occur.

The School of Engineering has engaged in far-reaching assignments. Among these have been a course for plant engineers and practicing engineers in Ceylon, a visiting professorship in electrical engineering at Madrid University, and teaching and research in Australia, Switzerland, Argentina, and Holland. During the summer of 1964 four students from different fields, under the supervision of a Stanford engineering professor and on contract with AID, spent three months helping develop small industries and businesses in Peru. An experiment in itself, it is hoped the Peruvian program will continue and expand to other countries so that more Stanford engineering students can gain this kind of internship as part of their professional training. The influence of these overseas interests is reflected in the fact that more than one-third of the foreign students enrolled at Stanford are enrolled in one or another of the university's engineering departments.

In addition to its ICAME program, the School of Business has conducted summer programs in management techniques in Iran, Ceylon, and New Zealand. The School, under an AID contract, established in Lima, Peru, the first graduate school of business administration in South America.

The School of Education, apart from its Comparative Overseas Education Center, is involved in a program to improve native competence in secondary education in Latin America, with the support of the Ford Foundation. Other members of the faculty are involved in the summer school in Guadalajara, Mexico, now administered primarily by the University of Arizona, which is attended by about thirty Stanford undergraduates each year.

The international activities of the School of Medicine have been concentrated in the Latin American countries, mainly because Stanford decided to enter the field of tropical medicine in 1955. A few years later, under a National Institutes of Health program, Stanford set up traveling fellowships, which enable about half the students in the medical school to do some tropical medical work in Central America or Brazil. These have produced satisfying results. For instance, Dr. Charles Beal, a former medical missionary, developed a "plastic bag" technique for maximum sterility under tropical conditions for emergency operations, and he and a group of Stanford medical students have demonstrated this in parts of Central America. Under the guidance of Dr. Quentin Geiman, brought in a decade ago to head Stanford's tropical medical program, student exchanges have been worked out with El Salvador and Venezuela. The school has also had a close institutional relationship with the Vargas School of Medicine in Caracas.

In the School of Law the international dimension is perhaps more visible than in the other professional schools. This is due in good part to Professor Carl Spaeth, who served for sixteen years as Dean of the Law School and continues to teach half-time as well as to head the International Legal Studies program. Professor Spaeth explained that the baseline for the internationalization of the law curriculum was about 1953. Up to that year law students who entered in the postwar years, although more interested in world affairs than their prewar predecessors, were mostly concerned with getting their degree out of the way. They took the courses offered and did not question the curriculum. Beginning about 1953, said Spaeth, law students began to indicate in subtle—and some not so subtle—ways that they wanted a broader array of course offerings than in the past.

With assistance from the Ford Foundation and other sources, an International Legal Studies program was begun in 1954. Over the years it has emphasized the legal aspects of relations between nations, the UN Charter, GATT, and the entire range of communications among states that regulate international politics, trade, and other relationships.

More recently, with support from the current omnibus Ford Foundation grant, the Law School began its program of Comparative Legal Studies. The focus of this is the domestic, or internal, legal systems of other countries, comparing and contrasting them with our own. The emphasis within the curriculum is on Italian law, the civil law system best suited for comparison with our own common law system, although faculty members with special interests have been assisted with research on legal problems throughout the British Commonwealth, Scandinavia, and the Soviet bloc. This research is then reflected in the comparative materials introduced into the standard courses on sales law, commercial law, anti-trust law, and so on.

The allocation from the Ford Foundation grant—$750,000—was also used to endow faculty appointments and to bring a series of visiting scholars to the Law School for one year at a time. In addition, the funds are used to bring foreign legal specialists to Stanford for further study. In conjunction with the International Legal Studies program, the South Asian and Japanese programs provided for a full year of legal study at Stanford for thirty-seven young judges, career law officers, and teachers of demonstrated promise from India, Ceylon, Burma, Pakistan, and Japan. In the 1965-66 academic year Italian law students will be brought to Stanford for the first time. The Law School has also played an important part in the creation, staffing, and programming of the Indian Law Institute at New Delhi.

All this has affected the law students, as their course work and career patterns show. Although no international law studies are required for the LL.B. degree, nearly all students now elect at least one of the four principal courses and seminar offerings. Before 1954 less than one-tenth of them on average registered for the one course then offered. Currently more law students are seriously interested in going into government service—State Department, AID, and so on—and a number take internships in the State Department and in programs of overseas service. In addition, more students are seeking jobs with firms that have overseas operations.

The Ford Foundation's grant to Stanford in 1964 for Latin American studies included some funds for pilot projects to be designed by the professional schools to encourage the involvement of their students in Latin American affairs. Professor Spaeth has advocated, especially in the Law School, the use of some of these funds to enable a few students to prepare for internships in Latin America. They would be selected at least a year before completion of their professional education so that they could use a summer for intensive language study and could then interweave appropriate courses in the liberal arts with their final year of law, business, or other school. One law student is already pursuing such a program.

IV

The wide range of Stanford's present commitments in world affairs was not arrived at either by design or central planning. The Stanford academic climate simply encouraged initiative and permitted international programs to flourish without central direction.

However, the very extent of Stanford's involvement made it difficult for the university fully to capitalize on its international capabilities without some form of all-university coordination. If Stanford can be faulted today, it is on the ground that so many years slipped past before this realization was translated into a policy and the mechanism to carry it out. The Stanford rejoinder to this criticism is that the passage of years gave the various departments and schools the opportunity for initiative, to find their own levels of interest and involvement—but this assertion is not offered with much conviction.

The Committee on International Studies

Within a very few years of taking office, President Sterling told us, "I had the feeling that too many things were going on in the international field at the university about which I and the administration knew nothing." His answer was to set up the President's International Committee, which met intermittently—and sometimes not for six months and more—and was headed by the President, the Provost, or a designated representative.

For almost ten years this committee continued in existence, not taking a really active role on campus, but by its very existence providing a reason for inaction on the part of those who felt a vague need for coordination in their international efforts. When C. Easton Rothwell was director of the

Hoover Institution, he was brought in as chairman of the committee, and for a brief time it gave promise of becoming something of a power center on campus, but when Rothwell left to become president of Mills College in 1959 the committee's role again declined.

That the committee gained a new lease on life and new authority was due in good part to the convictions and actions of a few individuals, chief among them Dean Wert, now Vice Provost and Dean for Undergraduate Education, who came to Stanford after a period with the Carnegie Corporation, and Carl Spaeth, then Dean of the Law School. Spaeth, after wartime service in Latin America and later in Washington, in 1946 was named Dean of the Law faculty at Stanford. In 1952-53 he spent his sabbatical in India for the Ford Foundation. More recently he served the foundation as a consultant on Latin America.

Wert, Spaeth, and a few others saw Rothwell's departure as a time for stock-taking. Some departments and schools were admittedly edgy about the committee, ineffective as it was, because they feared that the growth of a new campus entity might dilute their own authority. Others, particularly those with developing international programs, were unhappy that no means for campus coordination existed. The international committee then had no staff to carry out decisions even when arrived at, and the chairman was overloaded with his regular job. Several small Ford Foundation and other grants had been made to existing or new units within the university, but without correlation.

Sterling accepted the arguments of Wert, Spaeth, and others that at the very least the committee needed a designated, permanent chairman and a partial staff, and, after much searching, Emile Despres was persuaded to leave Williams and to join the Stanford staff for the 1961-62 academic year on a joint appointment, one half in the economics department, one half as chairman of the international committee. Recalling the arrangement, Despres said it was his understanding that there were to be no executive or implementation functions connected with the committee assignment, and that it would emphasize long-term planning.

The arrival of Despres, presumably not by coincidence, took place at the very time Stanford was assembling material for its preliminary submission to the Ford Foundation for an over-all grant for international studies, which exercise helped crystallize international thinking on the campus and encouraged the disposition to coordinate within the university. The East Asian specialists on the campus had begun to get together on their own, and their efforts were encouraged by a $225,000 Ford grant in 1957 to assist them in thinking in area terms. Likewise individual scholars came together in 1960 to establish a Social Science Committee on Latin American Studies. A similar coming-together took place in the School of Education. "This departmental initiative," we were told, "met with a responsiveness from the President's office."

As a well-known economist Despres retained consulting assignments that took up much of his time. And preparing the Ford submission turned out to be a far more detailed job than he had bargained for. At the end of a year as committee chairman he requested to be relieved of the job.

Carl Spaeth, who had meanwhile moved the Law School more into the forefront of international legal work, had earlier indicated to Sterling his intention of giving up the deanship, which he had held for sixteen years, and his desire to continue work in the international field. Having turned off-campus to get Despres, Stanford now turned to its own faculty. In August, 1962, Spaeth was offered and accepted the post of chairman of the Committee on International Studies on a half-time basis, allowing him to continue to teach in the Law School.

During the time Spaeth has served as chairman the Committee has taken on a structure and slowly and firmly spelled out its jurisdiction. It has no formal charter, and it takes its strength both from its apparent role within the administrative structure of the university and from the personality of its chairman.

From the administration's viewpoint the Committee on International Studies is responsible for continuing review and analysis of the university's role in international studies. It consists of eighteen members, appointed by the President, including representatives of the administration, senior faculty, and members from schools and departments throughout the university involved in international affairs, including the Schools of Business, Education, Engineering, Law, and Medicine.

As chairman, Spaeth serves in a staff capacity in close liaison with the President's office. The administration has made it clear that, as chairman, he will be called on to make recommendations on priorities with respect to new faculty appointments in international studies; to advise on overseas commitments negotiated by sectors of the university with governments or private foundations; to consult with the university librarian and the librarians of the several institutes and schools so that acquisition programs will insure an effective use of funds; and to encourage the development of teaching and research proposals for consideration by the Committee.

The Committee has been provided with an administrative budget— $37,000 per year—that permits the employment of an administrative assistant and one secretary, and occupancy of two small offices in the Law School. The office is charged with assisting the chairman, servicing the Committee, and maintaining current inventories of all international programs within the university. The Committee was granted a discretionary sum of $250,000 from the general Ford Foundation grant to allow it to start new international programs.

The Committee on International Studies meets about half a dozen times each year. However, much of the coordination is achieved by subcommittees that function on a regular or an *ad hoc* basis. Thus an East Asian committee, in existence before the Ford grant of 1962, was reorganized and continued as a subcommittee. This five-member East Asian Studies Committee acts as an executive committee for that area: a larger group brings together all faculty members interested in Asian studies. An African Studies Committee and a Latin American Committee have similar duties— facilitating communication among faculty members studying Africa (or Latin America); coordinating library acquisitions; introducing area studies into the curriculum; assisting in liaison with similar area studies at other universities; and advising the Committee on International Studies of the state and needs of African (or Latin American) studies at Stanford.

The chairmen of these area committees are members of the Committee on International Studies, and the area committees function as subcommittees of the parent body. Members of an area committee are selected only in part from the membership of the main committee, thus bringing in other faculty members and giving a greater number a share in charting the course of international studies at Stanford. In addition, a subcommittee on libraries was appointed. Headed by the Provost's executive assistant, it includes the director of the Hoover Institution and the acting director of the university library as well as the chairman of the faculty committee on university libraries and members of the faculty involved substantially in the regional and other special areas emphasized in the international programs. More recently a subcommittee was set up to look into the general economic and political aspects of relations among nations and regions throughout the world.

The fact that the Committee on International Studies was the chosen instrument to dispense the Ford Foundation funds granted in 1962 (according to the terms of the Ford Foundation grant letter, "it is understood that the University's Committee on International Studies will allocate funds to individual projects under this grant in relation to the general plans and priorities of the University's overall international program") greatly strengthened Spaeth's position as the new chairman, but he has not been content to have the committee act as a mere conduit of funds.

Several procedural mechanisms have been developed by Spaeth and the administration by which expenditures can be reviewed and coordinated, without being rigidly regulated. Before the beginning of each academic year the principal investigator for each project is expected to present to the committee a statement of his expenditures during the past year and his anticipated budget for the coming twelve to eighteen months. In addition, the committee's office receives copies of the monthly budget statements of each project. These can be checked against the original projections. As chairman, Spaeth is expected to report periodically to the President and Provost on the general pattern of expenditures.

The university has accepted the Committee's recommendation that Stanford begin gradually to assume responsibility for financing from general funds the incremental cost of the twelve or so tenure appointments resulting from increased international studies. Under this proposal Stanford assumes its obligation at a rate to increase from 10 to 20 per cent a year, beginning in 1965-66, until the additional positions have been gradually built into the university's budget.

The Committee also reserved to its members a discretionary role in selecting people for new appointments under the Ford grant. A memorandum was issued to all deans and department heads describing the search procedures to be followed in initiating international studies appointments: further it was specified that Spaeth countersign appointment papers for all persons appointed within the terms of the grant, to assure that the department concerned had conformed to the Ford Foundation grant. (This memo has proved so acceptable that its recommendations for consultation between department and regional group have reportedly been followed even for appointments not financed by the Ford grant.)

V

Stanford's proposal to the Ford Foundation for support of its international studies cited an agenda of basic policy issues facing the Committee for the next year or so. The range of problems then to be solved touched on most aspects of the university's international activities. The issues were:

1. What are the alternative methods of insuring liaison between the Committee and various area and problem study committees that will be directing Stanford's international programs?

2. What criteria should govern university decisions with regard to government, foundation, and commercial "service" contracts abroad?

3. Should there always be a demonstrable educational feedback, and how can the social and cultural insights being gained abroad by natural scientists and professionals contribute to education in the humanities and social sciences?

4. Can Stanford insure a judicious pacing of the acceleration process taking place in teaching and research on critical geographical and functional problems, giving consideration to the revolutionary changes in language teaching that developed during the pressures of wartime, and to the impact of Stanford's overseas centers in intensifying American competence within a short time?

5. How best can a balance be maintained between contemporary, problem-oriented research and fundamental research, guarding against neglect of the latter?

6. What role should an individual university play in feeding the tremendous scholarly output into the mainstream of the community?

7. What kind of relationship can most appropriately be established between the university and the Stanford Research Institute?

8. How can the ambivalent relationship between the university and the quasi-autonomous Hoover Institution be clarified?

9. How can Stanford capitalize still more effectively, both for students and for faculty, on the quantitatively and qualitatively rich resources of foreign students and scholars on the campus?

"Where Do We Go From Here?"

Some of these issues, and several others unanticipated in 1962, were confronted at a three-day "where do we go from here?" conference held in May, 1964, with several of the deans and all but one member of the Committee on International Studies in attendance. The keynote question posed by Spaeth was "How serious are we at Stanford about international studies?" While revealing a built-in tendency of some to resist the complications and intrusions of international affairs, the conference left no doubt that the university is serious in its commitments, and produced an ambitious program of action to be followed during the years to come.

Some of the items that landed on the Committee's agenda as a result of this conference are a content survey of courses that might have relevance for international studies; a data analysis of undergraduate programs; delineation of the advisory roles that subcommittees of the main Committee might play in curriculum planning by students and departments in the light of the first two items; a statement of the university's position about AID contracts; and coordination of faculty recruiting. Items being considered as a result of the conference include a plan for intensive training in critical languages for selected undergraduates, similar to the plan at Princeton; a degree program at the M.A. level, perhaps based on a separate center or institute, which would provide preparation for nonacademic careers in international affairs; strengthening the SRI to complement university activities in international affairs; and publication of an information handbook for international content courses available at Stanford, now being prepared.

Interuniversity Cooperation

Stanford, like most American universities and colleges, is prepared to further interuniversity cooperation and collaboration much more than it has done to date, according to President Sterling. Much of the signpointing will presumably come from the Committee on International Studies.

Stanford and Berkeley have already worked out modest collaborative arrangements. One such exists between the anthropology departments at the two schools for training graduate students on both campuses. The departments of economics have agreed on the desirability of collaborating on economic development study, and a Center for Overseas Projects in Economic Development has been proposed for the Bay area. A mechanism for collaboration in overseas activities between Stanford and the total University of California complex is now being designed by these institutions, patterned partly after the Midwest Universities Consortium.

Stanford is already involved in an interuniversity, interdisciplinary summer training program in anthropological field techniques for beginning graduate students. With the support of the National Science Foundation three training sites are being set up to orient graduate students in the behavioral sciences to the methods and problems of field work. At Oaxaca, Mexico, a site is being staffed by Stanford faculty; a similar site at Puebla, Mexico, will be the responsibility of the University of Pittsburgh. The third site, among the Shoshone Indians of Nevada, will be the responsibility of the University of Nevada. There will be twelve students at each site drawn from these three and other universitities; the twenty-four at the two Mexican sites in 1964 represented eight institutions.

In the autumn of 1964 President Sterling sent to the presidents of eighty-nine colleges and universities in thirteen Western states a proposal for a cooperative undergraduate program in the study of Chinese and Japanese languages and related area studies. The program would enable students interested in East Asia but attending institutions that do not offer Chinese or Japanese to pursue their language studies as undergraduates of their own college but in residence at Stanford. This would eliminate the need for smaller institutions to establish such departments, which are very expensive, and would also assure better and fuller use of the faculty and facilities at Stanford (which, in these language areas, are not overcrowded). Stanford proposed that a student spend the summer preceding his junior year and his junior year at Stanford, plus a possible second summer at Stanford. Both summers would be devoted to intensive language training, and a student would emerge from these fifteen months with a third-year-level competence in his language. In addition, he would have taken courses related to his area in the humanities and the social sciences. After the fifteen months at Stanford he would return to his home campus for his senior year and his A.B. degree. To protect against charges of piracy, Stanford will refuse to accept any such students as senior year transfers.

The response to this proposal—modeled on Princeton's "critical languages" program—was encouraging. Most of the institutions contacted responded, and most of them indicated interest in pursuing Stanford's suggestion.

Coordination of this dimension, which would cut across institutional lines and departmental pride, would be executed by the East Asian subcommittee of the Committee on International Studies. There is no question that the Stanford administration intends the Committee on International Studies to be both central and authoritative in the university's future. President Sterling told us that he "would be very happy to have the Committee run the international show."

"The Committee Is Here to Stay"

How successful Stanford will be in the international realm in future will depend in good part on how effectively the Committee functions. As chairman, Spaeth has many factors working for him. He retains top academic status, both from his years as dean of the Law School and as an active teacher. He knows from experience the strategies and tactics of dealing with foundations. He has a first-name relationship with President Sterling and easy access to the university's administration.

"I had sixteen years of preparation for the chairmanship of the Committee," says Spaeth, "and during that time a person can get to know the university pretty well. I learned about the attitudes of the faculty to, say, project research and about the attitudes of the administration. Whereas a newcomer might have plunged in and made mistakes, I had the advantage of long familiarity. In addition, the President and the administration were accessible to me because of my years as dean: I had an assured entree if and when needed. As Committee chairman I have simply tried to use these strengths and advantages to aid the Committee in the performance of its role."

Pockets of resistance to internationalization still linger on the campus, despite Stanford's long-time involvement. Economist Despres says that, although the professional schools are in general sold on international programs, in the humanities and sciences there are "enclaves of interest surrounded by areas of unconcern!"

Obviously there are loose ends to Stanford's international activities. There exist no fixed policies on the rate of growth of the foreign student population, or the total that can be accommodated or the desired mix between undergraduates and graduate foreign students. The overseas campuses have no direct tie to the International Studies Committee: this important student activity is not coordinated with the university's over-all international program, although the Dean of Undergraduate Education works closely with the director of the overseas campuses.

Spaeth's approach is to proceed by precedents, to set examples for cooperation and coordination that, in time, emerge as a fixed pattern of Committee responsibility and jurisdiction. All faculty members questioned on this point took it for granted that the Committee was the proper channel for new or expanded international programs; deans accepted as a matter of course that any international proposals would first be brought before the Committee on International Studies; President Sterling simply assumes that *all* new international projects at Stanford will come up to him through the Committee.

Emile Despres, having found the load as chairman more than a half-time economics professor could carry, now looks with satisfaction on this habit of communication and coordination that the Committee on International Studies has achieved. "The mechanics of coordination may vary in case to case from now on," he remarked, "but the habit has taken hold. The Committee is here to stay."

*   *   *   *   *

"Stanford," remarked President Sterling a few years ago, summing up the reasons it has so successfully internationalized, "has an institutional posture of receptivity toward various new ideas." Its first president, Dr. Jordan, said it more simply at the university's opening day ceremonies many years ago. "At Stanford," he said, the "finger-points all point forward."

Neither the direction nor the range of Stanford's present international commitments were arrived at by intensive central planning, nor were they undertaken conditional upon general financial support from external sources. Stanford's internal flexibility and encouragement of academic initiative provided the proper atmosphere in which international studies could flourish, and the major directions for growth have been marked by decades of research and interest in world problems.

The central problem confronting the university is how best to capitalize on these powerful capabilities and resources to make Stanford's international commitment increasingly effective. The core problem, in turn, has critical components. One is the need to achieve greater international involvement on the part of its professional schools. Another is the need for constant efforts at interdisciplinary integration and cross-fertilization in the international field. A third is the need to insure steady feedback from its overseas activities into the curriculum and into the over-all life of the university, particularly important in an institution where half the student body consists of undergraduates.

Finally, Stanford needs to determine the place of overseas assistance programs in the university's total commitment. Compared to its resources, it has done considerably less than many major American universities— certainly less than those covered in this survey—in assisting with the development problems of the emerging nations. The argument that Stanford has not entered into many such projects because of the possible drain on its resources that such programs represent is not entirely convincing. Other universities—Cornell, in particular, among those surveyed here—have devised an approach that both serves the institution's teaching and research requirements and fulfills its service functions.

The prestigious coordinating committee, the apparatus relied on by Stanford to achieve all-campus coordination of its international involvement, does represent all relevant sectors of the university—but representation is no guarantee that its components will make the best use of the university's resources in the international field. The Committee on International Studies has been functioning for more than a decade and has made substantial contribution to the development and coordination of the university's programs, but it may be necessary to strengthen further the committee's role within the administrative structure of the university or to explore new forms of organization to meet the major problems still to be solved.

MICHIGAN STATE

I

In his inaugural address on January 20, 1949, President Harry Truman gave voice to the policies that were to guide the United States through the awesome responsibilities thrust upon the country by victory in World War II. Point IV of Mr. Truman's declaration was a program to help the people of the underdeveloped third of the world help themselves.

"We must embark on a bold new program for making the benefits of our scientific advances and industrial progress available for the improvement and growth of underdeveloped areas," said the President. "Our aim should be to help the free peoples of the world, through their own efforts, to produce more food, more clothing, more materials for housing, and more mechanical power to lighten their burdens."

Within hours of the President's speech John A. Hannah, President of Michigan State College (as it was then named), acting in his capacity as President of the American Association of Land-Grant Colleges and State Universities, wired Mr. Truman and offered the association's complete and wholehearted cooperation in making the Point IV program effective.

President Truman lost little time in accepting the proffered assistance. Henry G. Bennett, President of Oklahoma State University, was named the first director of the technical cooperation program set up to implement Point IV, and John Hannah served for two years on the International Development Advisory Board that Mr. Truman established to formulate policy for economic and technical aid for the underdeveloped world.

Point IV thus marked the beginning of the deep involvement of American universities in world affairs. The federal government, having drawn heavily on the country's academic resources during the war, now discovered that American colleges and universities, especially those supported by public funds and moved by the desire to serve society, represented a reservoir of human resources available for assistance in implementing national policy in international affairs. Contracts were made with American universities to work with institutions abroad to help solve the development problems of the emerging nations. One of the first contracts was made with Michigan State.

In the years that followed American universities have struck two postures. Some profess to shun overseas contract operations, and some have willingly accepted such assignments as part of a university's legitimate functions. Michigan State has been a leader in the latter approach. As of 1964-65 the university—through agreements with AID or other government agencies, private foundations, foreign governments, and educational institutions—had cooperative programs underway with thirteen institutions in Asia, Africa, and Latin America and continuing contact and association with a much larger number. During the academic year as many as 215 Michigan State faculty members were on long- or short-term overseas professional assignments, many related to these projects, giving the university the top position among American universities for the largest number of teachers abroad.

II

While it has led the academic community as one of the largest operators of service and educational programs overseas, Michigan State has also pioneered in consciously using its international contract operations—its service function—to strengthen its two other basic functions, teaching and research.

President Hannah some years ago summed up the Michigan State approach: "Just as the problems we face as a nation are broad and not tied to a limited number of fields or disciplines, the Michigan State University approach to its technical assistance activities is broadly conceived. We have not, and we do not anticipate creating, relatively isolated pockets of international studies on our campus. Instead, we are trying to create a general environment and an international dimension which will permeate all relevant segments of the university over the years ahead."

This philosophy has had a profound impact on Michigan State. In the postwar period what had been a provincial college with parochial interests grew into a university of major dimensions and high standing. It is one of the best-known of the sixty-eight land-grant institutions, and ranks twenty-second among American universities in the number of Ph.D.'s awarded annually. Its international involvement is widespread, taking in almost every college and department: it has stimulated new areas of concern for the faculty, changed the nature of the faculty over the years, and altered the education of their primary charges, the students.

Physically the postwar growth has been phenomenal. The flood of veterans raised the enrollment from 5,284 in 1945 to 13,282 in 1946 and was an indication of what was to come. In the 1964-65 academic year Michigan State's enrollment was over 36,000, including its regional centers and its satellite campus, Oakland University, at Rochester, Michigan. Of these, 31,459 were enrolled on the main campus at East Lansing, a 4,900-acre development that stands adjacent to an additional 3,000 acres of experimental farms and research installations. Many of the students are undergraduates—about 81 per cent of those enrolled at the East Lansing campus. More than three-quarters of the undergraduates enter from Michigan high schools or as transfer students from Michigan junior or community colleges or other colleges and universities in the state. During the 1964-65 year there were 880 students from eighty-four foreign countries enrolled (plus fifty-eight foreign scholars from twenty-eight countries).

The university's academic staff numbers 2,235, including the Cooperative Extension Staff. Departments of instruction are organized into eleven colleges, which have more than 70 departments offering more than 200 different programs leading to undergraduate and graduate degrees. The colleges are The University College, College of Arts and Letters, College of Agriculture, College of Business, College of Communication Arts, College of Education, College of Engineering, College of Home Economics, College of Natural Science, College of Social Science, and College of Veterinary Medicine. There is also a School for Advanced Graduate Study.

Land-Grant Prototype

The Michigan State University of today can only be understood through its past.

A pioneering institution from the moment of its founding in 1855, it came into being to meet the practical needs of a frontier territory. President Hannah has described its origins: "The Michigan of 1855 had a total population of about 500,000 people, the great majority of them farmers. There were no roads worthy of the name, no railway network, no great industries. The legislature had met for the first time in the new capital of Lansing only eight years before. This was the frontier, with all the primitiveness and hardships the word implies. The great centers of population and learning were in the East. Colleges and universities of that date devoted their curricula primarily to a study of the classics, languages, medicine, and law. But among the hardy people of Michigan and other young states were visionary leaders who were not satisfied with the education offered by the older universities. Eighty-five percent of them were farmers. They felt a keen need for improved methods in farming in order to improve the quality and quantity of food for themselves and the growing markets of a developing America. So they petitioned the legislature to establish a college which would serve their needs, and what is now Michigan State University came into being."

Founded by law in 1855 as Michigan Agricultural College, it served as the prototype of the land-grant college system established by federal law under the Morrill Act of 1862. At the time of the act's passage the Michigan institution had been in existence as a state-supported venture for some seven years. In that time Congressman (later Senator) Justin Morrill had been impressed with the little college's accomplishments, and this was in his mind when he proposed legislation whereby the federal government would give a grant of public land to help establish similar educational institutions throughout the United States.

During its first hundred years Michigan State developed most strongly in the biological sciences, engineering, agriculture, and other fields closely related to its origins as a land-grant college. As the first college in the world devoted to teaching agricultural science, it pioneered in the new type of "practical" higher education under state auspices. In its agricultural extension conception it pioneered the "service" tradition by which a state-financed educational institution carried its resources to every corner of its constituency.

In 1925 the institution's name was changed to Michigan State College of Agriculture and Applied Science, and in the same year its first Ph.D. degree was conferred. In the next few years its graduate work was reorganized and strengthened, but in a state where the official state university—the University of Michigan at Ann Arbor—was established and powerful, the East Lansing institution had to wait another three decades—until its centennial year, 1955—before the legislature granted it the name Michigan State University of Agriculture and Applied Science (shortened to Michigan State University in 1964).

Turn Toward Internationalism

The years of World War II provided a watershed for Michigan State, as they did for many American educational institutions. They also coincided with the coming to the presidency of John Hannah, who in 1941 became the university's twelfth president. A product of the university's undergraduate school and a member of the faculty as an agricultural extension specialist in the first half of the 1930s, President Hannah came to office—after an additional six years as secretary of the Board of Trustees—as a vigorous champion of the land-grant philosophy, a firm believer that a university should serve the people.

In a quiet way Michigan State had already developed some international connections in its special areas early in its history. A steady trickle of foreign students had come to the college, attracted by its reputation in agriculture, engineering, and home economics. In 1908 a faculty member resigned to become president of the first school of agriculture set up in Brazil. But these activities, although forerunners of the widespread international involvement to come, made no great impact on the campus.

It was not until 1942, when the United States and its allies were retreating to gain time for eventual victory, that President Hannah and his colleagues reached the first of the decisions that were to put the international stamp on the university. As Mr. Hannah now recalls it, the consensus was that the end of World War II would certainly not leave the world the same as it had been in 1939, and that therefore the university should set about devising courses that would reflect anticipated changes in the postwar world. These courses would be introduced into the Basic College (now The University College) so that every incoming freshman would be exposed to them. Two major areas that had been neglected in the prewar days—Latin America and the Orient—were chosen for study emphasis.

The next step, President Hannah recalls, was to find competent scholars who could bring this international course content to the university. Within a few years Michigan State succeeded in bringing to East Lansing a distinguished Orientalist and an outstanding scholar from Brazil.

The end of the war and the onset of the Cold War reaffirmed Michigan State's decision to concentrate on non-European areas. The possibility in those pre-Marshall Plan days that Western Europe would follow Eastern Europe behind the Iron Curtain convinced President Hannah that the United States, to remain strong, would have to solidify its relations with Latin America. Michigan State would do what it could in this direction.

At the same time the postwar transition brought new international interests to the campus. In response to the national turn away from isolationism, Michigan State—along with many other American institutions—began to welcome many more foreign students, to play host to visiting foreign scholars and officials, to inaugurate study abroad by students and faculty, to expand course offerings in traditional international relations fields, and, in a variety of ways, to become more internationally oriented. A Foreign Studies department was established and language offerings were expanded.

A shift from this conventional pattern of international involvement became apparent with President Hannah's response to the Point IV proposal. "There was no specific decision at this point to enter into a long-term program of international involvement," Mr. Hannah explained, "but Michigan State made it known to President Truman that it was flexible and willing to experiment." Both President Bennett of Oklahoma State, who was later to lose his life in an air accident in Iran, and President Hannah were interested in seeing whether the land-grant philosophy could be applied to educational ventures abroad.

Because of its declared interest in Latin America, Michigan State chose to begin its overseas operations there. In 1951, under a contract with the new foreign aid agency, the Technical Cooperation Administration, the university undertook to work with the National University of Colombia in the development of two agricultural colleges in that country, at Medellín and in Palmira. This contract ran until 1958, at which time the Kellogg Foundation took over the sponsorship of technical aid to the two schools.

The Colombia project drew upon various departments of Michigan State's College of Agriculture, and at one time as many as seven Michigan State faculty members were in Colombia to advise, teach, and confer with the Colombian agricultural faculty. Many of the present Colombian faculty members have studied and earned advanced degrees at East Lansing and at other American universities as part of the program. In Colombia an agricultural experiment station, an extension program and a commitment to scientific agriculture remain as evidences of Michigan State influence. In the summer of 1960 faculty members from Michigan State played an important role in a Kellogg Foundation-sponsored special commission that looked into the overall prospects for higher education in agriculture in Colombia.

Michigan State's second overseas contract project followed close on the heels of the first. In 1951, at the invitation of the American Council on Education and the U. S. Department of the Army, the university "adopted" the newly founded University of the Ryukyus, which American military authorities had established on Okinawa. From 1951 on Michigan State has maintained an average of five faculty members on Okinawa to work with the Ryukyuan faculty. The MSU staff members have been drawn from the social sciences, agriculture, home economics, business administration, political science, public administration, education, engineering, and languages, and they have participated broadly in the growth of the Ryukyuan institution. This is now an important part of the educational structure of the Ryukyus, having expanded from a few temporary buildings to an impressive university center, and from a student population of less than 500 to a total enrollment of about 3,000.

It was Michigan State's hope that the University of the Ryukyus would adopt and adapt the land-grant principles of university service. This has only worked out in part, largely because Okinawa retains its close ties to Japan. When the university was founded, the attitude of its U. S. Army sponsors was to make it as non-Japanese as possible. Then, with the passage of years, the passing of the occupation mentality, and the changing conditions in the Far East, this intention was altered, and today the university is a combination of Japanese and American practices in its educational orientation. Of its 187 faculty members, about 40 have been educated in the United States, and most of the remainder in Japan.

In 1953 another overseas service opportunity was offered, and MSU again decided to participate. This time, at the request of the Getulio Vargas Foundation, a quasi-federal public institution in Brazil, and the International Cooperation Administration in Washington, MSU's College of Business and Public Service began a cooperative project in São Paulo, Brazil, leading toward the establishment of the first Brazilian school of Business Administration. Each year until 1964-65, when the program began to phase out, from four to nine São Paulo School of Business faculty members have studied at Michigan State and other American universities, and then returned to São Paulo to assume broader responsibilities there. By the end of 1963 some 30 Brazilians had received a Master of Business Administration degree from MSU and become full-time faculty members at São Paulo. The São Paulo school has been strongly oriented toward a teaching and an executive management program, and well over 500 Brazilian business men are now alumni of the institution.

In 1958 the Brazilian government decided to expand education in business administration to the University of Rio Grande do Sul and the University of Bahia. Michigan State and the School at São Paulo assisted in the development, and MSU professors are located at each of the universities. Meanwhile, Brazilians from the two universities have been trained at East Lansing.

In 1955 Michigan State entered upon what was by far the largest in size and scope of any of its overseas operations. This was its technical assistance program in Vietnam, carried out at the request of the government of the then new republic of Vietnam with the support of the ICA.

In 1957-58, when the program was at its peak, more than 50 Michigan State staff members were in Saigon. Their missions were to carry on training programs in the fields of public and police administration, including the establishment of training institutions, in-service training and research programs, assistance in administrative improvement through training and consultation, and the development of a public administration library. A National Institute of Administration was developed as a focal point for public administration developments, a center which grew to include its own night school with an enrollment of some 600 Vietnamese civil servants and a three-year degree program for 200 students. Police administration training activities were centered in several new institutions, including a National Police Academy and a staff officers' training school in Saigon. By the time the Michigan State contract ended in mid-1962 its consultants had put the Vietnamese police through special technical training courses in identification, communications, weapons use, and traffic control.

Service, Teaching, Research

The technical assistance contract in Vietnam represented a major commitment for Michigan State—and yet it had surprisingly little impact on the campus or among the faculty. To this day there has not emerged on the campus an adequate development of faculty resources in the area which Vietnam represents.

Recognition of a missing component had begun to disturb the university leaders even before the Vietnam project was begun, and by 1956 there was a strong concern on campus that Michigan State's overseas commitments were extremely heavy, and that insufficient attention was being paid to obtaining feedback from overseas projects and to the development of the international resources of the university on campus in teaching and research. There was concern not only over the extent of Michigan State's overseas commitments, but whether the university thoroughly understood what it was getting into in embarking on them. Faculty members pointed out that, important as the extension of university services abroad might be, they also had to enhance competence on campus through research and staff development; they had to be managed effectively; and they had to be brought into balance with other aspects of the university's international role. There was also a basic query about the advisability of any university undertaking programs in parts of the world in which it had no area studies base or geographic competence.

President Hannah had meantime extended his personal commitments. Having served for two years as President Truman's appointee on the International Development Advisory Board, he was appointed by President

Eisenhower as Assistant Secretary of Defense for Manpower and Personnel. He served in this post from February, 1953, through July, 1954, and in 1956 he made a survey of foreign aid programs in the Far East for the Foreign Relations Committee of the U.S. Senate.

Despite these off-campus activities, Hannah participated in the on-campus assessment of the university's overseas involvement and in the fall of 1956 he took a major step in systematizing the institution's international role. He appointed the first Dean of International Programs. The specific responsibility of the new Dean was to administer the university's overseas projects, on the one hand, and spur the development of the academic side of the international programs on the campus on the other. Both efforts were to proceed in an integrated and mutually reinforcing manner.

The man Hannah chose to head the new office was a rural sociologist, Professor Glen L. Taggart, who had many years of government experience in international work with the U.S. Department of Agriculture, as well as his university faculty experience. Taggart's conception of his new role rested on the conviction that in the future it would be inadequate for the university to undertake operating responsibilities overseas with a service motive alone: henceforth there would also have to be a clear-cut relationship to campus development, with opportunities for expanding knowledge through research and for increasing the effectiveness of faculty as teachers in the classroom.

The first step—in January, 1957—was to make the various overseas projects of the university (five in all at that time) the administrative responsibility of the Dean of International Programs. Each project continued to be tied closely to relevant colleges for subject matter guidance and support, with the exact arrangement varying from one project to another depending on the fields covered and the scope of the project.

Apart from the overseas projects, the international programs of Michigan State at that time consisted of some 400 foreign students from 64 countries, course offerings in political science, sociology, history, economics, and several other fields which have traditionally been internationally oriented, a limited number of international or cross-cultural faculty research projects, and a number of extracurricular student activities. The faculty included many scholars with an orientation toward the international aspects of their field and some with research experience overseas. The university's overseas projects had expanded the number of faculty members who had an extensive exposure to the underdeveloped areas of the world, although the pressure to fill its contracts had led Michigan State to hire some non-faculty members for its overseas assignments—a category of staff members which less-involved universities often slightingly refer to as "overseas mercenaries."

"Towards an International Dimension"

To many on Michigan State's administration and faculty the time seemed to have come for a serious look at the university's international involvement and the deliberate establishment of institutional goals.

In 1958 and 1959 the university organized faculty seminars for thinking through its objectives in the international sphere. Groups of faculty members, totaling 55 in all, were released partially or fully from other responsibilities to spend three months or more—supported by the university and a grant from the Ford Foundation—investigating and discussing Michigan State's appropriate goals in international training, research, and service. They were organized in five functional areas—politics and administration, economics and business, education, communications, and cross-cultural exchange. Their deliberations identified problems, goals, and projects in each area, and their combined reports—distributed in the form of a weighty document titled "Towards An International Dimension at Michigan State University"—were intended to serve as a plan for the university's future development in the international area.

The seminars reflected widespread agreement on the increasing importance of the international aspect at the university, and asserted several general guidelines for its future, such as:

1. A broad "international dimension" should be incorporated throughout the university's educational programs, since graduates of all fields should be internationally involved, actively or indirectly.

2. Certain academic strengths should be especially encouraged in order to contribute knowledge and provide educated specialists in the international sphere. At Michigan State these should include emphasis on the international aspects of economics and business, communications, politics and administration, education, and other fields which would reflect the needs of the country and build upon the international experience and academic strength of the university.

3. Research on international problems should be greatly expanded, particularly in the fields mentioned above.

4. Service programs should be continued and improved, but expanded only as they can contribute to the reinforcement of international training and research. In other words, overseas projects must increasingly serve the international academic goals of the university in addition to the goals of the sponsoring organization and the host country.

5. Primary emphasis at Michigan State should be along functional lines, rather than on area programs, but some area studies should be developed.

6. The international program should emphasize the expanding role of existing departments and colleges. Essentially decentralized administration should prevail, but a central integrating and coordinating system should provide leadership.

The faculty seminars had several other outcomes. They served to arouse wider interest in international work, and uncovered a readiness on the part of specific faculty members to undertake expanded roles in international research and training. They moved Michigan State closer to a programmatic and administrative system for its international activities. But, most important, they served to signal the Ford Foundation, which had shown serious interest in and appreciation for Michigan State's international objectives, that the university was determined to move ahead. Thus when Michigan State approached the foundation in the autumn of 1959 with a request for long-term developmental support, its aspirations were recognized with a five-year grant for $1 million beginning in 1960. The grant was to be used primarily to support individual and group faculty research in four functional areas: (1) politics and administration; (2) economics and business; (3) communications; (4) education and national development. Heavy emphasis was placed on interdisciplinary projects when feasible, and on strengthening the research component in overseas development by such techniques as assisting a professor returning from an overseas tour to complete and publish his research and providing means for graduate students to do their dissertation research while serving overseas on contract projects.

The Ford Foundation grant was to be used as seed money—to begin growth and to attract additional resources. In a sense, the funds were to serve as a means of binding some of the existing resources together and in so doing to make the whole more significant than the individual parts. The grant was also clearly aimed at strengthening academically the university's international efforts and at helping to balance the overseas operational emphasis.

The net result of the grant was greatly to strengthen the office of the Dean of International Programs, through which the foundation funds were to be administered. The coordinating role of the office was further solidified when the Ford Foundation on December 18, 1963, granted an additional $1,250,000 for the further development of the international program, making a total development support grant of $2,250,000 to be spent by Michigan State over a period of ten years.

III

Although its technical assistance programs in Colombia and Vietnam came to an end, Michigan State replaced them with several new projects—including a rural development program in Pakistan, an engineering education project in India, an agricultural program in Taiwan, and a new university, partially land-grant in concept, in Nigeria—until today its overseas contract operations, in number and magnitude, rank it among the leading half dozen American universities.

Pakistan Academies

At the request of the Pakistani government and the Ford Foundation, a Michigan State survey mission visited Pakistan in 1956 to look into the training needs and possibilities in connection with that country's so-called Village Aid and Basic Democracies program, aimed at providing political and general leadership at the village level to stimulate agriculture and industrial development and full utilization of resources on a community basis. As a result of this survey, under an agreement of 1957, Michigan State agreed to help develop two Village Aid academies, one at Comilla, in East Pakistan, and the other at Peshawar, in West Pakistan. These academies were to provide additional university-level education for rural development leaders.

The academies started virtually from scratch. Faculties were recruited from Pakistani applicants, and during 1958 most of them received training at Michigan State. The academies opened for classes in 1959, with six Michigan State staff members working with the faculties. Over the years a large number of MSU faculty members have been involved in the project, and a larger number have had contact with the Pakistani trainees during their stays in the United States.

Both academies have been actively involved in the rural development programs in Pakistan, and have undertaken instruction, research, and experimental demonstrations in the fields of cooperatives, agricultural production, local government rural credit formation, mechanization in agriculture, education, family planning, youth work, women's work, and related fields.

This marriage of the social sciences to public administration was no novelty to Michigan State, but it was very new to Pakistan, newly independent after a century of British colonial administration, and although the Pakistani government was sold on the concept from the beginning it was an uphill task to convince some Pakistani educators that two academies for village development had to be specially created to provide training for their middle-level administrators. Perhaps the most important factor in helping the academies get started was the fact that most of the Pakistanis instructed at Michigan State returned indoctrinated and dedicated to the belief that the academies could be agents of change and development in their regions, a conviction backed up by MSU consultants on the spot.

In the intervening years, the two academies have not developed evenly or in the same direction. The East Pakistan Academy at Comilla came under the direction of a distinguished and dynamic Pakistani, Akhter Hameed Khan, and has made itself a major force not only in the training of administrators but in the conduct of field research and the practical economic development of its surrounding area. Taking the MSU land-grant idea literally, according to Akhter Hameed Khan, the Comilla academy has successfully developed an area of 100 square miles around Comilla as a field demonstration, which has received international recognition as well as serving as a model for similar rural development efforts in other parts of the region.

As Comilla has been innovative, the Peshawar Academy has developed along more traditional lines, reflecting in part the cultural background of West Pakistan and in part the personal inclination of faculty members who take their standards from the University of Peshawar, which in turn identifies with the traditional academic values of a British university.

Audio-Visual in Brazil

From the autumn of 1960 until the project was phased out in the summer of 1964, Michigan State's Audio-Visual Center was involved in a cooperative effort with Brazilians to improve the instructional materials in Brazilian schools and universities and in industrial and professional training.

This project grew largely out of the personal involvement of Charles F. Schuller, the director of the A-V Center at East Lansing. Schuller spent two months in Brazil in the summer of 1960 at the invitation of an ICA colleague, who suggested he expore what MSU might do to prepare instructional materials not available in Brazil or translated into Portuguese. Schuller returned to Michigan State convinced that there was a role for audio-visual techniques in the underdeveloped areas, and on the strength of an ICA contract Michigan State was authorized to establish a new Brazilian Audio-Visual Center. Having worked for some years in business administration with the School of Business in São Paulo, MSU arranged to locate the new center on the University of São Paulo campus.

Three American advisers and a staff of 30 Brazilians manned the Center, and in its first three years—using a "train the trainer" technique—2,521 school administrators, principals, supervisors, and teachers had taken special study programs ranging from a few weeks to a year in length, and then went home to train their local staffs. In addition, the Center served as a major producing facility for graphic and photographic materials and educational motion pictures.

Schuller feels that the A-V program made a considerable impact before its end. For one thing, in 1963 the University of São Paulo introduced the first university-level course to be given in Brazil in audio-visual work. This step required the approval of the Brazilian Federal Education Council, which was given because of the reputation of the São Paulo A-V Center.

The University of Nigeria

In spite of its name, the University of Nigeria is not *the* national university of Nigeria: it is the regional university of the Eastern Region of Nigeria, and one of five federally supported universities in this most populous of the African nations. However, the University of Nigeria has one distinction not shared by the four others—it incorporates in its academic program some of the philosophy of the American land-grant institution, a brief but firmly planted heritage resulting from its sponsorship by Michigan State University.

The University of Nigeria, located in the countryside at Nsukka, some 40 miles north of the Eastern regional capital of Enugu, is in good part the personal creation of Dr. Nnamdi Azikiwe, now the President of the Republic of Nigeria and Chancellor of the institution which he brought into being. As a young man, Dr. Azikiwe acquired his higher education in the United States, where he worked his way through the university with odd jobs, and acquired an appreciation of vocational training and a respect for the dignity of work not normally found, even today, among educated Africans. Years later, during the struggle for national independence, he determined to bring to the region in which he was then Premier a university which would meet the needs of a broad segment of the emerging nation's population. Nigeria's first university, the University College of Ibadan, in the Western Region, had been established in 1948 by the University of London in the image of the traditional British university. Azikiwe determined to break with this classical model of a university for the elite. He found his own model partially in the land-grant university of the United States, with its blend of scientific and vocational as well as classical studies, and as early as 1955 he traveled to Washington and New York to seek assistance in implementing his plans to establish the University of Nigeria.

Unsuccessful in his approaches—neither government, foundation, nor private funds were forthcoming—Azikiwe returned to Nigeria, pushed a law through the regional legislature establishing a university and persuaded the Palm Oil Marketing Board to set aside money to finance it. His persistence impressed Washington, and in due course AID agreed to help. At Azikiwe's suggestion, the agency turned to Michigan State, and after a preliminary survey President Hannah agreed to assist in the launching of the new university. The new institution, in a uniquely Nigerian experiment, did not break completely with the British. On the ground that the standards and values of tradition should not be set aside, MSU persuaded the Inter-University Council of Great Britain, and later the University of London in particular, to become joint sponsor.

When the new university opened its doors during Nigeria's independence week in October, 1960, on a raw, newly cleared expanse of savannah land on the hills above the village of Nsukka, Azikiwe's summer home, there were two classroom buildings, a hostel block for students, and thirty-six senior staff houses. There was an enrollment of 220 students and thirteen faculty members. On June 15, 1963, Chancellor Azikiwe proudly conferred 150 diplomas on the university's first graduates. By 1964 the university's student population had increased to 2,500, of whom about 10 per cent were women, for whom university training until recent years was virtually taboo.

The senior faculty numbers 268, and, despite a deliberate effort to Nigerianize, it is still something of a little U.N., with seventeen nations represented. As of 1965 the Nigerian faculty members numbered 135: there were sixty-nine American faculty members, including the thirty members of the MSU advisory staff, as well as large groups of British, Dutch, and Indian faculty.

Currently there are faculties of agriculture, engineering, education, and business administration, as well as the traditional science, arts, social studies, and law. The physical plant, looking like that of any burgeoning American campus, has spread over 1,600 acres, and boasts thirty-three academic and administrative buildings, including ten student hostels, a library, a university medical center, a dining hall capable of feeding 2,000 at a time, and an Olympic-dimension stadium seating 30,000 spectators. The Nsukka campus also includes a Continuing Education Center, built with AID funds, which is comparable on a small scale with the Kellogg Center on the MSU campus and which offers adult groups special courses, seminars, institutes, and demonstrations.

At the branch campus at Enugu the University of Nigeria took over the facilities of the former Nigerian College of Arts, Science, and Technology, and currently provides for an enrollment of some 350 students. At this campus there is also the university's Economic Development Institute, established by MSU in 1963 as part of its AID-supported program to provide research and advanced training in economic development work for Nigerians. The Nsukka campus houses the Institute of African Studies, launched in 1963 and intended primarily for postgraduate research in Africana.

Under the terms of its AID contract, Michigan State's role at the new university is manyfold: (1) to seek out and train indigenous staff to replace the MSU advisers; (2) to provide advisory service in planning, organizing, and administering the university; (3) to organize and teach courses adapted to Nigerian students; (4) to encourage research on Nigerian problems; (5) to expand the bridge between the University of Nigeria and the region's secondary schools, government agencies, and agricultural and business groups; (6) to extend services of the university and its resources, in an adaptation of the land-grant approach, throughout the Eastern Region.

The assessment of Michigan State's involvement with the University of Nigeria varies with the point from which it is viewed. The university is a going concern, and has made a measurable impact on Nigerian education. Its graduates in the scientific and vocational fields have held their own with Nigerians trained elsewhere, and the steadily increasing demand for places at the university is limited only by available resources. Competing in 1965 with colleges of other African nations for UNESCO scholarships in graduate training, the University of Nigeria took top honors: its students won eleven of nineteen scholarships offered. In the university's Continuing Education Program, the first such effort in Africa, there are almost as many students as there are in residence, and no fewer than twenty-two extension centers in the region take education to the villages.

From Michigan State's vantage point, the balance is on the profit side. In the first year of operation a combination of administrative interference, academic snobbery on the part of those who looked down on land-grant education, and the frustrations of cutting through the bureaucratic jungle of a new nation led to some turnover among the faculty and administrators, but since then the relationship has been mutually satisfactory. In the five years of the university's operation a considerable number of MSU faculty members have had experience in Nigeria and then returned to the East Lansing campus. A high percentage of staff sent over on the MSU contract have come from the Michigan State faculty—a policy which the university has sought to follow since 1957. Of the thirty MSU contract staff stationed at Nsukka and Enugu during 1964-65, only six were not from the MSU faculty. In the reverse direction, well over twenty-five University of Nigeria faculty members have been involved in participant training programs in the United States. An MSU representative has served from the outset as Vice Chancellor in residence at Nsukka. Both sides had hoped to find a Nigerian qualified for the post, but for the 1964-65 academic year, when no qualified candidate had been found, Michigan State seconded its Dean of International Programs to serve as Vice Chancellor at Nsukka, an arrangement that is being continued through 1965-66.

The relationship with the University of Nigeria has also led to a summer student exchange program, known as MINEX (from Michigan State-Nigeria Exchange), which in the summer of 1965—the second year of its operation—enabled thirty MSU students and twenty-three Nigerians to switch schools for an eight-week period.

Institution-To-Institution

Simultaneous with its commitment to Nigeria, Michigan State in the fall of 1960 undertook cooperative work with the College of Agriculture of the National Taiwan University at Taipei, and with Taiwan's Taichung Provincial College of Agriculture (now the Chung Hsing University). The project, under the sponsorship of AID, called for Michigan State assistance by a variety of agricultural specialists and involved about five faculty members each year. During the term of the contract, fourteen Chinese faculty came to the United States for additional training. At Michigan State the campus affiliation was with the College of Agriculture.

In its relationship with the National Taiwan University, MSU has developed what it hopes may be a model for a follow-up to this type of overseas operation. Instead of merely phasing out the relationship at the conclusion of the technical assistance contract, the two institutions were able to get together and phase-over into an institution-to-institution relationship in which one supports the other. For the academic year 1965-66 MSU will send a specialist in American history to Taiwan, and the following year two junior faculty members from Taiwan will teach at MSU. For the time being, the two institutions are funding the exchange. Given outside financial assistance, MSU looks forward to the possibility of developing during the operational phase of any overseas program a "sister institution" relationship which could lead to exchange of faculty, exchange of students, and exchange of materials which could go on for many years into the future.

Under yet another AID contract Michigan State in 1961 began aiding two important Indian engineering institutes, one at Poona, the other at Guindy. The project was administered at MSU by the College of Engineering, which sent about nine of its faculty to India in an advisory capacity, and also brought some twenty Indian students to Michigan State for completion of their advanced degrees. This program was completed in mid-1964.

Other Overseas Projects

At the request of AID and the Turkish Ministry of Education, Michigan State specialists carried out a survey in late 1962 of that nation's facilities for higher education for business. Early in 1964 a contract was signed under which MSU undertook to provide a program of assistance to the Academics of Economic and Commercial Sciences located in four Turkish cities. The overall program, which is aimed at upgrading the quality and level of instruction in business administration, involves participant training, professor training and American faculty in Turkey.

In addition to its many technical assistance projects, Michigan State is engaged on a more restricted basis in international cooperative arrangements.

For almost fifteen years the university has worked with the Inter-American Institute of Agricultural Sciences, located at Turrialba, Costa Rica, under which rural sociological and social psychological research is carried on in Latin America. From time to time, MSU sociologists have conducted research, advised, and taught within the broad social science program of the Institute, and some of the Institute's faculty has pursued doctoral work at East Lansing.

In 1962 Michigan State signed a two-year contract with the research arm of AID to conduct a study on secondary and higher educational systems of Central American nations. The research part of the program progressed on a cooperative basis with the University of San Carlos in Guatemala, where a new Institute for Educational Research and Improvement was established, and recognized by the presidents of the five national universities as the regional center for Central America. Three Michigan State advisors were located in Guatemala and a number of short-term staff members were on the spot periodically for specific phases of the research program.

For some five years MSU's College of Education has rendered technical assistance to the Associations of American Schools in Mexico and Central America, providing special courses for teachers and administrative studies, consulting services, and instructional advisory services to the member schools of the associations. The schools themselves support the program, mainly with funds provided by the U.S. Department of State.

In 1965 Michigan State entered upon what it calls the early operational phase of two new technical assistance programs. One is the MSU-AID Thailand project, in which Michigan State has undertaken to strengthen the capacity of the Thai Ministry of Education and the National Educational Council in both short- and long-range educational planning.

The second new project is an AID-sponsored program in which MSU's College of Agriculture, supported initially for a two-year period, has agreed to provide technical assistance for the development of a College of Agriculture at Balcarce, Argentina. The intention is to develop a land-grant type of approach to agricultural education and research by integrating the functions of the new college with the existing Balcarce Experiment Station of Argentina's National Institute of Agricultural Technology.

Seminars at Cacapon

Thousands of foreign experts come to the United States each year seeking American know-how and then return home ready to contribute to the development of their own nations. But to pick up know-how is not the same as being able to pass it along, to communicate the acquired techniques to others. Recognition of this fact by AID, which is responsible for bringing a good many foreign experts to the United States under the designation of "participants," led to the decision some years ago to make a systematic effort to help the visitors apply their American training more effectively on their return home.

In 1958 AID turned to Michigan State, which had acquired a reputation in the communications field for its agricultural extension work at county and local levels in Michigan and by housing the National Project in Agricultural Communications, and charged it with designing a unique communications course that would assist the foreign participants in bringing about change in their home situations. MSU's response was an intensive week-long seminar, a communications "think tank" in which groups of returning participants are assembled at the end of their stay in the United States and put through an analysis of the processes of communication and the techniques by which they can initiate change on their return to their own countries.

Most of the seminars have been held at Cacapon Lodge, near Berkeley

Springs, West Virginia, which is convenient for the participants returning to Washington, D.C., after training at various parts of the United States. Michigan State has administrative responsibility for the seminars, but the staff members—more than 200 of them over a six-year period—have been drawn from more than forty colleges and universities, and from such disciplines as sociology, psychology, audio-visual, business administration, education, and communication research. Up to the end of 1964 more than 150 seminars had been held, and since 1958 well over 6,000 foreign visitors from more than seventy-five countries have taken part.

Altogether, about forty MSU faculty members have participated at one time or another in the Cacapon seminars, and some have gone back for repeat performances. A number who taught there became interested in the problems of cross-cultural communications, and a blossoming of the international dimension in the university's communications courses is attributable in part to the Cacapon experience. David Berlo, now the chairman of the Department of Communication, was the first director of the Cacapon center.

Some graduate students have been sent to Cacapon for brief periods of research, but some of the communications experts on campus feel that the unique research opportunities the project provided in such areas as the change process at work, role-playing, and communications techniques have not been exploited. The MSU administration has attempted to find research finance almost from the beginning of the program, but it was not until fairly recently—when the university was on the verge of giving up the program—that AID agreed to support some research at the center. When the contract comes up for renewal in the near future, MSU hopes to persuade AID to build a participant center on the East Lansing campus, which would facilitate both the debriefing and the research process.

IV

By 1965, the international dimensions set forth by the faculty seminars in 1958 and 1959 had become visible throughout the university, in its teaching, research, and service activities.

The top administration of the university is deeply and seriously committed to the expanded concept of service, by which its knowledge and expertise are made available in the national interest to help the developing areas of the world. But it has not overlooked its responsibilities to the students and the people of Michigan.

Many undergraduates come to MSU without having had any international exposure in high school: a high percentage have never been exposed to such simple tools as a public affairs magazine or a major metropolitan newspaper. In addition, many faculty members had little overseas experience prior to the university's plunge into international activities. It was in a melding of overseas experience for its faculty, leading to and contributing to curriculum changes at home, that Michigan State saw the prospect of enriching its academic program so as to ready its students for the challenges of the postwar world.

Today, more than 60 percent of the university's faculty have had overseas experience, in one capacity or another. Service abroad has widened faculty horizons and enriched the university curriculum by adding new courses, modifying old ones, adding new materials, or changing the curricular emphasis.

Curriculum Improvement

Michigan State is primarily an undergraduate institution. Only 5,000 of its 31,000 students on campus are pursuing graduate degrees.

The logical place to strengthen the international dimension in undergraduate education is in the heavy traffic courses taken by large numbers of students in the social sciences and the humanities in order to meet the general university requirements. At Michigan State this is in The University College. There, in a move which has had the broadest impact on the student body, MSU introduced in 1961-62 a basic revision of the three-term social science course, one of four general education courses required of all underclassmen at Michigan State. The revision, which was partially supported by the Ford Foundation grant, added greater emphasis on non-Western areas and the problems and processes of economic, political, and social change, and resulted in a new series of paperback texts, an eleven-volume Social Science Series, published in 1962. Some of the key faculty involved in stimulating and implementing the course revision were formerly engaged overseas in research or university contract projects.

The same origins were apparent in the internationally oriented courses that have been introduced in the Colleges of Business, Agriculture, Engineering, and Education, and in the departments of economics, agricultural economics, geography, and political science. Curriculum changes in an international direction have occurred in nearly every college of the university.

The international impact on the curriculum can also be seen in the undergraduate projects that were identified for attention at Michigan State during 1964 and 1965. These include:

1. The second major revision of the social science course in The University College, carried on during the summer of 1965.

2. A similar revision of the humanities course in The University College to include a non-Western orientation by devising a course in Civilizations and Institutions of South Asia, which may be generally offered in 1966-67.

3. The development of multidisciplinary instructional approaches to area studies, supporting the work of the university's Asian, African, and Latin American Studies Centers.

4. The creation of an upper division program in comparative cultures, jointly between the College of Arts and Letters and the College of Social Science.

5. The support of international programs in the professional schools, including the Colleges of Agriculture and Engineering.

6. Cooperation in developing international aspects in the program of the College of Education for students preparing to teach the social sciences in primary and secondary schools.

These six areas for development are intended to be complementary and reinforcing. Initially the entering undergraduate will have an opportunity to gain a broad international perspective through The University College instruction. The cross-disciplinary introductory area courses planned by the various centers will help him direct his attention to those facets of international studies that are most relevant to his undergraduate concentration. The specialized courses and curricula coordinated through the area centers will allow him to deepen his understanding of other cultures and geographical regions. As he progresses to upper division work, the comparative cross-cultural instruction will provide him with the analytical skills and perspectives to integrate his area concerns. If he is in a professional school, specially designed fifth-year programs, or undergraduate "area" minors, will relate to the emphasis in his profession. And if he is planning to teach in the social sciences or the humanities at the primary or secondary school level, the international context of these fields will be included in his preparation.

These efforts at curriculum revision have been supplemented by other new programs which, while less direct perhaps, lead to the same end.

Numerous courses on Africa emanate from the African Studies Center. There is a major field in Chinese studies, with Chinese language courses offered regularly. A course on American agriculture for foreign students is a regular offering, and in 1964 a course was designed in agricultural development and administration aimed at both foreign and American students, built around an interdisciplinary seminar. The journalism department offers a course in international journalism, and beginning in the autumn of 1965 a graduate-level seminar was devoted to mass communication and international development. A seminar on the role of education in the developing areas is now offered regularly, and a sequence of courses on international business management is offered. A senior-level, elective "Great Issues" course is taught regularly and has a substantially international content.

Other specific changes have been brought about by the international commitment. A center for teaching English to foreign students has been established at Michigan State, and is training teachers of "English-as-a foreign-language." A special librarian with overseas project experience has been designated international librarian and works with the area centers in establishing library priorities and expanding the international collection.

And, as a result of service abroad, the Counseling Center personnel have developed an international interest.

Efforts to achieve MSU's major objective of extending education about the non-Western world into more aspects of the undergraduate curriculum and to increased numbers of undergraduate students have taken many forms, but perhaps none to date has been as promising as the development which took place on campus in the spring of 1965. In a determined effort to counteract the problem of MSU's "bigness" and break through the impersonality of the multiversity, a special faculty committee recommended the establishment of a new, semiautonomous experimental college which will be limited to a maximum of 1,000 to 1,100 students, and will be housed within the academic residence halls that already exist at MSU. These are not only living complexes, but they also provide faculty counseling and some classroom and laboratory facilities. The objective is to attempt to give students some of the characteristics of a liberal education in a small college setting and still have the advantages of a large university.

Accepted by the administration and approved by the MSU Board of Trustees, the new college—named the Justin Morrill College, in honor of the sponsor of the land-grant system—opened with an enrollment of some 400 freshmen in the autumn of 1965.

It was the recommendation of the special faculty committee that proposed the college that its program be committed to a broad liberal education, with an in-depth study of a specific field, which would center around a substantial core of required courses and which would have international service and education as an underlying theme.

Area Centers

In a real sense, Michigan State University backed into its international involvement. When it undertook its first international activities in the postwar period, it had no foreign area study centers or strong competence in any particular geographic area abroad.

Despite its heavy commitment of personnel overseas for the past decade, Michigan State was slow to develop a corresponding institutionalized area concern. In the early years, this was due in the main to the opposition to area centers on the part of faculty members, some of whom regarded special area centers as irrelevant to the central concerns of the university. Other factors contributed to the lag in institutionalizing. One is the antipathy to the area approach on the part of some of the discipline-oriented departments. Another was the lack of any existing vested interest on campus for the interdisciplinary, area-oriented approach. Still another was the friction—encountered on many campuses with heavy overseas operating commitments—between the area specialists and the technical assistance practitioners.

These factors notwithstanding, the increasing interrelationship between faculty research, teaching, and overseas activities in recent years has made institutionalization seem natural and desirable. It was increasingly recognized, particularly in the Office of International Programs, that informal arrangements for cross-campus coordination would have to yield to more formally structured centers and institutes. Encouraged and nurtured by the Office of International Programs, three area centers and five functional institutes have come into being or are at various stages of development on the campus. The Office of International Programs has hewed to the belief that the management of international programs should be related as closely as possible to the component colleges. Thus all of the functional centers and one of the three area centers are located within colleges, although funds for their operation come through both the International Programs Office and the colleges concerned.

The three area centers are Africa, Asia (including both China and Southeast Asia), and Latin America.

The African Studies Center came into being in 1960 mainly because two or three faculty members had a strong interest in Africa and felt that a center would advance their interests on campus. NDEA funds, which MSU matched, were used to set up the Center. The Center coordinates and fosters the development of African studies in many relevant fields. At present, courses are offered in a number of departments, including economics, education, linguistics, geography, history, political science, sociology, and anthropology.

The Center is part of the College of Social Science. It is the only area center within a college but maintains close relations with the Office of International Programs and is physically located in premises of the office.

Course work and degree programs principally concerned with Africa are pursued in the discipline of chief interest, and the extent of coordination possible among fields is governed mainly by interdepartmental understandings. The Center does not grant degrees in African studies, but a concentration of courses on Africa with a social science divisional degree is possible.

The orientation of the Center is to sub-Saharan Africa as a whole, with special strength at present in West African studies. As one of the centers in the United States organized under NDEA provisions for the teaching of African languages, the MSU Center currently offers regular instruction in Hausa, Swahili, Bemba, such West African languages as Yoruba, Igbo, and Twi, and pidgin English. A significant activity of the Center is the publication of a new *Journal of African Languages,* sponsored jointly by Michigan State and the University of London. Currently, the Center is also sponsoring a research program designed to produce grammatical and course materials in West African languages.

The faculty of the African Studies Center is divided into core faculty and contributing and resource faculty, reflecting a division between the "purists" and the "activists." The core faculty comprises those who actually teach courses on Africa: with one or two exceptions, they have not been involved in the university's projects in Africa. The contributing and resource faculty is drawn from those faculty members who have had experience with or had their interests aroused by the university's project in Nigeria and elsewhere.

African Center personnel have been active in the development of the MINEX program, and have participated in the university's Peace Corps training programs for volunteers going to Africa. The MINEX program has apparently led to somewhat increased student interest in African Studies. The director of the African Studies Center has several times visited the University of Nigeria and has been involved in discussions of the MSU-University of Nigeria relationship, and the Center itself has been collaborating with a returned Nigerian program staff member in developing a leadership training program at MSU for staffing leadership training seminars in Nigeria. The Center has also benefited from the number of visitors who come to the MSU campus as a result of the University of Nigeria program, and, on the intangible side, has received support from the administration because of the interest in Africa generated by the University of Nigeria-MSU relationship.

The Asian Studies Center was established in 1962, and had its origins in the mutual interests of professors who had returned from assignments in Asia and began meeting informally. The MSU faculty now includes more than fifty members who have a major professional interest in Asia. The Center is located in the Office of International Programs, which undertook to provide financial support and encouragement until it could stand on its own.

The major purpose of the Asian Studies Center is to further knowledge and understanding of the countries of South Asia, Southeast Asia, and the Far East. The Center aims to attract students from the liberal arts and technical and professional schools to Asian studies, and, in accordance with their interests and capabilities, provide them with tailor-made programs and encourage them to become area specialists. It serves to correlate the offerings of the various disciplines on campus rather than functioning as a separate department. It also proposes to foster a research program utilizing the overseas projects of the university as centers where graduate students as well as members of the faculty may acquire field experience and basic data.

The Asian Studies program now is used as a core group for teaching and research. There is no interfaculty seminar, but there is an Asian Studies forum which utilizes visiting specialists for occasional seminars. There is no formal program with instruction in the graduate or undergraduate level, nor is there a major in the Asian field anywhere in the university. Most of the courses given are at the undergraduate level. In 1965 the Office of Education designated MSU as the site of one of five new South Asia Language and Area Centers to be supported by the NDEA.

A major in Chinese language and literature was approved in 1963, and work in Chinese anthropology has been carried out, but there has been a problem in widening the range of courses on Chinese studies because of a scarcity of faculty members in other disciplines. In Asian languages, Chinese and Japanese are taught and Bengali was added in 1964. Sanskrit was being taught for the first time in 1965.

There are two primary foci in Asian Studies—China and Pakistan. In Pakistan, where the university has maintained overseas projects for years, faculty members have had opportunities for research, and these interests will continue even after termination of the projects. By concentrating on China and Pakistan, members of the Asian Studies program feel they have a vested academic interest and expertise in these two countries, and they therefore look with some disfavor upon any attempt by Michigan State to accept service contracts in parts of Asia where faculty members do not have a prior research interest.

The Asian Studies Center has also begun a modest publication program, mostly reprints or speeches in brochure format.

Latin American Studies at Michigan State, organized in 1963, is the least structured of the three area centers. Like the Asian Studies Center, it is located physically in and supported financially by the Office of International Programs, which actually took the initiative some time ago in calling together faculty members with Latin American interests after a number of abortive efforts in which faculty members themselves tried to organize a program of Latin American studies.

The intention of the Latin American Studies Center is to develop a full curriculum in Latin American studies, with a full range of faculty. There are undoubtedly enough people on the Michigan State campus with competence in Latin America to provide such a program. At present, however, there is no effort to provide a degree program. The Center's aim is to enrich the curriculum in undergraduate work, and for the future to work toward a minor in Latin American studies. There is no continuing interdepartmental seminar in Latin American studies. Portuguese is not taught at MSU, although it is one of the major languages of South America and although Michigan State has had major AID contracts with Portuguese-speaking Brazil for a decade.

In a breakthrough into the research field, the Latin American Studies Center in the summer of 1965 was awarded a $400,000 AID grant to undertake an interdisciplinary study of food marketing in Latin America. During the two-and-a-half-year project, research will first be done in the San Juan area of Puerto Rico in an attempt to identify means of improving Latin American food marketing systems. In the second phase of the project, the researchers will analyze the food marketing system in a metropolitan area of a South American nation, probably Colombia. The objective of the study is to help coordinate rural and urban development by making the marketing systems more efficient to stimulate agricultural output and produce better food at lower prices.

Newest of the area programs at MSU is the Russian and East European Studies program, which was formally organized in 1965. As far back as five years ago the Office of International Programs tried a low-key effort to encourage faculty members with an interest in Soviet and East European affairs to organize a program, an effort which met with little response. In 1964-65 the Office of International Programs determined to be more systematic, and the newest venture is supported financially by the Office. Neither a center nor a full-blown area program, the new program, organized around a faculty committee, will offer the degrees of M.A., Ph.D., and Doctor of Education.

Next to be launched is a Canadian Studies program, a similar enterprise of a faculty committee, backed by university funds, which will organize a program of studies around the nucleus of a Canadian studies seminar which has existed at MSU for some years.

Functional Institutes

Concurrent with the development of the area centers has been the growth of functionally oriented institutes, each of which is located within a college or discipline (while encouraging participation of faculty from other schools on campus) and places major emphasis on research and the development of graduate programs. Both university funds and money from the Ford Foundation grants have been made available to assist the development of the institutes.

Four institutes have been organized and launched, and one more has been proposed. In a little more than a year of active operations, three of the four functioning institutes have been able to develop at least one major research project or contract.

The International Communication Institute, established within the College of Communication Arts, draws faculty participation from throughout the university's social science disciplines. Its primary objectives are: (1) promotion of research and training in international communication; (2) advancement of graduate study; (3) establishment of seminars and lecture series; (4) the development of library and research resources. The four main research areas which the Institute set out for study and support were: (1) cross-cultural communication, diffusion of ideologies, and technological innovations; (2) communication with illiterates and recent literates; (3) studies of the various means of communication used throughout the world; (4) research projects specifically related to instructional programs in international communication.

The academic year 1964-65 was the second full year of operation for the Institute, and the first in which real progress was made toward its objectives. Working with a specialist in the Indonesian theater, the Institute—on the principle that the theater is a communication channel in the cross-cultural sense—has supported the Department of Speech in developing several new courses on Asian and contemporary world theater. Support was provided for MSU faculty members to conduct studies of ideological commitment and change in five nations—Finland, Mexico, Costa Rica, Japan and the United States—and, in an agreement with the American International Association and its subsidiary, *Programa Interamericano de Información Popular* (PIIP), a communications research center has been established in San José, Costa Rica.

The major project involving the Institute is a four-year, $1,200,000 AID contract, signed in December, 1964, under which researchers from MSU will study the diffusion of innovations in rural societies at sites on three continents. Brazil, Nigeria, and India are the countries in which research sites have been selected.

The communication project is directed by Everett M. Rogers, who brought it with him when he left Ohio State University to join MSU. At MSU he serves as campus coordinator as well as project director, and he is also chairman of the board of international academic advisers which will formulate policy for the project.

"This is the largest study of communication in developing countries ever conducted," explains Rogers. "We hope the findings will make the process of change in these nations more rapid and more efficient." The aim of the project is to study the process by which new ideas in such fields as agriculture and sanitation are communicated to and adopted by villagers in emerging nations. Studies of rural villages in the host nations will attempt to identify community opinion leaders, innovators, effective channels of communication, and the various strategies used by change agents. About twenty social scientists in each of the host nations will assist the researchers in obtaining information. The MSU researchers will also train Americans and researchers in the host nations in methods for studying diffusion and communication.

As part of the project a Diffusion Document Center has been established at MSU to correlate the new data and assemble all available publications on diffusion. As outgrowths of this interest, the International Communication Institute is investigating the establishment on campus of an international development data bank, and has convened an all-university committee to study MSU's potential in the area of educational television for the developing countries. Once each term the Institute issues its own newsletter.

To capitalize on MSU's interest in and commitment to international education an Institute for International Studies in Education was established in 1964. The Institute has defined for itself four major purposes: (1) to develop methodologies for studying the problems of education in the developing nations; (2) to contribute to our fundamental knowledge of these problems; (3) to assist when possible in the use of this knowledge in the educational development of nations; (4) to assist MSU's College of Education to use overseas experience in order to enrich classroom teaching, curriculum, and research.

The director of the Institute, Cole Brembeck, conceives the organization's main task to be that of "building a strong link to the field through an overseas project and back again to the campus." The problem, as he sees it, is "how to enrich any technical assistance project overseas *from* the campus, and how to get feedback *to* the campus."

Michigan State may have devised a model answer to these requirements in its MSU-AID Thailand project, a two-year contract running to October, 1966, under which MSU will assist the Thai government in planning a comprehensive educational program for that country. The working relationship between the contract and the Institute is facilitated by the fact that Brembeck serves as campus coordinator for the Thailand project.

Working through the Institute, Brembeck has been able to build in to the AID contract several mechanisms to assist in the feedback process. For one thing, the project began with a seminar on educational planning in Thailand, held at the Kellogg Center in East Lansing in June-July, 1964, which was designed to add to both the ongoing work of educational planning in Thailand and MSU's understanding of the problems involved. Previously there had been a joint Thai-United States 1963 task force report and recommendations in the field of education and manpower planning. With the signing of the AID contract in 1964, the Institute introduced several additional feedback devices. One was the appointment of a faculty member as a director of research for the project, the first such appointment in any overseas technical assistance contract. Arrangements were also made to tie the work of MSU graduate students to the project, and three such students are scheduled to go to Thailand for research work. In another innovation, Brembeck instituted a campus "back up" team for the Thai project, a support group of faculty members, some of whom have had experience in Thailand and all of whom have experience in development work. The support team is intended to stimulate research ideas, to serve as an advisory group and a reactor to ideas coming in from the field, and, in part, to function as an orientation program for possible service in Thailand during the latter part of the contract. Finally, the Institute was able to persuade AID of the advantages of sponsoring a mid-term contract seminar, which will appraise the work of the first year and plan the work of the second.

The Institute for International Studies in Education is also the mechanism through which MSU is participating in the Inter-University Research Program in Institution Building, a cooperative endeavor of Indiana University, MSU, the University of Pittsburgh, and Syracuse University. Aided by an initial grant from the Ford Foundation, researchers—primarily from the four member institutions—will analyze the process of creating or reconstituting organizations in low-income countries which introduce new values, functions, and technologies, findings which are intended to aid and guide policy-makers and administrators concerned with building and modernizing institutions. As part of its contribution to the project, MSU has assigned a College of Education faculty member to undertake a ten-month study of the institutionalization of the professional education program at the University of Nigeria.

The Institute in the summer of 1965 also undertook its first cooperative venture with another institution, a joint seminar with the East-West Center of the University of Hawaii on the subject of "Cultural Factors in Educational Change." The Institute also has its own publishing program, and seven publications were in preparation in 1965.

The initiative for the formation of the third functional institute, the Economic and Agricultural Development Institute, came from members of the departments of agricultural economics and economics who were interested in the field of economic development.

Within a few months of its inception, the new Institute was given the administration of two research contracts with AID. One is a development of a research "map" to guide subsequent study and evalution of the U. S. Food for Peace Program, assessing the strengths and weaknesses of the program. The second contract grew out of an AID request that American universites having AID-sponsored technical assistance projects in Nigeria join in a cooperative research endeavor to study problems relating to the country's rural development. Four American universities are involved— Kansas State, Colorado State, Wisconsin, and MSU—in addition to the U.S. Department of the Interior and the Department of Agriculture, and the research consortium they have formed is being directed from MSU's Economic and Agricultural Development Institute.

A fourth institute, the Institute for International Business Management Studies, was established in the autumn of 1964, mainly growing out of the College of Business experience in Brazil and other parts of the world, and utilizing the existing resources of the Bureau of Business and Economic Research, which is part of the Graduate School of Business Administration.

A fifth institute, which would probably be known as the Institute on International Agriculture and Nutrition and would be located in the College of Agriculture, has been proposed and discussed at the faculty and administration levels. If launched by the university, it might concern itself with the relationship of mechanized agriculture to development, the production sciences, and the problems of food, food processing and nutrition, and so on.

Some of the functional institutes have made more rapid headway than others, but in all cases it has been made clear at MSU that they are experimental programs and that, while there has been at the outset a substantial commitment of university and other funds, the comparative progress made by each institute would vary widely depending on the commitment and initiative of faculty members who choose to associate themselves with them.

Library Resources

The book collections of the MSU libraries are approaching 1,000,000 volumes, about half of which are in the social sciences and half in the natural sciences. The early Michigan State emphasis on agricultural and engineering subjects has resulted in exceptionally good collections in those fields.

A core collection has been built up over the past ten years on the countries in which Michigan State has had contract operations—Pakistan, Taiwan, Nigeria, Okinawa, India, Vietnam—but the university's international librarian concedes that library holdings for the area programs, except possibly the Africana collection, do not yet compare favorably with collections elsewhere. The area committees in charge of the centers work closely with the library staff in their efforts to reach a level of acquisitions consistent with the teaching and research needs of the centers.

Like most universities faced with the problem of building up their library resources to match their geographic competence, MSU discovered that it takes time and money to build a collection adequate to support an area study program. From the librarian's point of view, the availability and development of library resources should be given first consideration before any new area program is started. According to its international librarian, these principles have been overlooked at MSU in the past and the university has been forced to use both general funds and some Ford Foundation grant money to boost its library resources.

The development of library collections for area studies is a task far more complex than generally assumed, because of the very nature of area studies. While they follow the traditional academic levels of undergraduate programs, master's degree programs, and doctoral-faculty research, their interdisciplinary aspect involves almost every academic discipline, and their library needs are very different from those of traditional academic programs. Depending on such factors as language, subject field, country, availability of bibliographies, and reference sources, most of the area programs require different types of publications and a different kind of library service. Even a modest undergraduate area program needs special publications, often in the vernacular, that are seldom obtainable in the regular domestic book trade. Graduate and faculty research needs require a mass of primary sources—government documents, unpublished reports, manuscripts, maps, periodicals, pamphlets, and backfiles of long out-of-print materials in Western and non-Western languages.

In addition, adequate reference and bibliographic work calls for trained librarians with the necessary area, subject, and language competence.

There is a serious national problem in staffing certain special areas with people qualified to catalog and service area materials and to render reference aid. At MSU, only two areas—South Asia and Latin America—have bibliographers with required background and training.

Despite difficulties, MSU has made a good beginning in the development of a Chinese reference collection and a working collection for South Asia. The Africana collection is still relatively small, but is steadily growing both in quality and quantity. Acquisition abroad remains a major problem, and MSU is experimenting with having faculty members on service abroad locate and acquire certain types of library materials for area programs.

Certain specialized projects have helped bring hard-to-get materials to the library. Since 1960 Michigan State has been a participant in the Latin American Cooperative Acquisition Project (LACAP), by which certain American universities buy materials in that area. Under the Farmington Plan—a project agreement entered into by some sixty major research libraries after a conference of their librarians at Farmington, Connecticut, so as to assure the availability in the United States of at least one copy of every new publication in the world of potential use in scholarship and research—Michigan State is the designated library to receive and catalog all publications from two African nations, Dahomey and Togo, and of all materials on psychology and occult sciences published in Western Europe. Michigan State, using U.S. Public Law 480 funds, also receives certain English-language publications from India and Pakistan, and is the depository for selected government documents from India, Pakistan, and Nigeria.

Overseas Research

The most persistent problem confronting universities that consider overseas projects an important part of their function is how to bridge the gap between the professional experience of a faculty member overseas and his work on the campus. This aspect of the feedback problem has continued to concern Michigan State, but the university has continually searched for productive ways to relate faculty experience abroad to academic development on campus.

This deliberate attempt to interrelate overseas and campus activities has led to a considerable expansion in the volume of research activities that have been made an integral part, directly or indirectly, of the overseas programs.

The main mechanism for encouraging international research is the Office of International Programs, which has an Assistant Dean for Research who is responsible for administering research grants from the Ford Foundation funds given to MSU for international studies. In the course of 1964-65 some sixty-five such research grants were awarded. Most of these, as a result of a specific policy of the Office of International Programs, were handled through the area centers and functional institutes.

The centers and institutes, while they are not all at the same stage of development, have progressed to the point where they can take over the task of screening and awarding research grants within their areas of specialization. This is in line with the Office of International Programs' policy of decentralization. Coordination is now achieved through a biweekly meeting of center and institute directors, who meet with the Office of International Programs representatives and informally discuss research projects under consideration. Further coordination occurs when each center and institute at budget time presents its overall requests for funds from the Ford Foundation grant.

The intention of the Office of International Programs is to drop out from direct sponsorship of research, except for those projects in the international realm that may be temporarily homeless or projects that, because of their nature, involve cross-university interests. Another area of research in which the Office of International Programs will take a continuing interest is the problem of transferring success, in techniques, personnel, contract arrangements, and so on, from one overseas project to another.

Recently Michigan State's efforts to strengthen the linkage between research and its overseas projects have included:

1. The assignment of doctoral-level research fellows to overseas projects to work with their academic advisors in the field. (This had been experimented with in prior years, but proved most successful in 1963-64, when three agricultural economists worked with the Economic Development Institute of the University of Nigeria.)

2. The provision of research funds for returning faculty members to complete writing, analyze data, and in other ways capitalize professionally on their period abroad.

3. The building into the overseas experience of the types of teaching and research activities that will enhance the contribution abroad and also strengthen academic ties to the home campus. This approach has worked successfully in a number of specific arrangements, such as the University of Nigeria, the educational research program in Guatemala, the agricultural engineering program at the National Taiwan University and, most recently, in the MSU-Thailand project.

4. The emphasis on Pakistan in MSU's Asian Center, and the center's interest in building the university's contract tie-in with the National Taiwan University into a continuing base.

5. The deliberate attempts to tie the programs of the institutes and centers to the university's overseas projects.

The centers and institutes themselves are components in feedback strategy, and through their programs they are supposed to create an environment on campus into which faculty members returning from overseas projects can willingly step. This is not expected to be a one-to-one arrangement in which a returning faculty member would fill the place of a faculty member setting off on an overseas project, inasmuch as there will always be faculty members anxious to return to their own campus niches, but the centers and institutes are intended to provide an interesting research and intellectual environment for returning faculty members who want to continue their interest in either functional or area problems with which they have been dealing while overseas.

Study Abroad

Michigan State has not joined the parade of universities offering large-scale study abroad programs, but it has a number of sharply focused programs designed to send students abroad for a portion of their undergraduate or graduate work.

In 1960 the university established its International Doctoral Fellowship Program, which provides opportunities for advanced graduate students to do their dissertation research overseas with a tie-in to a local university project. Through special arrangements, each graduate student works under the general guidance of a professor located at the overseas project, although the student continues to be responsible to his regular doctoral advisory committee. The research done is supposed to be of use to the overseas project, and it also serves as the dissertation research project for the candidate. Ford Foundation funds helped to launch this new program.

In an effort to provide opportunities for undergraduate language study abroad at minimal cost, Michigan State in 1961 began to work cooperatively with the European Language and Educational Foundation located in Zurich, Switzerland. The foundation, financed by the MIGROS organization, a Swiss marketing cooperative, maintains European Language and Education Centers (ELEC) for intensive language instruction in Switzerland, Spain, France, Germany, Italy, Austria, and England. MSU students could study the languages at the intermediate and advanced intermediate levels in France, Germany, Italy, or Spain while immersed in the cultural and daily life of these countries.

The main drawback to the ELEC program was that it was not affiliated with local universities, and MSU students who attended were not guaranteed credit for their work. On return to East Lansing they could take an examination for academic credit in MSU courses comparable to those taken abroad, and the amount and type of credit given depended on the test results.

In the summer of 1965, based on a number of years of experience with the ELEC Centers, MSU entered on an expanded and improved arrangement. Three MSU professors went to Europe, one to each of the ELEC Centers at Cologne, Paris, and Madrid, and some 150 MSU students were signed up to attend. Credit will be given for work done at the Centers. Frankly experimental, the program will be evaluated as the result of the summer experience, but it is MSU's hope that it can be expanded into a year-round program, and that up to 150 students can attend for a semester at a time.

In the summer of 1964 Michigan State inaugurated MINEX, an exchange program between itself and the University of Nigeria, a project developed on the East Lansing campus jointly by the African Studies Center and the administrators of the University of Nigeria project. For the first summer the five-week course was made available to all students at MSU, and the thirty-one who enrolled represented many departments and colleges in the university. The cost to the students was $740, and the program was subsidized by a grant from the U.S. Department of State's Bureau of Educational and Cultural Affairs. The special courses given at Nsukka for the MSU visitors were accredited by Michigan State. They included such subjects as "Nigerian Society in the World," "Politics of West Africa," and "Geography." They were taught by Nigerian professors.

Financial drawbacks—few Nigerian students have the money for brief journeys to the United States—make a genuine exchange program difficult, but for the summer of 1965—with the aid of another grant from the Department of State—MSU and the University of Nigeria were able to work out a program involving students from several universities.The MSU contingent of thirty students was opened to students from the member universities of the Midwest Universities Consortium, and at the University of Nigeria were given interdisciplinary course work "distinctly African in nature." In addition, the American students undertook field trips to supplement the course material. The twenty-three Nigerian students brought to MSU could enroll for one regular credit course, and in addition were given a specially designed course in American living and were taken on tours throughout the state.

Still another summer exchange program designed to involve MSU students in areas where the university has been operating is the MREP program (from *M*ichigan State-University of the *R*yukyus *E*xchange *Pro*gram), which was inaugurated on an experimental basis in the summer of 1965. Some twenty MSU students and ten faculty members from MSU and Michigan high schools were selected to study for five weeks at the University of the Ryukyus and to tour Okinawa and Japan. Both the MSU and high school faculty contingents enrolled for a seminar workshop dealing with Japanese and Okinawan topics. The student contingent enrolled for five-week junior- and senior-level courses in the culture, political systems, and economic development of Okinawa and Japan. Credits are transferable to MSU.

Foreign Students

In the 1964-65 academic year, Michigan State had on campus some 880 foreign students from eighty-four countries, and ranked fifteenth among American universities in the total number of foreign students enrolled. Approximately 65 percent of them were at the graduate level. Canadians (158) made up the largest single group, with Indians (92) second, Chinese (51) third, and Iranians (47) fourth. Brazil led in the number of Latin American students with 29, and Nigeria, with 33 students, provided the largest delegation from Africa.

The foreign student population at Michigan State University is viewed as a responsibility, a challenge, and a resource. The university's foreign student program, an integral part of the international program, emphasizes all of these and has taken important steps to fulfill and realize all three.

An Assistant Dean in the International Programs office is responsible for improving and developing exchange programs for Michigan State University students generally, including the foreign student program on campus. Working under him is the exchange program coordinator (former foreign student adviser) and several other persons concerned with foreign students. In general, however, administration of foreign student matters is the same as for all other students. Admissions, academic records, counselling, and advising are all handled on a normal basis within the university. The Assistant Dean becomes involved in special cases and in the development of policy.

Emphasis is on expanding the interest and ability of normal organizations, such as the Counselling Center, to provide necessary services to foreign students. Special orientation programs are conducted, a newsletter for foreign students and alumni is distributed regularly, and special extracurricular activities which tie together the American and foreign students are encouraged. Written guides are being prepared, covering important areas of concern to the foreign student during his stay at MSU.

Several years ago Michigan State established a special English Language Training Center, administered within the Department of English and the College of Arts and Letters. The Center provides intensive training to improve English language ability so that foreign students can perform effectively in the classroom. The Dean of International Programs has helped to establish the Center and keeps in touch with its development but does not have administrative responsibility for its operation.

The foreign student at Michigan State University is generally provided the same type of program as all other students. Certain essential aids to social and cultural adjustment are provided. These are kept at a minimum, the theory being that the foreign student should be an integral part of the total campus community, rather than kept apart.

Of particular significance in recent years have been the steps to make use of the foreign students as a resource. One development in this direction has been in the African language program, where language informants drawn from the African students on campus are an essential element. More broadly, the student government International Cooperation Committee now provides orientation and personal assistance to the foreign student, and offers special opportunities to socialize and "intellectualize," with benefits flowing in both directions. The committee requires all participating American students to undergo eight hours of orientation, conducted by faculty members. All International Cooperation Committee work with foreign students is managed and financed by student government.

Both the foreign students and a segment of the American community have benefited from two extramural programs. The first is a professional growth and development program arranged between the Boards of Education in the greater Lansing community and the International Programs Office. Credits for professional growth are given to the sixty-five high school and elementary teachers who participate in this twelve-hour seminar. The emphasis in this program is on important social-psychological considerations in crosscultural relations. Selected graduate foreign students are asked to serve as resource persons under the leadership of Michigan State University faculty members.

The second extramural program is one in which carefully selected foreign students are utilized as resource persons for teacher workshops on social science curriculum in out-state areas, where face-to-face contact with representatives from other cultures is infrequent. These workshops require a considerable amount of preplanning so that the foreign resource persons will have a reasonable idea about the teaching materials being used by the teachers. The opportunity for the foreign students to work closely with high school teachers and learn more about the American education system is both rewarding and interesting.

An active multinational United Nations group, an international club, and various nationality groups continue their important contributions to the extracurricular, cross-cultural life on campus. The International Relations Club has been revitalized, and several other groups with an international orientation meet regularly.

At most universities in the United States foreign graduate students are admitted on the recommendations of the graduate admissions officers in the various departments and colleges to which they apply. This procedure is increasingly inefficient, resulting in uncoordinated admissions with no relation to total university enrollment, but it also throws on the graduate admissions officers the responsibility of keeping abreast of the multitude of educational systems in the world and of interpreting adequately the academic credentials presented with applications for admission, a responsibility for which few admissions officers are equal.

In an effort to avoid the pitfalls of this approach, the Assistant Dean of International Programs at Michigan State recommended in 1964 that the university's Central Office of Admissions be requested to assume primary responsibility for the admission of foreign graduate students, in addition to its present responsibility for foreign undergraduates. It was further recommended that the Admissions Office and the Assistant Dean of International Programs develop an accepted procedure to coordinate the most effective use of the special talents of the two offices as they bear upon the admission of foreign students.

Under this proposal the Admissions Office would be given authority for the final decision to deny admission if there is lack of evidence of either adequate financial resources or of sufficient academic preparation for the intended course of study. The applications from foreign graduate students would go first to the Central Admission Office and be thoroughly appraised by the staff specializing in foreign admissions. Observations on various factors—an interpretation of the academic performance of the student in his home country, a scrutiny of the proposed course of study in relation to previous training and experience, and an appraisal of financial resources— as well as the recommendation of the Central Admission Office would then be transmitted to the appropriate department, which would decide which potential students to admit from those regarded as generally admissible by the Admissions Office. If the Admissions Office determines that a student is not generally admissible for graduate or undergraduate work, the credentials would not be forwarded to the department and the student would be notified accordingly.

Such a procedure would put Michigan State far in front in terms of establishing a rational policy for the admission of foreign graduate students. Despite the fact that the proposal cuts across departmental and college privileges and traditions, the university's Graduate Council took it under discussion during early 1965 and went so far as to recommend the employment of a professional admissions counselor skilled in the interpretation of foreign educational credentials in order to screen foreign graduate applicants, a long step in the right direction.

International Campus Environment

The influence of the international program at Michigan State is seen not only in teaching and research but also in the international content of campus and community service activities.

Performers from India, Korea, Japan, Haiti, and South Africa have appeared at the university as part of a special Asian-African,Latin American yearly concert series arranged by the African, Asian, and Latin American studies centers. About half the concerts put on in the lecture-concert series feature international performers.

Early in 1964 three student organizations, the Michigan State University Student Government, the National Student Association, and the International Relations Club, combined to put on a three-day campus conference under the title of "Winds of Change in the Emerging Nations." MSU faculty were the main resource people, but name speakers were brought to the campus and the meetings were so well attended that a similar conference on Population Pressures was held early in 1965, at which about 4,500 MSU students and faculty and delegates from other schools attended the three-day seminar.

Every spring one of the most popular campus activities is the International Festival, sponsored by the International Club and held in the Auditorium, where students from foreign lands represented at MSU put on displays and tell their fellow students and the people of Michigan of their home countries.

Apart from the International Club—which has about 625 members, half American students—and the various language clubs found on many campuses, Michigan State has wide variety of international or internationally oriented clubs and associations, ranging from an Association of African Students and student clubs for Iranian, Indian, Pakistani, Arab, and Chinese students, to a Caribbean Club, a Campus U.N., and even a group known as *Les Gourmets,* who are by definition international in their appetites.

The campus communication facilities—the daily student newspaper, *The Michigan State News,* WMSB-TV, WKAR-AM and FM radio stations— do a fairly professional job of coverage of the international activities in and around the university. WMSB-TV, which shares a channel with a Michigan commercial station and is on the air for some $38\frac{1}{2}$ hours per week, is a member of NET, the National Educational Television network, which programs heavily in international subject matter. The Michigan State television station is also used to broadcast programs designed for preschool and elementary age children, and the Continuing Education Service of the university also utilizes its facilities to broadcast informal college courses, many of which have an international element. One year it carried a thirty-nine-week series of telecasts on "Sub-Saharan Africa." *The Staff Bulletin,* known as the "blue sheet" on campus, carries an average of three international items per issue.

Despite the visible international content in the newspaper and in the radio and television facilities, some communications experts on the campus feel that Michigan State has not made a systematic attempt to use the facilities to create more interest in international affairs both on campus and in the community and state. One reason for this would seem to be that the facilities are separated from the academic side of the university, and are run by the administration on the justification that they reach an audience off campus.

A special effort is made to keep in touch with the university's overseas alumni. A bulletin titled *News* (spelled out in six languages) *From Michigan State University* is periodically sent to all alumni overseas, keeping them up to date on the university's activities.

As a direct outgrowth of this international campus environment, MSU was an early practitioner of the "teach-in" technique which spread across the United States and to other areas of the world in the spring of 1965. Less publicized was MSU's gesture in pioneering a student-to-people program, in which MSU students and faculty collected funds and "adopted" a Vietnam village, providing schoolrooms and a medical clinic. When Vice President Hubert H. Humphrey appeared on campus on June 1, 1965, to launch the program, more than 2,000 Michigan State students and faculty turned out. Within a week the MSU idea had spread to almost 100 other American campuses.

International Extension

For some time it has been evident that more could be done to thicken the international content offered in MSU's Extension and Continuing Education program. Its programs and courses reach nearly every community in Michigan, but until recently a relatively small percentage was devoted to world affairs. The expansion of the international and non-Western component in these courses was identified as a target of emphasis for both the Office of International Programs and the Continuing Education program, and in September, 1964, they brought the problem squarely into range with the establishment of an office of International Extension. Physically located within the Continuing Education and Cooperative Extension services of the university, the new office derives one-third of its finances from the Office of International Programs and works closely with it in its daily operations.

In its first year of existence, the new office undertook a wide variety of assignments. It participated in the planning of the MINEX and ELEC exchange programs, and it is anticipated that the coordinative functions of MSU's future exchange programs will be housed in the Office of International Extention. In the summer of 1965 it conducted two training programs for Peace Corps volunteers, one of them a community development program for volunteers going to Chile, the other for volunteers going into agricultural extension and rural development work in Nigeria.

In the autumn of 1965 the Office of International Extension inaugurated a new Peace Corps program, the first of its kind in the United States, under which qualified P.C. volunteers will have the opportunity to work for a master's degree and for Michigan teacher certification while carrying out their Peace Corps assignment. Known as the MSU-Peace Corps Masters in Education program, it was designed by the Peace Corps in response to a request by the Government of Nigeria for additional professional secondary school teachers. MSU will organize both the academic program on campus and in Nigeria. While in Nigeria volunteers will acquire MSU credit through independent study, supervised teaching and seminar work— under the direction of MSU faculty members in Nigeria. Following twenty-four months of service in Nigeria, the volunteers will return to MSU for an additional term of study to complete their degree and certification requirements. Returned P.C. volunteers with Nigerian experience will supplement the MSU teaching faculty. Through the program, which is admittedly a pilot project, it is hoped to develop individuals who desire a career of teaching overseas as well as to attract to Michigan teachers who can bring a knowledge of the developing nations into the state's high school curriculum. Volunteers who qualify will be certified for teaching in the secondary schools of Michigan, and these certificates are reciprocal with those of most states. During the first period of the program, from thirty to sixty P.C. volunteers will be trained.

Stimulating community interest in world affairs became the second major responsibility for the new Office of International Extension. In the summer of 1965 it put on a Resources conference, bringing to East Lansing the chairmen of many international community committees from throughout the state for the purpose of widening their knowledge of existing international programs and resources. For the winter of 1966 the office plans a study tour of Africa for Michigan community leaders, an exposure intended to encourage individuals to return home and develop community groups with international interests where they do not already exist. And, in its own bailiwick, the office hopes to assist in the development of a World Affairs Council in Lansing and East Lansing.

To enlist faculty support and participation in its efforts to bring world affairs home to the people of the state, the office has also compiled a faculty list, a compendium of international interests and experience, with specific reference to the extension activities in which faculty members would be willing to participate.

V

Much of the leadership for the development of the international programs at Michigan State has been provided by staff members who have returned from overseas assignments. Project-experienced personnel, for instance, fill the following positions: several key posts in the International Programs Office, the chairmanship of the Latin American and Asian studies centers, the directorships of the International Communication Institute and the Institute for International Studies in Education, key committee posts in the social science course revision, and assistant deanships for International Programs within the Colleges of Education, Agriculture and Engineering, and The University College. In addition to these formal roles, numerous returnees have been effective in faculty discussions and decisions which have led to specific developments in the campus international program. In many of the developments, particularly in the College of Agriculture, they have provided crucial leadership.

The Office of International Programs

Ultimate concern for all international aspects of the university's development is centered in the Office of International Programs, headed by the Dean of International Programs.

Both programmatically and administratively, the role of the Office of International Programs has evolved largely in accordance with the guidelines suggested by the faculty seminars of 1958 and 1959. Programmatically, there is a constantly reinforcing relationship between the various components of the university's international activities. Administratively, a unique blend of centralization and decentralization has developed over the years, a combination of decentralized action and initiative and central administrative leadership. This is based on the concept of a pluralism of centers of authority in international program activities, with decisions made close to the points of participation and action. The International Programs Office, while it stimulates and encourages many activities, administers few directly.

As the first international coordinating mechanism to be developed on a university campus, the Michigan State system has been observed by other universities and portions of it have been introduced elsewhere. However, the Michigan State arrangement for handling its international activities has evolved within its total institutional environment, and would have to be adapted to serve effectively elsewhere, just as MSU itself has adapted its area and functional centers from successful experiences on other campuses.

Symbolizing Michigan State's commitment in the international field is the new building, opened in 1964, which was erected to house the Office of International Programs. The building stands near the new geographical center of the campus, and provides facilities for the Office of the Dean of International Programs, the foreign student exchange program, the three area studies centers and several of the overseas project coordinators, as well as seminar rooms and other facilities.

Structure of the Office of International Programs

The Office of International Programs consists of the Dean, an Associate Dean, Assistant Dean (research), Assistant Dean (overseas operations), Assistant Dean (exchange programs), Assistant to the Dean (administration), and secretarial and supporting personnel. This seems to give the office almost as many deans as the Chase Manhattan Bank has vice presidents, but each has a well-defined function.

The Dean of International Programs is responsible to the administration of the university for all activities the university undertakes overseas in the international field and for the development of academic programs, including research, in the international field throughout the university.

The Associate Dean is concerned with all matters within the Office and acts in the Dean's place during his absence. He is particularly responsible for the Ford Foundation grant, but is also involved in overseas project activity, the development of the campus research and academic program, and the general administration of the OIP.

The Assistant Dean (research) exercises a loose coordination of the international research activities of the area centers and institutes and, in addition, initiates and organizes research on subjects and problems related to the overseas operations of the university and of central concern to the international program but which are not logically a part of the research program of any center, institute, department, or college.

The Assistant Dean (overseas operations) is responsible for an overview of the university's contract operations overseas, although the coordination of the various operations is achieved mainly through a biweekly meeting of the campus coordinators, with the Associate Dean of International Programs in the chair. The Assistant Dean (overseas operations) also issues a monthly bulletin, *Overseas Report,* which describes the changing international activities at MSU and is intended to keep those on contract operations overseas in touch with developments on campus. In time, this newsletter may be enlarged to serve as a publication covering all the activities of the Office of International Programs.

The Assistant Dean (exchange programs) is responsible for developing international exchange programs for MSU students. In general he is concerned with the improvement of the foreign student program of the university and the development of all aspects of the university's work related to foreign students and the sending of American students abroad for study. In carrying out this function he works with several faculty committees. Working under him, in addition to his assistant, is the Educational Exchange Coordinator (formerly Foreign Student Adviser).

The Assistant to the Dean (administration) is concerned with the Office budget, the maintenance of all administration aspects of the operation of the Office, the procedures and policies pertaining to personnel, budget, planning, programming, and so on, of the contract projects. He also serves as coordinator of the University of the Ryukyus project.

How the International Programs Office Functions

The Dean of International Programs reports to the president of Michigan State on all matters pertaining to overseas projects; to the provost for international developments involving the campus, such as area centers, institutes, research, and curriculum; and to the vice president for Student Affairs on foreign student matters.

However, two important procedural mechanisms would not show up on any table of organization of the university's decision-making structure. One is the fact that it is clear that the Dean of International Programs has direct access to the president of the university whenever he desires it. This fact is well known on campus. The second is that the weekly meeting of the eleven deans who head the various colleges of the university and the Dean of International Programs provides a convenient channel for communication and the development of consensus. This outlet is no longer as important as it was in the early years of the international activities, when it was necessary from time to time to sell the deans on new developments in the field. Now all but a few of the deans and most of the leading administrative officials of the university have had intimate contacts with the international programs overseas, a uniformity of experience that certainly did not occur by happenstance.

The responsibilities of the Office of International Programs include both line and staff functions. The primary line responsibility relates to overseas project operations, in that all project administrators are administratively responsible to the Dean of International Programs as the president's representative for international programs.

The principle seems clearly established at Michigan State that *any* new international projects or programs must be cleared through the Dean of International Programs. The formal authority over existing programs is exercised in two ways. Most of the univeristy's overseas projects are college projects, which—even if they draw some participating faculty from more than one department or school—are administered by one given school at the university. The campus coordinator for such a project is located in the school, and the school has virtual autonomy for operating the project, with control by the Office of International Programs exercised primarily through informal consultation. The amount of consultation generally depends on the personalities involved. Other overseas projects are known as "university overseas projects" and these are directly affiliated with and administered by the Office of International Programs. Their name derives from the fact that they generally draw upon a number of different colleges and departments on the home campus. The campus coordinators for these projects are responsible to the Dean of International Programs, and recruiting for them is carried out by the Office of International Programs in negotiation with the deans of the various schools involved.

There does not seem to be at Michigan State either a trend or an attempt to centralize administration of all overseas projects in the Office of International Programs. Although the center of gravity for overseas operations has moved to the Office, the most recent overseas project to be initiated is college-based, like the majority of such projects on campus, and even the present Office of International Programs-administered university projects have programmatic ties of varying strength to the schools whose faculty are involved.

The responsibility of the Office to improve the effectiveness of overseas projects is exercised primarily in two ways: (1) through the latent—but seldom exercised—power of the Dean of International Programs to veto various moves by project administrators in the schools, including appointments of specific faculty to overseas contract parties; (2) through the meetings (biweekly) of all the campus coordinators, representatives of the Office of International Programs, and certain others, such as a representative from the university's business office who specializes in overseas contract matters.

The strengthening of research and academic programs is clearly defined as a staff function of the Office of International Programs. The influence of the Dean and his staff in this field is exercised partly by consultation and discussion (informally or through many *ad hoc* committees), partly through the mechanism of the area centers and institutes, and partly by the force of outside funding whose disposition the Office of International Programs controls, particularly those resources deriving from the Ford Foundation's 1963 grant and Michigan State's share of the 1964 Ford Foundation grant to the four-university Mid-West Universities Consortium for cooperation in international programs and research.

Like a moving staircase, the Office of International Programs has continually evolved and modified and improved its methods of communicating and coordinating the international realm at MSU. In its early years, in addition to numerous *ad hoc* meetings, the transmission belt upon which the office relied for the communication of policies, decisions, and information within the university was the International Programs Advisory Committee, on which sit representatives not only of the colleges—and in some cases the deans themselves—but also of the library and other elements of the university. However, in contrast with the advisory committees of senior deans and department representatives found at some universities, the Michigan State representatives are generally middle-level faculty, and the committee is often headed by the Dean of International Programs himself. In some cases, the college representative on the committee serves as assistant dean responsible for international programs within the college: and if the university undertakes projects which are primarily staffed from the personnel of a specific college, the assistant dean for international programs within that college typically serves as coordinator for the contract on campus.

This system, utilizing the advisory committee and the assistant deans for international programs within the colleges, evolved in response to the desire of the Office of International Programs to meet several concerns—(1) to improve the effectiveness of overseas program operations; (2) to increase the breadth of international involvement; (3) to improve the feedback from the university's overseas experiences into research and teaching on campus.

The passage of time, and in particular the rapid development of the area centers and functional institutes, downgraded the role of the advisory committee as the major means of communication among the various components of the university engaged in international activities. During 1964-65 the meetings of the advisory committee were accordingly reduced to once each term, and in their place the Office of International Programs instituted a biweekly meeting of the directors of the area centers and institutes.

Also meeting biweekly, but on alternate weeks to the sessions of the center and institute directors, the campus coordinators of the overseas contracts are brought together by the Office of International Programs. Although liaison between the two committees is provided by the common presence of International Programs Office personnel, the need for closer coordination will grow as the institutes and centers become more closely affiliated with overseas operations and in the next evolution of its operations the office expects to bring the two committees together for a joint monthly meeting. The overall advisory committee will continue to meet once each term.

Organization for Overseas Projects

Each overseas project at Michigan State has a coordinator who is responsible for administrative matters to the Dean of International Programs and, for program matters, to the dean of the appropriate college, if the overseas project is primarily related to the subject matter and personnel of one college. In the case of projects involving a number of colleges, such as the University of Nigeria project, the coordinator is directly responsible to the Dean of International Programs for both administration and program.

The coordinator works with department heads throughout the university to locate the personnel needed for overseas assignments. If the coordinator of a project in agriculture needs a staff member from, say, the College of Education, he works with their Assistant Dean of International Programs in locating the appropriate person from the college.

All personnel and budgetary matters affecting the overseas contracts are approved by the Dean of International Programs. However, as a college gains experience and develops its own expertise in the international field, its reliance on the Office becomes less. Nonetheless, on administrative matters where personnel and finances are involved, the Dean of International Programs, acting on behalf of the president, continues to have final responsibility.

When a faculty member takes part in an overseas project he does not go on leave. He continues to accumulate time toward a sabbatical leave. His salary transfers to the project account, which is under the jurisdiction of the coordinator of the project.

Within the university's business office there are one or more persons specifically concerned with the university's overseas contracts. All financial matters pass through this office. Matters of contractual interpretation are discussed with coordinators, representatives of the Office of International Programs, and the business office, and clearance through the business office is necessary before the signing of any contracts.

Forward Planning

There is still some campus opposition to the university's overseas involvement. As one center director phrases it, "Some colleges and departments still have not tuned in on the international program now underway." This opposition is lessening as the years go by. Faculty discussion can still be heard about whether a university should take on overseas obligations equal to its staff and facilities or undertake a contract assignment and then build up the staff and facilities to meet the challenge. But even this argument is becoming less real as Michigan State has extended its areas of competence with each contract completed.

For a time overseas service was looked upon by some faculty members as a drawback to promotions and salary increases, and staff members who went overseas felt that they were often bypassed on the academic ladder. Now the balance has been reversed, and international service is, on the whole, a plus factor in determining promotions, salary advances, and departmental chairmanships throughout the university.

In the spring of 1964 and again during the same period in 1965 the Office of International Programs assembled at a Michigan resort several of the deans, some of the faculty and most of those involved in the direction and management of the various international programs of MSU for a three-day retreat, known as a "Forward Planning Seminar," to identify opportunities for program development, examine broad policy issues, and set forth long-range development plans. The discussions have provided the International Programs Office with a continuing agenda, and it is the intention to make them annual affairs.

Among the problem areas which emerged from the discussions at the 1965 sessions or from follow-up sessions back on campus are these:

1. An examination of the role of international programs in MSU's professional schools, such as Human Medicine, Veterinary Medicine, Business, Engineering, and Education.

2. How to insure a continuous supply of top personnel for overseas assignments, and follow up by having them bring back academic substance related to their overseas experience which can be effectively fed into the instructional and research programs on campus.

3. How to build bridges from the operational phase of an overseas contract to a long-term, meaningful relationship between MSU and the overseas institution concerned. If an institution-to-institution exchange is the result, how can this be funded for a considerable period of time?

4. The need to strengthen the dialogue between the university's overseas projects on the one hand and its centers and institutes on the other. In a

related sense, can MSU find a better way to share the experiences gained on each of its overseas projects with all the others? In other words, how do you overcome the prevailing tendency for each of a university's overseas operations to find its own way, even while traveling ground that has already been trod in some other part of the world or by personnel from another unit on the ever-expanding and ever-more-complex home campus?

5. The need for systematic studies of the relationship at MSU between foreign students and domestic students, a survey long overdue on the national scene. Are the courses which Michigan State offers its foreign students those that will, in fact, prepare them appropriately for their roles back in the home culture? What are the reasonable limits of special services and extra care that a university such as MSU should expect to expend on its foreign students?

6. What can Michigan State achieve educationally by establishing study opportunities abroad that cannot be achieved at home? Should MSU serve its needs in this field by either officially cooperating with another institution which has already established a program which fulfills its needs, or by merely recommending to its students such programs if they are open to students of other universities? Given the size of its enrollment, is an overseas study program involving only a few score students adequate for Michigan State? Should such a program be made available to and brought within the price range of hundreds of students, particularly undergraduates, at a time?

7. The need for a systematic orientation program for project personnel and research personnel going abroad.

In this key area, the prescreening and indoctrination of faculty chosen for overseas assignments, Michigan State has perhaps made as much progress as any other university in the field.

One thing is certain: there is no agreed-upon formula guaranteed to prepare university (or any other) personnel for overseas service. MSU has over the years experimented with (1) organized briefing programs for one project, (2) interuniversity programs for several projects, (3) person-to-person briefing sessions, and has concluded that, on balance, the personal orientation effort is as good as any.

In the summer of 1961 MSU organized and participated in a training and orientation program known as TOPS, which brought together a small group of professors and their wives from three universities and several other organizations, all of whom were departing for projects overseas. The conclusion was that the TOPS approach yielded no measurable advantage over other briefing attempts, but the Midwestern Committee on Institutional Cooperation (CIC) undertook to study the possibility of establishing a continuing training program. The CIC turned to MSU for the leadership in organizing such a program, but after a period of time in which other member universities appeared less than interested, Michigan State redirected its proposals to the Midwest Universities Consortium for International Activities (MUCIA). As a result of its own experience, Michigan State put before the consortium board a proposal for a long-range, continuing effort in orientation and training which it hopes will be implemented in the summer of 1966.

Michigan State increasingly looks to interuniversity cooperative efforts to boost its international programs. The main cooperative activity at present is in MUCIA, a corporation incorporated early in 1964 with a $3,500,000, five-year Ford Foundation grant to enable Michigan State, Wisconsin, Indiana, and Illinois universities to strengthen their campus programs and their ability to perform effectively abroad. The consortium is intended to supplement and complement the international programs of the member institutions. It can also give financial assistance to enable member universities to overstaff in order to provide a margin of faculty to spare for overseas assignments. The consortium can also assist in the pooling of resources on certain overseas projects when any one university might not have sufficient staff or facilities to carry out a project on its own.

In the faculty seminars of 1958 and 1959 which set the long-range guidelines for Michigan State's internationalism, it was anticipated that ten to fifteen years of intensive effort would be required to achieve the broad international dimension and establish the centers of intensive effort toward which the university should strive. After the first five years, those who have paced the university's international involvement found that progress had been more rapid than anticipated.

The deans of the International Programs Office are frank to admit that they and the administration have pursued a deliberate strategy in drawing the university deeper into the international area. Looking back, they distinguish at least four tactical decisions, each of which was intended to spread and reinforce the international dimension over the total university. The seminars themselves were planned efforts to engage and interest key faculty members in the unfolding possibilities of increased internationalism. The next stage was faculty commitment, an ever-widening involvement of individual faculty members in overseas projects, assignments abroad, and overseas research. The third stage in the campaign was MSU's determination to build on its strengths, to capitalize on its land-grant experience when and where possible, and to limit its area specialization to geographic regions where it could claim some competence to avoid spreading itself too thinly across the world. The fourth tactical decision was the approach of the Office of International Programs. Jurisdictionally operating from a central position of strength, the office has refrained from relying on this and instead has pursued a policy of patience mixed with persuasion. It has sought not to create threats to the academic establishment at Michigan State. It has avoided head-on clashes with entrenched academic departments and disciplines reluctant to internationalize. "We are not out to win battles," explains one of the deans of the office, "we are in this to win a war."

Even in such delicate areas as curriculum revision the long-range strategy of involving the total university in the international dimension has begun to show results. Widespread involvement of faculty members overseas over the years has served to develop people within particular departments who are conscious of the need to bring more universal, non-Western content into the classroom. This results in a change or an infusion of new material into a course here and there, and gradually a broader concern develops. It becomes legitimate and necessary for a larger number of faculty to consider the non-Western content in many courses where it would not otherwise be considered.

This is what the Office of International Programs refers to as the building up of a critical mass of involvement, so that when it occurs it brings about changes across the broad front of the university's activities. Once such a mass has been built up, the moves toward internationalism begin to come about without the office necessarily being aware that they are taking place. Several steps to increased internationalism take place every month, all across the university, and the office hears about them only casually.

The best example of this was the recommendation of a special faculty committee—some of the members of which had contact with previous international programs, either overseas or on campus—to establish the new Justin Morrill College with international education as a central theme. The Office of International Programs was not involved in determining the theme. In fact, it was not aware that the international dimension would be a focus of the experimental college until it was announced. To the Office of International Programs, this was evidence that Michigan State had reached critical mass.

*   *   *   *   *

More than any other of the universities included in this survey, Michigan State appears to have deliberately built upon its international activities as a means of moving the institution up to major university status. In a few short years it has lifted itself from a provincial college with an agricultural orientation to a university of national stature and worldwide recognition.

Looking back over this Operation Bootstrap, three forces can be seen to have combined to provide the leverage. One is the personality of its president and the initiating role he has performed in the university's internationalization. The second is the fact that President Hannah has had the support of a small but committed group of international-minded members of his faculty and administration. And the third source of strength has been the fact that the president, his administrators, and a portion of the faculty have held to a deliberate strategy, a long-range plan to internationalize the institution.

The course chosen—a succession of technical assistance contracts overseas, involving many of the university's professional schools—has not been without cost. Within the academic community the image projected by MSU—as an institution over-eager for overseas involvements and often overextended in its areas of competence—has become almost a cliché. MSU faculty members are understandably sensitive on this point.

The image is unjustified: if it ever applied, it is now well out-of-date. It may take some time to blur away at the edges, but it should fade more rapidly as the academic community comes to realize that Michigan State in the past year or so has accomplished more than perhaps any other American university—certainly more than any of those included in this survey—in building a continuing relationship, a feedback to its campus, between its activities abroad and its teaching and research functions at home. In contrast to those universities where the international program development consists of an isolated area center or international facility, Michigan State has moved in the direction of achieving a real international dimension throughout the institution.

As MSU provided a model in its early creation of a centralized administrative apparatus to coordinate its international activities, a functional step that has been followed and adapted by several other universities, so its pioneering efforts in internationalizing its curriculum and in providing linkage between its field projects and its campus learning and research could serve as models for its sister institutions in the United States.

TULANE

I

History, tradition, and geographic location have combined to give Tulane University both a strong international bent and a natural and logical involvement in Latin America. Situated in the great world port city of New Orleans, which ranks second in the United States in total tonnage, Tulane stands at the cultural, educational, and economic crossroads of the Americas, at the gateway between the vast Mississippi Valley and the Hispanic lands to the south. Moreover, New Orleans is the only city in the United States which was both a French and a Spanish colonial capital, and Louisiana's legal system is partly derived from continental Europe and thus related to that of Latin America.

Located in the residential part of a city where French, Spanish, and early American architectural styles have been preserved, Tulane has absorbed some of the distinctive atmosphere of the old city and its earlier civilizations. But with well over a century of its own history behind it, Tulane seems to wear its heritage as naturally as the moss that hangs from the live oaks around its 180-acre campus. As an urban university, it is far more cosmopolitan than most, reflecting the mixed cultures and permissive atmosphere of the city in which it stands.

A southerly orientation was evident from the very founding of the university in 1834, nineteen years after the Battle of New Orleans, when seven young physicians of the city established the Medical College of Louisiana to combat the "peculiar diseases" afflicting the area—principally cholera, malaria, yellow fever, and parasitic infections. Inasmuch as those diseases were common to Latin America and infection from there often caused epidemics in New Orleans, the study led in that direction. Tulane physicians took the lead in the study of tropical medicine, making the university today one of the principal centers for research and instruction in that field.

A privately administered, nondenominational institution, Tulane does not have the same demands for public service that stir state-supported institutions, but the service motive, particularly in the medical field, has nonetheless been part of Tulane since its inception. Its School of Medicine offers a degree in tropical medicine and is one of the two Southern schools (the other being North Carolina) offering a degree in public health.

Tulane has always regarded itself as an institution of distinctive service, doing many things which were not done, or could not be done as adequately, by other agencies. One of its chief goals, which receives growing emphasis, is the preparation of faculty members for universities and leading colleges, primarily to serve the southern region of the United States. But in this objective, Latin America is also a natural and logical region of service, and numbers of graduates are faculty members of Latin American institutions. Special graduate programs for potential foreign university teachers in law and medicine are well established, and nearly all the participants in the medical program and about half those in law have come from Latin America. In addition to students enrolled in those curricula, however, Latin American students are currently pursuing graduate study at Tulane in a number of fields, including business administration, social work, engineering, anatomy, anthropology, biochemistry, economics, English, microbiology, physiology, physics, sociology, Spanish, and zoology. Of the foreign students on campus during the 1964-65 academic year, 164 were from Latin America (sixty-eight as undergraduates). Twenty-one Latin Americans held faculty appointments.

II

Few evaluators of educational standards would rank Tulane among the top 20 American universities. It is not one of the traditional centers of excellence, but by the same standards no Southern institution has yet managed to break into the charmed circle. However, if it is in the second rank nationally, Tulane is certainly one of the half dozen leading universities of the South and preeminent in its immediate region. It is one of the six Southern institutions whose graduate programs and scholastic standards have won them membership in the restricted ranks of the 41-member Association of American Universities (the other Southern institutions being Duke, North Carolina, Virginia, Vanderbilt, and Texas). It ranks in the top twenty American institutions receiving NDEA fellowships, and in 1963 ranked eighth in the nation in the number of its graduates obtaining Woodrow Wilson fellowships. It has a faculty to student ratio of one to twelve.

Of the six universities surveyed by EWA case study teams, Tulane is by far the smallest in terms of student enrollment. Fall enrollment in 1964 numbered some 5,500 full-time and 2,250 part-time students (most of the latter being adults enrolled in evening classes in University College). Of the full-time students, some 3,200 were undergraduates, who were in turn subdivided into some 2,100 men attending the component schools and colleges of Tulane and 1,100 women enrolled in the coordinate Sophie Newcomb College, the first women's college in the country to be coordinated as part of a university. Tulane's full-time faculty includes some 800 with the rank of instructor or above and about 200 assistants and other ranks.

The Tulane University of Louisiana—to give it its official name—consists of ten colleges and schools which offer undergraduate, professional, and graduate courses. The College of Arts and Sciences is for male undergraduates only. Newcomb College is for women. All other units in the university are coeducational. The Schools of Architecture and Engineering admit undergraduates, and the Schools of Law and Medicine admit students after a minimum of three years of undergraduate work. Graduate training is carried on in the Graduate School itself, which offers advanced programs in the liberal arts and sciences, education, engineering, basic medical sciences, and social work; the Schools of Business Administration and Social Work; the graduate division of the School of Law; the division of postgraduate medicine; and the division of Hygiene and Tropical Medicine (accredited as a school of public health). The tenth unit is University College, an integral part of the campus, which offers primarily evening undergraduate courses for adults.

History and Heritage

One of Tulane's deans describes the university as "cosmopolitan in nature, privately endowed, and located in a Southern city, and trying as rapidly as circumstances will permit to overcome its deficiencies." This capsule characterization sums up several of the factors which have weighed heavily in Tulane's past and figure prominently in its future planning.

From the moment of its founding, it was accepted that Tulane had a special obligation to the area in which it is located.

Its conception was an act of faith on the part of seven young doctors in the old city of New Orleans. Determined to lift the standards of their profession, particularly in the tropical diseases peculiar to the area, and disgusted with some of the quackery which then passed for medical education, they joined together to create a center where young medical men could be taught and trained. They began in a Congregational church (now the site of the Sheraton Charles Hotel) in 1834, and in return for volunteering their services to the city's Charity Hospital were granted a square block of land in downtown New Orleans. There they built the Medical College of Louisiana. Thirteen years later this became the medical department of the newly chartered, state-operated University of Louisiana, and a law department was added to the medical nucleus. Four years after this promising start a collegiate department, forerunner of today's College of Arts and Sciences, was added, but the Civil War closed the university and the aftermath of the conflict brought critical financial problems.

At this point, some fifty years after the institution's beginnings, Paul Tulane entered the city's educational life. A native of New Jersey whose family came originally from France, Tulane came to New Orleans in 1822 at the age of twenty-one and in time became a wealthy merchant and real estate investor. From one of his factories in New Jersey he shipped clothing all over the country (he is credited with introducing the ready-made suit to America). After his retirement to Princeton, New Jersey, Tulane decided to do something for education in the city which had given him success, and in 1882 he organized a group of New Orleans business and community leaders into the Tulane Educational Fund, provided it with the then yearly income of $38,500 from his real estate holdings in the city and charged it with "building or fostering of an educational institution for the white youth."

The administrators of the hard-pressed University of Louisiana let it be known that they were not averse to some type of cooperative arrangement with whatever institution might be founded by the administrators of the Tulane Educational Fund, but two years of hard negotiations ensued because Mr. Tulane really wanted to found a technical school, not an academic institution. However, when he learned that a technical school could not be established tax free, he accepted the University's offer to be incorporated. In 1884 the state legislature turned over the property and control of the University of Louisiana to the board of the Tulane Educational Fund, and the university, now a private institution, was renamed The Tulane University of Louisiana in honor of its benefactor.

Until 1893 the little university remained crowded into its downtown premises. Almost a decade earlier the Great Cotton Exposition had been held in what was then the edge of the town and is now the city's famed Audubon Park. This aroused interest in the city's outskirts, and Tulane's board, in what it thought was a prudent move, bought fifty-five acres of low, swampy land from a rice and sugar plantation at the edge of town. This was intended to serve Tulane "for all eternity," but each decade since the university moved to its new location it has had to purchase acre after acre of high-cost residential land to keep up with its expansion.

Paul Tulane's connection with the university that bears his name had a disappointing climax. From his gesture in giving his New Orleans real estate earnings to the university, it was assumed that he would also provide for it upon his death. His New Orleans friends rushed to Princeton when news of his death reached them, but no will or codicil was found, and under New Jersey law his estate was divided among his nearest relatives, with nothing for the university that bore his name.

Tulane and the State It's In

For all its ties of trade and tradition which New Orleans had with Latin America during the early decades of this century, Tulane remained a regionally oriented, Southern educational institution until after World War II. However, in the decade that followed, Tulane emerged as a university with wide national interests and strong international ties, particularly in the inter-American field.

The Medical School, which had pioneered from the outset, again led the way in adjusting to changed world circumstances after 1945. During the last years of World War II it was one of the American medical institutions which developed short courses on tropical medicine, particularly parasitology, for the U.S. armed forces and for contingents from allied countries to the south. This experience encouraged the Medical School to ready itself for greater international involvement in the postwar period, and drew it into early cooperative efforts with medical authorities in Latin America.

Simultaneously, forces were at work—within Tulane and throughout the

South—that gradually brought about a complete change in the character of the university, both in faculty and students.

From 1947 to about 1953 there was a thorough turnover of faculty, which brought in younger scholars from different parts of the United States, many of whom had international interests. There was a deliberate effort to strengthen the graduate work of the university. Early in his presidency, Rufus C. Harris—who served as President from 1937 to 1961—made known his intentions to improve Tulane's graduate position, and he had the backing of the administrators of the Tulane Educational Fund, as Tulane's trustees are called, but the wartime years made this impossible. Prior to World War II, Tulane offered Ph.D.'s only in the basic medical sciences, and the university in those years could not count on more than some two hundred graduate students. In their postwar appraisal, the administration and trustees deliberately decided to add depth to the graduate program. By 1954 the Graduate School had some three hundred students. Today, a decade later, it has more than one thousand. The number of Ph.D. degrees conferred in the period 1958-63 was 229 percent greater than that for 1948-53, and the rate of increase was the highest of any member of the Association of American Universities (and compared with 64 percent for the whole organization). The Ph.D. degree may now be earned in thirty-two fields at Tulane, as compared to fewer than ten before World War II, and the master's degree in thirty-eight—mainly in the social sciences and humanities.

In time, this deliberate attempt to improve the university's standards—in the period 1954 to 1959, according to campus observers—altered the makeup of the Tulane student body. Prior to World War II, Newcomb College was "a finishing school for nice Louisiana young ladies," as one dean described it. The College of Arts and Sciences was in those days largely devoted to turning young men from Southern families into prelegal and premedical students. Today, with admission standards jacked up and tuition as high as any other private Southern university, the student body is more varied, more competitive, more aware. Deliberate efforts are made to recruit students from outside Louisiana and the South. In today's Tulane, only 24.6 percent of the students list New Orleans as place of residence, and 12.4 percent come from other Louisiana communities. About one-third of the student body comes from other Southern states, and the remainder from almost every state in the union and from 57 foreign countries. The total enrollment of foreign students during 1964-65 was 320, with about two-thirds of these in the graduate schools.

By every meaningful index of higher education—the expenditure per pupil in public institutions, college enrollment in proportion to population, expenditures on research and educational development, and so on—the South lags below the national average, but the regional gap is slowly narrowing and as it has narrowed so it has brought changes to Tulane and the role it plays in its region.

At the turn of the century, Tulane supplied a major proportion of the undergraduate educational opportunity, not only in New Orleans but in a large area of the deep middle South. This is no longer true. Today, Tulane's undergraduate student body constitutes less than one-quarter of the total undergraduate enrollment in higher educational institutions in its home city. In 1962-63 it had only 6 percent of the undergraduates enrolled in all Louisiana colleges and universities. Although a moderate increase in Tulane's undergraduate enrollment is contemplated, the university feels that more important than its quantitative contribution is the influence on neighboring institutions of the high quality programs of undergraduate study at Tulane, a multiplying effect achieved through its preparation of teachers for higher educational institutions and its cooperative ventures with other colleges and universities in the area, including Negro colleges.

Another development that concerns Tulane is that, despite the absolute and relative growth of graduate education in the South during recent years, an increasing proportion of superior students of the region are going elsewhere for their advanced study. Although 24 percent of the nation's college enrollment is in the South, only 13 percent of national fellowships go to students who use them at Southern institutions. The percentage of students awarded national fellowships in Southern schools has declined overall since 1958 from 17 to 13. In 1960-61 about five out of every ten southerners receiving Woodrow Wilson fellowships attended non-Southern graduate schools: in 1963-64 the proportion was nearly eight out of ten.

Tulane believes, therefore, that only the development of strong regional institutions into major national universities offering education of high quality will enable the South to retain its native talent as well as attract talented young students from other regions.

A special problem for Tulane, along with other educational institutions in the South, is to provide opportunities for Negro education.

A forced policy of segregation, a legal requirement imposed by the terms of Paul Tulane's endowment, which provided education for "the white youth" only, worked until recent years to limit Tulane's cosmopolitan character. It discouraged nonwhite foreign students—"there is no question that the problem of race affected our involvement with foreign students," concedes Tulane's President Herbert E. Longenecker. In theory at least, the racial bar at the university made it ineligible for certain kinds of AID contracts in which nonwhite participants were involved, although in fact President Longenecker contends that "Tulane has had relatively few relations with AID mainly because the kind of contracts AID offers do not lend themselves to Tulane's requirements." Most AID proposals have been rejected, explains the President, because they have been "regarded as a diversion of the university's real interests."

Another consequence of the racial barrier, it is conceded by President Longenecker, is that "Tulane does not have too much direct involvement with African nations at this time."

The administration and faculty—including both southerners and northerners—for many years opposed the segregation policy resulting from the Tulane bequest, and a few years ago—in a move quietly instituted—they succeeded through court action in setting aside the color bar provision. There are some fifty Negro students enrolled in the various schools and colleges of the university today, about half of them doing graduate work, and many more in University College.

Tulane's act of desegregation may divert some of the university's funds and interests from the international dimension. The university has for some time cooperated with Dillard, a Negro university in New Orleans, on faculty research and publications, but—like most of the other newly desegregated Southern institutions—Tulane is now ready to increase its efforts over the next few years in assisting with the upgrading of Negro education in its region.

III

For a small university Tulane offers a surprisingly wide range of international activities. A conscious and planned interest in the international component in education seems to pervade the administration, department heads, and most faculty members. Faculty with research interests on foreign problems or areas and with overseas experience exist in most if not all departments. The ratio of foreign faculty visitors and foreign students to their American counterparts is higher than the national average. Course content of an international nature can be found in the curriculum of most departments.

These factors, taken together, serve to make the international dimension visible to the Tulane student.

Dr. Joseph E. Gordon, acting Dean of the College of Arts and Sciences, believes that the increasing internationalism has had a measurable impact on Tulane's students, particularly over the past five years or so. For one thing, there has been a heavy growth in majors in political science, and a corresponding increase in the numbers of Arts and Sciences students going on to do either graduate or professional studies. Dr. John R. Hubbard, Dean of Newcomb College, remarked on a similar impact observable among his female students. The percentage of students enrolling in English, music, and other traditional courses for college women is declining, while the proportion majoring in political science, sociology, anthropology, and foreign languages is increasing, as is the number going on to graduate studies.

Dean Gordon enumerated at least four reasons why, in the liberal arts colleges at Tulane, the international dimension had visibly increased in recent years. One is a strong political science department, staffed with popular faculty members and offering courses which have had a personal appeal to many students. Another is the growing strength of the combined sociology-anthropology department, which has been expanded over the past few years by the deliberate addition of faculty with international experience and interests. A third is the popularity of the program of the American Universities Field Staff, a joint reportorial venture of certain American universities—of which Tulane was one of eight founding institutions—which brings highly qualified observers from key areas throughout the world to lecture and discuss foreign affairs on the campus several times each year. The fourth reason, and the one which Dean Gordon believes has given the greatest stimulus to the university's international activities, is Tulane's version of the Junior Year Abroad.

Junior Year Abroad

The Tulane-Newcomb Junior Year Abroad program, known as JYA on campus, offers superior students (grade average of at least B) an opportunity to spend their third collegiate year at major European universities (and one in the Middle East) following courses of study for which they will receive credit toward their degrees. Students chosen may enroll in specially selected universities in France, Spain, Germany, Italy, England, Scotland, Ireland, Wales, and Israel. Each student takes courses under the regular faculty of the overseas university, for which full credit is received at Tulane. Students are encouraged to elect courses in their major fields which are not available at Tulane or at other American universities. Enrollment in courses which duplicate or are similar to those offered at Tulane is not favored. Every effort is made to fit students into the academic framework of the foreign institution rather than to "export" courses which are requirements on the Tulane campus.

The country and university to which a student is sent are determined by his interests and field of specialization. Tulane now maintains relations with approximately forty European universities to which students have been or can be admitted through the JYA program. The European emphasis reflects the interest of the JYA's proponents at Tulane. So far, no serious effort has been made to extend a JYA relationship to universities in Latin America, Asia, or Africa.

Most students live in dormitories with European roommates, but they may live with European families if they wish. A Tulane professor-in-charge accompanies a group to Great Britain, where the largest contingent goes, and remains in residence in London throughout the year: another professor-in-charge travels with a second group to the continent and is in residence in Paris. Usually not more than two Tulane students are sent to any one overseas university.

There is keen competition for the JYA at Tulane. The ratio of applicants to places is usually about three to one. Each year about seventy qualified students are chosen to go abroad after selection by a faculty committee, which considers both the academic record and the personality of the student applicants. Expenses, including round trip transportation, generally do not exceed the cost of an academic year in residence at Tulane, and most scholarships and loans may be applied to the JYA.

While the program is mainly intended for liberal arts students, superior students in the Schools of Engineering and Architecture and the Graduate School may also be chosen, and prelegal and premedical students are also eligible if they follow a four-year rather than a three-year preparatory curriculum. Transfer students from other universities must spend at least one year at Tulane to be eligible for the program.

The JYA is largely the creation of Dean Hubbard of Newcomb, now on leave from Tulane to serve as deputy chief of the U.S. AID education mission in India. Recalling the origins of the program, Dean Hubbard remarked that when he first came to Tulane in 1953 he found "remarkably little interest in international affairs, given the university's background and location." A historian himself, specializing in British history, he approached the University of Birmingham in England and succeeded in placing two Newcomb girls for a year abroad. The JYA was born from those modest beginnings, although it was met with some skepticism. A New Orleans newspaper facetiously announced Hubbard's program under the general headline: NEW NEWCOMB DEAN WANTS TO GET RID OF HIS STUDENT BODY.

Each year an increasing number of Newcomb girls participated in the JYA, and about five years ago it was decided to extend the privilege to male undergraduates in the College of Arts and Sciences. For the academic year 1964-65 there were twenty-one Newcomb girls at various British universities and nineteen Arts and Sciences students, plus one each from the architecture and engineering schools. A similar 50:50 ratio of male and female Tulane students prevailed at other universities overseas, but in time the Arts and Sciences College, with its larger enrollment, is expected to outnumber the Newcomb nominees.

Dean Hubbard draws a sharp distinction between university programs for travel abroad and Tulane's policy of carefully placing selected students in appropriate universities overseas. "We believe in total immersion for our students, rather than just sprinkling," he says.

This approach has been justified by the results achieved over the eleven years of the program, Dean Hubbard believes. "When the JYA takes, it takes deeply," he remarked, commenting on the impact on Newcomb students exposed for the first time to a culture other than their own. The majority of the participants in the JYA are Southern students: for instance, of the seventy-one overseas during the 1964-65 academic year, sixty were from Southern states, and of these thirty came from Louisiana, Alabama, and Mississippi. Abroad—most of them for the first time—they have been exposed to the diversity of peoples at European universities, and borne their share of questioning about American racial problems.

Dean Gordon also notes "an almost 100 percent change in outlook" among his students returning as seniors after a year abroad. By far the largest share of these come back with a new desire to return overseas or enter into international service careers. Dean Hubbard agrees. "The returning students are much more mature," he says. "The only readjustment necessary is when they find it difficult to work back into the spoon-fed system of American education."

Tulane is now engaged in a systematic study of the impact of its JYA, but meanwhile those connected with the program are convinced that its results are measurable. Dean Gordon believes there is a close correlation between participation in JYA and the desire to continue graduate studies: he estimates that between 75 to 80 percent of those who have been on the JYA go on into graduate work, as compared to about 50 percent of the remainder of the student body.

Recently inaugurated by Tulane is a program of student exchange at the graduate level with the University of Strasbourg, in France, and the Free University of West Berlin, which began with the 1965-66 academic year. Tulane is also exploring the possibility of a faculty exchange program with the Free University of West Berlin.

Foreign Students

Because of the close-knit layout of the Tulane campus, in which the buildings are grouped around about five large city blocks, foreign students enrolled at the university seem to make an impression out of proportion to their numbers. They are housed in the dormitories with other students, and no attempt is made to "cluster" them according to nationality. About half of the 320 foreign students on campus in 1964-65 were from Latin America. Second most numerous were European students, but an increasing number each year are students from Taiwan and India. More than one-third of the foreign students are enrolled in the various branches of the Medical School. The ratio of foreign admissions in the graduate and professional divisions over undergraduate admissions has been increasing year by year, and currently more than two-thirds of the total foreign contingent is made up of graduate students. This increasing emphasis on graduate work has been accompanied by a change in the type of Latin American student coming to Tulane. Few playboy sons of wealthy Latin American families now apply for admission: foreign graduate students, with few exceptions, come to Tulane on scholarships or assistantships.

Until about eight years ago, admitted Dr. John H. Stibbs, Dean of Students, Tulane had "a fairly casual admissions policy" for foreign students. Then in 1958 the university established an International Office under a full-time director, Dr. Samuel S. McNeely. Fluent in Spanish and several other languages, McNeely has made several trips to Central and South America to visit universities there. As director of the International Office, he counsels and assists foreign students and assists the Office of

Admissions in selecting and screening undergraduate foreign applicants. However, he does not pass on the admission of foreign graduate students, who are admitted by the graduate departments and schools, although he serves these divisions in an advisory capacity. He also evaluates academic credentials earned in foreign educational systems and makes recommendations on allowable credits. An extension of the International Office, with a half-time advisor, is maintained in the School of Medicine.

Dr. McNeely also teaches English to those foreign students who require it. Difficulty with the English language remains a major obstacle to the academic progress of many foreign students and Tulane, like most American institutions admitting students whose first language is not English, utilizes several means of coping with the problem, such as tutoring, summer courses, and even classes for wives of students.

Tulane has pioneered a method of handling foreign students with language problems which may be applicable to other universities which have adult education or extension divisions on campus.

Foreign students deficient in English usually have difficulty carrying the full load of a university course. Dean John P. Dyer of Tulane's University College some years ago worked out an arrangement with McNeely in which the International Office recommends certain foreign students each year for admission to University College, where they are given a reduced course load but with heavy emphasis on English. At the end of the year, if the foreign student has made sufficient progress, he is admitted to the regular university courses. About forty of the foreign undergraduate students at Tulane during the 1964-65 academic year were taking this special course.

"Many arriving foreign students need this year of reduced load," explains Dean Dyer. "It accommodates them to the university and helps them learn American academic ways. The program gives the foreign student a way into the American university, and yet gives him time first to develop his language capacity and, second, to cope with a different educational system. For one thing, the whole method of class discussion—the give and take of the American classroom—is a new experience to most foreign students."

The problem is usually to convince the foreign student that this is the program he should take. "Most of them are too proud to admit that they cannot carry a full load and do not have full command of the language," admits Dean Dyer. However, the fact that University College is an integral part of the Tulane campus, and that the special students reside in the dormitories and participate in all university activities and are in all respects indistinguishable from regular Tulane students has assisted in the program's acceptance.

In many cases, the reduced-load program means the addition of up to a year of undergraduate studies for the foreign students taking part in it, but in view of the fact that finance does not seem to be a limiting consideration to most foreign undergraduates at Tulane this has not worked against the program. Both McNeely and Dyer hope to see it extended in the future.

Housing and hospitality are two areas in which the International Office assists foreign students in adjusting to living in New Orleans. Foreign undergraduates, on arrival, go through the usual freshman orientation program, but they also get a special orientation as foreign students. A Tulane student committee, the Cosmopolitan Committee of the University Center, functions throughout the year to provide cultural and social opportunities for the foreign visitors, and through the Community Hospitality Committee a number of families in the city serve as individual hosts to students from other countries, providing them with home hospitality and community experiences. The foreign students have responded with organized activities of their own. A few of them banded together to form a soccer football team, and then went on to organize a New Orleans league competition, which the Tulane team proceeded to win—to the cheers of their fellow students.

Campus Internationalism

An international overlay is apparent at many points on the Tulane campus.

The weekly student newspaper, *The Tulane Hullabaloo,* gives prominent coverage to any international affairs activities oñ campus, such as the presence of foreign visitors, the reports of American Universities Field Staff lecturers, the activities of foreign students, and the participants in the JYA. Staff interest in international affairs is directly correlated with the fact that most senior staffers on the paper have participated in an overseas experience, usually the JYA.

As a member of the A.U.F.S., Tulane is served by four visiting lecturers, experts who return from prolonged assignments in their special areas overseas and then move from campus to campus among the member institutions, spending up to ten days on each campus, where they are available for addresses, classroom lecturing, graduate research consultation, and talks with individuals or groups of students.

Tulane alumni are scattered over almost every country on the globe, and like most alumni they tend to recede into memory over time and distance. Tulane has been able to do more than most universities, however, in maintaining an association with its alumni in one country, Mexico. The university's choir has performed in Mexico City for a number of years, and its members are usually housed by the alumni. In 1963 the get-together was enlarged into an annual Tulane education conference, which brings together in Mexico City leading cultural figures and educators from both sides of the border, along with many of Tulane's eighty-six alumni in Mexico. This effort aroused so much enthusiasm that Tulane would like to repeat it elsewhere in Latin America where there is an alumni colony. Another proposal which Alumni Director Beatrice Field has under consideration is an alumni newsletter in Spanish. Miss Field is also a believer in the possibility of using the university's alumni for counseling individuals abroad who are considering attending Tulane. With one or two Tulane graduates on the staff of many major hospitals and medical schools in South America, the Medical School in particular might benefit from such alumni assistance. So far, however, this remains a possibility to be explored.

Language Laboratory

In 1960 Tulane's language department received a grant from the Office of Education for a three-year program of curriculum research and revision to determine the extent to which audio-lingual programs could be used in the college curriculum. It was also to compare the effectiveness of monitored versus unmonitored language work. Final testing was completed during 1964, on the basis of which a report was prepared.

Tulane's own findings were so encouraging that after two years a portion of the experimental work was shifted into regular courses in Spanish and French, accounting for from two-thirds to three-fourths of the language students. After a third year of experimental work the department introduced a similar program for German language training. There has been some work done in Russian and an intensive course has been programmed. In Portuguese language training, half is being done by the traditional methods, half by the new techniques.

Latin American Studies

Among international studies at Tulane the predominant area of program interest is Latin America. Until recently, that interest centered on Mexico and Central America and Tulane's strength was really found only in these areas. Specific areas of long-term interest and scholarly expertise are centered on Mexico, Honduras, and Guatemala but in the postwar period there has been a conscious effort within departments to broaden area coverage in faculty and curriculum. The Latin American area concern now includes Portuguese and Brazilian interest.

The liberal arts divisions at Tulane offer approximately eighty to ninety graduate and undergraduate semester courses of Latin American content, not counting introductory language courses or others only partially related to Latin America. They comprise instruction in anthropology, art, economics, history, legal systems, political science, Portuguese, sociology, and Spanish. A student may choose such courses as individual electives or include them in a specified curriculum of Latin American studies, Brazilian studies, or a departmental subject such as history or language. In addition, many other courses are related partially to Latin America or have direct application to that area. Among these are basic language courses, American musicology and history, and various courses in the social sciences, botany, geology, and zoology.

About fifteen faculty members in the social sciences are primarily concerned with Latin America, and several specialize exclusively in that region. The departments of art and music each have a Latin American specialist.

Latin America may be selected as a major field of concentration in study for an M.A. or Ph.D. in history, anthropology, sociology, political science, and other fields. The department of Spanish and Portuguese is strong enough in Latin American literature to allow concentration in that field in the curriculum leading to the Ph.D. degree. Its faculty includes full-time members who are natives of Argentina, Brazil, and Chile, and visiting professors from Latin America as well. Offerings in the department are presently being substantially strengthened, especially in Portuguese.

Area studies are a relatively new development in American academic life—interest in such programs first appeared in American colleges and universities in the years immediately before World War II—but Tulane was an early organizer of the area study concept. Further, although other universities have tended to create new area studies centers to match the shifts in national and public interest from one trouble spot to another in Asia and Africa, Tulane has remained faithful to Latin America since the mid-1920s—even though for much of this time the area has been taken for granted or neglected by the rest of the United States.

As far back as 1924 Tulane established a department of Middle American Research for the purpose of collecting materials on and conducting advanced studies in anthropology, archaeology, botany, ethnology, history, geography, linguistics, and products of Mexico, the Central American Republics, and the West Indies. That year, in a gesture demonstrating the close "town and gown" relationship between the trade interest of New Orleans and the academic concerns of the university, Tulane was given an initial grant of some $300,000 by Samuel Zemurray, a one-time poor immigrant who had made good as president of the Cuyamel Fruit Company and later president of the United Fruit Company. The Zemurray grant was used to sponsor numerous expeditions and individual research projects, to publish a series of monographs and papers on Latin America and to conduct reconnaissance in the field as well as archaeological excavation and restoration. In 1938 the department of Middle American Research was renamed the Middle American Research Institute.

One of the new institute's responsibilities was to cooperate with other departments in the establishment of a comprehensive course of instruction in Middle American studies, but an interdepartmental committee set up to bring this about had hardly begun to function when World War II brought such planning to a halt.

After the war the Carnegie Corporation stepped in to encourage certain American universities to reorganize their instructional and research programs in Latin American studies, and Tulane was a natural candidate for the Carnegie grant given in 1947. Included in the Carnegie project were the University of North Carolina, which was to specialize in Argentina and the West coast of South America; Vanderbilt University, which was to concentrate on Brazil; and the University of Texas, which was to make Mexico its special area of interest. Tulane was to emphasize primarily the Middle American and Caribbean areas. The Tulane interdepartmental committee was reorganized and restyled the Committee on Latin American Studies, and that same year (1947) an undergraduate and graduate level program in Latin American Studies was offered. Designed to provide a broad regional approach to Latin America and to give the student a general knowledge and understanding of that region of the world, it was intended to meet the demand for men and women especially trained for careers in Latin America in such fields as business and commerce, communications, government foreign service, research, and teaching.

An undergraduate electing this program—in the College of Arts and Sciences for men or Newcomb for women—follows the B.A. curriculum and meets the requirements for a major in a single department. In addition, the student completes the minimum of twenty-four semester hours of work dealing specifically with Latin America, divided among at least four departments other than that of the major.

A student in the Graduate School may take the M.A. degree in Latin American Studies. The curriculum consists of thirty semester hours in Latin American content courses, with a minimum of twelve hours in one department. The student writes a thesis developing a regional topic and must pass a reading examination in Spanish and also in either French, German, or Portuguese.

Tulane claims that of the Latin American studies programs established in Southern institutions, its effort was one of the few that "took." In any event, when the first five-year Carnegie grant expired in 1952 it was renewed for another five-year period. It was not continued after its expiration in 1957, but the program has been sustained and expanded by the university.

In 1962, with the aid of a matching grant from the Office of Education, Tulane established a Language and Area Center for Latin American Studies. The Center is coordinated with the Latin American Studies Program and the university's language laboratory, and strengthens them by aiding in offering additional courses and by adding to personnel, library holdings, and equipment. The courses which it has added to the curriculum deal mostly with South America.

With the establishment of the Center, offerings in Portuguese were multiplied and a program leading to the M.A. in Brazilian studies was initiated.

Slavic Studies

The study of Slavic languages was begun at Tulane in 1960, and languages offered now include Russian, Serbo-Croatian, and Bulgarian, with the emphasis on Russian. It is also possible to take courses in Slavic Studies, ranging through history, economics, and linguistics. About forty to fifty students are involved, with more graduate students than undergraduates participating. Four undergraduate courses and ten graduate courses are given. No Ph.D. degree is offered, although the faculty specialists in Slavic studies are anxious to find the financial support necessary to expand the library holdings and course offerings to enable them to offer a Ph.D. program.

The beginning Russian language course is split into two sections, one of which utilizes the tapes and techniques developed by Tulane's language laboratory, the other the traditional method. The superior students are those using the laboratory course.

In Russian literature the courses cover the period from 1800 to the present. For 1965-66 the department plans an interdepartmental colloquium covering history, language, and literature dealing with "Russia at the turn of the century."

International Studies

Within the framework of their standard degree programs, both the undergraduate and graduate divisions at Tulane offer courses designed to meet the international interests of the students or to provide special competence in the international field.

The history department's international program is appropriate to a university of Tulane's size. The department has a faculty of twenty-three and the enrollment is relatively small (200 undergraduate majors and 62 graduate students in 1964-65). The department has concentrated in United States, European, and Latin American history, and in the latter it must rank among the top centers of the country.

The international program and interest of the economics department is consciously limited, reflecting the belief that the tools of economic analysis are usable in all areas and do not require an area orientation by specific economists working in an interdisciplinary context. Two members of the department have international interests and teach courses in international trade and the economics of Latin America. The department is also studying the implicatons of foreign trade for the economic development of the port of New Orleans and its hinterland. As far back as 1948 Tulane's combined sociology-anthropology department offered a course in African anthropology, and two or three years later the university added to its staff two anthropologists who where specialists on Africa and American Negro anthropology. Interest in Africa thus predated by some years Tulane's desegregation. However, the department plans in at least two areas—expertise on Africa, and the study of race relations in the South—to do more intensive research in the future than it has in the past.

In the meantime, the department has undertaken three separate projects in the social problems involved in public health in Latin America. The initial project, growing out of the parallel interest of the Medical School in Colombia, was the assembling of sources for the development of correlation maps for biological and human ecology in that country, a project that will result in a published volume of studies and maps in a few years. The second study is of human ecology in the Cauca Valley of Colombia, where graduate students have selected research sites for their dissertations. The third, currently going on, is a two-year survey financed by the U.S. Atomic Energy Commission of the demographic, ecological, and relocation problems associated with the possible construction of a new canal through Colombia or Panama.

The international interests of the department of political science extend well beyond the normal disciplinary interest in international relations and comparative politics. The department is responsible for an honors International Affairs Program, which prepares students for careers with public or private agencies concerned with international relations or for advanced study in the field of international affairs. Students in the program are required to maintain a B average, and must write an honors thesis, a supervised project which may include field training with a public agency. An International Affairs Certificate is given with the B.A. on completion of the program. About ten students at a time, out of some ninety political science majors, are enrolled.

The program is not pushed by the department because there is no need to emphasize international affairs among the students, according to Professor Henry L. Mason. "At times the emphasis on international affairs is almost overwhelming," says Mason. "We have far too many would-be foreign service officers and hope-to-be foreign correspondents applying for the number that can eventually be employed." Mason, who is on sabbatical leave to teach at the Free University of Berlin in 1965, has one complaint: he deplores the fact that so few Latin American students coming to Tulane seem interested in Latin American studies. "They are seemingly simply not concerned about their own countries," he says.

School of Medicine

Tulane's School of Medicine was the first in any of the territory added to the United States after independence, and was the only one permanently established in the Gulf states for nearly sixty years. It played a major role in ridding New Orleans and the Gulf plain of the tropical diseases that once infested the area. Its interest in these diseases persisted until it became one of the world's principal centers for their study. Tulane physicians headed

the first Cuban Yellow Fever Commission, were instrumental in dissemi-
nating Dr. Carlos Finlay's theory of transmission by mosquitos, and participated in the experiments which substantiated the theory. It was at Tulane
that the malaria parasite was first propagated in the laboratory.

The early southward orientation of the Medical School is now deeply
rooted, and although Latin America is by no means the sole overseas
interest, it is a chief area of concern and all the instruction is applicable to
some portions of the region. The division of Tropical Medicine and Hygiene, which functions also as a division of Graduate Public Health, has a
full-time faculty of more than thirty members, most of whom have had
experience in Latin America. *The American Journal of Tropical Medicine
and Hygiene* and *Dermatologica Tropica* are edited in the department.

Over the years, faculty members have directed or taken part in numerous medical research and control projects throughout Latin America. In
one country—Colombia, where in recent years more than twenty-five Tulane medical faculty members have served as consultants, or directed or
participated in research—Tulane's activities constitute possibly the greatest
contribution any single American institution has ever made to the health of
an entire nation.

Tulane's tie-in with Colombia goes back to 1953 when, in response to a
request by the Colombian government to the United States government, a
committee—headed by Dr. Maxwell E. Lapham, then dean of the
School of Medicine at Tulane, and now provost of the university—carried
out a survey of the status of medical education in the country. As a result
of the survey, the Colombians asked the U.S. foreign aid agency (ICA) for
technical assistance in improving their medical education and research and
Tulane was chosen to carry out a five-year contract, which was later extended. Over the course of years the Colombian government contributed
much of the cost.

The program began in 1955, and all departments of Tulane's Medical
School were enlisted in a program of cooperation with seven medical
schools in Colombia, involving faculty training, modernization of educational methods, and development of curricula. The program also provided
training opportunities at Tulane for young medical graduates planning to
become full-time members of the faculties of the Colombian schools. More
than sixty Colombians took from one to three years each of training at
Tulane during the life of the contract, and some twenty-five consultants
from Tulane spent periods of from six weeks to three months each in
Colombia. During the first five years of the contract Dr. Ernest Carroll
Faust, world-renowned parasitologist from Tulane, lived in Colombia as
resident field coordinator with headquarters at the Universidad del Valle in
Cali.

Although this particular program came to an end in 1963 it had lasting
results, and Tulane hopes that the objective of improving the health of an
entire nation might provide a model for other South American countries in

the field of medical education. The success of this interinstitutional program in Colombia was a prime reason why Tulane was one of six American universities that in 1960 received substantial grants from the National Institutes of Health for the establishment of overseas centers for medical research and training. Colombia was designated as the locus for Tulane's operation, and in 1961, in cooperation with the Universidad del Valle, Tulane established its International Center for Medical Research and Training at Cali, Colombia. It has a staff of some thirty-five Colombians, headed by a Tulane graduate physician from Argentina.

The work of the Center involves not only several departments of Tulane's Medical School but the department of sociology and anthropology and the School of Social Work as well. Projects planned or in progress relate to the basic problems of Colombian health, some in the area of public health and epidemiology, some in infectious diseases and microbiology, others in the area of nutrition and metabolism.

Tulane is hopeful that, on the basis of a highly favorable prognosis of results expected, the grant from the N.I.H. will be renewed for a second five-year period.

A program pioneered by Tulane's Medical School is the Biochemistry Training Program for Foreign Fellows, a unique training scheme which has been conducted at Tulane each year since 1957 with the support of the Rockefeller Foundation.

The program provides individualized, twelve-month courses of study for postgraduate foreign students who need to strengthen their knowledge of chemistry and biochemistry before beginning advanced graduate work in the medical sciences in the United States. Foundation officials realized that many young medical graduates, particularly from Latin America, were encountering serious difficulties in postgraduate work in the United States owing to deficiencies in their prior chemical and biochemical education. A special course of study was seen as a necessary preliminary step toward their advanced education.

Organized by the department of biochemistry within the framework of the Graduate School, the program is tailored to strengthen each student's preparation in the basic medical sciences. In addition, students may supplement their study with courses in mathematics, physics, genetics, human physiology, histochemistry, and advanced biochemical techniques. Special instruction in English is also given.

Students participating in the program are expected to serve on the faculties of medical schools when they return to their own countries. More than 80 percent of the participants so far have been from Latin America, and about 40 percent of them have continued their advanced study at Tulane. Support from the Rockefeller Foundation has been extended to the program through 1967.

School of Law

The law of Louisiana is embodied in a civil code derived from the Roman law through the Code Napoleon. But Louisiana is also a member of a federal union of common-law states, and the common law has influenced the Louisiana code. Tulane's School of Law thus sits at a junction of two of the great legal systems of the world, and since early in the present century it has offered a course of studies to prepare students for practice in both civil and common law jurisdiction. It is the only law school in the United States in which a student may choose between the two systems for concentration in study toward the Bachelor of Law degree.

Comparative law is emphasized throughout the curriculum, and is treated not as a separate field in which a few courses are offered, but as a way of approaching and teaching all law. Tulane also offers masters' degrees in both civil and common law and a doctorate in comparative law.

This emphasis on the comparison of two legal systems makes Tulane's Law School exceptionally attractive to foreign students, and a good many Latin Americans attend because the course prepares them to practice in their own jurisdictions as well as gives them an insight into the legal system of the United States. For some years, about 10 percent of the registration in the school, undergraduate and graduate, has been from foreign lands. In the 1964-65 academic year, of the 325 students in the school, sixteen were foreign graduate students, all of whom were at Tulane on a fellowship basis. For most of them, their present intention is to teach law in their homelands.

A logical outgrowth of the comparative approach which characterizes the school is the Institute of Comparative Law, which Tulane founded in 1949 in order to carry on research and training in the field of foreign and comparative law. The Institute encourages research and publication of materials on comparative law, and coordinates the work at Tulane with that undertaken by other agencies and institutes concerned with comparative law. An important part of its work is related to Latin America, but it also draws visiting faculty and lecturers from France and other parts of the world where the Napoleonic civil code obtains.

Since 1959 the Institute has published the semiannual *Inter-American Law Review,* in both English and Spanish, as the first bilingual law journal devoted to the Western hemisphere. It is edited by a Mexican legal scholar, Rodolfo Batiza, who also occupies the chair of Latin American Legal Studies.

Dean Cecil Morgan and Professor Ferdinand F. Stone, director of the Institute, would like to undertake more exchange programs with Latin American law students and faculty. A few years ago they held successful seminars for groups of Argentine lawyers who visited Tulane for six-week courses. This experience highlighted one problem in dealing with Latin American legal schools. Most of the faculty are lawyers who make a living commercially and teach on the side: an exchange teaching arrangement thus represents a considerable financial sacrifice, even when it can be arranged.

Other Professional Schools

A number of Latin Americans have attended the Tulane School of Social Work over the years, and at least sixty graduates of the School are known to be practicing their profession in their home countries.

Requests have been received from several schools of social work in Latin America for opportunities to continue the training of some of their faculty. Some of this is done by correspondence, but the school would like to find the financial support to enable it to develop a consultative service for Latin American schools and social agencies.

In order to make the services to such institutions more effective, a committee of three Tulane School of Social Work faculty members was formed in 1962 to develop policies and activities in connection with Latin American and other Spanish-speaking lands. Each of the members is a specialist in a different field of social work, and is also fluent in Spanish.

In the summer of 1964 the school conducted a summer course for its own students in Mexico City, the objective of which was to make a case study of that country's social welfare legislation and its implementation.

Tulane's School of Architecture, while it has no program specifically designed for Latin American students, nonetheless has attracted in recent years the highest percentage of students from that region of any of the university's undergraduate divisions. Partly this is due to the fact that three of the school's faculty members are fluent in Spanish and have had extensive professional experience in Latin America. Latin American architects are frequently on campus as visiting professors.

The School of Business Administration, now entirely a graduate school, offers fifteen semester hours of Latin American content courses in economics, resources, and trade. It has two bilingual faculty members who devote most of their attention to Latin America, one in resources and the other in economic problems and international trade.

However, the Business School—which until last year housed the economics department—is not exactly enterprising in the international field. On two occasions, 1960 and again in 1962, the School put on a three-week institute for Mexican business executives in mid-career, designed to bring visiting Mexican businessmen up to date on American developments in business administration. By all accounts, the program was enthusiastically received by visitors and Tulane participants alike, but there has been little if any initiative on the part of the Business School's faculty to repeat the project or put it on an annual basis.

This attitude is reflected in the relative absence of foreign students in the Business School. There are some applications, but few are admitted—

about two or three each year—partly because few are prepared to undertake a graduate program in business administration, but also because the problems of dealing with them are burdensome to a graduate faculty.

Library Resources

Tulane's postwar expansion of doctorate fields has put a heavy strain on the university's library resources, and a new general academic library is being constructed to expand the present library.

In the major program area of Latin America, Tulane has several special advantages. The Howard-Tilton Memorial Library (the central library) some years ago was designated the principal depository in the United States for material currently published in El Salvador, Guatemala, Honduras, and Nicaragua, an assignment undertaken under the Farmington Plan. Publications obtained are made immediately available to other libraries on loan. Besides the four countries named, Tulane assumes secondary coverage for Costa Rica.

In addition, the library of the Middle American Research Institute contains distinguished collections on Central America and Mexico totaling more than 75,000 volumes, among which are many rare titles, as well as unusual manuscript collections numbering in the thousands. Because of its traditional involvement with Latin America, the library of the Medical School is rich in materials on tropical medicine and public health, and the library of the Law School is similarly stocked with source materials pertaining to every country in Central and South America.

National librarians, surveying this accumulation of library resources, rate Tulane's combined collection of materials on Latin America as one of the three or four best in the country.

In other foreign areas the library holdings are less impressive, and although the total library budget has steadily increased and the departmental allocations improved, Tulane finds that it must spend considerable sums yearly on library resources merely to keep even in relation to competing institutions. For instance, during 1964-65 the budget for history acquisitions was doubled over the previous year, to a sum of $20,000. But during the same year one campus of the University of California spent $50,000 for its history book acquisitions, and a prestigious Eastern university spent $110,000 merely for books in new areas of history.

Research Institutes

Tulane's interest in Latin America quite naturally spilled over into the field of music, and in 1961 the university established the Inter-American Institute for Musical Research for the purpose of promoting scholarship and publication in the music of the Americas and encouraging graduate study in the field. The Institute is the personal creation of Dr. Gilbert

Chase, a renowned musicologist who joined the Tulane faculty in 1960 and now serves as director of the Institute. The archives are built around his personal collection, said to be the largest collection in private hands of manuscripts, scores, books, recordings, and other material related to the music of the Americas. Dr. Chase directs a graduate seminar on Problems in American Music, dealing with the basic principles which apply to the music of North and South America, and graduate students have tackled such esoteric inquiries as the use of the Gregorian chant in the Spanish mission schools of the southwest United States before 1800 and an investigation of French influence on American musical composition. Under the Institute's direction, the first inter-American conference of musicology, bringing together musical scholars from North and South America, was held at the Library of Congress in 1963.

The Middle American Research Institute, of which Dr. Robert Wauchope is director, has curtailed the role it plays in the Latin American field, in which it pioneered for Tulane and the American university community. For some years, supported by its endowment, the Institute maintained its own research staff, sponsored expeditions and promoted research. Now, in a more limited approach, it functions as a center for coordination, promotion, and publication of research by faculty members and graduate students—but even this role is restricted by financial pressures. The staff of the Institute is limited to the director and administrative, editorial, and art assistants: faculty members in several departments, who work with the Institute, are designated as research associates.

As the colleges and departments at Tulane added Latin Americanists to their faculties, the Institute extended its scope to include fields such as political science, economics, and art history, but the division of labor that now prevails is that the Institute has prime responsibility for the research function, while the Latin American Studies Program provides instruction.

The Institute is currently engaged in two major projects, which involve expenditures of more than three-quarters of a million dollars; funds are from extramural sources, including the National Science Foundation, the American Philosophical Society, and the National Geographic Society. One is the excavation of the Maya site of Dzibilchaltun in Yucatan, an unusually extensive area occupied for more than 3,000 years. The other is the compilation of a definitive, eleven-volume *Handbook of Middle American Indians,* of which Dr. Wauchope is editor-in-chief and to which more than three hundred scholars in many countries are contributing articles.

The Institute is a separately endowed division of Tulane, but the Zemurray endowment—which yields only $22,000 per year now—is wholly inadequate for present needs, and the Institute more and more concentrates on major projects supported by outside funds. Its operation—apart from the externally financed projects—is on a hand-to-mouth basis, and last year, with its small staff overtaxed by the two projects in which it is involved, it closed its museum gallery. It had previously turned the administraton of its specialized library over to the general library, cut publishing to one small monograph and supported no faculty research in history, political science, geography, art history, cultural anthropology, or language and literature—all fields to which it had contributed when it was a grant-making institution. Crates of research materials and museum pieces remain unopened on the Institute's premises because there is neither the money nor the space to handle them.

Expansion of the work of the Institute would thus appear to hang on foundation funds or other external assistance.

Where the Primates Are

As the Middle American Research Institute pointed the way to international study and service in the 1920's, so Tulane expects that two of its new international research facilities will make significant contributions in the decades ahead.

One is the Delta Regional Primate Research Center, a new division which was set up in 1962 by a grant from the National Institutes of Health to provide "the major resource in the central south for research basic to human health that either requires or can best be undertaken with primates." The Center, a group of laboratory buildings erected near Covington, Louisiana, across Lake Pontchartrain from New Orleans, is run by Tulane but is available to facilitate research by scientists from six other regional universities which are associated with Tulane in the Center's program. These are Louisiana State University, Loyola University of the South, and the universities of Mississippi, Alabama, Arkansas, and Texas. The Delta Center is one of seven primate centers which have been established by the N.I.H. across the nation. The others are at Harvard, Emory University, the University of California at Davis, and the Universities of Oregon, Washington, and Wisconsin.

The primary aim of the Delta Center is the establishment of an integrated program of comparative biological research in primates that is directed toward the solution of health problems in man. Work will be done primarily with chimpanzees, monkeys, and other primate animals, and in a year or two, acccording to Dr. Arthur J. Riopelle, the Center's director, Tulane expects to have at least five hundred primates.

This brings the Center squarely into international affairs, for Tulane has set up its own "catching teams" to do field research in Southeast Asia, Africa, and South America—"where the primates are," according to Dr. Riopelle. "We are trying with our own 'catching teams' to cut human contact to the minimum," he explains. "Usually the animals shipped commercially to the United States have been so handled by humans that by the time they arrive here they are already infected with the diseases we want to study under laboratory conditions." In Southeast Asia, the Center has sent a representative to work with the SEATO laboratories in Bangkok. In Central America, the Center intends to develop a relationship based on the long ties which Tulane has with the Universidad del Valle in Colombia. In Africa, a Tulane "catching team" operated in the Congo under the auspices of the *Institut pour la Recherche Scientifique en Afrique Centrale,* and was interrupted from time to time by the rebellion round about them.

The second area of new international research expansion is the Tulane University Computer Center. "A few years ago," explained President Longenecker, "we made a deliberate decision to go into the computer business." The results surprised even the administration. From a $200,000 program at the outset, the Computer Center has grown over the past two and a half years to a $1,500,000 operation and two major components. One, the Computer Laboratory at the uptown campus, is used as a problem-solving tool by students of engineering and business administration and as a research tool by faculty members in the social sciences, humanities, and engineering. The other unit is the Biomedical Computing System, operated by the School of Medicine and used in connection with health-related research projects. At least one of these investigations has led the Biomedical computing unit into international assignments.

The computers were initially used to work on problems of nutrition and large-scale feeding, and in time they were computing menus for hospitals and other large public institutions, cutting food costs by as much as 25 percent. Two airlines expressed interest, and the Food and Agriculture Organization of the United Nations explored the use of computer studies for working out diets for the less-developed areas of the world. At the close of 1964 the Tulane Biomedical Computing Station was awarded a contract from the U.S. Interdepartmental Committee on Nutrition for National Defense to compute the nutritional resources in Guatemala, Paraguay, Costa Rica, northeast Brazil, and Nigeria, a study intended to "meet the nutritional needs of the underdeveloped countries in terms of the best utilization available of indigenous resources."

Computers are also installed at the Primate Center—run by the staff, but keeping animal records in the form of "animal diaries"—and at several other units of the university, and the administration—pleased at the payoff to its decision of a few years ago—contemplates establishing a division of Computer Sciences at Tulane.

IV

In any one year, according to a Tulane administrator's estimate, several hundred Tulane faculty members, researchers, or representatives may be abroad as consultants, research workers, teachers, and trainers in foreign areas either on individual study projects or departmental programs of broader significance. During 1964, for instance, Tulane faculty members were on extended projects or assignments in Brazil, Chile, Colombia,

France, Formosa, Germany, Great Britain, Guatemala, India, Iran, Italy, New Guinea, Nigeria, Sweden, and the West Indies Federation.

However, most of these efforts take place on a personal or at best departmental level. One faculty member, questioned as to how he saw the development of the university's international dimension, replied that the direction and the depth of international involvement seemed to be up to the individual faculty member as he pursued his own interests, idiosyncracies, and inclinations of the moment. As a faculty member, he said, he was not so much aware of any university *direction* as he was of an administration attitude which seemed to say, "Tell us where you want to go"—to the individual faculty or department head—"and we'll help you."

This shades something from the truth, but it reflects the fact that Tulane has no all-university channel by which various faculty or departmental projects in the international field become tied together in an institutional sense. No administrative structure exists to coordinate all the university's international activities, and President Longenecker candidly remarked that in many cases the only way he was made aware of a venture abroad was when a courtesy copy of a report was sent upward, generally after the project had been completed. However, the office of the Vice President in charge of Development and the Provost's office report that they are practically always advised of contemplated programs of research ventures abroad and are frequently asked to suggest means of support. In addition, the Provost, Dr. Maxwell E. Lapham, formerly the Dean of the Medical School, has a general responsibility for keeping on top of the international dimension, at least in an informational sense, on behalf of the president.

In the course of recent years a number of mechanisms have been developed at Tulane to coordinate separate programs or areas, but to date no overall attempt to centralize its international activities has been made. Tulane has not yet undertaken to compile a roster of faculty members with their backgrounds, subject strengths, interests, and availability for assignments abroad (except for a Ford Foundation submission for Latin Americanists), an exercise which some other universities regard as one of the first steps toward centralization of international activities.

The International Office set up to serve the needs of foreign students has, since its inception, carried responsibility for the programming of international visitors to the Tulane campus, and, as New Orleans is a city which few official visitors to the United States like to miss, these almost daily visitations impose a strain both on the office and on the university—not to mention the costs of hospitality for visits ranging from periods of half a day to several weeks. In a year as many as six hundred foreign observers will visit the Tulane campus. Because it exists, there is a tendency for the International Office to be given assignments—working with the Peace Corps, or arranging short courses for visiting foreign scholars—that would normally fall to a centralized international program office, but the director of the Office and his small staff conceive their main responsibility to be the care and counsel of foreign students.

Because of its long history of overseas involvement as well as its physical separation from the main campus, the Medical School has some of the characteristics of an independent operation. Some faculty members are inclined to feel, privately, that the Medical School has too long dominated Tulane's Latin American interests at the expense of other disciplines, although this would not seem to be sustained on the evidence.

The Law School likewise operates, particularly in Latin America and through its Institute of Comparative Law, in a manner somewhat independent of the overall university, although its involvement is small compared to that of the much larger Medical School.

Imbalances in the availability of extramural funds for creative scholarship led a few years ago to the establishment of the University Council on Research. Acting on applications of faculty members, the Council awards leaves of absence at full salary, summer grants, and other funds for research.

The Latin American Studies Committee is an informally constituted body made up of all members of the faculty in the humanities and social studies who teach Latin American course content. Its chairman, Professor William J. Griffith, was appointed by the president of Tulane and has indefinite tenure.

The committee was originally created to administer grants made by the Carnegie Corporation: then it planned the programs for the bachelor's and master's degrees and obtained required approval from the curriculum committees in the affected instructional departments. It also assisted interested departments in finding Latin American specialists. With the two Carnegie grants exhausted, the nature of the committee's work altered. It now performs functions analogous to those of a department operating in the College of Arts and Sciences, Newcomb College, the School of Business Administration, and the Graduate School. It offers independent studies work, presents an occasional candidate for a baccalaureate degree with honors, and administers programs leading to the B.A. and M.A. degrees. It is under the administrative supervision of the provost, but its small budget is provided through the office of the dean of the College of Arts and Sciences.

Like the Middle American Research Institute, the Latin American Studies Committee is also on short finances, and this has contributed to its weakened position on campus. One department head no longer works through the committee—except on academic matters—and directly seeks foundation and administration support for his department's expansion. In fairness, it must be noted that the committee's chairman spends much of his own time searching for fellowships and funds to enable graduate students and faculty to pursue field work.

Area studies programs are expensive and almost invariably require out-

128 The University Looks Abroad

side financial assistance in order to thrive. Tulane's program was initiated and grew to its present stature through the Carnegie grants, and despite substantial Tulane support it seems unlikely that it will be able to hold its own against other, upcoming centers of Latin American studies unless it receives additional large-scale outside assistance from foundations or other agencies. Most of the other centers of excellence in Latin American studies at American universities have now received substantial outside assistance, mainly Ford Foundation grants, and the result has been an intensified competition for scarce resources and the best faculty, a competition in which an unassisted Tulane program could slowly fall behind.

The department heads and program directors in Tulane's Latin American area feel that they have over the years built up small, solidly based academic programs, with logical and sufficient international content, and they voice real disappointment that such a quality program has not received uninterrupted foundation support.

On one point the chairman of the committee and some of the faculty are adamant: they are dead set against the conventional area program approach which many universities have adopted and which foundations have tended to favor. They regard the large, problem-oriented and centrally administered program of some of the major universities as of doubtful academic quality, and in an institutional pattern that Tulane does not want to follow. Foundations in general have admittedly placed their grants for area studies in institutions where the structure, on the infusion of a sizeable sum of money, promised a rapid and impressive expansion of enrollment and research and was likely to influence if not encompass the entire university.

Tulane's administration, while it may in time—because of the pressures of diverting more and more of the university's funds to support an international program—have to come down on the side of a more centrally run Latin American studies program, is inclined for the moment to support the position of the committee's chairman and those who adhere to his approach.

This position reflects in some ways the administration's own approach to the problem of devising a suitable all-university mechanism for coordinating Tulane's international activities. President Longenecker is acutely aware that, in the individual forays of faculty members all over the world and far-ranging departmental research projects (among the more than 700 undertaken by the university each year), a certain amount of wasted effort and duplication of work is inevitable. Yet, mindful of the diversity within the university and respectful of departmental and divisional autonomy, no total institutional coordinating structure has been attempted by the administration.

President Longenecker has his sights fixed on other problems, many of which appear more urgent than his organization chart. For one thing, Tulane is engaged in a drive to raise $18,400,000 from private sources, the target which the university set itself to meet a Ford Foundation challenge grant of $6,000,000 over a three-year period from April, 1964.

Still ahead lies the prospect of more active collaboration with neighboring or regional educational institutions and a massive effort to help raise the standards of Negro higher education in the area. Soon after assuming the presidency of Tulane in 1960, President Longenecker took off for a three-month tour of Latin America to familiarize himself with the university's activities there. Much impressed with the university-to-university relationship which Tulane had worked out with the Universidad del Valle, he returned to the United States convinced that more American and Latin American universities should be entwined academically. During 1964, when he served as president of the Council of Southern Universities (consisting of nine Southern institutions—Virginia, Duke, North Carolina, Emory, Vanderbilt, Rice, Texas, Louisiana State, and Tulane), he proposed that they form a consortium, similar to the four-university consortium of Midwest universities, to support each other in strengthening their graduate offerings to students from both the United States and South America. In the meantime, however, all these institutions hurdled the barrier of racial segregation and the Council has decided to concentrate on improving Negro education, from preschool to graduate work. For some time to come, in Longenecker's opinion, this commitment will work against Tulane and the other Southern institutions undertaking joint overseas operations.

President Longenecker is conscious of the gaps in Tulane's international competence. He is under pressure from some faculty members to set up an African studies program on the ground that no major university in the United States should be without such an area interest, but he realizes that this would require either a serious diversion of university funds or a substantial foundation grant.

The president's own inclination is to "deepen, not widen" Tulane's international activities, to build on its strength rather than follow academic fashions into new areas. He believes that Tulane will be called upon for increasing involvement in international affairs and he has publicly committed the university to this course. "While Tulane's Latin American interests will be dominant," he has written, "the university must strengthen its capabilities involving other areas."

Whether this can be achieved without devising a tighter institutional structure for the university's international activities remains to be demonstrated. President Longenecker confesses that on several occasions over the past year or so he has explored with his administration colleagues the possibilities of achieving more correlation in the international field. Each time, he said, the idea of making one person so responsible has been discarded because, as he put it, "in order to keep track of Tulane's Latin American activities alone the person would have to be a second president or a second provost."

With an administration that is no more than one deep at any level, this may be Tulane's way out. Other universities far larger than Tulane, with problems more complex and programs more varied in the international field, have sought their solution in appointing "a second president or a second provost" in the person of a dean or director of their international programs.

*   *   *   *   *

While it has achieved a remarkable upgrading in less than a score of years, and in that time has transformed itself from a regionally oriented Southern school in pre-World War II days into a university with regional, national, and international responsibilities, Tulane has still not organized itself to draw maximum advantage from its international activities. The impression persists that it has been perhaps too content to rest on its ties of trade and tradition to Latin America, and that it has therefore fallen somewhat behind—except in the medical field—in bringing its historical involvement in Latin America up to date in terms of that area's present-day needs and interests. Thus its Latin American program, while solidly based on literature, language, history, and anthropology, has nonetheless not kept even with competing programs offered by the half dozen American universities that share the front rank among academic centers that emphasize Latin American studies. The interest is there, on the part of administration, faculty, and students—but the sense of a need for coordinated effort seems to be lacking. The development and conduct of international programs has been and remains essentially on a departmental basis.

The components of what Tulane has in the Latin American field are good, however, and their basic quality should in time be recognized and rewarded with continued government, foundation, and private support.

In at least one field—the design of special course work for foreign students who may be deficient in English or lack the qualifications for full-time college work—Tulane has pioneered approaches which could well be copied by other American institutions concerned with "the foreign student problem."

WISCONSIN

I

At the University of Wisconsin even the telephone system reveals a great deal about the institution and the way it operates. Each department, school, and college seems to have its own approach to the instrument. One department operates a switchboard and extension phones in faculty offices; another has a central phone and a few booths in the halls; still another department accepts only incoming telephone messages for its faculty members.

Of the six universities visited by EWA case study teams, the University of Wisconsin appears to be the most permissive, the most faculty oriented, the most seemingly diarchial in its organization. Although not as extreme as the German or Dutch universities, where the concept of academic freedom for the individual scholar has been carried to the point where the academic and administrative staffs are sometimes scarcely on speaking terms, at Wisconsin many departments are strong power centers, almost colleges in themselves, and decision-making is still largely in the hands of faculty committees. In fact, Wisconsin statute books still carry an early piece of legislation which specifically states that "the immediate government of the colleges of the university is entrusted to the faculties thereof."

And yet, as one dean puts it, "the University of Wisconsin is more administered than it looks. It may appear to be permissive, but, under the surface, the administration is there." This, according to Fred Harvey Harrington, the university's president, is administration "from the bottom up." Administration "from the top down" is more likely to be found in pure land-grant institutions or newer establishments where a liberal arts faculty has not been entrenched from the outset. At Wisconsin, the only combined state university and land-grant institution among the six visited, the liberal arts faculty has been strong from the earliest days of the university and the administration's technique is to encourage faculty initiative, to support faculty strengths and interests while at the same time providing guidance and direction without seeming to do so.

This approach—taking account of the acute sense of departmental pride, coupled with a high degree of faculty independence—today overlays the entire range of the university's international activities. It also has shaped the university's organizational structure of its international programs, and explains why Wisconsin has moved cautiously, in its own good time, to develop a centralized administrative apparatus to deal with its international dimension.

II

The University of Wisconsin is now well into its second century as one of the nation's leading state, land-grant institutions. Its official Founders' Day is marked as February 5, 1849—a year after Wisconsin became a state—and it began as a small classical academy and college of the New England type. When its first college class—consisting of two students—graduated in 1854, there were forty-one students in attendance and fifteen in the preparatory course.

Today the University of Wisconsin consists of two major campuses—the main campus clustered along the shore of Lake Mendota in the capital city of Madison, and the University of Wisconsin-Milwaukee—with three basic colleges, five professional schools, and some ninety departments. In addition, the university has been carried to the boundaries of the state with nine University Centers located in cities throughout Wisconsin, where freshman and sophomore instruction is offered. The far-ranging Extension Division, through correspondence courses, special classes, institutes, and other activities, has pushed the university's institutional reach well out into the world. The student body on the Madison campus now numbers more than 21,000, and there are more than 41,000 students on all campuses.

By any measure of institutional quality, Wisconsin has for long ranked high in the national standings of major universities. A *School and Society* survey of a few years ago ranked it fourth among American institutions in the number of doctorate degrees awarded in the past century, and third among institutions in the 1950's. It has consistently rated near the top in winning Woodrow Wilson national fellowships and National Science Foundation fellowships.

"The Wisconsin Idea"

The concept of the land-grant university in the years after the Civil War added another dimension to American higher education. To the instruction of students and to research, both as an adjunct to teaching and as a goal in itself, was added the concept of using the unique strengths of a university's faculty and facilities for solving the problems of its state. In this area, the University of Wisconsin pioneered and became both a national and international leader. At Madison the idea that the boundaries of the campus were the boundaries of the state, and that knowledge should be put to work in every possible way for the advancement of society, became proudly known as "the Wisconsin idea."

Relations between state and university in Wisconsin have always been close—if not always friendly. When, in 1848, Wisconsin became a state, its constitution provided for "the establishment of a state university at or near the seat of state government," and the first State Legislature specified with considerable precision the scope and character of the projected institution. Steps toward providing an institution of higher learning with an endowment of lands in the public domain had been taken by Wisconsin's Territorial Legislature as far back as 1837. With the passage of the Morrill Land-Grant Act of 1862, Wisconsin took a giant step toward acceptance of the philosophy that service to the community should be one of the three functions of a university. The Morrill Act, one of the first forms of federal aid to education, granted the state of Wisconsin 240,000 acres of public land for the encouragement of agriculture and the mechanic arts, and in 1868 the university added a professor of agriculture to its faculty and put into active operation its agricultural department.

Progress was slow, but by the turn of the century the enrollment in agriculture accelerated and the department began to enlarge its off-campus activities. The feeling of Wisconsin citizens that their university was an arm of the state made them look to it for specialized aid, and the university responded with bulletins, farmers' institutes, short courses for farm youth, and the development of a general extension program.

In time, "the Wisconsin idea" came to be applied to other fruitful areas. During the era of the Progressive Party and Governor "Fighting Bob" La Follette, when Wisconsin led the nation in its approach to political reform and social justice, the university—not without doubts on the part of some of its faculty members and vigorous criticism by conservatives throughout the state—played a role of importance. Legislators and university professors cooperated in framing and administering state laws for the regulation of corporate wealth, in strengthening political democracy to break machine-dominance, and in designing labor legislation to promote social justice. Members of the Wisconsin faculty served on the regulatory commissions set up by reform legislation. The doctrine of service to the state, the land-grant concept, was further refined to the point where the university entered into large-scale sponsorship of research of obvious economic benefit to the people of Wisconsin.

"The Wisconsin idea," thus applied, helped establish the University of Wisconsin's reputation for being at the forefront of higher education. Liberal circles throughout the United States hailed it as—in the words of one crusader—"an experiment station in politics, in social and industrial legislation, in the democratization of science and higher education," and in 1912 Theodore Roosevelt declared that "all through the Union we need to learn the Wisconsin Lesson." Other institutions, both in the United States and abroad, began to be influenced by "the Wisconsin idea."

All this was not accomplished without a full measure of strife. The university was bitterly attacked by La Follette's opponents on the ground that it was a hotbed of radicalism and that it was taking part in political controversies. Hence, when the Progressives were defeated the university faced the problem of a working relationship with a party and a governor hostile to it. In the years of Republican state rule, liberals complained that academic freedom was in danger. Relations with the La Follettes deteriorated when an internationalist faculty signed a round-robin letter condemning the elder La Follette for his opposition to American entry into World War I. During the depression years criticism, charges, investigations, threats, and muckraking beset the university from all sides, and it was not until 1937, when Clarence A. Dykstra, formerly city manager of Cincinnati, was brought in to take over the presidency, that Wisconsin—state and university—put its divisive wrangling behind it.

"The Wisconsin Idea" Abroad

At the 1958 inauguration of Conrad Elvehjem as President of the University of Wisconsin a fellow educator, Grayson Kirk, now President of Columbia University, recalled that Wisconsin and its university had pioneered in the use of professors in government. Declared Kirk: "There is need for a Wisconsin Idea for the whole world."

The need to export the Wisconsin concept of service beyond the state and national level to all areas of the globe had long been felt by individual faculty members at the university, but the university itself, perhaps because of the buffeting it had received in the years between the wars, was somewhat behindhand in getting involved in the new dimension of world affairs. In the years after World War II it also had to contend with the national rise and fall of a Wisconsin phenomenon, Senator McCarthy, and minor pinpricks from the American Legion and a legislative inquiry into Communist influences on the campus.

For the past sixty years or so Wisconsin has attracted more than its share of foreign graduate students, most of whom found their way to the university because of the reputation of Wisconsin specialists. One such specialist was Professor Joaquin Ortega, who—about a quarter of a century ago—began to attract students from Latin America. Another was Paul Knaplund, a European-born professor of history, who became a well-known British Empire historian. Three economists—John R. Commons, E.E. Witte, and Selig Perlman—served as magnets for students from all over the world. Still other specialists—among them Gustav Bohstedt, an expert in animal husbandry, John Kolb, a rural sociology specialist who became interested in Latin America, and Conrad Elvehjem, a biochemist who became the university's president—established wide-ranging reputations.

All through the 1920's and 1930's Wisconsin was particularly strong in history, political science, and the social sciences, and many of the university's internationalists were to be found in those departments. Foreign language departments were also strong and established.

Wisconsin has always put heavy emphasis on research work, and in due course Wisconsin professors followed their bent out beyond state boundaries as individual researchers or consultants on projects abroad. World War II provided the watershed: many of the faculty members who returned to the campus after serving abroad brought back a new concern about the state of the world. Robert L. Clodius, currently Vice President for Academic Affairs, was in the U.S. Navy until 1946 and later served as a specialist for the State Department in Latin America. "You have to be 'welfare-oriented' to be in education in the first place," Clodius now says, "and many of us on our return to Wisconsin after the war felt that helping other countries cope with their problems was at least an alternative to shooting wars."

Singly or in small teams, Wisconsin faculty members ventured into the new dimension of worldwide service, but for the most part they went on leaves or personal commitments, without organized university support. It was what President Harrington now calls "the gunshot approach," unfocused and propelled by the interests of individual faculty members. Several faculty members were active in the immediate postwar years at the Seminar in American Studies at Salzburg, Austria. Harrington served as a director of the Seminar and Edwin Young, now Dean of Letters and Science, and William Gorham Rice of the Law School taught at the Seminar in its infancy after World War II. Professor Robert Hattery, now at Indiana University, spent a year on leave from Wisconsin as assistant director of the Salzburg center. The former Dean of the School of Education, John Guy Fowlkes, served in India as educational advisor to the late Prime Minister Nehru in 1954-55. Clifford Liddle, professor of education at Wisconsin, took time away from the university to serve as chief education officer of the Technical Cooperation Mission (the Point Four program) in India. His colleague, Marshall Clinard, a sociologist, worked for the Ford Foundation in Delhi developing neighborhood council experiments in Indian slums. In Indonesia a Wisconsin anthropologist, Milton Barnett, carried out a research and planning assignment for the Council on Economic and Cultural Affairs, exploring interdisciplinary approaches to the problems of Indonesian communities, and in Seoul a communications specialist from Wisconsin, Maurice Iverson, labored to introduce audio-visual materials into the Korean educational system.

An exception to this almost casual, individualistic approach to the international realm was the development of Latin American studies at Wisconsin. Largely because of the personal interest of certain faculty members, Wisconsin organized as far back as 1930 an undergraduate major in Hispanic Studies, thus giving it the longest continuous history of an integrated, interdepartmental program of Ibero-American studies among major universities in the United States.

Other than in Latin America, however, Wisconsin's approach to international activities continued to be episodic and personal until well after the end of World War II. "It was the good old Wisconsin way of each scholar going his own way and the university helping him out," recalls Vice President Clodius. There was no direction from the administration and very little staff assistance for any of the international ventures and projects attempted.

A contract in India involving the College of Engineering and the entry of the department of economics into Indonesia with Ford Foundation

support were the first breakthroughs into university—as against individual
—commitments to international activities.

The College of Engineering in 1953 entered into an agreement with the
International Cooperation Administration (ICA) of the U.S. government
for the improvement of engineering education in India. Seven Indian educational institutions were provided with guest lecturers from the United
States, received equipment and supplies, and sent their own staff members
to this country for study. This contract was terminated in 1959, but a
special program of assistance to Bengal Engineering College and the University of Roorkee was continued through 1964 under the auspices of
AID.

In 1957 the department of economics began a program for the establishment of a faculty of economics at Gadjah Mada University, Indonesia,
under Ford Foundation assistance. However, even this contract grew out of
a personal rather than a university relationship. A Ford executive, interested in creating a faculty exchange relationship with Indonesia, persuaded
a personal friend, Edwin Young, who was then head of Wisconsin's economics department, to explore the project. Young and a colleague, after a
preliminary survey in Indonesia, returned and convinced the economics
faculty to undertake the assignment. The persuading reasons, Dean Young
now recalls, were several: (1) it offered the economics department an
opportunity to experiment abroad; (2) it was felt to be a "good thing" for
the university to be involved in the foreign area; (3) it would help establish
good relations with the Ford Foundation; (4) there happened to be a
faculty member who was interested in heading up the Wisconsin venture in
Indonesia.

The project involved providing American professors for teaching and
consulting at Gadjah Mada University, selecting Indonesian economics
students for study in the United States, and training Indonesian students
through joint research efforts in that country. From the program's inception
up to the 1964-65 academic year, seventeen faculty members teaching
twenty-five separate subjects and thirty-six fellows had been sent from the
University of Wisconsin. The faculty exchange with Gadjah Mada University was terminated in 1963: however, the fellowship program was extended to provide continued interim teaching in areas where help was still
needed.

Looking back, Dean Young concludes that the Indonesian project provided great value for the time and effort invested. First, it established at
Gadjah Mada a first-rate economics department. Second, it made a considerable impact on Wisconsin's economics department. It led to changes in
the Wisconsin economics curriculum as professors returned with their horizons broadened; it provided new experiences for the faculty; it brought
Indonesian graduate students to the Wisconsin campus and provided field
assignments in Indonesia for Wisconsin graduate students. The feedback is
measurable today in terms of an internationally experienced economics

faculty: of the full professors now in the department, twenty have had experience abroad in one form or another and only seven have had no experience in the international field.

The experiences in India and Indonesia also provided new impetus for the old public service aspect of the university and encouraged it to broaden the international scope of its services, to extend "the Wisconsin idea" abroad. By 1960, when then Vice President for Academic Affairs Harrington, accompanied by Professor Young, made a round-the-world tour to check on "the Wisconsin idea" in action, the administration went squarely on record in support of the new dimension of worldwide service.

"The United States is permanently involved in world affairs. So is the University of Wisconsin, in line with its tradition of state and national service," declared Harrington on his return. And in March, 1961, the Board of Regents set forth its policy in a statement:

> With the passing years, the welfare of the people of Wisconsin has become increasingly tied to national and international developments. It is logical, therefore, that the scope of the Wisconsin Idea should be broadened. The years ahead certainly will see the University of Wisconsin more active on the national and international scene, in the public sphere as well as in research and instruction.
>
> We recognize that the university's first responsibility is to Wisconsin and its residents. But the university must look outward if this obligation is to be fulfilled. Thus we as Regents declare that the university should welcome students from other states and from foreign lands. These out-of-state students are an educational and cultural asset to our Wisconsin students, and make a substantial economic contribution to our state.
>
> The university's contributions to international understanding also shall include exchange of students and faculty, official visits, research applicable to problems of underdeveloped countries, and similar functions it is uniquely able to perform. The interdependence of the world's people, the ease of travel and communications, the rising importance of other cultures, and the quest for peace have tended to make the globe our campus. This trend we encourage.

III

As if to make up for lost time, Wisconsin in a few short years has become fully engaged internationally. Its international dimension today includes most of the conventional activities—and a few that are unconventional or unique, such as its Land Tenure Center, its Comparative Tropical History program, its International Theater program, and the "law in action" approach of its Law School.

International Course Content

The university-wide interest in the international component of higher education is reflected in the instruction Wisconsin now provides. There are undergraduate and graduate courses, correspondence and adult education offerings in every aspect of global affairs. Wisconsin now offers instruction in more than thirty foreign languages, and provides a wide choice of courses in international relations, U.S. foreign policy, international trade and finance, the geography and anthropology of all the continents. There is a wealth of offerings in comparative studies—in education, in the economics of development, in sociology and history. All freshmen in the College of Letters and Science are required to take a year-long course, Freshman Forum, a weekly lecture and discussion session (also broadcast on the state's radio network) which deals with major problems in world affairs, such as economic aid, population control, disarmament, nuclear proliferation. Seniors in the same college are required to take a course called Contemporary Trends, lectures which attempt to summarize or focus the knowledge the student has gained in his undergraduate experience in relation to the scientific, technological, social, and economic changes of today's world.

Undergraduates may major in Asian, Hebrew, Ibero-American, Indian, Scandinavian, and French area studies, in addition to the numerous language areas, or they may major in international relations. Although the latter major is not primarily vocational, it provides a training program for students interested in preparing for a career with the U.S. Foreign Service, commercial concerns abroad, international banking, foreign press service, or teaching and research in international affairs.

International relations have a key place in the Integrated Liberal Studies program, in which Wisconsin pioneered. Inaugurated in 1948, the I.L.S.— which drew some of its ideas from the university's Experimental College headed by the late Alexander Meiklejohn—is a core program, an introduction to Western civilization, which seeks to interrelate by a specially designed, closely knit sequence of studies the diverse elements of a liberal education. Open to a limited number of some 300-400 freshmen each year, it is an optional two-year program which, in the final semester, includes a course on "The International Scene," aimed at arousing student awareness of the larger world with which American society interacts.

Foreign Students and Faculty

The foreign student enrollment on the Madison campus is approximately 1,400 students, of which 80 percent are in the graduate schools, principally those of agriculture and the natural sciences. This puts Wisconsin in fourth place among American educational institutions (behind only the University of California, New York University, and Columbia University) in the number of foreign students enrolled. Foreign student enrollment has remained at about the same level for the past few years. Wisconsin has no fixed limit on foreign student enrollment, and has not enunciated a policy on numbers. However, early in 1963, at the request of the president, the associate dean of the College of Letters and Science, C.H. Ruedisili, embarked on a study of the university's foreign student enrollment and the programs of other universities and organizations in this field. Grown to book length, the study when published will provide recommendations to the president and a faculty committee on most aspects of the foreign student program.

An Office of Foreign Students and Faculty, established as part of the Division of Student Affairs, meets particular needs. Staffed by a part-time director and assistant director, the office provides counsel on problems of personnel and adjustment, supplies financial assistance and arranges for certain undergraduate scholarships which are provided by the university and by contributions from the student body. The office also prepares and distributes at the beginning of each semester a directory of students of foreign citizenship.

Foreign faculty members on the Madison campus number from 150 to 200 annually, with the largest number being affiliated with the university's Enzyme Institute and the Mathematics Research Center, which the university operates in cooperation with the Department of the Army.

Foreign students have been around the Madison campus for so long and in such numbers that their presence is almost taken for granted. No special housing is provided for them. Some years ago the university had an International House, but it did not prove successful, and the present university position is that foreign students will better integrate into the campus and community if they do not have a special area set aside for them.

The International Club has a paid adult advisor whose duties are to aid the foreign students in any way possible during their entire stay at Wisconsin. The Foreign Students Office, working with the International Club, arranges for visits and lectures by foreign students on an intrauniversity as well as on a wider state basis (although this does not seem to apply to the foreign visitors who come to the university's extension division). However, a systematic attempt is made to introduce foreign students, through visits and discussions, to other campuses and communities around the state.

The administration indicates its general support of foreign students on the Wisconsin campus by providing free tuition for those whom the Wisconsin students, by their contributions, provide room and board, and there are a few special scholarships.

The university is now on occasion using its foreign alumni to help screen prospective applicants in their own countries. This is done through the graduate school or through departments, however, and not through the university's alumni office.

Junior Year Abroad

Wisconsin was not an early starter in the American academic race to establish undergraduate study abroad programs, the uncoordinated scramble by which American universities and liberal arts colleges have over the past decade staked out more than 120 different programs for their undergraduates to study at a variety of foreign institutions. By 1960, when Wisconsin first ventured into the field with an experimental program, more than fifty programs were already operating, and by 1962-63, when Wisconsin embarked on its first conventional junior year abroad arrangement, the number of academic year abroad programs offered by American institutions had doubled.

The early programs of foreign study were largely for nonprofessional students, but in 1960 the Carnegie Corporation—alert to the increasing importance of technology on the international scene—gave Wisconsin a modest grant to experiment with foreign study for engineering students, and an arrangement was worked out with an outstanding Mexican professional school, the Instituto Tecnologico y de Estudios Superiores de Monterrey. Beginning in 1961-62, Wisconsin engineering students with superior academic records were chosen to spend their junior year at Monterrey. From 1962 to 1965, the Wisconsin students were joined by engineering students from the Case Institute of Cleveland. The counterpart to this activity—Monterrey junior-year students participating at Wisconsin under the auspices of the program—was added in 1963-64.

At Wisconsin, eligible students are informed of the program at the end of their freshman year, and those who wish to participate register for an intensive Spanish course (oral emphasis) in their sophomore year, preparatory to the study of engineering in the foreign language. Participants, selected jointly by the Wisconsin and Monterrey faculty, then attend a summer language session at Monterrey before they enroll there in the fall for the regular academic year. Full credit is granted for academic work completed at Monterrey.

The Wisconsin-Monterrey program is intended to broaden the scope of training through close contact with another culture and language. The students travel widely in Mexico and become acquainted with Mexican customs and home life. Exchange students from Mexico have an opportunity to learn about the United States through the personal experience of studying at an American professional school and living and traveling in the country.

The program is small—only seven or eight Wisconsin students have joined with an equal number from Case Institute each year—but a modest student and faculty exchange has resulted between Wisconsin and Monterrey, and Wisconsin staff members have visited their Mexican counterparts in advisory capacities. There are some doubts, however, whether the program can be continued in its present form. It does not receive more applications than it can fill: in fact, its organizers have actively to recruit qualified students to fill the available places. The main reasons are that engineering students are not traditionally oriented toward foreign study, and that they are usually engrossed in meeting their technical course requirements. Subsidiary reasons working against the program are that students must decide in their freshman year on a commitment for the junior year, and that the summer language preparation eliminates summer job opportunities. Finally, now that the original Carnegie Corporation support has ended, the Wisconsin end of the program is being operated largely on university funds, which are not normally available for overseas or non-United States purposes. However, the program's success has led to consideration of other cooperative programs with Monterrey: both the College of Agriculture and the physics department are exploring a junior year program with Monterrey. Students who have returned from the course show a pronounced degree of maturity. There is a steady demand for graduates of the program by American business and engineering firms with Mexican operations.

Wisconsin's college year in India program is an academic program established in 1961 by the department of Indian Studies. It combines a summer of language training on a university campus in the United States with a year of academic training in an Indian university. Applicants are selected in their sophomore year from Wisconsin and other institutions—the Associated Colleges of the Midwest joined in the program for its first three years, but dropped the arrangement at the end of the academic year 1964-65—and go to India for their junior year. Preference is given to applicants with a B average or better, and the factors weighed in selection include: (1) a career plan indicating that a year in India would be useful academically and intellectually to the student; (2) an ability to withstand and benefit from the psychological strain of living in a different culture; (3) an interest and aptitude for intensive language study. The summer language preparation consists of either Hindi, Urdu, or Telugu. The overseas program includes further language study, an optional course from Wisconsin's M.A. syllabus, and an independent field project, conducted under the supervision of an American director and Indian professors at each center. Wisconsin's current Indian affiliations are with the Delhi School of Social Work at New Delhi, the Hindu University at Banaras, and Osmania University at Hyderabad. About seventeen juniors are accepted each year.

The first three years of the program were supported by grants from the Carnegie Corporation, but in 1964 the State Department agreed to underwrite it for an additional two years, using blocked currency accumulated in India, Public Law 480 money, from the sale of U.S. foodstuffs.

Having started late, Wisconsin profited from the experiences of those institutions which found themselves running foreign travel programs to meet the demand among students and faculty for study abroad programs. The university determined to create an academically sound study-abroad opportunity for Wisconsin students, and in March, 1960, created a Junior

Year Committee of faculty members to investigate the feasibility of junior year abroad programs. Two committee members toured Europe in the fall of 1960 to examine possible sites. They settled on France. The following year the University of Michigan agreed to join with Wisconsin in plans for a junior year program, and a proposal for support was submitted to the Carnegie Corporation. A sum of $60,000 was granted for a three-year experimental program to be conducted by the two universities and to commence in the academic year 1962-63.

In September of 1962 the Wisconsin-Michigan program was formally initiated at the ancient University of Aix-Marseille, one of the most distinguished French universities (founded in 1409, suppressed by the French Revolution and replaced by various faculties in Aix and Marseille, and then reconstituted as a university in 1896).

The program consists of a full year of academic study for forty to fifty students. Although jointly administered by Wisconsin and Michigan, students from any accredited American institution are eligible to apply. To be considered, an applicant must have had a minimum of two years of college French, a grade average of B or better, and a good score on the MLA proficiency tests. Approximately twenty students are selected·from each university each year, along with a resident director and a visiting professor. These latter appointments rotate between the two universities. The students travel to France at the end of August each year and begin intensive language training and cultural orientation at Aix until regular classes begin in November. Students then enroll in either Aix for courses in French language and literature, philosophy, history, classics, and so on, or—in mathematics and the sciences—at Marseille. Students are housed either in dormitories, small hotels, or private homes. Essential costs are kept to a minimum so that the student's basic expenses for the academic year do not exceed those at either Madison or Ann Arbor by more than about $200. Scholarships, loans, and grants-in-aid normally available in the United States can be applied to the program in France.

At Wisconsin the program is administered by a part-time director in the Office of International Studies and Programs. Wisconsin rates this program an outstanding success, although it is conceded that it has problems. The students at Aix have experienced some difficulties in keeping up with the regular academic program for French students, but weekly seminars are held under the direction of the resident director to supplement the academic work of the American students and efforts are made continually to raise the academic level of students going over in the program. The Wisconsin-Michigan juniors are expected to compete on an equal scholastic level with French students and hopefully to excel. Although French majors are not required, the bulk of the students going overseas in the program —73 percent in 1964-65—are French majors. Most of the students from the United States are women.

However, there is considerable feedback to the Wisconsin campus. The returning students are very advanced in language and literature: almost all of them continue into graduate studies. Under the arrangement with Aix, either a visiting Wisconsin or Michigan professor is offered as a guest lecturer for a year, and administrators and faculty from Madison and Ann Arbor visit Aix from time to time to maintain the link with the home institutions. And, finally, there is extracurricular feedback in the form of campus publicity, cultural programs, broadcasts, and television shows about the junior year in France. Wisconsin would like to work out a cooperative program with Aix whereby French students taking American studies would come to Madison for academic work, but such an exchange has so far been very limited.

The success of the junior year in France encouraged Wisconsin and Michigan in 1964 to join with Wayne State University of Detroit in a similar program for a junior year in Germany. This program consists of a full year of academic study at the Albert-Ludwigs University in Freiburg, at the edge of the Black Forest. Wayne State had operated its own program in conjunction with Freiburg since 1960. About fifteen Wisconsin honor students participate each year in the study program, which concentrates on language and literature. The regular academic session at Freiburg is preceded by an intensive five-week course in German conversation, reading, and composition. Two years of college German, a B average or better, and a passing score on the MLA proficiency tests are required for admission, and all instruction is in German. A resident director from one of the American universities oversees the program in Freiburg and provides tutorial help when needed.

"Our Campus: The World"

As the boundaries of the University of Wisconsin have literally spread to the far corners of the world, so the world has come back to the Wisconsin campus.

Wisconsin was a pioneer in radio transmission—in 1917 station 9XM went on the air from a physics laboratory on campus—and its station WHA was the first educational radio station established in the United States. From its early days its program content has been heavily international. As far back as the early 1930's it began carrying commentary and cultural programs provided by the British Broadcasting Corporation. It now carries programs from France, Holland, Sweden, and South Africa, in addition to those from Britain. Although its audience is the state of Wisconsin and not merely the Madison campus, WHA frequently coordinates its programming with university interests. For instance, beginning in the 1963-64 season, the station has carried a weekly interview series, orginated and arranged by the Office of International Studies and Programs, which was designed to broaden interest in the work of the university's area programs, under the title of "Our Campus: The World." Through its unique statewide network of educational radio stations, programs with an international dimension are made available to every home in the state.

WHA-TV, begun in 1954, was the third educational television station to be established in the United States, and its programming has followed the paths traced out by radio in the state. It regularly televises the Wisconsin School of the Air, in which foreign students are introduced to schoolchildren in Madison and the surrounding area. In 1964-65 it introduced a weekly foreign film festival, in which foreign film imports were shown ("using sex to sell international affairs," as one WHA staffer called it) and then discussed by a university film expert and student commentators. Another innovation attempted by WHA-TV is to take episodes from stock American television programs, such as "Gunsmoke," in which the action and gestures are fairly understandable, and then dub in, say, German language. The idea is to help adults brush up on their foreign languages, but the WHA men believe their doctored tapes could also be used for supplementary language work in high schools.

Another Wisconsin venture which has an important cross-cultural impact on the campus is the program in International Theater, which was begun in the autumn of 1963 with financial assistance out of the Ford Foundation grant to the university. The program intends to offer study and training in the history of theater and dramatic literature, worldwide in scope, embracing both Western and Eastern cultures, and the course is accompanied by dramatic productions intended to tap the traditions of various cultures and areas.

The International Theater program has begun its activities with the Asian theater, particularly the theater of India, China, and Japan, and it came into being at Wisconsin because an authority on the Asian theater, British-born Professor A.C. Scott, was available as acting director. A graduate program is offered, and in the 1963-64 academic year there were twenty-nine students enrolled, most of them working on doctorates, preparatory to teaching. The program is designed to work in cooperation with the departments of physical education (dance), English (speech and drama), and Indian Studies. Asian dance and drama specialists, as well as Asian theater directors, have visited Madison to give technical demonstrations and performance analyses. Its inauguration in 1963 was marked by a month-long Far Eastern Festival—under the auspices of the student Union —which brought to the Madison campus Shanta Rao and her dance company from India, Suzushi Hanayagi, Japanese classical dancer, and Kimio Eto, the blind performer on the ancient Japanese stringed instrument, the *koto*.

Language and Area Study Programs

In a progress report to the Ford Foundation in August, 1964, on the state of the various foreign area and international programs at Wisconsin,

the Office of International Studies and Programs wrote: "These programs
have achieved a position of high acceptability with faculty, students and
the state at large; area and international programs are beginning to loom
large on the Wisconsin scene."

There are two reasons why, in a few short years, a group of isolated and
unknown study centers have become conspicuous and respected enterprises
on campus. One is the university administration's growing and visible
commitment to area study programs. The other was the fact that the bulk
of the $1,200,000 five-year grant given by the Ford Foundation to Wiscon-
sin in March, 1962, was to be applied "for graduate training and research
in non-western and other international studies." Wisconsin's area studies
programs then were in position to take unique advantage of the Ford funds,
and the timely grant enabled them to make special forward surges.

The growth of interest in Ibero-American Area Studies can be measured
by the increase of students in the program. In 1961 there were fewer than
twenty-five students majoring and minoring in this area, whereas today
there are approximately 115 participating both at the graduate and undergraduate levels.

The Ibero-American Studies Program at Wisconsin (formerly called
Hispanic Studies) was organized as an undergraduate major in 1930 and
later expanded to include a major at the M.A. level and a minor at the
Ph.D. level.

In 1959, a Luso-Brazilian Center was established at Wisconsin under
the National Defense Education Act, designed to promote the study of
Portuguese at the graduate level and to provide area courses representing
the Portuguese-speaking world. The Luso-Brazilian Center was incorporated into a Language and Area Center for Latin American Studies established in 1962, under the NDEA. Thus the Spanish-speaking and Portuguese-speaking worlds, which are the focus of the Ibero-American Studies
Program, find an administrative home in the Latin American Center.

The program has two fundamental objectives: development of strength
in academic departments for teaching and research in the Hispanic and
Luso-Brazilian sides of the program which will benefit the undergraduate
and graduate offerings of the university; and the assisting and encouragement of graduate study and faculty research in Ibero-American studies by
providing a coordinated framework within which special interests may be
pursued.

The Language and Area Center for Latin American Studies is organized
as an interdepartmental program with a committee representing the cooperating departments. The members of the committee as well as the administrators of the program ordinarily teach at least one course in the
program. In addition, the Center's director—working out of a small office
provided by the Office of International Studies and Programs—maintains
contact with the chairmen of departments participating in the program so

that they are informed of the Center's needs and budgetary arrangements. The activities of the Center have regularly been extended to undergraduates and about half the total enrollment is in the undergraduate major. Currently there are about thirty students working toward an M.A. degree in this area program. There are now fifteen candidates for a Ph.D. in other departments who are obtaining credits in the minor field of Ibero-American Studies. In addition, there is a sizable enrollment in language programs offered by, or in conjunction with, the Center. The graduate program in Ibero-American Studies is the same as that of the Center. Graduates of this program have entered careers predominantly in government, the Peace Corps, and college-level teaching. The program has regularly offered courses in economics, anthropology, history, geography, political science, Spanish and Portuguese, structural and historical linguistics, and Spanish, Portuguese, Spanish-American, and Brazilian civilizations. More recently, the departments of sociology, rural sociology, and music have contributed offerings. The program has had courses in Spanish and Latin American art given by visiting professors, is contemplating an offering in Latin American law, and hopes to add course work in Spanish-American dialectology.

The Center has undertaken its own student recruitment program, a necessary step. Area studies in general face the problem of grounding students in several disciplines, as well as a language in sufficient degree to enable them to do field work and interdisciplinary research in graduate programs. With the rapid expansion of knowledge and basic requirements, it is increasingly desirable to get the language requirements satisfied as early as possible. Therefore the program has begun working with teachers of Spanish in the high schools of the state, informing them of the area program and enlisting their cooperation in directing it to the attention of their best students.

The program and the Center have plans for growth and improvement. The Center has begun publication of a journal, the *Luso-Brazilian Review*. More graduate fellowships, additional staff, further library acquisitions, and the development of suitable teaching materials are needed. Part of a 1965 Ford Foundation grant given to Wisconsin to strengthen its Latin American studies has been used to set up a Center for International Business Research, to concentrate on comparative studies of industrial organization, business in developing societies, labor organization, and labor relations—with emphasis on Latin America. The Center has been set up as a combined function of the Ibero-American Studies program, the School of Commerce, and the Industrial Relations Research Center.

The African Studies Program at Wisconsin is the youngest of the area programs. In 1957 Professor Philip Curtin, later to become first chairman of the Program, joined the department of history; under Professor Curtin's leadership, a program of Comparative Tropical History was initiated in 1959, of which Africa was, of course, a part. Formal organization of an

African Studies Program did not occur until 1961. The first nucleus consisted of representatives for an African specialty from the departments of history, geography, and political science.

Although the orientation of the program is broadly historical, centering on the development of the African cultural tradition and its influence on modern African life and problems, it provides an opportunity for graduate students in the humanities and in the social sciences to explore Africa from the view of various distinct disciplines—anthropology, history, geography, linguistics, political science, and journalism. The African Studies committee—faculty members teaching courses or seminars principally concerned with Africa—operates on the belief that graduate students and more advanced researchers should be first of all fully trained in their own disciplines. The aim of the committee is to make available interdisciplinary area training which it believes is essential to successful research in African studies in any one of these disciplines. Graduate study of Africa can be carried out jointly with the African Studies program and the program in Comparative Tropical History of the history department or with the program in the Politics of Developing Nations of the department of political science. The following programs are available: a certificate in African Studies to all students who meet all requirements for an M.A. degree in a major department in the university; a minor field in African Studies is available for Ph.D. degree candidates in a discipline who desire interdisciplinary training in African studies. Undergraduates with an interest in Africa may work toward a B.A. in African language and literature, with appropriate courses in other disciplines; or they may plan a program to emphasize the study of Africa, while meeting the major requirements of another department.

The decision to give formal recognition to an African Studies Program represented a commitment by the university to place priority on the recruitment of qualified staff members (either by retraining existing staff, or recruiting new faculty) in the major social science and humanities disciplines, to expand the program beyond its initial history base. There has been since that time a very rapid expansion, both in faculty members with a special competence in Africa, in the number of Africa-related course offerings, and in the number of graduate students specializing in Africa in fields other than history.

Another landmark in the development of the program was the formal establishment of a Department of African Language and Literature in the spring of 1964. The program of instruction in Swahili and Xhosa required some departmental base; these languages could not be conveniently added to any other existing department, and the African Studies Program desired the added flexibility which separate departmental status for its language program would provide.

The stress of the African Studies Program is on graduate instruction, although undergraduate course offerings are provided in all fields represented on the African Studies Committee. The goal is to include the entire continent in its scope, although it was not until 1964-65 that a specialist in the North African area was added. It is recognized that equal depth and coverage cannot be given to all parts of the continent, and that what is done best will be a function of the particular training and experience of the staff members at any given time. However, the program has decided against any explicit emphasis of one region over another.

The goal in developing the program is to include a staff member with an African specialty in all of the social science disciplines, within the humanities, fields of music (African ethnomusicology), and art history, and to strengthen the language training in the three major languages of Africa now offered at the university (Swahili, Xhosa, and Arabic). Further, in departments with the heaviest concentration of students specializing in African Studies, such as anthropology, history, political science, and geography, the goal is to include at least two staff members with African specialization, in order to maintain continuity of course offerings with larger enrollments during the frequent periods of faculty leaves and field research. In addition, the Schools of Law and Education are both committed to developing instruction in research in the African field.

So far, the enthusiasm generated about African affairs on campus has been such that some thirty-five teachers and graduate students have formed a Wisconsin Africanists' Association and begun issuing their own mimeographed newsletter. At least fifteen of the members planned to do field work in Africa during 1964-65.

The Russian Area Studies program is deeply rooted at Wisconsin. Interest in Eastern Europe in the prewar years lodged in the department of Polish language, which in turn was created because of the large Polish population in the state. As the Soviet Union tightened its control over the captive nations of Eastern Europe, attention focused on Russia itself. Professors whose primary concern was Russia were added to both the history and the political science departments, and Russian language was emphasized.

In 1957-58 these professors, together with Harrington, then Vice President for Academic Affairs, took an active interest in developing a wider program of Soviet studies. At the end of 1958, the first Russian Area Studies program was formally established. An interdepartmental committee of faculty members concerned with the area integrated the several courses offered by the departments of history, Slavic languages, political science, and geography into a program of study at the graduate level.

The present program is designed to give graduate students interested in the Soviet area a double opportunity: first, to acquire a general knowledge of the area through integrated study of Soviet history, government, politics, foreign policy, economics, language, sociology, law, literature, anthropology, and geography; second, to gain specific knowledge of some aspect of the Soviet area through intensive study of one of these fields. The primary aim of the program is to train Ph.D. degree candidates for research and teaching at the college level in the field of Russian studies. Several complementary objectives have been recognized from the outset. These include: emphasis and encouragement of faculty research; training students for careers other than college teaching, primarily journalism and secondary education; extending the pervasive benefits of development work in audio-visual and other teaching methods; and the public service advantage to be gained from having specialized and reliable information available to local mass media, civic groups, and general adult education activities.

There are now nineteen full-time faculty members involved in Russian Studies. They are hired by their departments and are on department payrolls for tenure, but most of them spend at least half their time teaching in Russian Studies.

Wisconsin's Indian Area Studies program is not so new in content as it is in concept. A few of the courses offered now had been offered previously, but the designation of Wisconsin six years ago as a Center for Indian Language and Area Studies under the NDEA enabled the university to pull together its facilities for advanced study in such disciplines as anthropology, comparative literature, economics, education, history, linguistics, philosophy, political science, and sociology with special reference to India.

Indian Studies now has thirteen faculty members of academic rank and offers degrees on all three academic levels, an undergraduate major, an M.A. degree and Ph.D. minor, a Ph.D. in Buddhist Studies and, beginning in 1965-66, a Ph.D. in Indian language and literature. The undergraduate program is primarily in language and literature. The M.A. in Indian Studies requires language work to an advanced level, and takes two years for students entering without previous work on India, one year for those with adequate undergraduate preparation. The graduate student preparing for college teaching or professional research in any of the disciplines, with a specialization on India, earns a Ph.D. in his discipline, complemented by an M.A. in Indian Studies. Language is central to the program, which offers Hindi-Urdu, Telugu, Kannada, Sanskrit, Tibetan, Pali, and Buddhist Japanese. In 1966-67 a new course will be offered: the study of Oriya.

A doctoral program, the first in the United States that leads to a Ph.D. in Buddhist Studies, was established as part of the Indian Area Studies program in 1961. The objective is to train scholars and teachers to deal with Buddhism as a component in the social, cultural, and religio-philosophical history of Asia. A unified interdisciplinary curriculum equips the student to handle Buddhist canonical languages (Sanskrit, Pali, Chinese), doctrine (religious concepts and philosophical systems), and social studies (Buddhist institutions, cult, and social history). In addition to the intrinsic, ancient appeal of Buddhism, the student gains an appreciation of its significant role in the ideological drama of contemporary Asia.

As with African, Indian, and Soviet area studies, courses and specialists in many of the areas of East Asia are of long standing at Wisconsin.

However, it was the increasing recognition of the importance of Asian developments in international affairs, coupled with the interdisciplinary nature of East Asian studies, that led to the establishment of an East Asian Studies program at the university in 1962.

An East Asian program had been organized about 1954, but on an *ad hoc* basis, and it ran an undergraduate minor program and an occasional minor graduate program. As a result of the Ford Foundation grant in 1962 the program was formalized. A Ph.D. degree minor program is now offered to students in all disciplines who are especially interested in Asia. Special opportunities are offered in the associated departments for concentration on Southeast Asia, Inner Asia, China, and Japan. Future plans call for an interdepartmental M.A. in Asian Studies, but no degree beyond this. At present, there are sixteen members of the East Asian staff teaching in the program and approximately seventy students.

As far back as 1875, a forerunner of Wisconsin's Scandinavian Studies was established as a language department emphasizing the teaching of Norwegian, an innovation attributable to Wisconsin's strong Scandinavian tradition. Some educators of the day looked upon the course as today's equivalent of baton-twirling—"I suspect they reacted as we would today if someone told us the university was originating a course in Patagonian," says Professor Harald Naess, the present head of the Scandinavian Studies department, quoting the department's founder—but when one of the department's members wrote a book which was favorably received, the teaching of Norwegian won sufficient support to survive.

A formal Scandinavian Studies program was instituted at Wisconsin in 1949 (with Scandinavia being defined as including Denmark, Finland, Iceland, Norway, and Sweden). The program is designed to impart a general knowledge of life in Scandinavia, with emphasis on social and cultural conditions against a geographical and historical background. The department provides an opportunity for the acquisition of a Scandinavian language as a tool for speaking and reading; a systematic study of the literatures of the Scandinavian nations, both in the original languages and in translation; courses in the history, government, and international relations of Scandinavia; and graduate study and research leading to an M.A. degree or a Ph.D. degree minor in Scandinavian Studies.

The eighth of the area studies programs at Wisconsin is the department of Hebrew and Arabic Studies, which provides the opportunity for the acquisition of Hebrew and Arabic as classical and living languages, the systematic study of Hebrew literature in the original Hebrew and in translation, and the study of other Semitic languages such as Aramaic, Syriac, Ugaritic, and Akkadian. Courses are designed to train students, teachers, members of the Armed Forces, and candidates for the foreign service in the language and cultures of the Near Eastern peoples. Advanced courses are adapted to the needs of students seeking higher degrees who wish to specialize in the Bible, Ancient Near East literature, including Jewish and

Islamic studies, Semitic philology, archaeology, history, and theology. Research in Judeo-Arabic texts is also available.

Library Resources

The university is well served by the extensive Western language collections of the Memorial Library and the supplemental collection of the nearby Wisconsin State Historical Society, but in the book and periodical collections of the more exotic areas of the world the university labors under some limitations. Although state funds help to support the acquisitions program, they are nowhere near enough to enable the library to acquire the scarce, old publications demanded by the area study programs, most of which are growing increasingly more expensive as the competition for them increases. Also, in order to mount a first-rank area program, Wisconsin—having started late in some areas—must catch up with the acquisitions of institutions whose programs have been in existence for a longer period of time.

Another problem is the Parkinsonian impact of area programs on the library's staff: acquisitions in foreign languages usually require bibliographers to handle them, and it is difficult to find staff with both library and language competence. Prior to 1959 at Wisconsin, one person handled all area programs. Then the growth began: a bibliographer was added to handle Indian studies; in 1961 an African bibliographer was added; in 1963 a combined Indian and African bibliographer was secured; in 1963 an Hispanic bibliographer was found; and by 1964 a Slavic bibliographer, and two bibliographic assistants, one in Japanese and one in Chinese, were added to the staff.

Growth is evident in the numbers of titles on hand, bringing with it the inevitable problems of space and handling. In 1959 there were 7,000 titles in Indian Studies; by 1964 this had been increased to 14,500. In 1961 there were 5,400 items in African Studies, in 1964 a total of 11,519. There was an annual increase of 20 percent in 1961-62 and 30 percent for 1962-63.

The ability to order foreign library materials through dealers and their catalogs is becoming more difficult. In 1961-62 Wisconsin ordered 62 percent of its foreign items from catalogs, but in 1962-63 only 55 percent. This necessitates more expensive travel by the librarians to buy materials on the spot and comb the archives abroad for materials which might be microfilmed.

Land Tenure Center

Wisconsin's Land Tenure Center, established in 1962 as a cooperative research and training program of the American nations, AID, and the University of Wisconsin, is a prime instance of "the Wisconsin idea" being applied well beyond the borders of the state. It was set up—supported mainly from a contract with AID—to administer an effective research organization engaged in the comparative study and analysis of the economic, social, political, and administrative aspects of land ownership, land tenure, and the agrarian structure in Latin America. Training through research is part of this activity. Scores of promising young men and women from the Latin American countries and the United States have taken part in research projects on campus or with the senior staff in Latin America to gain experience for future work in developing nations.

Like many international activities at Wisconsin, the Land Tenure Center represents an extension of interests from the Madison campus to the world at large. It is based on a solid foundation of long-time study of land problems, which grew out of issues of land settlement and resource management in the state of Wisconsin. Nearly a half century ago a course was organized at the university to foster study and research on land problems. Many of the ideas and research results of this early period are contained in the book, *Land Economics,* by Professors Richard T. Ely and George S. Wehrwein. During the same period John R. Commons was developing his ideas of institutional economics with research directed at public policy, social security, collective bargaining, and public administration. As far back as the mid-1920's the university launched a periodical titled *The Journal of Land and Public Utilities.* During the depression years whole areas of middle and northern Wisconsin became rural slums, as poverty and dispossession despoiled the land and drove families from the farms. Again Wisconsin professors became involved, sometimes on their own, often working through the state legislature, in providing solutions: land was reforested, and rural planning and rural zoning were introduced to close down the marginal farms and resettle the farmers. This experience, which involved faculty from the Law School as well as from the College of Agriculture, gave Wisconsin and its university worldwide recognition in the field of land tenure. Its journal was continued, but in the 1950's its title was changed to *Land Economics.* The reputation of the agricultural economics department of the College of Agriculture, where the specialized interest centered, began to attract foreign graduate students and specialists to Madison.

In 1951, when the then Mutual Security Agency convened a conference on land tenure, with delegates invited from around the globe, the logical locale was Wisconsin. Thirty-eight foreign lands sent delegates and some of the delegates either remained on at Madison to study or returned later. In the years that followed Wisconsin specialists in land tenure were in demand at international meetings, and their appearances abroad usually resulted in more foreign students finding their way to the Wisconsin campus.

The 1951 conference, according to Professor Raymond J. Penn, who served until the summer of 1965 as director of the center, broke new ground by combining the talents and interests of agricultural communicators with agricultural economists and rural sociologists in a common desire to bring about land reform by working down at the local, community level. Up to that point, sociologists had tended to look down their noses at the agricultural journalists, but at Wisconsin they came to respect each other and work together. Later, when the Land Tenure Center was established, the academic specialists turned to the university's extension experts for the techniques and know-how in teaching more productive agricultural methods in Latin America.

The central administration of the College of Agriculture, then conservative in outlook, took no interest in this new specialty, but a few passionate believers in the agricultural economics department—mainly Professor Penn, Professor Kenneth H. Parsons, and, for a short time, Vice President Clodius, who was then in the department—generated sufficient enthusiasm to persuade the university administration to institutionalize their interest in land tenure in the form of a center. They were joined by individual faculty members from other disciplines, such as Professor Jacob H. Beuscher of the Law School, an expert on the law of land use and natural resources who has done a prodigious amount of extracurricular work in preparing testimony and legislation for the state.

In 1962 a grant from AID established the Land Tenure Center. The contract was renewed in 1964, but on an annual review and budget basis with support promised to 1969.

Because changes in land tenure and agrarian structure have economic, political, and social ramifications, the research of the Land Tenure Center is by nature multidisciplinary.

The Land Tenure Center is not a curriculum or a department in the ordinary university sense. It is a coordinating and service facility to aid the university in carrying on an integrated program of research and training. This is carried on though the departments of agricultural economics, rural sociology, law, agricultural journalism, political science, commerce, Ibero-American Area Studies, geography, anthropology, and others.

It became quickly evident through this undertaking that Latin American administrators, students and policy makers wanted more than just the research results called for under the contract. They wanted interpretations, a chance to learn analytical procedures, and consultation in taking bold new steps forward.

Research has centered on Latin American development problems and policy issues. In Chile, for example, a University of Wisconsin researcher and a young Chilean are studying agricultural productivity and investments in labor and equipment on large farms. One study evaluated voluntary reform programs now being tried on some large farms in central Chile. The young Chilean co-worker has since been asked to assist Chile's Frei government in developing plans for agrarian reform. This is an example of how not only the research but the training are put to immediate local use.

In Colombia a young law scholar worked side by side with national and international legal experts to help draft a new water use code for Colombia. His understanding of water use control came from studies underway as a part of the Land Tenure Center research.

Information obtained from studies of rural areas of Colombia is pointing up the importance of local and rural organizations in the growth, stability, and development of rural communities.

These examples illustrate how research into social problems can be oriented to public policy and problems of change. More than twenty research workers are engaged in similar activities in Latin America at the present time.

The Center's imaginative approach is best illustrated by its development of technical documentary films, a series of 16 mm. films for teaching purposes that are made available through the university's audio-visual film library. Flying over the areas where land reforms were at work convinced Center personnel that a series of before and after films could provide a new kind of research technique to document rural conditions and land tenure relationships. Produced in cooperation with the Center's research workers in the field and shot in some instances by the university's film experts, they add an important visual dimension to written documentation.

Comparative Studies

Wisconsin's program on the histories of tropical countries is unique.

Established in 1959—with the financial support of the Carnegie Corporation—as the Comparative Tropical History program, its first purpose is to meet the growing need for research scholars and teachers in the histories of Tropical America, Africa, South Asia, Southeast Asia, North Africa, and the Near East. The central focus of the program is the historical fact that a period of European rule or influence has been the most important single factor in the recent history of these regions and that they have gone through a period of rapid cultural change without losing their cultural traditions. The historical experience of the four areas is therefore comparable; they have become the emerging nations of the 1960's, sharing a common set of problems and aspirations.

While the common factor of European intrusion provides an element of comparability, the Wisconsin program centers not on the European activities but on the changing patterns of society in each of the tropical areas. The program is oriented toward the Ph.D. degree, and at present there are some fifty students participating in it. A Ph.D. candidate chooses one of the four tropical areas for major specialization. In this area he is expected to have command of the relevant languages and research techniques and to be acquainted with the methods and contributions of other disciplines. Another area is chosen for secondary specialization. Finally, the student is expected to have a broad, and admittedly more superficial, knowledge of other non-Western areas in the modern period. The department of history offers year-length introductory courses in the history of the five tropical areas in the modern period. In addition, a year-length course in "The Expansion of Europe" provides a general survey and comparative analysis of all five areas. Each of these six courses is accompanied by a parallel graduate seminar, in which the comparative and analytical approach is stressed. More specialized training is provided by a series of one-semester advanced courses, such as the history of Mexico, the history of Brazil, the history of Bantu Africa, the history of West Africa, the history of South India, or the history of Indonesia. All graduate students go abroad for field research.

In the autumn of 1964 Wisconsin launched a second comparative program, Comparative Tropical Economics. This is a heavily research-oriented seminar which takes up one central theme—such as the response to economic incentives in differing cultures, the role of foreign entrepreneurs in economic development—and brings in faculty members on an *ad hoc* basis from such departments as economics, agricultural economics, or the School of Commerce as the subject warrants. The innovator of the program is now seeking foundation support.

Population studies are, by definition, comparative and at Wisconsin it has been recognized that population and its problems cut across many fields. The Population Committee of the university—founded in the early 1940's—recently reorganized its course offerings to make the program more interdisciplinary, and its advisory committee includes representatives from disciplines as diverse as anthropology, urban and regional planning, and wildlife management.

Professional Schools

The pioneering ventures by the College of Engineering and the department of economics in undertaking service contracts abroad have now been followed by virtually every school and department at Wisconsin.

The economics department is continuing its support to the faculty of economics at Gadjah Mada University, in Jogjakarta, Indonesia, backed, as it has been for seven years, by a Ford Foundation grant. In addition, the program has been widened to take in a consortium of American institutions —the University of California at Berkeley, Harvard, and Wisconsin— which is under contract to the Ford Foundation to maintain academic continuity with the faculties of three Indonesian universities, the University of Indonesia at Djakarta, Nommensen University at Medan, and Gadjah Mada. This involves occasional short-term visits to Indonesia by selected representatives of the American universities concerned in the program. In 1964 the economics department at Wisconsin also signed an AID contract, terminating in 1967, under which three or four Wisconsin economics faculty members and half a dozen research assistants will cooperate with various institutions in Southeast Asia in helping to formulate more effective plans for economic growth in the area.

Dean Young, as an outgrowth of his earlier interest in Indonesia, was the prime mover in setting up, under the economics department, the Center for International Labor Studies. This unit in 1964 began a one-year study of comparative labor market behavior and manpower distribution in Japan and India.

The field work under which the College of Engineering provided assistance to seven Indian educational institutions—a program which originated in 1953 and continued under successive U.S. foreign aid agencies (TCA—Technical Cooperation Administration; FOA—Foreign Operations Administration; ICA—International Cooperation Administration; and, finally, AID) terminated in the summer of 1964. Eight summer schools for engineering college teachers were carried on with assistance of the University of Wisconsin in the summer of 1965 in India. Wisconsin will continue until the summer of 1966 to handle Indian students sent to the United States as participants in a training program. To date, 165 Indian engineering college teachers have received advanced education in the United States under the program.

The college's director of foreign programs, Merton R. Barry, calculates that altogether Wisconsin's engineers have supplied about sixty-seven man years of professional service (teaching and consultation) to Indian engineering schools under the contracts since 1953, an investment which—whatever it has achieved in Indian education—has been completely justified from Wisconsin's viewpoint. It has developed a core of internationally competent professionals at the university's engineering school, and greatly strengthened the international public service motive in the school. It has also brought the school into close collaboration with the Indian Studies program, which has assisted the engineers in selection and orientation for staff assigned to India and with the School of Education, which has developed special courses for Indian students coming to Wisconsin under the engineering program.

Recognition of the value of the program to engineering education in India is attested to by strong requests for continued collaboration by the Indian engineering colleges, the Ministry of Education of the Government of India, and AID.

Wisconsin's school of journalism is one of the nation's oldest: courses in journalism were first offered at the university in 1905. It also has the reputation of being an internationally oriented school, due in good part to its director, Professor Ralph O. Nafziger.

Nafziger, midwest born and trained, has had no overseas journalistic experience himself—"I'm a sublimated foreign correspondent," he says—but from his early years on the staff at Wisconsin he has shunned the traditional approach to journalism teaching, which too often seems to consist of courses in type makeup, advertising, and city and state reporting taught by unsuccessful weekly newspaper publishers. At the University of Minnesota, where he taught before coming to Wisconsin, Nafziger developed a pioneer course in international journalism and he brought it to Wisconsin with him, influencing a generation of journalism graduates. In more recent years he has taught at the Free University of Berlin and participated in numerous international conferences on journalism: he has also brought to his staff several journalism teachers who have had experience abroad as newsmen. One staff member, Dr. William A. Hachten, associate professor of journalism, has taught and studied international communications in Western Europe and Africa. He will be in charge of a new course and a seminar which will deal largely with communications in developing nations.

Wisconsin's journalism school confers the degrees of M.A. or Master of Science in journalism. The Ph.D. degree can be earned under an interdisciplinary program leading to the Ph.D. in Mass Communications or under a joint program with one of certain other departments of the university.

The program in Mass Communications is another Nafziger innovation intended to provide training in mass communications theory and experience in research techniques of the area. A modest Mass Communications Research Center has been set up in three rooms tucked away in the aged journalism building, and a University of Illinois communications specialist, Professor Percy H. Tannenbaum, has been brought in to head it. Using a modest sum from the Ford Foundation grant of 1962, Tannenbaum in 1964 embarked on a research project which goes by the mouth-filling title of the Structural Correlates of Written Message Comprehension Study. Its purpose is "to examine the relative generality or specificity of structural correlates of written message comprehension in a sample of different languages," including those spoken in Mexico, Canada, Belgium, Denmark, England, Finland, France, Germany, Greece, Italy, Lebanon, and The Netherlands. In lay terms, what it means is that Tannenbaum's specialty is a study of linguistics, finding common symbols in different cultures. The search for symbols led him into a study of attitude changes and this, in turn, led to a study of resistance to attitude changes in different countries.

The Medical School, in addition to its primary objectives—the education of physicians and the furtherance of medical research—willingly shoulders a wide variety of service responsibilities for the community, the state, and the nation. Until recently it has not regarded these responsibilities as extending to other lands.

At the urging of Vice President Clodius that they "get into international affairs," the medical faculty set up an international committee in July, 1964, headed by Dr. Anthony R. Curreri, professor of surgery, director of the division of clinical oncology, and chief surgical consultant to the U.S. Army, an appointment which compels him to travel about the world. Curreri confesses that it is an uphill job to persuade fellow medical men that they should accept service responsibilities abroad. In the first place, there are limited faculty resources and great need for them at home. In the second, there is an ingrained resistance for career reasons: promotion in the university medical field hinges on research, study, and publications, and this appears to mitigate against service abroad.

"How can one change this attitude," asks Curreri, "and arrange that a person can receive credit for helping people? Those who go abroad for service reasons are often regarded by their fellow faculty members in the medical field as being second-class citizens. Wives want to know 'Will someone use my husband's lab when he's abroad?' " Curreri believes the only answer is that the university administration—which is firmly in favor of service abroad—must succeed in convincing the medical faculty that its members should accept the obligations of service abroad, without loss of academic status.

Dr. Curreri has proposed a three-way program. The basic idea is to send a team of Wisconsin medical men to a selected foreign country to demonstrate how an American hospital team works together. The teams would deliberately include younger doctors and interns, to offset the fact that many foreign-trained doctors are inclined to slight their younger colleagues. The team visit would then be followed up by the exchanges of young staff members, to enable young foreign medical men to come to Wisconsin and to give Wisconsin's young medical students experience overseas. Curreri conceives this approach as applying not to the newly emerged nations, where hospital facilities are sometimes nonexistent, but to the middle-level nations, where Wisconsin teams could supplement the work of going institutions and then pull out in a year or two.

Under an AID program Wisconsin's School of Commerce is cooperating with the University of Carabobo at Valencia in Venezuela, to strengthen the commerce faculty at that school. In 1964 the School of Commerce took on another assignment in cooperation with the Bank for International Development. At the request and expense of La Bolsa (the National Securities Exchange of Argentina), Wisconsin's Commerce faculty will set up a series of seminars in Argentina to train and inform businessmen, inform bank officials, and train bank technicians. And, as mentioned earlier, the School of Commerce has joined with the Ibero-American Studies program to set up a Center for International Business Research to make comparative studies in Latin American business affairs.

These service and research involvements for the Commerce school have recently been enlarged but its interest in world affairs goes back a generation and more. The dean of the school, Erwin A. Gaumnitz, is an internationalist who has seen wartime service in Washington and done consulting work in South America, and one of his predecessors, Chester Lloyd Jones, aroused the school's interest in the problems of international trade, particularly Latin America, in the years before World War II. One of the Commerce faculty, Professor Edward E. Werner, spent more than three years working in and supervising the economics project at Gadjah Mada University in Indonesia. When he returned he became a half-time assistant to the Dean of International Studies and Programs, but he retained his joint appointment with Commerce.

Going down his faculty man by man, Dean Gaumnitz remarked that ten out of perhaps fifty members, associate professors and above, had either official, contract, or personal experience abroad, and that a further ten members had a general interest in international affairs. About twenty faculty members concentrate largely on domestic problems.

However, in Dean Gaumnitz's view, the changes brought about in the Commerce school by its increasing involvement abroad have been substantial. They include: (1) a new dimension to the course content and the conception of new courses, such as new developments in international marketing and finance, and transportation economics, taught on a worldwide basis; (2) the strengthening of the faculty (if the school were faced with two equal candidates for a teaching position in, say, marketing, it would now pick the man with foreign experience, said the dean); (3) an enrichment of the school's library with international materials; (4) contacts with various arms of the government; (5) the addition to the staff of foreign faculty members.

Wisconsin's Law School is proud of its pioneering. It was the first state law school in the United States; it was the first law school in the Middle West to adopt the casebook method of instruction; and it was one of the first to respond to the challenge to legal scholars laid down about a half a century ago by Roscoe Pound, formerly Dean of Harvard Law School, when he exhorted them to abandon the security of their libraries, end their isolation, and join with other social scientists in looking at real-life socio-economic-legal problems in order to determine how the law in the books compared with the world of reality.

In answer to this challenge, Wisconsin's law faculty joined hands with its agriculturalists and economists, immersed themselves in the state's problems of land tenure, utility regulation, conservation, and so on, and helped draft legislation and push through reforms. Out of this experience came the Law School's "law in action" program, a deliberate effort to move the legal scholars out of the classrooms and into field research, especially that relating to the use of rural lands, farm tenure, and farm credit. At the same time members of the law faculty, headed by Professor Beuscher, took an active part in worldwide work on land tenure.

It was a logical extension of this interest, therefore, when in 1962 the law faculty unanimously decided to implement an international "law in action" program, with emphasis at first on Latin America, and to embark on a long-term study of the legal problems of agrarian reform in the underdeverloped world.

Each year four Wisconsin law students are selected to work in Latin America, observing agrarian problems on the spot. Professor Beuscher, who feels that law graduates in Latin America would also benefit from a period of applied work before beginning to practice, has proposed a similar "law in action" program for the students of the University of Chile's Law School.

The School of Education has always encouraged its faculty members to take on overseas assignments, then return to the campus for a few years. The feedback contributes to the school's determination to add more emphasis to research into educational problems. "Our goal is to make Wisconsin's School of Education the leading world center for research in education," says Dean Lindley J. Stiles.

Two major service projects overseas are contributing to the research feedback. In 1962 Professor Milton O. Pella of Wisconsin participated in a summer program in science and education, sponsored by the Ford Foundation, which was held at the American University in Beirut, Lebanon. Out of this grew his proposal to the foundation for a program of leadership training for science teachers in the secondary schools of the Middle East, which formally began in 1963 in four nations, Lebanon, Iraq, Jordan, and Syria. Participants are selected in each country to spend two years of postgraduate training in the United States. They then return to their own countries for research and other work in academic science, after which they are returned to the United States to complete their degree requirements and receive a doctoral degree.

Late in 1964 the School of Education embarked on a larger assignment. Under a grant of approximately $2 million from the Ford Foundation, the School of Education undertook an extensive primary teacher education project in Northern Nigeria to help that region improve and expand its primary education (an area in which, at present, only 14 percent of the children of primary school age are in school). The project was planned cooperatively by the Northern Nigerian government, AID, the Ford Foundation, and the University of Wisconsin.

The grant will support a teacher-training program at seven teachers colleges, which will be involved in in-service education in primary schools and in other teacher-training programs in these seven colleges. It is anticipated that innovations which have proved to be effective in the United States will be given careful consideration for use in Nigeria—such as team teaching, programmed instruction, and the use of audio-visual materials and language laboratories. Assistance will be given to Ahmadu Bello University in its developing Institute of Education to enable it to train teachers to replace the Wisconsin team in teachers colleges. Wisconsin's responsibility is to provide no fewer than thirty-two professional staff, including four professors in a central staff which will work with the regional Ministry of Education.

In a research-service arrangement which it hopes will become a pattern for future AID-university contracts, Wisconsin also proposes to have a limited number of graduate students from its African Studies Program spend time doing field research on the education project in Nigeria.

The School of Agriculture is a latecomer into the international field, even by Wisconsin's standards. Its conversion did not occur until 1963-64 and then only because a handful of faculty members, prodded by the sympathetic administration, kept pushing for an international commitment.

The College of Agriculture made its reputation—as one of the best in the country—on the caliber of its research and its service to the state. Success in these areas reinforced its conservatism: neither area required it to venture into the new realm of international service.

There were exceptions to this view within its faculty, particularly among the agricultural economists and agricultural journalists. Their enthusiasms were shunted off into the Land Tenure Center, which was brought into being despite a coolness on the part of the College of Agriculture. Individual faculty members in agriculture established their own cross-disciplinary relations on the campus, and found international outlets outside their own school.

The inauguration of the new administration of President Harrington and Vice President Clodius set a new tone for Wisconsin, and the College of Agriculture in time came to realize that its responsibilities were no longer coterminous with the boundaries of the state. At least some of the initiative in pressing his more conservative colleagues came from Clodius, who had been an agricultural economist before moving up to the administration. Two main arguments were used to persuade the reluctant agriculturalists. One was that, with a shrinking agricultural population in the state and a new sense of world involvement on the part of those farmers who remained, the responsibilities of the College of Agriculture had likewise shifted. The other was that the longer Wisconsin delayed entering the international field the farther behind it was falling in the competitive standings with agricultural schools which have global operations. With the administration pressing from one side and a sizable minority of the agricultural faculty agitating on the other, the opposition decreased and in the autumn of 1963 the then dean designated one of the internationalists on his staff, Professor Edwin E. Heizer, as director of a new International Agricultural Programs Office in the school.

Heizer's first step was to ask for a convocation of the agricultural faculty to outline the possibilities open to the school in international service. Through a contact initially made by Clodius when he was in South America for the Department of State, Wisconsin for several years had filled a chair in economics at the University of Rio Grande do Sul, Brazil, a post financed jointly by the State Department and Wisconsin. Heizer persuaded his colleagues to set up a faculty committee to go to Brazil and make a feasibility study of the possibility of extending this relationship between the two universities. The then dean of agriculture, as well as the chairman of the department which would be expected to contribute the largest number of personnel, were persuaded to serve on the committee.

The conversion was complete when the committee returned and recommended a greatly expanded program of cooperation which would initiate and develop an agricultural research program at Rio Grande do Sul University and furnish participant training in the United States for prospective Brazilian staff members of the university. An AID contract was quickly worked out and in January, 1964, Wisconsin undertook a two-year assignment to provide up to eight agricultural faculty members and two project associates for work in Brazil. Heizer now has a waiting list of faculty members willing and ready to go!

A few months after taking the plunge in Brazil, the College of Agriculture undertook a three-year AID contract to develop an agricultural research program for the new faculty of agriculture of the University of Ife, in Nigeria's Western Region. A staff of fourteen Wisconsin agricultural faculty men, representing most disciplines in the school, will be sent to Ife, where they will provide at the outset two-thirds of the university's agricultural faculty, and up to eight young Nigerians will be brought to the United States for training under the contract.

The drain on the Wisconsin agricultural staff in one year has been severe. Unlike some institutions, the College of Agriculture has not had time to overstaff—to hire additional faculty to provide a margin for overseas assignments—but Heizer hopes to lean on exchange arrangements worked out with other members of the Midwest Universities Consortium (the universities of Illinois, Indiana, Michigan State, and Wisconsin) for the next year or so. On one point the school is firm: any service contract undertaken shall be done with Wisconsin agricultural faculty only. It does not intend to hire outsiders to make up or complement the Wisconsin contingent on any foreign contract.

Whatever the problems, the international dimension in the College of Agriculture is now to be seen. A new dean, a pronounced internationalist, took office in September, 1964. Heizer's office, with its International Agriculture legend on its door, is central and prominent, and students are already coming in to ask how they can get involved in international agriculture, both while in school and later. The next step at Wisconsin is to devise courses to meet their needs. There are some three hundred foreign students enrolled in the College at present, and they make up about one-third of the graduate students in agriculture.

Heizer is optimistic about the impact of all this. "If in ten years we are not a stronger, more versatile agricultural faculty," he says, "then we've made a mistake. But it is my feeling that we will show solid results in that time. For instance, because of our work in Nigeria, the University of Wisconsin will have outstanding courses in tropical agriculture within ten years." There is another bonus which is more immediate. "There has really been very little liaison on campus between the social scientists and the 'production scientists,' such as those of us in agriculture," explains Heizer. "Some of this liaison is now being accomplished on the job in our foreign contract operations. We are finding common strengths and common problems while we are in the field, yet many of us didn't even have a speaking relationship while we were here on campus."

In addition to the major service operations abroad, most departments and schools at Wisconsin seem to have worked out special relations with various institutions and areas abroad. Among these are: a faculty exchange program between the departments of pediatrics at Wisconsin and the University of Chile at Santiago: a research and graduate training program on cacao in Costa Rica carried on by the department of entomology in cooperation with the Interamerican Institute of Agricultural Sciences at Turrialba, Costa Rica: collaborative studies in neurophysiology between Wisconsin's department of physiology and the Instituto de Fisiologia of the University of Chile; a cooperative research program in experimental nuclear physics with the University of São Paulo, Brazil; and various international programs carried on by the department of veterinary science in Canada, Panama, Ecuador, Brazil, Turkey, Colombia, Mexico, Venezuela, and Argentina.

Extended Education

Wisconsin's Extension Division, one of the largest in the United States, has always been far in front of the rest of the university in its willingness to be involved in the world. Access to learning is the essence of "the Wisconsin idea" and the Extension Division has been one of the main vehicles for carrying it beyond the Madison campus. The original philosophy of the division, explained Charles E. Wedemeyer, now the head of instruction and evaluation, was to serve first the state, then the nation. "And almost before we knew it, we were serving the world."

Correspondence instruction, a European idea which first flowered in the United States as part of the educational and cultural programs of New York's famed Chautauqua Institute, found early support at Wisconsin. Soon after the university's founding, friendly professors were corresponding with students around the state who couldn't continue their education because they were too poor or had to help on family farms, and in 1891 a formal correspondence program was instituted. Today, with some 450 course offerings making it one of the largest operations of its kind in the United States, the correspondence program at Wisconsin serves students in some eighty different foreign lands. Altogether, some 12,000 correspondence students are enrolled in Wisconsin courses. Many of these are foreign students, and a good many are civilian Americans living abroad, but more than 1,000 of them are members of the U.S. armed forces who enroll in university-level correspondence courses.

Wisconsin's long experience in the correspondence field led the U.S. Army to turn to Madison in 1942, just after our entry into World War II, and ask the university to set up on an emergency basis what became the

United States Armed Forces Institute (USAFI), which quickly set in motion an enormous correspondence instruction program for persons in active service in the various branches of military service. After the war, USAFI remained in Madison, off-campus and independently run, but it still relies heavily on Wisconsin correspondence instruction, and every year more than 100,000 servicemen are enrolled in USAFI courses taught under the Wisconsin contract.

The impact on the campus is highly visible, in the shape of bulging mailbags that deposit up to 2,000 lessons a day from either USAFI or the correspondence courses upon the Extension Division, which in turn relies upon some 450 faculty members, graduate students, and townspeople to correct the papers. Other faculty members are involved in designing courses, either at the USAFI-level, or noncredit and credit courses geared to the Wisconsin curriculum. Altogether, counting the USAFI contract students, the correspondence branch services 163,000 mailbox students yearly.

The Extension Division was called upon to cope with the educational bulge of returning veterans in the postwar years of the 1940's, and during those hectic days more than thirty extension centers were set up around the state. A smaller number of larger, permanent centers have since become the full-fledged University of Wisconsin Center System—a coordinate partner with the other major components of the university. These centers have been used as models in India to help meet the educational needs of that nation.

The reputation and educational efforts of the Extension Division are worldwide. It has been studied, copied, and used as a model and a training resource in dozens of nations of the world. Both its subject matter specialists and its educational process experts have girdled the globe. Its students in any recent year have represented from one-half to two-thirds of the new nations of the world. Wedemeyer, sought after as a correspondence study expert, has aided Venezuela in establishing a correspondence educational program vital to its isolated hinterland. Staff from the division's Institute of Governmental Affairs have consulted and taught in Nigeria and India. Brazil, Argentina, Korea, and Uganda are a few countries where on-site efforts by the division's subject matter experts have been undertaken.

The Extension Division also operates the International Cooperative Training Center, housed in the Extension building, under a contract with AID. The Center provides training in cooperatives to adult students from the developing nations, who are sent to Madison either as AID participants, or as nominees by their governments or local cooperatives, or else attend privately.

The Center came into being because the Cooperative League of the U.S.A., of which former Congressman H. Jerry Voorhis is director, persuaded AID to set up a central source to provide information and training for people from all over the world who were coming to the United States to find out how to organize and operate successful cooperatives of all kinds. As a state Wisconsin has been a leader in cooperatives and its university was a logical choice when the Center was established in 1962. Students attend seminars, in groups of eighteen to fifty at a time, which last for sixteen weeks, including eleven weeks of classes and four weeks of field observation work in cooperatives in Wisconsin and elsewhere in the United States. In the autumn of 1965, the courses were lengthened to twenty weeks. Up to June, 1965, the Center had trained 513 participants from fifty-five different countries.

Many other shorter training courses are conducted by units of the Extension Division. The Center for Advanced Study in Organizational Science, the Institute of Governmental Affairs, and the School for Workers are regular hosts for large numbers of foreign trainees sponsored by AID, the U.S. Department of Labor, and other national government agencies. Foundations increasingly call upon the division for overseas work.

Experience in handling an expanding demand for education has made the Extension Division extremely receptive to new teaching ideas and experimental techniques, approaches of which some of the more conservative academics in the university itself are hardly aware.

Many small high schools in Wisconsin do not have foreign language teachers. Concern for equalizing educational opportunities has led the division to offer French, German, Russian, Spanish, and Latin by correspondence instruction, supplemented by monthly visits to the classrooms of the instructors and by tape recordings. In some schools, the division utilizes the tele-lecture technique, by which a telephone and an amplifier make the teacher as accessible to a group of students as if he were in the room. Tests show no statistically significant difference in achievement in comparison with regular classroom methods. As schools become capable of providing their own instruction, they cease to depend upon the Extension Division.

IV

Wisconsin's immersion in the international field and its development of administrative procedures to deal more adequately with the problems inherent in international activities were directly influenced by two factors, one external, one internal.

The outside influence was the catalytic intimation from the Ford Foundation that it was prepared to grant substantial sums to certain universities in order to help step up their international programs. "There is no question," recalls Vice President Clodius, "that the Ford Foundation approach helped us to pull our university structure together."

Wisconsin was asked by the foundation late in 1960 to prepare a survey of its existing international programs and to indicate its willingness to shoulder the financial burden of increased costs after a foundation grant, if forthcoming, had ceased. In October, 1960, the university had appointed a

Committee on Area, Language, and International Programs, which included many of the campus internationalists, such as Harrington, then Vice President for Academic Affairs, Clodius, Clifford Liddle, of the School of Education, and Chester S. Chard, an East Asian specialist. Henry B. Hill, a historian, was appointed chairman of the committee. By March, 1961, the committee had compiled an impressive itemization of the programs of an international nature then in operation at the university, some twenty in number, and at the close of the year the compilation was used as the basis for a request to the Ford Foundation for support for the university's area programs, support for comparative and international studies, and support to increase the involvement of the professional schools in international studies.

With the submission made to the foundation, the original committee was discharged, and in January, 1962, the university established the Office of International Studies and Programs. Hill, who had headed the committee, was installed as Coordinator of the office. Two months later came the news that the Ford Foundation had granted Wisconsin $1,200,000 to support its international activities, and a Ford Advisory Committee of faculty members was appointed to allocate the funds among the program components.

The internal changes were simultaneously at work. Wisconsin, which had tried both home-grown and imported presidents in the course of its often stormy history, had been under the control of distinguished scientists as its presidents since the close of World War II. When Edwin B. Fred, a Wisconsin bacteriology professor, retired as president in 1958 he was succeeded by a native university product, Conrad A. Elvehjem, who had graduated from Wisconsin and served as chairman of its biochemistry department. The social sciences and humanities faculty members had long chafed under the succession of science presidents, and their choice for the post in 1958 had been Harrington, whom President Fred had brought in to his administration as a special assistant to strengthen the influences of the social sciences and humanities. Acknowledging this undercurrent of faculty feeling, President Elvehjem made Harrington his Vice President for Academic Affairs and later Vice President of the university. A specialist in U.S. foreign relations, Harrington did what he could to encourage greater university involvement in the world around it.

In the summer of 1962 President Elvehjem died, and the "Young Turks" on the faculty who had pushed for Harrington in 1958 put on a whirlwind campaign among fellow faculty members, the Regents, and the public. On the day of Elvehjem's funeral the Regents announced that their search for a successor had ended almost as soon as it had begun—Fred H. Harrington was appointed the university's fourteenth president. Clodius, one of the "Young Turks" who had supported Harrington, was made Vice President for Academic Affairs, with prime responsibility for the university's international affairs.

Office of International Studies and Programs

Under the Harrington-Clodius administration, the Office of International Studies and Programs was enlarged, and provided with project assistants and staff. "In no time at all," recalls Professor Hill, "items which formerly went into the President's waste basket began coming in my direction—and they've been coming ever since."

The office's description of itself is that "as an administrative unit, it provides the structure necessary to coordinate the financial and administrative aspects of planning and development as well as providing the necessary support for individuals and groups participating in area programs. In addition, the Office of International Studies and Programs presents an integrated approach to the foundations, government, and other agencies to initiate and gain financial support for research in international studies."

The office allocates funds provided by the Ford Foundation grant. Until it was phased out of existence in the spring of 1965, an Advisory Committee of the Ford Foundation Grant—operating in conjunction with Hill's office—authorized expenditures of funds to initiate new projects as well as those of the existing area studies programs or to support worthy research projects undertaken by various departments or individual members. The Ford Advisory Committee gave advice and made policy, and while it usually followed the line of Hill's office, did not regard itself as a rubber stamp.

The office has made at least two surveys of faculty personnel interested in current or proposed international programs, and in 1963 published a *Directory of Faculty Personnel with International Academic Interests,* probably the first of its kind undertaken by an American university. The plan is to issue the directory every two years, with yearly supplements. Among other duties performed by the office is the coordination of the lectures and other activities of the American Universities Field Staff, of which Wisconsin is a member university.

In January, 1965, an Office of Foreign Visitors began to function under the jurisdiction of the Office of International Studies and Programs. Its purpose is to coordinate the details—conferences, meetings, visits throughout the state, housing arrangements, and campus welcomes—of the visits of foreign faculty and other foreign visitors (nonstudent) to the university.

Structurally, Hill's office is attached to the office of the Chancellor, Robben Fleming. However, for all-university, all-campus matters, Hill reports directly to Vice President Clodius. Administered out of Hill's office are the Junior Year Abroad programs (managed by a part-time assistant in Hill's office) and the funds for the various area programs. Hill has a staff of one assistant, Professor Edward E. Werner, who remains on a joint, 50:50 basis with the School of Commerce, plus five project assistants and the usual secretarial services. The office itself occupies a modest two-room suite in the new Social Science building and nearby are five tiny offices housing the various area studies and the Center for Developing Nations.

The Center for Developing Nations

The Center for Developing Nations was launched at Wisconsin in the autumn of 1964 as a reflection of faculty concern that the university required more adequate machinery to handle proposals arising from agencies outside the university and involving several faculty members and cutting across college or departmental lines. Late in 1962 the desire to achieve a more coordinated approach to the possibility of providing research and services for the underdeveloped nations led to the appointment by Clodius —at Hill's request—of a faculty committee representing most of the schools and departments likely to be involved in overseas contracts. It went through several name changes—the Committee on Tropical Public Service, the Committee on Public Services of Newly Developed Nations, and finally the Committee on Research and Services for the Newly Developing Nations. Part of its mission was to come up with recommendations which would be incorporated in the proposal which a consortium of four Midwest universities were to submit to the Ford Foundation for a grant to assist them in promoting cooperative efforts in carrying out overseas programs, but at the same time the Wisconsin committee went on to recommend that their university take a greater part in the realm of foreign technical assistance. In its report to the university on January 1, 1964, the committee spelled out the rationale for committing Wisconsin to increased assistance in the underdeveloped areas, set forth the conditions ùnder which faculty members should serve overseas and recommended the establishment by the university of a Center for Research and Services for the Newly Developing Nations.

The recommendation of a Center was accepted by the university and in the spring of 1964 Vice President Clodius named a new committee, with a fortunately shortened title—the Committee on Developing Nations—to act as an advisory body for the new Center, to perform as a screening committee for the university's relationships with the Midwest Universities Consortium, and to encourage interested faculty members in the development of individual or group programs of research and service in the newly developing nations. At the outset of the academic year 1964-65, the Center for Developing Nations was formally established, with Professor Edward E. Werner, Hill's assistant, as its director.

The Center is intended to work closely with Hill's office, but without being part of it, a jurisdictional arrangement made easier by its physical location as part of Hill's office and by the dual role played by Werner as Center director and Hill's assistant. Since the Center's formation Werner has, among other things, compiled a resume of Wisconsin's international projects, expanded a roster of faculty with international interests—which will be combined with similar information from the other schools belonging to the Midwest Universities Consortium—and contributed to the publication of a revised directory of faculty with international experience and interests. Werner also assisted the School of Education in planning a five-day orientation program for faculty members participating in the teacher education project in Northern Nigeria, a precautionary procedure which is overlooked or downgraded to a low priority by most universities and colleges engaged in overseas assignments. It is Werner's intention to do a follow-up survey with the participants on their return from Nigeria to determine how effective the original briefing proved to be.

For the future, Werner has plans for a graduate seminar for returning Peace Corps volunteers, scheduled for the autumn of 1965, and the preparation of an administrative field manual covering many aspects of overseas operations. Mindful of the need to communicate with University of Wisconsin personnel on overseas projects, he is also exploring the idea of a Center newsletter. As Center director, Werner also assists Hill in working closely with faculty members and groups in advising on proposals for submission to the Midwest Universities Consortium and other agencies.

The University of Wisconsin–Milwaukee

The administrative structure which has evolved at the University of Wisconsin to deal with its international dimension includes the separate but equal Office of International Studies and Programs at the University of Wisconsin–Milwaukee.

The University of Wisconsin–Milwaukee—formed in 1956 by a merger of the Milwaukee Extension Division with the Wisconsin State College and, later, Milwaukee Downer Seminary—is now to all intents an autonomous operation, both in its academic offerings and in its approach to international activities.

A 1964 report of the Regent's Committee on the Future of the University of Wisconsin–Milwaukee declared that "it is the aim of the University of Wisconsin–Milwaukee to achieve major national university status within the next fifteen years." President Harrington predicts that, if adequate faculty and facilities are provided, the Milwaukee campus within ten to fifteen years will enroll as many students as now are enrolled at Madison. At present there are just over 12,000 enrolled at Wisconsin–Milwaukee, and of these up to 250 are foreign students or short-term visitors. About two hundred faculty members out of a resident faculty of some seven hundred have been involved in international work. The curriculum has a pronounced international flavor. Excluding courses in foreign languages (and there are nearly one hundred of them), the Wisconsin–Milwaukee catalog lists about seventy-five individual courses in which large emphasis is placed on the world outside the United States.

As a relatively new university and therefore less encumbered with vested academic interests, it was far easier to establish the international dimension on the Milwaukee campus than at Madison. In general, the Milwaukee faculty represents a younger generation, educated in the war and postwar years, and therefore more aware of world affairs. In addition, however, Wisconsin–Milwaukee deliberately decided a few years ago that the shortest route to achieve major university status was to concentrate on its international commitments. The Regent's Committee report specifically listed as one of the "new directions" for the university the following: "UWM will give special attention to international studies and programs. Research and service programs must involve UWM faculty and students directly in the problems of government, economic life, and cultural development in countries beyond our borders, particularly the non-Western cultures."

The result of this, over the course of a few short years, has been a vigorous pursuit of programs and activities which emphasize the university's institutional concern with the world around it.

The Milwaukee campus is the location of one of the four national year-round Peace Corps training centers in the United States. Under contract to conduct six training programs annually, Wisconsin–Milwaukee up to December, 1964, had completed a total of thirteen of them, and had turned out more volunteers for more countries than any other university. Aided by some $2 million in Federal funds, the university has fully committed itself to Peace Corps training: it has adapted an apartment building on campus to house the P.C. volunteers as well as apartment facilities for the full-time language staff engaged in P.C. training. The P.C. training contract runs to 1968.

The university's association with the Peace Corps extends beyond the actual training of volunteers. It has set up a program of special assistantships, internships, and fellowships for qualified graduate and undergraduate students who have successfully completed P.C. training and service, and it awards academic credit for Peace Corps work overseas. In the autumn of 1964 Peace Corps director R. Sargent Shriver announced that Wisconsin–Milwaukee would undertake with the Corps cooperative research programs, overseas project development and supervision by faculty specialists, and the establishment on the campus of new sequences of undergraduate and graduate studies to prepare Americans for effective overseas service. Only one other university (Hawaii) thus far is participating in this new P.C. program.

The School of Education, one of the strongest elements emerging from the 1956 merger, has played a leading role in Wisconsin–Milwaukee's international activities. In the academic years 1962-65 it has undertaken no fewer than twenty-eight different programs, most of them in the Latin American area. The 1964-65 school year was the third of the School's training programs for the development of comprehensive high schools in

Venezuela and the Dominican Republic, a project supported by AID and the Ministry of Education of Venezuela. It carries on a continuing relationship with the University of Antioquia in Medellín, Columbia, exchanging faculty and materials; it operates a summer faculty exchange with the University of Puerto Rico; and it provides M.A. training for students from the University of Ceara, in Brazil. Under an arrangement with the U.S. Office of Education, the School puts on three-month seminars for foreign teachers brought to the United States under the International Teacher Development program, and it plays host to a number of short-term projects under which foreign visitors come to Milwaukee to study classroom techniques, educational administration, and community relations.

In 1965 Wisconsin–Milwaukee was designated an undergraduate NDEA Latin American Language and Area Center. This new Center will complement the NDEA graduate center in Latin American Language and Area Studies at Madison.

Wisconsin–Milwaukee is also the site of the Center for Advanced Study in Organization Science, a special unit devoted to research, consulting, and midcareer studies, which was founded in 1954 at the University of Chicago as the Center for Programs in Government Administration. Moved to Milwaukee in 1962 and renamed, the Center puts on national and regional programs of continuing education for upper-level government executives. Under AID contracts, the Center has so far put on two training courses for administrators from developing countries, the first, in 1963, for Afro-Asian administrators, and the second the following year for Indian administrators.

The speed with which Wisconsin–Milwaukee has established itself as an international-minded university owes much to the presence there of the Institute for World Affairs, which was begun in 1960 as a cooperative undertaking of Wisconsin–Milwaukee and the university's Extension Division to stimulate the interest of students, faculty, and the community in the field of world affairs. The Institute also assists and coordinates world affairs programming by community groups throughout the state.

The Institute's former director, Donald R. Shea, is a member of the Wisconsin–Milwaukee political science faculty, and it was in part due to his success in giving the Institute a country-wide reputation that the Peace Corps and other government agencies turned to the burgeoning Milwaukee campus to carry on their training programs. In October, 1963, in recognition of this role, Shea was named Dean of International Studies and Programs at Wisconsin–Milwaukee and an Office of International Studies and Programs was organized as a counterpart to the Hill office at Madison. In August, 1964, Hill's title was altered to correspond to that of Shea, Dean of International Studies and Programs.

The Madison and Milwaukee international offices are coequal in structure, and autonomous in operation, but efforts are made to dovetail the evolution of their programs. A measure of coordination is achieved by the fact that Shea reports through the Chancellor of Wisconsin–Milwaukee to Vice President Clodius at Madison, and the two offices keep contact through phone consultation and frequent conferences. Joint projects have not figured in the activities of the two offices—except for a certain amount of joint recruiting for some overseas projects and a joint inventory of faculty on both campuses engaged in international activities, currently being conducted—but both the Madison campus and Wisconsin—Milwaukee have plans for increasing the cooperation in the international field between the two institutions.

The Wisconsin Approach to Coordination

At both the Madison and Milwaukee campuses the administration is squarely behind the university's increasing internationalism. In his public speeches and private meetings with the faculty, President Harrington underscores the university's commitment to the world. Vice President Clodius, who retains overall responsibility for international matters because of his own personal interest, says: "The university is international and everybody knows it. The problem is no longer one of arousing the interest of departments or colleges. Budget is the only limiting factor in undertaking more international activities."

At the Madison campus, older, larger, and more permissive than the newer institution at Milwaukee, the presence of the Office of International Studies and Programs appears to the outside observer to be less visible and its impact on the university less noticeable than at Milwaukee. This, explains Dean Hill, is in keeping with the Wisconsin tradition. His office deliberately underplays its potential centralizing role because, as he puts it, it is part of the Wisconsin system that "all international programs are faculty-initiated, faculty-oriented, and, as far as substance is concerned, faculty-directed."

The role of the administration, particularly that of his office, says Hill, should be confined to "housekeeping." The basic idea of the office, he feels, "is to make life for those faculty members involved in international activities as fruitful and simple as possible." The Hill office does not intend to administer or direct any program. "It is university policy," says Hill, "that international programs should be decentralized to the maximum and administration reduced to an irreducible minimum." This is in keeping with the Wisconsin tradition of a "lean" administration. In time, hopes Clodius, the university hopes to "decentralize to the point where every college and department in it will regard the international area as its own responsibility and will not expect some central office to run the ball for it."

In the meantime, however, it is admitted that until that ideal is realized some mechanism is required to coordinate and facilitate the activities of the university in the international field, even if only to provide information on a need-to-know basis for the administration. And some of those engaged in international activities at the university admit that departments and units occasionally miss the opportunity to benefit from the cross-fertilization of ideas and experiences that come with a somewhat more centralized direction.

In response to these needs the university in June, 1965, moved a step closer to centralization. The two advisory faculty bodies which had existed in the wings of the international programs, the Advisory Committee of the Ford Foundation Grant and the Committee on Developing Nations, which had been mainly concerned with screening proposals for submission to the Midwest Universities Consortium and other agencies, were phased out of existence. In their place is a new, overall advisory body, the Committee on Plans and Policies for International Activities, with Dean Hill as its chairman, which will survey and inventory on a continuing basis the University of Wisconsin's role in the international field. This body will have as its first major responsibility the preparation of a submission to the Ford Foundation for a renewal of Wisconsin's 1962 grant for international support. Within the overall committee will be a "group," functioning as a subcommittee in all but name, drawn from those with interest in the Center for Developing Nations, which will have prime responsibility for projects with the Midwest Universities Consortium and other development activities.

The university is also making an attempt at tighter centralization in the acceptance of government or foundation contracts. Departmental contracts for outside services, such as those with AID, must be approved by an assistant to the Vice President. It is understood that the Hill office will review such contracts in advance and that no such contract will be signed without Hill's approval. Although the Office of International Studies and Programs does not tell the School of Agriculture, for example, how to administer a contract in, say, Nigeria, Hill is more and more able—because of his contacts with government agencies and foundations—to point out research opportunities and other details which would otherwise be missed.

The next correlative step, which Hill has in mind for the academic year of 1965-66, is to convene a monthly meeting of all the campus coordinators, the administrators of AID and other service contracts, with the directors of the various area studies programs. Through this mechanism, Hill hopes to bring about a closer relationship between overseas programs and the university's area studies, by which students in area studies will be utilized on the research functions of overseas undertakings.

That Dean Hill reports to Chancellor Fleming and to Vice President Clodius on all-university, all-campus affairs and has the ear of President Harrington is known across the campus. Plans for the new administration tower which will be built on campus include an entire floor set aside for the Office of International Studies and Programs, directly under the offices of the President, Vice President, and Chancellor. "The faculty knows that the Program Office has direct connections to the central administration and that it is to the Program Office that the administration turns to for advice on international matters," says Hill. A specialist in French history, Hill is a respected scholar on campus: he has made a point of retaining his faculty status, but he has time now for only one seminar course. Insofar as these factors carry weight with an otherwise independent-minded faculty, they assist in the quiet performance of his office's role.

President Harrington sums up the Wisconsin approach to an administrative apparatus to handle its international dimension as one based on "coordination, liaison, and agreement, instead of on coercion and direction." He believes that the Wisconsin approach offers a viable alternative, particularly to institutions with strong liberal arts foundations, to tight, centralized control from the top.

"It has taken us longer to get organized than at some universities," he concedes, "but we believe that as a result of our approach our faculty members are as personally committed and the university is as genuinely involved as any in the United States. International activities are accepted at Wisconsin as part of the total university."

*   *   *   *   *

Of the six universities included in this survey, the University of Wisconsin is the only one which is both the official state university and the land-grant university of the state. As such, it has a long tradition of service to the community.

With this heritage, it might have been expected that Wisconsin would have emerged earlier as a leader in international service, in a continuation of this long-established tradition. Instead Wisconsin, relative to its size and competence, has lagged behind such institutions as Michigan State in shouldering technical assistance assignments overseas, and it is only in comparatively recent years that the university's professional schools have entered the technical assistance field in a major way.

As a university in which faculty influence has always been powerful, if not predominant, Wisconsin's experience underlines the need to enlist faculty members at all levels in any progress towards internationalizing the institution. Faculty resistance may have been a factor in the university's delayed entry into international assistance programs. More certainly, a respect for faculty sensitivities caused the administration to move cautiously in developing a centralized structure to coordinate the university's international activities. And yet a good part of the initiative for internationalization at Wisconsin—for instance, the newly founded Center for the Developing Nations—appears to have been generated at faculty level.

One result of this dyarchical approach to internationalizing is that a certain amount of time and several opportunities have been lost. Wisconsin's School of Agriculture, for example, which was once preeminent in its field of agricultural research and agricultural extension, is a late starter in international agricultural development work.

Over the course of the twelve months between the autumn of 1964 and the autumn of 1965, however, the University of Wisconsin moved farther along toward real all-campus coordination of its international activities than it had during the four-year span from 1960 to 1964. The administration and faculty may look forward to the day when central direction will wither away, when all colleges and departments of the institution are so thoroughly involved in the world that they will move about in their own international orbits. But until that time both administration and faculty seem tacitly to recognize that the university will go through a period of more rather than less centralized direction from the top in the international field.

CORNELL

I

In the roster of American educational institutions, Cornell University—which celebrated its centennial in April, 1965—represents an almost unique merger of two great educational traditions, those of the European humanistic-oriented university and the American land-grant college.

This merger embodies in Cornell today the interaction of the approach of its two founders—the practical vision of Ezra Cornell and the intellectual creativity of Andrew D. White.

White was American born, but a product of an older culture: devoted to learning, steeped in the arts and humanities, he was a professor who lived in the world of ideas. He had long dreamed of founding an educational institution that would be "a worthy American university . . . a nucleus around which liberally minded men of learning . . . could cluster, a center from which ideas and men shall go forth to bless the nation during ages."

Ezra Cornell, who came from humble beginnings and had little formal education, was a practical and energetic businessman imbued with a Quaker conscience. Having made a fortune through his investments in Western Union and other enterprises, he concluded: "My greatest care is how to spend this large income to do the greatest good." His decision was to use his personal fortune for the support of education, but he determined to build an educational institution which would turn away from the pattern established by earlier American universities, with their sectarian sponsorship and curriculum copied from an English college. Instead of pursuing conventional academic ideas, he proposed to offer *any* intellectually qualified person instruction in *any* subject, an aspiration which now appears on the university's great seal: "I would found an institution where any person can find instruction in any study."

White and Cornell met when both were serving in the Senate of New York State at Albany. There they conceived the plan to build a university together. The Morrill Land Grant Act of 1862 had provided for gifts of public land to colleges that would teach agriculture and the mechanic arts. White and Cornell won the approval of the state legislature for their plan to combine the public land awarded New York State under the federal act with private resources contributed by Ezra Cornell, initially half a million dollars and his farm overlooking Cayuga Lake at Ithaca, New York.

Cornell University was chartered in 1865. It opened three years later, with twenty-six professors on the faculty and 412 students, and with Andrew D. White as its first president. A startling innovation in education, it brought new fields of study into its curriculum and shattered the myth that there was only one revealed course of study suitable for university curricula. It offered courses in agriculture, engineering, and veterinary medicine on a level of equality with such traditional subjects as classics and mathematics. It was the first nontechnical school to introduce engineering courses. It offered the nation's first courses in American history and had the first university press. In this century, Cornell continued its academic pioneering by founding the first schools of electrical engineering, hotel administration, nutrition, and industrial and labor relations.

The result today is a university of national and international stature. In size, compared with other American universities, Cornell is medium. It has a student body of some 13,000 from fifty states and eighty-four nations, and a faculty numbering more than 1,650.

The structure of the university is a unique mix of public and private support. Cornell is essentially a privately endowed university under the direction of an eighty-man Board of Trustees, but with four of its fifteen schools and colleges (Agriculture, Home Economics, Veterinary Medicine, and Industrial and Labor Relations) operated under contract as units of the State University of New York. Coeducational and nonsectarian, it is both the land-grant university of New York State and a member of the Ivy League. The main campus is at Ithaca, with the medical college and nursing school in New York City, an aeronautical research laboratory in Buffalo, and research and field stations scattered around the world.

II

The international dimension of Cornell became visible early in its history. In 1868, the university's first year of operation, the student body included five students from abroad, one of them from Russia. As early as 1870, Chinese was being taught at the university. In 1918 a Cornell alumnus, Charles Wason, a successful businessman who became interested in China and directed his book dealer to collect every book in English on China, gave his unique collection to the University, along with a $50,000 endowment to add to the titles. This became the nucleus for what has now become one of the outstanding collections in the world of Chinese language material and material in other languages on China, Southeast Asia, and Japan.

Cornell's physical involvement overseas also developed far earlier than at most American universities. As the result of a personal relationship between the American faculty members of the University of Nanking in China and Cornell's department of plant breeding, a program was established in 1924 under which Cornell agricultural experts worked in China until 1931. Crop yields were increased and Chinese students were trained in genetics and plant breeding to carry on the improvement of crops. This was one of the pioneering cooperative efforts between universities directed toward increasing a nation's food supply, and was the first notable example of the university-based technical assistance programs which became the standard technique in dispensing U.S. foreign aid after World War II.

The Impact of World War II

To an even greater degree at Cornell than at most other American universities, World War II represented a time of challenge and focus in relation to international, and particularly non-Western, studies. Cornell became one of the institutions most deeply involved in the development of the U.S. Army's Specialized Training Program, which trained language and area specialists for the armed services. Cornell was one of the ten "core" campuses where the program was established in 1943. This experience, together with the existing research and teaching strength of the university in particular non-European areas, and the long-standing international inter- ests of many faculty in the agricultural and related schools, led to Cornell's taking a more definite and distinctive posture toward its own international involvement, and toward the postwar growth of area studies in particular, than was the case with many other American universities in the same period.

Two decisions taken near the war's end were of significance in this connection. The first was the development of a unified organizational pat- tern of teaching foreign languages and literature which remains almost unique in American universities. Instruction relies heavily on the oral-aural "spoken approach" developed in World War II. Under this program a division of Modern Languages, staffed almost entirely with trained linguists who work with ninety native-speaker "informants," is responsible for vir- tually all teaching of the twenty-two European and other modern languages currently taught on campus. All instruction is concentrated in an intensive one-year basic language course and in a second-year composition and con- versation course taught in the language. Literature courses are offered only in other departments: the respective departments of German, Romance, and Russian Literature and the department of Asian Studies for courses with reading and instruction in the given language or the division of Litera- ture (which offers no majors) for reading courses with reading based on translations.

The second decision, taken in 1946 but since superseded by expansion in other areas, was to concentrate the intensive development of Cornell's scholarly resources in the Asian field—on China, South Asia, and South- east Asia. While Asian Studies thus remains a major program at Cornell, subsequent decisions and faculty interests have expanded the university's programs into other geographic areas.

Field Stations Abroad: The Cornell Peru Project

The two decades following World War II brought expansion and diversi- fication of Cornell's international dimension, both on campus and overseas. The area studies programs, in part because of the unusually large role played by anthropologists and linguists in their development, have consistently involved a very strong overseas field research component which, in turn, attracted foundation support by the late 1940s and early 1950s. At that time, Cornell field stations were already established in Peru, the Philippines, India, Thailand, and Indonesia.

The Cornell Peru Project was unplanned and unanticipated, but over the period of the past dozen years it has developed as a remarkable experiment in social change and a prime example of the close relationship between theoretical and applied research. In the late 1940s, Cornell's department of sociology and anthropology received a grant from the Carnegie Corporation of New York to conduct comparative studies of technological change in India, Thailand, Canada, the southwestern United States, and Peru. The site chosen for study in Peru was the Andean *hacienda* of Vicos, a vast manor or estate of about 40,000 acres located in a valley known as the Callejón de Huaylas, some 250 miles northeast of the Peruvian capital city of Lima. Attached to the mountainside manor, but owning none of it, were 1,700 Quechua-speaking Indians who had been bound to the land as serfs or peons since early colonial times, living under a system that was near-feudal. A public manor, a type not uncommon in Peru, Vicos belonged to the state, and was rented out to the highest bidder every five or ten years. The renter, or *patrón,* usually absentee, held almost absolute economic, political, and judicial power over the area, and—because he did not own the land—was not inclined to improve it for the future. Each household on the manor, in return for the privilege of scrabbling out a bare subsistence from the rocky soil of the mountainside, had to contribute one peon to the manor's labor force for three days of each week, and also provide the manor with free services as cooks, watchmen, shepherds, household servants, and grooms. Most Vicosinos suffered from malnutrition, education was almost wholly lacking, and all hope had long since been drained from the community. All protest movements had been squelched by a coalition of the landlords, the clergy, and the police. After some four hundred years of their marginal existence, devoid of any responsibility for handling their affairs, the Indians of Vicos had an antipathy to change.

For two years a Peruvian anthropologist, Dr. Mario Vazquez, lived in Vicos and conducted a study of its social system as part of the overall Cornell study. During this time it became evident that there would be no social change to study in Vicos unless some outside force initiated it. Late in 1951, through a fortuitous circumstance—the industrial firm renting Vicos on a ten-year lease went bankrupt when the lease still had five years to run—this opportunity presented itself to Cornell. The university assumed the role of *patrón,* rented the *hacienda* for the five-year period, and determined to conduct its own experiment in modernization. In collaboration with the Peruvian Indianist Institute, Cornell embarked on a program of induced technical and social change to see whether an unproductive, highly dependent manor could be transformed into a productive, independent, self-governing community able to take its place in a modern state.

The Cornell Peru Project, or the Vicos project, as it became known, was under the founding direction of a Cornell anthropologist, Dr. Allan R. Holmberg, a man of long experience in Latin America and interested in the plight of the Andean Indians. The problem he confronted—whether the Indians of Vicos could be helped to develop economically and socially— had to be solved without any large infusion of funds and without a great number of personnel. In fact, no more than two Cornell graduates and two Peruvians were at any one time assigned to the *hacienda* for purposes of the experiment.

The program of change centered on four major areas: economics and technology, nutrition and health, education, and social organization. Some of the worst features of Vicos life—the free labor services performed by the serfs—were eliminated at once. By introducing modern farming methods, farm production was almost doubled and money made available from it for other changes. A clinic and modern health practices were introduced. Schooling was made available, so that most of the children instead of a mere handful attended. In time, control of Vicos was gradually shifted to an elected group of *hacienda* residents. By 1957, when Cornell's lease expired and it willingly stepped aside as *patrón,* Vicos had a fairly solid economic underpinning, the wealth base had been considerably enlarged, and the members of the community had assumed complete responsibility for their community affairs. After four hundred years of peonage, the residents were substantially masters of their own land and lives—almost.

Five more years elapsed before their accomplishments were made secure. In 1957, when Cornell's lease ran out, the university recommended to the Peruvian government that it expropriate the property from its title-holders, the Public Benefit Society of Huaraz, in favor of the indigenous inhabitants. Local power elites, determined to keep the land from the Indians, threw every possible legal block in the way of the title transfer, and even the central government, many high officials of which were *hacendados* themselves, hesitated to alter the *status quo,* but after years of uncertainty the cumulative pressures exerted by Peruvian supporters of Vicos and U.S. government officials prevailed and agreement was reached for the direct sale of the manor to the Vicosinos. Thus the community actually gained control of its land and affairs in July, 1962.

When Cornell gladly relinquished its lease of the manor in 1957, it continued its role of advisor to the Vicos Indians and to the Peruvian Ministry of Labor and Indian Affairs. Cornell Peru Project personnel stayed on in the revitalized community in the role of scientific advisors and observers. Project research continued to be oriented toward the informational needs of the Peruvian government. Thus when Peru in 1959 created the National Plan for Integrating the Aboriginal Population, superseding the Peruvian Indianist Institute, Cornell continued to collaborate with it. This new agency has carried on an official government program of development at Vicos since Cornell ceased being the manor *patrón,* and has adopted Vicos as a pilot project for other communities.

The initial success at Vicos brought the Cornell Peru Project additional foundation support for an expanded research program in the Andean region in 1959, and Cornell at that time undertook investigations designed to enable it to generalize about Peru on a national scale. The project at Vicos served first as a field training program for anthropologists and other social scientists from Cornell, but it has also provided an anthropological field station where scientists and social scientists from a number of other institutions could collect data pertinent to a wide range of specialties. The project has always operated with an "open door" at Vicos. Peru's largest university, the University of San Marcos, has given its students training at Vicos and other communities under study by Cornell Peru Project personnel. The Peruvian National Agricultural University, located at La Molina, near Lima, has also begun to make use of the Vicos field station in its student training programs in recent years.

The Carnegie Corporation, which financed the bulk of the development work of the Cornell Peru Project, undertook in 1960 to finance another experiment in undergraduate education in world affairs. In order to expose a number of American university students to the harsh realities of rural Latin America, the foundation provided Cornell, Harvard, and Columbia (joined in 1962 by the University of Illinois) with funds to conduct an interuniversity summer field program. The basic idea was to have selected undergraduates participate in ongoing social science field projects abroad. Cornell's anthropological study in the Callejón de Huaylas of Peru provides the intensive field experience desired for these students from the participating American universities.

Owing in large measure to the extensive work of Cornell in Peru, the university was chosen as the center for the training of members of the Peace Corps to be sent to that country. Since the summer of 1962 approximately 380 Peace Corps volunteers have studied at Cornell. In the autumn of 1962 the Cornell Peru Project contracted with the Peace Corps to study the impact of its volunteer programs upon rural Andean Indian communities. In 1963 the project also undertook for AID to study the feasibility of Cornell's assuming an Indian integration program in Peru, Bolivia, and Ecuador.

Field Stations Abroad: The Cornell-Los Banos Program

Cornell's tradition of international interests pervades the whole university, but it has always been especially strong in the College of Agriculture. At the beginning of the century, Cornell had attracted agricultural students from eleven foreign countries, and over the past half century there has been a steady increase in the number of foreign agriculture students, especially from Asia, the earliest of them stimulated by scholarships from the Boxer

Indemnity Fund and the services of one of Cornell's presidents as chairman of the first Philippine Commission. Today, about one third of the foreign students attending Cornell are in agriculture, and one out of every three foreign graduate students at Cornell studies in the College of Agriculture.

With this background, it was to be expected that the most extensive postwar program in which Cornell has been engaged overseas was a project of the College of Agriculture. This was the Cornell-Los Banos project, financed initially by the U. S. International Cooperation Administration and later by AID, in which the College of Agriculture of the University of the Philippines at Los Banos, which had been devastated by World War II, was rebuilt and strengthened for effective service to the Philippines and other countries in Southeast Asia. Between 1952 and 1960, fifty-one U.S. professors—thirty-five from Cornell, including seven department heads, and nine who were Cornell-trained—served in the Philippines for a year or longer. In addition, eighty-three faculty members from Los Banos were sent abroad for additional training and a majority of them studied at Cornell. An experiment station was established, teaching programs were improved, and the Los Banos College of Agriculture was revitalized—advances intended to benefit the entire economy of the Philippines.

The Center for International Studies

By the mid-1950s, apart from its commitments in Peru and the Philippines, Cornell had projects underway in such diverse fields as overseas rural extension and international legal studies.

About this time the university's Social Science Research Center—still in existence—held a series of interdisciplinary faculty seminars. Out of these discussions came an awareness of the increasing involvement of Cornell in international programs, the widespread commitments of departments and colleges of the university, and of the obvious gaps which existed in the planning and coordination of these activities. Within the university there was a growing faculty concern that too much international involvement might strain its resources, and a disposition to make certain that whatever international commitments Cornell entered upon would fit in with the overall academic objectives of the university, the training of scholars and research.

This campus concern led to the formation of a Cornell Faculty Committee on International Affairs, and the committee's recommendation—a resolution calling for the creation of a Center for International Studies—was approved by the faculty council in May, 1961, and reported to the Board of Trustees soon after. On July 1, 1961, the Center came into being, and Professor Mario Einaudi, chairman of the department of government, assumed the position of director.

This concern within the Cornell family coincided roughly in time with a suggestion by the Ford Foundation that, as a general practice in the future, universities should present their requests for financial support as a development plan for the entire international component rather than as piecemeal requests for funds for individual projects.

Immediately upon its creation, the Center for International Studies began negotiations with officers and staff of the Ford Foundation on behalf of Cornell. The Center assumed the responsibility for presenting a single comprehensive request to the foundation for assistance in making international studies a permanent part of the university's academic programs. Under a Ford Foundation program initiated in 1960, twelve other universities had previously received general grants to strengthen international studies.

During the summer of 1961 the staff of the Center met daily with members of the Cornell community concerned with activities directly or potentially eligible for support from the foundation, and a consolidated application for financial support was presented in the autumn of 1961. Further negotiations took place, and on March 23, 1962, the Ford Foundation announced a grant of $3,250,000 to Cornell. This was to be used over five- to ten-year periods for the support of international programs and to be administered under the general supervision of the Center for International Studies. Most of the grant funds were earmarked: $950,000 over a ten-year period was made available for the support of the Southeast Asia program; $800,000 over a ten-year period was for the support of the China program; $800,000 over a five-year period was for support of Cornell's program in International Agricultural Development; and $700,000 over a five-year period was for direct use by the Center and for the support of other programs relating to non-Western areas. The grant funds were to be used for new faculty positions, faculty research, travel, compensation for visiting scholars, research assistants, library expansion, fellowships, publications, and administrative support.

III

Cornell's current international involvement covers a multiplicity of academic programs, with allied research projects, service contracts, and foundation-supported activities. To a very large extent, they have developed from concerns of the various disciplines, colleges and professional schools of the university and are a natural outgrowth of the historical development of Cornell. Taken together, they reflect an immersion in international and cross-cultural affairs which now covers a good part of the university.

Area Studies

Area studies at Cornell are discipline-based, research-oriented, graduate programs for training largely in the behavioral sciences. The essential components are disciplinary depth, multidisciplinary breadth, and language competence.

On the assumption that there is no substitute for vigorous disciplinary training, it is in a discipline in which the student receives his degree. Area studies comprise a minor program in a disciplinary field. The area program is multidisciplinary, in order to provide the student with the broad background and understanding necessary to do research in a complex society other than his own. Knowledge of the language which is the native tongue and literary medium of the people being studied is considered essential both for research and as a key to the acts and thought processes of that society.

An area study committee at Cornell is composed of members from the various disciplines and fields who have specialities in the particular geographical area. The committees offer multidisciplinary seminars, and are responsible for seeing that there is the breadth of courses needed properly to round out an area program. The fact that Cornell's area programs are the cooperative effort of faculty members from diverse disciplines and professional schools has resulted in the programs receiving strong and sustained support from the regular departments of the university.

Faculty members are appointed in their respective departments and their teaching responsibilities are determined by the department. As a rule, faculty members at Cornell teach both undergraduate and graduate courses and courses within the geographical area specialty as well as other courses within their own discipline.

In general, area studies at Cornell are graduate programs, with minimal effect on undergraduate education. The exception is Asian Studies, in which the university offers an undergraduate major.

Research in the field is another important characteristic of the Cornell area programs. The university has developed and maintains bases in the Philippines, India, Indonesia, and Latin America for faculty and student research. Having faculty in areas of university interest assures supervision for graduate student field research.

The Latin American Program

The Latin American Program, while relatively new as a coordinated program, serves as a model of the broad program of studies, research, and service which the university would like to achieve in all its area studies.

The Latin American Committee is now composed of seventeen faculty members, drawn from four colleges and ten departments of the university. Thus it coordinates an existing complex of teaching, research, and overseas activities that originated in the several colleges and professional schools. In addition, the committee serves as a catalyst to stimulate the development of interest in, and commitment to, the study of Latin America in those segments of the university, and in those academic institutions throughout

New York State, where Latin America has not received primary attention. These catalytic activities include: (1) the encouragement of the appointment of Latin American specialists to faculty positions in various disciplines; (2) the provision of funds and staff services to expand the library's acquisition program in the Latin American field; (3) the allocation of research funds to faculty in fields not yet represented in the Latin American Program, thus encouraging research projects that might result in a continuing commitment to the Latin American field; (4) participation in the Columbia-Cornell-Harvard-Illinois summer field research program to interest promising undergraduates in Latin American studies; (5) the staffing of a summer seminar on Latin American studies for faculty members in New York state institutions interested in developing a competence in Latin American studies. The summer seminar is jointly sponsored by Cornell and the State University of New York's enterprising Office of Foreign Area Studies.

The Latin American Program is the teaching arm of the committee. Its course offerings constitute a minor field of concentration for graduate students seeking the M.A. or Ph.D. degree. It offers sixteen courses directly pertaining to the economy, polity, and society of Latin America, in addition to a full complement of instruction in the Spanish, Portuguese, and Quechua languages.

The committee elects a director to serve a three-year (renewable) term. The full committee meets monthly, but has several subcommittees to deal with curriculum, finance, library, lectures, and special events. All members of the committee are competent in the Spanish language, and all are eligible to serve as members of graduate student masters or doctoral committees, representing Latin American Studies.

The strength of the Latin American Committee on campus stems from the fact that it was a natural outgrowth of and a response to a felt need at the university. Throughout the 1950s more and more faculty members from various colleges at Cornell independently became involved in Latin American research and scholarly contacts. With their research tending to concentrate on the West coast of Latin America, particularly on the Vicos field station, the need for closer interrelation and cross-disciplinary exchanges of information became more apparent. On the administrative level, the personal contacts and knowledge acquired by one faculty member in Latin America could be immensely helpful to other faculty members about to embark upon research in the same area. Agricultural specialists discovered that it was difficult to deal with purely technical matters without benefit of the experience of social scientists. Social scientists found it difficult to cope with community problems without attention to agriculture. Within the social sciences, sociologists, labor relations specialists, and economists found that research in relatively unknown societies often required the theoretical and methodological skill of the sister disciplines as well as linguistic skill and awareness of historical processes.

By 1956 these concerns led Cornell to set up a planning committee on Latin America. Its study resulted in several important conclusions: (1) that an interdisciplinary area program of Latin American studies as a minor field would be desirable both for faculty and for graduate students; (2) that competence in one language would open doors to at least twenty separate political entities in Latin America; (3) that a certain amount of subarea concentration would be advantageous because much of Cornell's work had been in the Andean region.

In 1958 the committee proposed to the Graduate School that a Latin American Studies minor field be created, and this recommendation was formally accepted. In 1960 the program applied for Title VI NDEA support and was awarded four NDEA fellowships. With the addition of a specialist in Latin American history, the Latin American Studies program was officially announced in 1961. A program director was selected, and the first graduate students began their minors.

The position of strength achieved by the Latin American Program in a few short years was further shored up in June, 1964, when it was awarded a supplementary grant of $550,000 by the Ford Foundation to support the program for a three-year period, making possible a major expansion of research and graduate training. In 1965 the program was further strengthened by the establishment of a Latin American Language and Area Training Center under the NDEA.

Cornell's commitment to Latin American Studies was dramatically underlined when the university designated the academic year 1965-66 as the Cornell Latin American Year, a bold effort to focus the attention of the entire university community on a single dimension of Cornell's involvement with a major world area. This is first and foremost a conscious effort to achieve internal coordination and communication, to reinforce the conviction that the university's involvement in the area is the business of the whole university. If the Cornell Latin American Year is a success the university will in future make parallel efforts to direct its attention as a whole successively to other new dimensions in which it is engaged.

The extensive experience of Cornell faculty members in Latin America constitutes the base of the Latin American Year. Conferences, lectures, and seminars will treat significant contemporary political, economic, and social issues. Leading Latin American scholars, statesmen, and cultural representatives will visit the Ithaca campus. Art exhibits, concerts, and photographic displays will originate at Cornell and, in some instances, be circulated throughout the United States. Major publications relating to the program will be released during the year.

Asian Studies

Since 1870, when the first Chinese language course was taught at Cornell, the interests of the university in Asia have been greatly expanded.

Thus, while Latin American Studies may be broader in concept and while there is a medium-sized program in Soviet Studies and a developing interest in an African program, area studies at Cornell are naturally heavily centered in Asian Studies.

The department of Asian Studies in the College of Arts and Sciences serves to coordinate for the entire university the diversified and substantial academic resources for instruction, training, research, and publication on Asia, as these are developed in the several other departments and divisions of Cornell.

Cornell's concern with Asia includes agricultural development in China, Southeast Asia, and South Asia; applied work in linguistics and in anthropology in South Asia and Southeast Asia; city and regional planning and community development studies in India, Laos, and the Philippines; work in industrial and labor relations in Southeast Asia and India; research on demography in China and on nutrition and public health in South Asia and Southeast Asia; studies of educational development in modern China and of political socialization in Communist China; and, for New York state social studies teachers, a special summer program on Southeast Asia and China, conducted in cooperation with the S.U.N.Y. Office of Foreign Area Studies.

Since 1946 Cornell—building on its strengths—has concentrated the intensive development of its scholarly resources in the Asian field on China, South Asia, and Southeast Asia. As a means of strengthening its work on these contiguous and interrelated regions, the university maintains three multidisciplinary area and language programs—teaching, research, and administrative units of the department of Asian Studies.

Among the more than thirty faculty members of the department are specialists in anthropology, art, bibliography, economics, government, and international relations, history, history of art, linguistics, literature, psychology, public administration, and sociology. Other professors in the various divisions of the university who have a special knowledge of Asia also participate in the work of the department. Some of these (especially those in agricultural technology, nutrition, and similar fields) have had years of valuable experience in the Orient. Visiting experts, many from Asia and Europe, are regularly brought to the campus to supplement the work of the resident faculty in Asian Studies.

Under Title VI of the NDEA, three Asian language and area centers have been established at Cornell. The East Asian Language and Area Center deals with China and Japan; the South Asia Center with Ceylon, India, and Pakistan; and the Southeast Asian Center with all the countries of the intervening region.

An important function of the department of Asian Studies is to offer undergraduate courses in the languages, history, culture, and contemporary development of the countries of East, Southeast, and South Asia. Approximately 25 percent of the undergraduates in the College of Arts and Sciences elect at least one of these courses, as do many students from other colleges of the university. A few students each year are accepted as majors in Asian Studies with concentration usually in one of these areas—China, Japan, South Asia, or Southeast Asia.

Cornell and its department of Asian Studies have also developed both formal and informal extramural associations designed to facilitate the work of the staff and students. Notable among these is a unique British-American cooperative endeavor, embarked upon in 1962, which involves Cornell with two specialized schools of the University of London, the School of Oriental and African Studies (S.O.A.S.), and the London School of Economics and Political Science (L.S.E.). At Cornell the joint program involves the China Program and the Southeast Asia Program. Supported by American and British foundation grants, the project—known as the London-Cornell Project—is designed to develop research on social, political, and economic institutions and related processes in China and Southeast Asia, and at the same time to train a new generation of social scientists specially equipped to carry out such research. The schools concerned share their faculties of nearly sixty specialists, their language teaching, research, and other resources to conduct a combined program of graduate training and field research. Student exchange is coupled with the circulation of staff members between the two universities, and in one year as many as fifteen postgraduate students from the two universities will be conducting doctoral field research within the project's scope.

The size of the graduate body is kept small. A usual ratio is about one hundred graduate students (some of whom may be doing field research abroad) to more than thirty faculty members.

Cornell offers no advanced degrees in Chinese, South Asian, or Southeast Asian Studies as such. Unless he is carrying a major or minor in Chinese, South Asian, or Southeast Asian history, in Asian art history or in Chinese literature, the student is expected to elect Asian Studies as one of his two minor fields. Within this field he may concentrate his area study on China, South Asia, or Southeast Asia.

Southeast Asia Program

Southeast Asia is generally understood to include eight countries—Burma, Malaysia, Indonesia, Laos, Cambodia, North Vietnam, South Vietnam, and the Philippines. Cornell's Southeast Asia Program, which registered its first candidates for advanced degrees in 1951, has become one of two major Southeast Asia area and language training programs in American universities (the other is at Yale). Nearly one-quarter of the doctoral candidates in the United States who are working within the disciplines of the social-sciences and humanities and whose dissertations center on Southeast Asia are currently at Cornell; and more than a quarter of the doctorates in these fields granted by American universities during the past decade were from Cornell. The Southeast Asia collection in the Cornell library is claimed to be the most extensive in the United States and probably in the world. Under the Farmington Plan, the Cornell library several years ago was designated as the principal repository in the United States for publications from the countries of Southeast Asia.

The Southeast Asia Program has grown steadily since its formal launching in 1951. After World War II the accelerated programs on Southeast Asia instituted during that conflict were incorporated into the curriculum, with particular emphasis on anthropology. In 1947, community studies were undertaken in Thailand and Burma, focusing on the social problems that arise when modern technology is introduced into nonindustrial societies. Then, in 1950, support from the Rockefeller Foundation enabled Cornell to establish a formal Southeast Asia Program, which had four objectives: to train experts on the area to do the teaching, research, and public education needed in the United States; to provide knowledge of the area for government officials; to train scholars from the Southeast Asian countries; and to initiate coordinated, interdisciplinary research programs centered on specific problems of the region, particularly in the social sciences.

The Southeast Asia Program also introduced a concern for the area in the undergraduate curriculum of the university. In addition to the twenty-two language courses open to undergraduates and graduate students, there are a number of nonlanguage programs, primarily for undergraduates, that have a substantial Southeast Asian component.

A large number of foreign service officers, military attaches, and personnel of other government agencies have been trained under the program. Also, graduate students from universities unable to provide special language and area training frequently come to Cornell for a year's work prior to undertaking research in the field.

The graduate level of the program is geared to Ph.D. candidates, and the M.A. degree is reserved primarily for those who cannot secure sufficient funds to carry on to the Ph.D. or who appear unable to complete its requirements.

Under a grant from the Ford Foundation, the Southeast Asia Program has also been involved since 1954 in what is known as the Modern Indonesia Project. This series of studies in depth and breadth of social and political conditions in that country deals with the political organization of villages, the attitude of the Chinese minority, and Soviet relations with the Indonesian Communist Party. The project also published an Indonesian-English dictionary, the first comprehensive work of its kind, and has translated Sukarno's *Indonesia Menggugat* ("Indonesia Accuses"), which the Indonesian President has described as one of the most important formulations of his political thought. A substantial portion of the research in the project was carried out by Indonesian scholars, and as a direct result of the program the number of Indonesians undertaking research in the social sciences has substantially increased.

South Asia Program

The South Asia Program (which covers India, Pakistan, and Ceylon) was established at Cornell in 1961, as a successor to the India Program of the 1950s. Doctoral dissertations are normally based on research under faculty supervision abroad. As a relatively small area program, the South Asia Program has concentrated heavily on graduate training as well as research.

The strength of the South Asia Program rests on the work done by Cornell in the language field since 1950 and on the extensive programs of social research which Cornell faculty and graduate students have carried on in rural Indian communities over the past decade. In 1950 the teaching of Hindi was introduced at Cornell, and in 1960 the university was named one of the seven language and area centers for Hindi and Urdu supported by the NDEA. In addition, Cornell received an NDEA grant to develop a teaching text for elementary Sinhalese, for which there was no teaching material available in any Western language. Cornell will thus be the only American university to offer instruction in these three major languages of South Asia, i.e., Hindi (India), Urdu (Pakistan), and Sinhalese (Ceylon).

The China Program

Cornell has been a pioneer in the development of Chinese studies in the United States: five years after its founding a course in the Chinese language was offered.

The China Program, as currently constituted, is both a comprehensive area training institute and a sponsor of major research. It brings together faculty members from eight fields of the graduate school. It also insures a significant place for Chinese studies in the regular curriculum of the under-graduate College of Arts and Sciences. In any given year about five hundred undergraduates at Cornell complete one or more courses in some aspect of Chinese civilization.

The need for comprehensive research on contemporary China assumed particular importance with the establishment of the Chinese People's Republic. In 1950 Cornell established a graduate China Program, and in 1957 a decision was made to concentrate a major teaching and research effort upon contemporary China. Between that year and 1962 no fewer than nine faculty appointments were made in the area of Chinese Studies, bringing to twelve the number of faculty specializing in this area.

While the number of students entering the China Program for doctoral training has increased markedly in the past few years, the fact that mainland China is closed to American citizens has brought a problem of field research for graduate students. Most research has thus had to be concentrated on Taiwan, Hong Kong, or the expatriate communities in Southeast Asia.

It was to provide a center for academic research and offer services and facilities for professional scholars working in Hong Kong that Education and World Affairs, with a special grant from the Carnegie Corporation, established the Universities Service Center in that city in 1963.

Soviet Studies

Soviet Studies at Cornell had an early start, then lapsed, and only came back into being relatively recently, in 1961. However, since that time the program has doubled in faculty and students.

Despite a long interest in Soviet studies and Soviet affairs, Cornell failed to capitalize on this and upon its wartime experience with the ASTP, which became the forerunner of later academic centers for the study of Russia and other foreign areas. The university's wartime interest was not renewed until 1961, when a small-scale faculty coordinating group established the Committee on Soviet Studies.

At that time the Committee made a conscious decision not to launch a full-scale program for the study of all phases of developments in the U.S.S.R. There were several reasons for this: (1) Cornell's already extensive commitments to other costly area programs; (2) the fact that exisiting major academic centers on the Soviet Union were fairly adequately meeting the country's felt needs in the field; (3) the fact that no way was found to identify interdisciplinary interests and structures which would effectively span the wide range of faculty members and departments represented; (4) the failure to secure for Cornell an NDEA grant for a Russian language and area studies center.

In the meantime, the committee worked on two problems: course offerings in the Russian language, and library holdings of books and periodicals in Russian. In 1963 a new department of Russian literature was established.

In order to develop and maintain a quality program of Soviet studies, the committee laid down certain guidelines. It would place its emphasis on the Soviet Union and not on Eastern Europe; it would emphasize the Russian language; it would not offer an interdepartmental seminar or a Soviet Studies major or minor; and it would place the emphasis on graduate students, with no attempt to organize offerings for undergraduates. As an illustration of its special emphasis on the Soviet Union, the committee engaged in a detailed study of the modernization processes in the Soviet system, with particular emphasis upon the dissimilarities to Western modernization and to its impact upon the underdeveloped countries of the world.

Informally, the Committee on Soviet Studies has become a coordinator for Cornell's small but active flow of different kinds of visitors from the U.S.S.R. Some are participants at Cornell in the U.S.-Soviet exchange of graduate students. There is also an exchange of middle-level and senior faculty members, as well as leading Soviet scholars invited directly by Cornell. In all these activities, the committee—in the absence of its own secretarial staff—relies heavily on the Center for International Studies.

The effort to maintain a limited but high-level Soviet Studies program at Cornell is not without its problems, the most serious of which is where to draw the line between minimum requirements and attractive facilities that will draw and retain capable graduate students and able faculty. One difficulty is the discovery that it costs about the same in library acquisitions, staff, and services to support a limited program as it does for a major program.

African Studies

The limitations which plague Cornell's Soviet Studies program apply equally to African Studies. The Committee on African Studies was organized by the Center for International Studies in 1961 so as to bring together a small group of faculty concerned with the university's facilities for graduate study and research on Africa. The committee is under the chairmanship of Victor Turner, formerly of Manchester University, and consists of three other full-time Africanists. Instruction is offered in Ibo and Yoruba, and in general linguistics.

With direct financial support from the Center for International Studies, the committee has been concerned with building library resources in order to round out an African collection that will meet basic minimum criteria. Following an intensive survey of the library's holdings, Cornell carried out an accelerated acquisition of African materials during 1962-63. The problem of enriching the library's resources in African materials highlighted the dilemma which Cornell, along with many other American universities, faces in the proliferating field of area studies—the choice between comprehensiveness and ineffectuality, or between an undertaking which will meet the university's needs and yet not involve it or its faculty members in new commitments and new burdens. With its deliberately limited approach to Soviet and African studies, Cornell may have found a satisfactory way out of the dilemma, but this has not yet been established.

Library Resources

The Cornell libraries rank among the top ten largest American university collections, with a 1965 total of 2,577,296 volumes. Until recent years the major foreign sources of library acquisitions were the countries of Western Europe, but as Cornell extended its areas of principal concentration to other parts of the world the library staff has given greater attention to acquisitions from those areas.

Although Cornell had the Wason collection on China since 1918, it was not until 1962-63 that a major expansion in acquisitions of Chinese material was undertaken, a program which has added some 25,000 volumes to the Wason collection and made Cornell one of the principal centers for Chinese materials in the United States. Cornell holds the Farmington Plan assignment for materials from Southeast Asia, as well as the assignment for Peru. In addition, Cornell has been a participant since its inception in the Latin American Cooperative Acquisition Project, a program through which a group of libraries in the United States has undertaken to broaden and strengthen the acquisition of library material from Latin America. This group finances the travel of one person throughout Latin America to search and purchase library materials for member universities.

Graduate area programs pose difficult and expensive problems for most university libraries, and Cornell's is no exception. The more exotic the area, the more difficult the problems of staff, space, acquisitions, and handling, in addition to finances. Area studies faculty and students comprise a very small percentage of the total student body at an institution such as Cornell, yet the needs for space, staff, and funds for acquisitions are highly disproportionate.

When dealing with exotic programs, the language problem becomes particularly difficult. This is especially true with the great number of languages involved in a Southeast Asian program. Acquisitions also create problems of space. When Cornell's present library building was laid out, there was but one area program. The addition of other area programs has brought on crowding in the acquisition and cataloging areas, and the stacks are being rapidly filled.

The International Agricultural Development Program

Cornell's College of Agriculture, one of the land-grant and state-supported units of the university, has a long tradition of both international involvement and community service. It was logical, therefore, that it should develop its own contemporary international focus, related to other Cornell programs, but oriented more toward service and development.

At the same point in time, 1961, when other academic departments and colleges at Cornell were reviewing the future direction of their international involvement, a similar concern developed in the College of Agriculture. However, with the background of work at Nanking and Los Banos and the personal involvement of many of the agricultural faculty members in overseas enterprises, both the international and the service concept came through considerably stronger than in the rest of the university. Since the initial contact with Nanking University in 1924, no fewer than 160 active and emeritus professors of Cornell's College of Agriculture have served in eighty-nine countries around the world. In 1961 a faculty committee of the college was established to appraise its future international role, and in 1962 the committee's recommendation took shape in the form of a new International Agricultural Development Program, recognized and supported with funds from the state of New York as the fourth dimension in the organizational structure of the college, in addition to resident instruction, research, and extension.

A director of international agriculture was appointed in 1963 to coordinate existing programs and to emphasize international agriculture. An advisory committee was also established, composed of department heads and several professors of agriculture. As a consequence of the new program, an undergraduate program in international agriculture was established, as well as a minor field in the graduate school.

This systematic approach of the College of Agriculture has resulted in a significant international program, blending together an overseas function with teaching, research, and graduate training, and an undergraduate teaching program on campus. It has been able to attract funding, in addition to normal university sources, from the Ford Foundation and the Rockefeller Foundation.

The major objectives of the International Agricultural Development Program are to develop further: (1) a comprehensive program for educating American and foreign undergraduate and graduate students to work in international agricultural development; (2) a program of basic and applied research in the biological, natural, and social sciences applicable in the low income countries; (3) a program of direct cooperation with universities in other countries to help develop their staffs and facilities; (4) an exchange of graduate students and professional staff members between Cornell and the cooperating institutions abroad.

The graduate faculty in International Agricultural Development is currently composed of thirty-three professors in the College of Agriculture and six professors from the College of Arts and Sciences, the Graduate School of Business and Public Administration, the Graduate School of Nutrition, and the School of Industrial and Labor Relations.

Undergraduates may major in one of more than fifty subject fields and, through a core of courses and seminars, including languages, they can be prepared for specific work in international agriculture. A graduate student in agriculture must be competent in one or more subject matter fields in agricultural and related basic and applied sciences. If he is preparing for overseas service, he first selects a field of specialization for his major and may then choose one of his minors in international agricultural development. This program involves language training and may include overseas research experience. The courses offered enable him to apply subject matter specialization to foreign situations.

In addition to the more than twenty courses available in the College of Agriculture, there is an intercollege seminar on international agricultural development. This course was designed to promote communication among staff and the graduate students of the various disciplines with the hope of developing a better understanding of the relevance of the several sciences to agricultural development.

With assistance from the Ford Foundation, the three social science departments—agricultural economics, rural education, and rural sociology—have developed a research and teaching staff whose members specialize in international agricultural development and offer a group of fifteen courses for the training of undergraduate and graduate students. Six of the rural social scientists are members of the Latin American, South Asian, and Southeast Asian area studies staffs of the university. They facilitate coordination of the College of Agriculture's foreign area-oriented training with that of the total university. Staff members in rural social science pursue a program of research which involves participation by graduate students. The Ford Foundation grant has facilitated the sending of students abroad for their doctoral dissertation field research. This contributes to needed research in the country to which the students go, to the training of the students under realistic field conditions, and to the fund of knowledge on international agricultural development.

The College of Agriculture's major overseas program in the graduate education program is an outgrowth of its earlier relations with the College of Agriculture of the University of the Philippines (Los Banos). Begun in 1963, it is a cooperative program, financed primarily by the Ford Foundation but with additional support from the Rockefeller Foundation, and is due to run for five years, with an expectation of continued support. It involves exchange of faculty and graduate students for teaching, research, and extension and some for postdoctoral work. American graduate students go to the Philippines after a minimum of two years of study at Cornell. They serve as teaching and research assistants and do their thesis research under the direction of a Cornell visiting professor or consultant working cooperatively with Filipino professors. After two years of research these graduate students then return to Cornell for a final year of study and preparation of a thesis.

Carefully selected Filipino graduate assistants, after a minimum of two years of graduate study at Los Banos, come to Cornell for two years of advanced studies. Doctoral candidates return for their thesis research to Los Banos, where it can be done under the environment in which they will work in the future. Professors from the Philippine College of Agriculture also have an opportunity to come to Cornell or to another American university for professional improvement and advanced study. Associated on the Los Banos campus is the International Rice Research Institute, constructed with funds provided by the Ford Foundation and operated at Los Banos by funds from the Rockefeller and Ford Foundations.

Other international involvements of the College of Agriculture at Cornell have included three faculty members serving with the university's AID project at the University of Liberia; an exchange of rural sociology graduate students with the Agricultural University at Wageningen, The Netherlands; and undergraduate student exchanges with the Agricultural College of Sweden and with the University of Buenos Aires.

The College also provides each summer—with support from the Rockefeller Foundation—a nine-week on-campus orientation program for foreign graduate students who have been accepted by American universities. This breaking-in period permits students to get comprehensive training in English and become familiar with American education and agriculture before embarking on their formal studies. And as one of the two largest colleges of agriculture in the United States—a distinction it shares with Iowa State University—Cornell's College of Agriculture plays host to a steady stream of foreign visitors and scholars. It has its own Foreign Visitors Office which handles all short-term visitors to the college and also processes all graduate and undergraduate applications to Cornell for participants nominated by AID and the Food and Agriculture Organization of the United Nations for enrollment in the Colleges of Agriculture, Home Economics, and Veterinary Medicine. If the objectives of the applicant are approved, applications are forwarded to the Admissions Office. The Foreign Visitors Office also assists with housing and then checks the progress of the students to make sure that the objectives outlined in the applications are being followed. Between July 1, 1964, and the end of June, 1965, the Office handled 379 visitors from thirty-seven countries.

The International Agricultural Development Program periodically puts on a predeparture orientation course for persons going to the Philippines on the Cornell contract. (This is the only contract which Cornell has involving significant numbers of departures at the same time: orientation for other contracts is handled on an individual and *ad hoc* basis.) Three orientation sessions of two hours each are held for all participants and their wives. The first session seeks to acquaint all participants with the objectives of the program—why Cornell is in it and what it hopes to accomplish— and to dispose of logistical and housekeeping details, such as travel, clothing, furniture, and household equipment required. The second session concentrates on the Philippines, a bird's-eye view of the nation, its history, culture, customs, and people, and the background of the University of the Philippines. The third session, to which is usually invited an outside expert who has lived for some time in the less-developed lands overseas, is given over to consideration of the personal and personnel factors essential for success in overseas service.

Within its International Agricultural Development Program, Cornell's College of Agriculture has developed an overall, long-range plan in the international field. With the successful launching of the Philippine project, the college now hopes to establish a similar relationship with a South

202   *The University Looks Abroad*

American university which would also permit close ties to the ever-increasing Latin American interests of Cornell. Sometime in the future lies the establishment of a third base for overseas agricultural operations, probably in Africa.

Professional Schools

The New York State School of Industrial and Labor Relations, another of the Cornell units operated under contract with the state, has a wide range of international activities and studies. These are structured around two separate subdivisions of the School. One is the department of International and Comparative Labor Relations, an academic unit, and the other is the division of International Activities, an administrative and operating unit.

The department of International and Comparative Labor Relations consists of some thirteen faculty members whose research interests include the study of international labor problems and who, in some cases, also offer courses in this area for graduate and undergraduate students. At the present time, the department offers a minor in International and Comparative Labor Relations for Ph.D. and M.S. candidates, and some discussion has taken place regarding the advisability of developing a major in the field at some future date. During 1964-65 the following courses were taught: International and Comparative Labor Problems I and II; Social Problems of Industrialization, Comparative Economic Systems—Soviet Russia; and Industrial Relations in Latin America.

The division of International Activities is responsible for the development, supervision, and coordination of international and overseas academic and training programs in labor relations, which include at present the continuation or phasing out of work initiated in previous years in Chile, Puerto Rico, and India.

In Chile the division has carried out a five-year undertaking, extended to a sixth year through September, 1965, in agreement with AID, to establish an independent program of resident teaching, research, and extension in industrial and labor relations at the University of Chile. Under the contract, long-term Cornell staff members have served at the university, a core library of labor relations materials—one of the finest in Latin America—has been built up, and Cornell-trained researchers and faculty members now teach labor relations courses at both the undergraduate and graduate levels at the University of Chile. Extension activities have been carried on with certain trade unions in the country, and seminars held for both blue- and white-collar workers in Chile.

In a similar program in India, progress has been much slower, due in part to staffing problems but mainly to the changed national situation created by the Chinese invasion of India. Initially, the Cornell school undertook at the bidding of the Ford Foundation the development of a

Central Institute for Labor Research in India, but for two years the prospects were discouraging. Cornell, the Ford Foundation, and the Government of India agreed that their cooperative relationship would continue through the academic year of 1964-65 in order to assess the future of the project.

In a joint undertaking with the Labor Relations Institute of the University of Puerto Rico and with the financial support of the Marshall Foundation, the division of International Activities for three years carried on a Training Program for Labor Educators in Puerto Rico. In addition, several groups of Latin American trade union education specialists were trained in ten-week programs at the Labor Relations Institute at Rio Piedras. As of 1964-65 the training of labor educators began to diminish in importance as a training priority, but the division at Cornell believes that similar training programs could be undertaken for organizers, researchers, and press and public relations representatives in the labor field.

Not part of the program of the division of International Activities but developed within the School of Industrial and Labor Relations is the Liberian Codification Project, under the directorship of Professor Milton R. Konvitz. For some years Konvitz and his project staff have laboriously drawn up and codified new civil procedure and criminal procedure law for the Republic of Liberia. Drawn along modern lines and based upon the best and most efficient models that comparative studies have produced, the new codes derive from Liberian institutions and needs. Konvitz has also undertaken several specific studies of Liberian laws, and the Cornell University Press publishes the volumes of the *Liberian Law Reports.*

The Graduate School of Business and Public Administration has both an overseas operation and a growing academic program in international studies.

In 1961 Cornell signed an ICA (now AID) contract to assist the Management department of Middle East Technical University at Ankara, and to provide three interrelated programs of support. The first was to send to METU professors either from Cornell's BPA School or selected by Cornell as visiting staff members, to serve at Ankara for periods of one year to eighteen months. The second obligation was to accept suitable students from METU for graduate study at Cornell. Some of these have already completed their M.B.A. degrees and are now teaching at METU, and by the end of the academic year 1965-66 Cornell will have trained a total of twelve METU staff members who, on their return to Ankara, will provide a solid teaching nucleus for the department of Management. The final responsibility of Cornell was to select a basic library in business administration and economics for the METU library.

Although Cornell's BPA School for a number of years offered course work in international studies, this had relatively low priority in the academic program. As of a year or two ago, this emphasis began rapidly shifting, and an expanded program in International Development and Foreign Operations has been initiated. Students taking this concentration take the basic core in administration required of all students, supplemented by course work in foreign operations of public and private organizations, comparative administration, and development administration. The balance of the student's time is taken up in either one of the area programs or in international studies offered by the various departments of the College of Arts and Sciences, the School of Agriculture, or the School of Industrial and Labor Relations.

Cornell's Law School offers an LL.B. with specialization in International Affairs, and the School's courses in the international field, open to all law students, include Admiralty, Comparative Law, Comparative Constitutional Law, Conflict of Laws, International Law, Legal Problems of International Transactions, and Litigation of Business Disputes—Domestic and International.

Cornell's program of international legal studies has received most attention, however, for two projects in which the university's Law School has pioneered. One is the summer conference on international law, financed through a grant from the Ford Foundation, which for some years has brought together teachers of law, private practitioners, and government officials who are particularly concerned with international law. A second innovation is the General Principles of Law Project, a series of seminars and discussion papers which explore the feasibility of finding and formulating a common core of standards, principles, and rules prevailing in the contract law of the world's major legal systems. Foreign scholars have prepared papers commenting on how numerous concrete factual situations would be handled under their various legal systems, after which the participants have gathered—mainly at Cornell—for seminar sessions lasting for months of discussions and redrafting, aiming at a comparative, worldwide study to be published in 1965.

Cornell's Medical College is engaged in several international studies, but it is not involved in a major way overseas. One study, a field investigation of the possible roles of migratory birds as intercontinental disseminators of the so-called arbor viruses, utilizes a laboratory in Mexico City with field extensions. Another project, conducted with professors at the University of Bahia, Brazil, is to provide training in tropical diseases and to conduct research on certain questions having to do with diseases of tropical areas, initially on typhoid fever. A third project with international applicability is an ambitious, seven-year study among the Navahos to study the process of modernization of cross-cultural and language barriers using improved medicine broadly as the chief modernization element.

The School of Education has no major overseas commitments. No program of teaching, research, or public service involving persons going overseas or coming from overseas is being operated by the School. However, the School can nonetheless claim a steady growth of involvement in international affairs. It has a respectable quota of foreign graduate students in residence—between forty and fifty most years—and of its comparatively small staff of some thirty-five, one-third have had overseas experience in recent years, many of them on assignments sponsored by the university or its contract colleges. The faculty is interested in developing an overseas commitment in educational administration, organization, and teacher education, provided the right setting can be found.

The Cornell University College of Engineering is another component which has no current overseas teaching or research commitments or other substantial relationships involving foreign institutions. Two activities are international. The Graduate School of Aerospace Engineering operates a contract with the Office of Scientific Research of the U.S. Air Force for participation by selected Japanese professionals in certain aspects of research carried on by the School. And for some years individual faculty members of the College of Engineering have provided consulting or resident teaching services at the Universidad del Valle at Cali, Colombia.

Concern within the College of Engineering as to its future policy on international education led to the selection of a faculty committee to prepare a study to advise the Dean of the College. The committee's report has been under review during the 1964-65 academic year.

The principal international commitment of the College of Architecture is the production of two volumes of essays by city and regional planners in Poland and Yugoslavia, a project of a special University Committee on Comparative Planning which was organized under the Center for Housing and Environmental Studies.

The New York State College of Home Economics is engaged in a collaborative effort with the Ghana Ministry of Education to develop a four-year college-level home economics education curriculum at Ghana's Winneba Training College. The Ghana-Cornell Project, as it is known, developed out of an intercultural program put on in 1961 by the U.S. Department of State and AID during which half a dozen prominent women educators from the United States, including the Dean of Cornell's College of Home Economics, conducted two ten-day workshops in East and West Africa on "Problems of Education of African Women and Girls." African women educators from fourteen countries took part in them, and a subsequent visit to the United States by a party of African women educators led to a formal request from the Ministry of Education in Ghana for help from the faculty of the College of Home Economics in Ithaca.

The project as designed is intended to benefit both Ghana and Cornell. The curriculum is based on knowledge of Ghanaian family living practices in order that teachers can be prepared for leadership designed to raise the level of living in Ghanaian homes. Such education will help women adjust to a drastically changing society and help them increase the productivity of the total family in a society where expanded agricultural production and rapid industrialization are considered imperative. The project is also expected to contribute to the effectiveness of teaching home economics for students at Cornell by providing experimental work in the preparation of teaching materials, research in curriculum development in a different culture, and testing the universality of certain principles of home economics subject matter.

The College of Home Economics is convinced that its subject matter is uniquely suited to make a significant impact on the physical and emotional health of people in the underdeveloped countries and on their levels of living. The experience in Ghana and a study of similar possibilities in Liberia led the College in 1964 to appoint a faculty member to head up an Office of International Commitments and Programs in order to coordinate and promote its activities in the international field.

The Graduate School of Nutrition carried out a small-scale international training program in nutrition in Peru, an AID contract which was discontinued in 1963. This work provided a background for further work in international nutritional investigations, and in 1964 the School initiated a limited field training program in applied nutrition in Guatemala, a program assisted by grants from the National Institutes of Health, and the Williams-Waterman Foundation. The School's program of International Nutrition also offers a course on programs and problems of international nutrition for graduate students of the School and of the College of Home Economics. It has also offered a seminar on food and population, mainly attended by graduate students in agricultural economics, rural sociology, and education.

Cornell's School of Hotel Administration, relatively small in number of students, is an international attraction. For some years it has led the undergraduate divisions of the university in the percentage of foreign student enrollment, and it is second only to the larger College of Agriculture in the number of foreign students enrolled. In one year it may have as many as fifty-five to sixty foreign students, representing some twenty-five nations. Hotel and restaurant men visiting the United States gravitate to Cornell, often in contingents of thirty and more at a time, and the School's summer sessions always attract representatives from foreign nations. The School is under constant pressure to assist and advise in establishing schools, workshops, and training sessions in foreign countries, but most of the requests have to be turned down because it does not have the faculty and staff available for overseas commitments.

Projects and Programs

The main all-university technical assistance program at Cornell is the Liberia project, a contract entered into in 1962 with AID and the Government of Liberia to develop the University of Liberia into an institution of more acceptable educational standards so that it might produce trained personnel to fulfill the requirements of the country's economic and social development. The contract differs from the usual American college or university undertaking, in that it involves all segments of the university and its activities rather than a single department or college.

Cornell's interest in Liberia goes back to 1960, when its representatives were dispatched by ICA to study the University of Liberia and make recommendations to assist in the development of that institution. Established as Liberia College in 1862, and in continuous existence since that time, it became the University of Liberia by legislative action in 1951. At the time the contract was written, the somewhat grandiose plans put forward in Monrovia contemplated relocating the university from the capital to a new site some eighteen miles in the country, where a modern university, complete with recreational facilities, student housing, and faculty housing, would be constructed. Cornell's recommendation was that a better sequence would be first to concentrate on the upgrading and development of the university in its present location, and leave for the future—when many more students will have been prepared for university instruction in the developing elementary and secondary school system—the erection of a new plant.

Under the contract, Cornell has provided up to eleven faculty members at any one time, most of them Cornell faculty or former Cornell students, for periods of from four months to two years.

Cornell's International Population Program, which has attracted many overseas students, was initiated in 1962 to concern itself with the complex of issues resulting from the population explosion around the world, with particular attention to the problems created by the massive movement of the rural peoples to urban centers. The program is a research and training program in social demography. It is housed in quarters provided by the Center for International Studies, and the financing for fellowships and research was provided by the Ford Foundation for a five-year period and the NDEA for the first two years.

Increasing demands from all parts of the world for demographic skills, the growing quantity and quality of international statistics, and the inability of traditional demographic theory and techniques to cope with many of the applied problems stemming from world population growth suggested the need for a program designed to develop broad demographic skills in comparative population analysis. Because of the strength of its area programs, Cornell was able to devise a training program for demographers with economic, sociological, social psychological, and general methodoilogical skills. Graduate students majoring in demography-ecology within the department of sociology normally take a minor in one of the area programs and another minor in research methodology, social psychology, agricultural economics, or economics.

The program has also sponsored and developed field and census research in those countries from which it draws students. Currently, two Latin countries are being studied in some depth—Peru and Puerto Rico. In Peru—selected because of Cornell's extensive anthropological work at Vicos—the program has carried out studies of fertility and attitudes towards fertility. These, in turn, led to a joint project with the International Population Program and CELADE (Centro Latino Americano Demografico) to make a series of comparative studies of fertility and attitudes related to fertility in seven or more Latin American cities.

Puerto Rico is a laboratory for demographic study. It has a longer history of good censuses and vital statistics than most Latin American countries; its small size and homogeneity make it relatively easy to study; and its rapid social and economic development over the past two decades provides a convenient time period covering its entry into and transition through a stage of modernization.

In cooperation with the Puerto Rican Planning Board, Cornell's I.P.P. is engaged in a series of ecological studies of fertility which should have implications for future field and census studies in other nations.

The generalizations emerging from both the ecological and field investigations in Latin America, the backbone of the I.P.P., must be tested for validity for other regions at comparable stages of economic development and with highly different cultural patterns. Thus, the I.P.P. intends to make a parallel study of a census tract analysis of fertility variations in San Juan, Puerto Rico, and Cairo. Similarly, fertility field studies in Latin American nations will be complemented by a comparable investigation in Turkey.

Capping this field work is Cornell's data bank, the Cornell Demographic Inventory of annual statistics of vital events, economic levels, and other related social and economic data for each nation in the world, compiled on punch cards. Electronic data processing makes possible immediate information retrieval for time series or comparative purposes.

A program established by the Center for International Studies is the Modernization Workshop, an effort which began in 1962 in order to make use of much of the research material of the major area programs. Taking as its major project the functional study of low income countries, the Workshop brings together a small group of faculty members for discussions during the academic year, drawing on their experiences acquired through a variety of overseas and research activities for the study of the processes of modernization in low income countries. The product of these discussions has been a joint manuscript on the modernization process, analyzed in terms of the discipline of each of the Workshop associates, but oriented around a common conceptual and theoretical focus, a book which will be published in 1966.

In 1963 the department of anthropology contracted with the office of Technical Cooperation and Research of AID to accelerate the process of analysis and reporting of results of its long-term project on Comparative Studies of Cultural Change. As a result of this new interest, Cornell investigators returned to carry out updated field research in areas and communities in which they or their colleagues had worked years ago—in the hills and tribal areas of northern Thailand, in India, at Vicos, Puerto Rico, Japan, Brazil, Nigeria, and Nova Scotia.

International Course Offerings

A wide variety of courses of instruction with international content is offered in the academic departments of Cornell's schools and colleges, notably in the Arts and Sciences, Agriculture, Business and Public Administration, Home Economics, Industrial and Labor Relations, and Law. Specialized instruction at the graduate and undergraduate levels is also available in the university's area programs.

As a service to students and faculty with a prime interest in international content courses, the Center for International Studies prepares a biennial catalog, a separate survey of courses of instruction in international studies offered at Cornell. This was attempted for the first time on a university-wide basis for the academic year 1964-65. The survey first lists courses offered in programs of special concentrations; it then presents a listing of courses by departments, which is cross-indexed with the offerings of the area programs.

The division of Modern Languages offers instruction in no fewer than twenty-two languages, as well as linguistics and special attention to the teaching of English and French as foreign languages overseas. Under a Ford Foundation grant given at the end of 1962, the division is engaged in a seven-year program to strengthen its resources in applied linguistics and the teaching of English as a second language (TESL). As part of this program, Cornell linguists have aided in the development of TESL centers in Italy, in India, and—in a consortium with Brown University and the University of Texas—in the educational system of Egypt.

Study Abroad

Cornell has no formal study-abroad program. Individual students interested in studying abroad may contact the International Students Office, the placement office, and the Graduate School for information, but even this is not systematically organized in one place. The College of Arts and Sciences does not enter into formal arrangements for student exchanges.

The College of Agriculture operates two limited but successful one-for-one exchanges with the Agricultural College of Sweden at Uppsala and with the faculty of Agriculture and Veterinary Medicine at Buenos Aires. The Swedish-Cornell exchange is now in its tenth year. Satisfaction with these restricted efforts led the agriculture faculty at Cornell to establish an *ad hoc* committee on undergraduate study abroad, which was expected by late in 1965 to have investigated the possibilities and recommend what the official College of Agriculture policy should be concerning study abroad.

Foreign Students

In terms of numbers of foreign students enrolled Cornell ranks twelfth out of some 1,800 institutions in the United States: in terms of percentage of foreign students in relation to its total enrollment, Cornell ranks fourth in the United States, tied with the University of Chicago.

During the 1964-65 academic year, Cornell had 1,020 foreign students on campus from eighty-two countries, the largest number ever to enroll at Cornell. This was an increase of 7.2 percent over the 1963-64 year, mainly because of a larger number of continuing students rather than an increase of new foreign student arrivals.

Foreign students thus make up 8.1 percent of the total student population of the university. The three largest national contingents are from Canada (163), China (92), and India (92). Undergraduate foreign student enrollment (286) represented 3.1 percent of the total undergraduate enrollment, while foreign graduate students (734) made up 72 percent of the foreign student enrollment and comprised 24.8 percent of the total number of graduate students enrolled. Of the foreign undergraduates, the highest percentage of total enrollment continued to be found in the School of Hotel Administration (12 percent), followed by the College of Architecture (6.6 percent) and the College of Agriculture (4.4 percent).

The approach that Cornell takes to its foreign students has been spelled out by David B. Williams, the director of the university's International Student Office.

"Our program at Cornell has expanded both by design, and by virtue of the increase in the number of foreign students and faculty coming to this university," reported Williams. "These people are temporary guests and visitors in the Ithaca community, a community increasingly aware of its opportunity to share in the exchange of persons program. More community involvement has meant that Main Street, Ithaca, is now meeting Main Street, Seoul, or Helsinki, or Quito to a much greater degree than ever before."

University, student, and community facilities are blended to meet the special needs of Cornell's foreign students. An International Student Office, essentially a service office, serves as an information center on all programs related to foreign students and is responsible for counseling on personal matters such as housing, financial aid, employment, immigration, transfers to other institutions, and liaison between student and sponsors. In addition, the Office also supports and encourages the efforts of Ithaca and the Cornell community in developing meaningful programs involving foreign students. It runs a Speakers' Bureau for foreign students and supports a Host

Family Program through which foreign students can be matched up with hospitality offers from families on campus or in the community.

Every arriving foreign student—having been previously provided with prearrival orientation literature—goes through a four-day formal phase of orientation which is student-planned and directed, coordinated wherever possible with the International Student Office and community groups. Volunteer assistance during this period comes from the International Committee of Student Government, the International Committee of the Student Union, and the International Hospitality Committee of the Campus Club (faculty wives), responsible for operating an Emergency Greeting Group, the Host Family Program, International Wives' Friendship Groups, and English classes for wives of foreign students and staff.

During the year, international student activity is coordinated by the International Committee of Student Government, which in turn works with the various nationality clubs on campus, maintains liaison with the major organizations on campus, and runs a program of International Interns to develop leadership by American students in the international student area. In addition, communication with foreign students while on campus is attained through the cooperative efforts of the International Committee of Student Government and the International Student Office in publishing two periodicals, *Dateline,* a monthly newsletter that goes to all foreign students on campus, and *Internationally Speaking,* a forum-type publication, published six times each year, which enables students to express their opinions and report on international affairs and activities.

IV

Cornell's Center for International Studies, established in 1961 to ensure the most effective development of the university's international programs, occupies a suite of offices on the second floor of Rand Hall (above the computer center), where it provides space for the London-Cornell Project, the International Population Program, and other associated activities.

The Center itself does not have a separate faculty nor does it offer instruction. Instead, the projects and research activities in international studies as well as the various programs and committees associated with the Center draw on the participation of the university faculty. In addition, the Center brings to Cornell visiting faculty, postdoctoral research fellows, and distinguished visiting academic and professional personnel in the area of international studies.

How the Center Functions

Relatively new as university institutions go, the Center is still evolving its administrative role and operating style.

According to a 1962 university description of its functions, it is intended "to coordinate the various programs, to initiate new programs and research, to effect the maximum influence of the international programs upon the undergraduate curricula, and to advise and assist the university on contract commitments in international activities sponsored by governmental or private institutions." In addition, the Center has the responsibility for administering under its general direction the Ford Foundation grant of $3,250,000 given to Cornell to strengthen its international studies in 1962, and a second grant, a sum of $550,000 given by the same foundation in 1964 to support Cornell's Latin American Program for a three-year period.

Several of the area programs were established on campus prior to the Center's arrival on the scene and the high degree of autonomy they enjoyed was reflected in the fact that the 1962 Ford Foundation grant carefully allocated specific sums to the ongoing programs, while noting that the grant would be "under the general direction of the Center." The 1964 grant to the Latin American Program was more explicit: it was to be administered "under the general supervision of the Center." Any further foundation grants would undoubtedly be channeled through the Center.

The fact that this potentially divisive matter of funding has proceeded smoothly at Cornell is due in good part to the Center's staff and method of operation.

The staff of the Center consists of a director and an associate director, both of whom are active members of the university faculty, and of a full-time administrative aide and secretary. Director of the Center is Steven Muller, associate professor of government, who succeeded Professor Einaudi in January, 1962. A Rhodes Scholar who received his Ph.D. from Cornell, Muller is a specialist in comparative government and political theory and the field of arms control. The Associate Director is John Mellor, professor of agricultural economics, who has been active in agricultural development work overseas, particularly in India.

While all of the administrative expenses of the Center are borne by Cornell, its initiating activities in the international field—such as sponsorship of research, seminars, publications, and visitors—are made possible by the allocation to the Center of $700,000 over the five-year period of the initial Ford Foundation grant.

The central, policy-making body for the Center is its executive committee, a relatively large group, headed by the provost, and consisting of twelve faculty members appointed for staggered three-year terms by the president, and another twelve members active in university administration. In practice, the Center serves to provide leadership for the development of the university's international activities. Through the executive committee, administrative and faculty viewpoints are expressed on various alternatives for international program development, priorities are established, and plans are discussed. The Center, through its director, provides assistance to departments and colleges on the campus, stimulates consideration of the various issues in the international field which the university confronts, and in this way helps bring about sound program development. The director also serves as liaison for the university in discussions with the government and foundations on international matters, seeks outside support for Cornell's programs and provides information. By no means passive, the Center actively pursues the establishment of international activities which are considered to be academically sound and worthwhile in the judgment of the executive committee. The Center is informed of all plans and projects in the international field originating in various departments or colleges before approval is granted by the university, and the Center's director is able to influence decisions.

When the provost, in response to the university's growing international commitment, appointed a faculty committee in 1964 to consider the question—"What shall be the basis for Cornell's future involvement in overseas research operations?"—the Center's director was named chairman. The committee's recommendations firmly underpinned the position of the Center in its relations to the administration and to the faculty. The basic recommendation read: "Proposals for overseas commitments, whether originating in a single unit of the university or in more than one unit, will first require departmental and college approval and then be submitted to the university administration. The university administration will consult with the staff of the Center for International Studies on all such proposals. The Center for International Studies is prepared to be of assistance to units and individual faculty and staff members in preparing proposals and acquainting them with relevant resources and interests within the university. To take advantage of the Center's services, persons planning overseas programs are encouraged to contact the staff of the Center in the exploratory stage."

Subsidiary recommendations were that the Center should extend and complete a faculty roster, initiated in 1962, and compile an area reference file which—organized by country—would record all the activities being carried on in the country by Cornell faculty and administrative units, the names of all Cornell faculty members with experience or special knowledge in the country, and the names of all nationals of the country with previous ties to Cornell, either as students, visitors, correspondents, colleagues, and the like. In addition, it was suggested that the Center embark on the compilation of a handbook on problems of overseas activities, based on experiences of faculty from Cornell and elsewhere, which would describe typical problems and means for dealing with them encountered in academic and scientific work abroad. A form of predeparture orientation, the handbook would serve to alert the faculty or staff member contemplating overseas involvement to the kinds of adjustments he might expect, thus encouraging him to seek needed information and consultation in advance.

In its final recommendation, the committee suggested to the provost that the executive committee of the Center be charged with preparing a report evaluating the strengths and weaknesses of Cornell as a whole in the realm of international activities, a report that would examine the nature and extent of the university's present commitments, point to existing or potential interrelations between programs, evaluate resources within the university for future development and call attention to possible blind alleys and major opportunities. On completion, the report would be circulated and discussed by the faculty.

Within the Center itself, the main concern is with academic and research development rather than with technical assistance programs. This does not mean that Cornell is not interested in service contracts overseas. The university combines within itself the traditions of the academic, the land-grant, the extension, and the public service concepts, and therefore many of its faculty members and some of its overseas activities are motivated by the ideal of service. However, it is also true at Cornell that there is hardly any faculty member—including those in the land-grant and state-contract units of the university—willing to undertake an overseas project unless that project has a clear-cut research-teaching relationship to Cornell, either to the individual faculty member, his department, or the university.

Subscribers to this approach, the director of the Center and his associates believe that only when overseas research is a real element in an overseas service contract should Cornell enter into any such contracts.

One thing is clear: the Center is to be a nonoperating organization. It will not be used to manage overseas operations or contract projects. Some thought has been given in the administration to a contract arrangement, such as Cornell has with the Aeronautical Engineering Laboratory in Buffalo, by which an outside service organization would undertake the technical, administrative, and managerial aspects of an overseas service contract, leaving Cornell faculty free to contribute expertise and develop research. This would provide the university with a means of engaging in service contracts, but keeping them at arm's length, an arrangement that is more attractive on paper than in practice.

Activities of the Center

Apart from its sponsorship of the Committee on Soviet Studies, the Committee on African Studies and support for the Modernization Analysis Workshop, the Center has developed other activities.

Beginning in April, 1963, it issued its *International Studies Bulletin,* a mimeographed monthly which is a who's who in international affairs on the Cornell campus, an informal listing of faculty changes, new appointments, visiting lecturers, and so on, that is sent to all teaching and administrative staff.

During 1964 the Center assumed direct administrative responsibility for two research projects. One is the preparation of an English-Indonesian dictionary, supported by a four-year grant from the Ford Foundation. The other, supported by a two-year grant from the Russell Sage Foundation, is the preparation of a manuscript entitled *The Making of the New Soviet Man,* by Professor Urie Bronfenbrenner, professor of Psychology and of Child Development and Family Relations.

Another Center venture which proved most successful was a Current Affairs Film Series, inaugurated in 1963 and repeated in 1964, which made available to the university community free of charge a series of films, mostly newsreel footage of international events from World War I to the Suez and Hungarian crises of 1956. The audience response was so overwhelming that the films had to be moved in 1963 from a small room to the main campus auditorium, and were viewed by capacity audiences.

In the summer of 1964 the Center's executive committee reaffirmed its intention to make the Center a research-oriented institution. The Center's staff lost no time in launching a modest publishing program, issuing a series of occasional booklets or research papers, original monographs by members of the university faculty on subjects of special international interest.

The Center prepared and presented the application for foundation support for Cornell's Latin American Year, 1965-66, and the Center is cosponsor with the Latin American Program in presenting the year-long activities which will mark the university's involvement in that area.

In 1962 and 1964 Cornell ran a training program for Peace Corps volunteers headed for Peru. In 1963 a similar program was operated for volunteers going to Sierra Leone. In each case, the staff of the Center and faculty closely associated with the Center were involved in the training projects.

Over the course of the past few years a number of distinguished visitors have been brought to the Cornell campus with the sole or partial sponsorship of the Center, and the Center has sponsored or cosponsored seminars and conferences of international subjects, some of which have attracted national attention. Among the visiting professors in international studies have been Arthur Lall, former Ambassador of India to the United Nations, and—in 1964-65—Vladimir Dedijer, Yugoslav historian and biographer of Tito.

Recreating a Sense of Community

The initial charter for the Center stipulated that it had a three-year tenure, with the proviso that its status and existence would be reviewed at the end of that period. In November, 1964, the Cornell administration— after a careful and extended consideration of the recommendations of the Center's executive committee—reconfirmed the role of the Center and its leadership for a new five-year term. No substantial changes were made in its organization. The executive committee, large and unmanageable as it is, continues as the central policy-making body. However, greater efficiency has been achieved by the creation of several standing subcommittees that meet more frequently than the executive committee and report to it. The most important of these are: (1) a program committee, which regularly brings together, every fortnight or so, the directors or chairmen of the several area programs or committees as well as the directors of international activities of at least four of the schools and colleges; (2) the finance committee, which has authority to review and discuss the budgets, not only of the Center itself, but also of the associated area programs within the university; (3) the committee on overseas operations and research, which reviews proposals made anywhere in the university for overseas contracts or other activities involving groups of people from the Cornell community.

The executive committee's status report, and its acceptance by the administration, constituted a solid vote of confidence in the Center. Only one aspect was left undefined: the right of the Center to make clear decisions by itself. As constituted, the Center gives advice to the university, and the university makes the decisions. In a jurisdiction-conscious institution this might lead to divided authority, but at Cornell the slight ambiguity in the Center's position is offset by the weight of several factors operating in the Center's favor. One is that the Center itself leans heavily to the academic. It is headed by individuals whose roots are in their departments, and whose academic qualifications are well accepted by their colleagues. This in itself helps avoid two sources of conflict—the "administration versus academic," and "the service motive versus the academic"—which often beset institutions trying to organize their international activities. The second strength is that the Center has been demonstrably successful in obtaining foundation grants, and has acquired over the years the know-how in preparation of submissions for outside funds, a special skill which carries over to its other activities and bolsters its prestige and influence on campus. And, finally, the Cornell administration has indicated clearly that it intends to operate its international programs within the framework of the Center, and that it intends the university community to respond accordingly. As a token of its intentions, the administration in its successful Centennial Campaign, which raised $75,580,000, earmarked the sum of $1 million of endowment for the Center, the income from which will be used for administrative purposes of the Center and as seed money to attract further foundation and other support.

As the president, provost, vice presidents, deans, departmental chairmen, and others increasingly refer their problems to the Center, so the recommendations of the Center will become more authoritative. However, its influence is felt more through consultation and persuasion than through the exercise of hierarchical authority.

Looking back over three short years of its history, the Center can claim to have rationalized the structure of international studies at Cornell, and to have consolidated and supported the achievements of the two postwar decades.

Looking ahead, the Center's staff has charted several areas for prime attention over the next few years.

One is an essentially tactical effort to weave the university's professional schools as closely as possible into the international program.

The effort to involve the professional schools is targeted for 1966. At the same time, Muller and the Center hope to lay the foundation for an equally important area of concern—the effort to spread what is still at Cornell primarily a faculty and graduate program in international activities down into undergraduate education, not just in the College of Arts and Sciences but throughout the university's undergraduate colleges.

The third preoccupation for the Center is the problem of communication both within the university and throughout the university community. "In the area of international studies, badly fragmented in most places, as are so many other disciplines and pursuits," says Muller, "our effort is to recreate communications and a sense of community." It was with this as the intent that the Center prepared its concept of Cornell's Latin American Year, an attempt to achieve a feeling of total university involvement by focusing on a single dimension of the university's activities. This search for a means to restore a sense of community to the university will continue to underlie much of what the Center does. For as Muller puts it, "it is part of the creed of the Center that Cornell is still a university rather than a multiversity."

* * * * *

The overall impression of a survey of Cornell is of an effective university moving in a steady manner toward an international dimension of real consequence. An educational innovator since its founding days, it has not devised a highly structured format for its international activities, but certain characteristics are outstanding and worth noting by universities now moving into unknown ground over which Cornell has already traveled.

Although not as faculty-oriented as the University of Wisconsin, for example, Cornell has nonetheless proceeded in its international involvement only so far and so fast as its faculty has been ready to go. This is particularly noticeable in its approach to area studies, which have achieved their present strength because they have evolved purely out of faculty interest and commitment and were not grafted on the university by the administration, because they are broadly representative of the whole university, and because they depend on departmental cooperation and appointments rather than on an independent faculty.

A second characteristic has been Cornell's willingness to settle for a limited approach to area studies in the case of its African and Soviet studies centers, a case of tailoring its prestige to fit its resources.

The major drawbacks to overseas technical assistance projects have always been that they, by definition, divert university resources and that they disrupt the teaching and research programs on the home campus without providing equal or even adequate professorial or scholarly compensation.

Research in the field has long been a hallmark of Cornell's international programs, going back at least to 1924 and its collaboration with China's Nanking University, and in its approach to technical assistance programs Cornell may have found the pattern which avoids these drawbacks while sacrificing none of the institution's strengths and interests. The best instance of this approach is Cornell's cooperative program with the University of the Philippines (Los Banos), under which faculty and students in many disciplines take part in research and training programs in both countries.

On one characteristic of its international program, Cornell can be faulted. In its determination to stay clear of "operating" functions, the Center for International Studies has not worked systematically at maximizing the benefits the university could draw from its international involvements. This is due to the fact that the Center is research-oriented, and because the university has preferred to operate with decentralized administration of its overseas projects. Except for the internal efforts of the International Agricultural Development Program, no real mechanism exists by which the various programs and activities interact one upon the other, or upon the university as a whole. The provision for feedback to the campus is therefore minimal, and when it does take place it is apt to be casual rather than systematic.

If there is one common conclusion that can be drawn from this six-university study, it is that a university—to obtain full advantage from its overseas involvements—must work at the task. Cornell has not yet put its head down to this job.

INDIANA

I

In a letter to a friend in the Ford Foundation, an Indiana University faculty member attempted in the spring of 1964 to sum up his university's commitment to international affairs in personal terms. "The president, the chancellor, and the deans," he wrote, enthusiastically, "are as at home in Lima or Sarajevo or Nairobi as in Bloomington, Indiana."

The president, the chancellor, and the deans could accept his compliment as a statement of fact. In the years since World War II the international dimension of higher education has been increasingly recognized as part of Indiana University's responsibility in teaching, research, and public service. In the ten years since 1955 the university has shouldered several dozen assignments around the world and carried out world affairs programs on its campus, for and in cooperation with AID, the Department of State, the Defense Department, the U.S. Office of Education, and the foundations. In a remarkable program of cooperative efforts with other educational institutions in the state, Indiana University has influenced a substantial improvement in the teaching of foreign languages in Indiana public and parochial secondary schools, upgraded the secondary school training of history and social studies (including world affairs), and enriched the international curriculum in undergraduate education in more than three-fourths of the state's colleges and universities. And over the past decade it has welcomed to Bloomington, where the university was founded in 1820, thousands of foreign students and a steady stream of international visitors, turning the small southern Indiana town into an important cultural center of the Midwest.

Birdseye, Bangkok, and Bloomington

That this international involvement has taken place in a state long known for its ingrained isolationism and conservative politics is in itself remarkable. Even more remarkable is the apparent fact that the international bent of the state-supported university has had the blessing and active participation of the people of Indiana.

How this has been brought about has been explained by the Chancellor of Indiana University, Herman B Wells—(B is his middle name, so it takes no period). A practicing internationalist who is at home anywhere in the world, Mr. Wells served as acting President in 1937, President from 1938 to 1962, and as Chancellor since then. During that period—in the approving words of one of the deans—"he has infected the whole university and influenced the entire state" in the direction of increased internationalization of its education.

During the Wells presidency, and under that of his successor—Elvis J. Stahr, who took office in 1962—the university's administration has operated on the principle that the university must relate to the community it serves, the state of Indiana.

"Through the years," said Mr. Wells, "Indiana University has tried to preach the gospel that to be a university of the first rank in this day and age, it must keep its eye on Birdseye *and* on Bangkok, and, of course, on Bloomington."

Birdseye is a small village in southern Indiana. "Birdseye is our constituency," remarked the Chancellor, "but there is more than one Birdseye. The steel workers of Gary are Birdseye; the Indiana Federation of Women's Clubs are Birdseye; the State Chamber of Commerce is also Birdseye. And the colleges and high schools of Indiana are among the most important of our Birdseyes. Birdseye can thus be reached in many different ways."

As a state university, dependent on the legislature for 40 percent of its yearly operating budget, Indiana University has at least three factors favoring it in influencing its statewide constituency. One is that it is constituted by law as head of the state's public school system, giving it a legitimate leadership role in improving the quality and content of the educational system of Indiana. Another is that a high proportion of its undergraduates are home-grown products: 82 percent come from Indiana high schools. The third is the fact that a high percentage of its graduates remain within the state and, in due course, many of them achieve positions of influence and status in their communities. In some towns it is not at all unusual to find that the mayor, the doctors, and not a few of the lawyers, businessmen, newsmen, and other opinion leaders are IU alumni, a circumstance that is not lost on the legislative representatives.

Indiana University is the university of the state but—unlike most state universities—it does not offer a full range of professional education. It has no schools of agriculture, engineering, or veterinary medicine, for instance. For the state of Indiana these functions are provided by Purdue, a land-grant university. IU, however, offers two hundred majors of academic concentration in 106 departments in ten schools and colleges. At its 1,850-acre main campus at Bloomington, a wooded layout typical of southern Indiana and regarded as one of the most beautiful college campuses in the United States, IU maintains its College of Arts and Sciences; Junior (Freshman) Division; Schools of Law, Education, Business, Music, Health-Physical Education—Recreation; and its Graduate School. At Indianapolis, fifty-one miles north of Bloomington, the university has its School of Medicine, School of Dentistry, School of Nursing, Division of Social Service, and the evening division of its School of Law.

From its modest beginnings in 1824, when it opened as the State Seminary with one professor and ten students in two courses, the Bloomington campus has grown to an enrollment in 1964-65 of some 20,000 students. In addition, more than 12,800 full-time and part-time credit students were enrolled in the nine regional campuses which IU maintains throughout the state. These regional centers, which serve the functions of junior or community colleges for the state (although they also offer many junior and senior courses for regular students and adults), are located at Indianapolis, Gary, East Chicago, Fort Wayne, South Bend, Kokomo, Jeffersonville, Richmond, and Vincennes. The center in Richmond is operated jointly by Earlham College and Indiana University: the Vincennes center by Vincennes University and IU.

The total faculty of Indiana University numbers approximately 1,900 full-time and 3,000 part-time teachers, and of these more than 300 have had experience in foreign areas.

Not one of the traditional centers of excellence, Indiana University in the momentous years since World War II has raised itself into the top rank of American academic giants. In size it ranks eleventh in the nation, and by many measures of strength among modern American universities it must be rated near the top. Thus, in a 1965 listing of leading graduate schools, graded on such measures as the presence of students and faculty who had been singled out for recognition as fellows or scholars, Albert H. Bowker, Chancellor of the City University of New York and President of the American Statistical Association, ranked Indiana University among the top ten institutions for excellence in social sciences and humanities.

II

Indiana is one of the oldest state universities west of the Alleghenies. When it was founded by law in 1820, four years after the admission of Indiana to the Union, Indian territory began just five miles northwest of Bloomington. Established as the State Seminary and then renamed the Indiana Seminary, the little institution had made such progress in the number of its students that by 1828 it was raised to the dignity of Indiana College. By 1838 its continued growth and increasing importance in the state led the legislature to confer upon it the name and style of Indiana University.

The Impulses of Early Internationalism

There is no ready explanation as to why a small frontier college should grow into a university with a worldwide reputation and strong international commitments. Yet the impulses which have moved the university into the forefront of the international field have been present since its founding, and for the most part they are traceable to strong personalities who have left their mark on IU.

In the autumn of 1829 Andrew Wylie came to Indiana College as its first president, a post he held until 1851, and in the tradition of that day he came not only as president but also as professor. As the Indiana Seminary, the curriculum had been solely in the classics, but President Wylie taught the senior class in the new college and lectured to them on a variety of subjects, including constitutional law and political economy. By 1838 he had added moral science and international law.

The Wylie tradition of teaching subjects with an international content was continued by David Starr Jordan, the international-minded scholar from Cornell who took over the presidency of Indiana in 1885 and remained there until lured away in 1891 to the presidency of the new Stanford University in California. Jordan used to lead parties of his students on studies abroad.

Out of these early influences came a strain of IU graduates who distinguished themselves in international work or service abroad. One such was Joseph Wright (for whom a campus quadrangle is named), an early governor of Indiana, who became the first U.S. Minister to Prussia and was prominent in helping to found the first Methodist Church in Germany. Another, John Foster (for whom another quadrangle is named), graduated from IU in 1855, went into international law and career diplomacy after the Civil War, served as Minister to Mexico, and later became Secretary of State. His grandson, John Foster Dulles, who lived with him as a youngster, followed in his footsteps as Secretary of State sixty-one years later. Still another IU man, Walter Q. Gresham, rose to become Secretary of State, and others in the same period served abroad as American ambassadors.

Around the turn of the century another influence came to the fore, the "missionary" impulse. This manifested itself at different universities in various forms. At Princeton, for instance, it took the form of being the intellectual godfather of colleges in the Middle East. At Indiana, in a sort of early form of the Peace Corps, it sent graduates hastening to enlist in international YMCA, church, and mission work all over the world, an impulse which continued to move IU students right up until the outbreak of World War II.

Some of these early overseas venturers were responsible for yet a third influence which has contributed to Indiana University's international coloration. When the Philippine Islands came under U.S. authority in 1898 after the Spanish-American War, the country was swept by an impulse— partly out of guilt for the method of their annexation—"to educate the Filipinos, and uplift and civilize and Christianize them," in the words of President McKinley. This early version of a technical assistance project sent a whole stream of IU graduates out to teach and work in the islands. Many remained there, and others came back to teach at Bloomington. Because of these personal contacts, a number of Filipino students found their way to Indiana, and when they returned home moved into positions of influence and authority. Many prominent Filipinos today are IU alumni. This connection with Indiana has flourished over the years, and today there are cases of third-generation Filipino students studying at the university.

Another important impulse for international involvement was the research of individual faculty members. One such project was the important study carried on by Indiana University Professor (now emeritus) Paul Weatherwax regarding the evolution of the corn plant. These studies took him to many parts of Latin America, where he is today known as well as he is in the United States.

The Impact of International Teachers

As the decades passed, other influential teachers left their impact on the university and its student body. One was Professor Amos Hershey, a political scientist who took an intense interest in international affairs and served as one of President Wilson's advisers at the Versailles Conference. A popular teacher, he had many disciples among the students, and a number of them went into international work and diplomacy.

But in the years between the two world wars, when Indiana and the Middle West went isolationist, the university went through a quiet period. In the great Ku Klux Klan revival of the 1920's, when the Klan controlled political offices in several states, the organization ran Indiana, and Wells recalls when he was an undergraduate at IU seeing the local Klavern parade up Fifth Street and through the campus in a gesture to intimidate professors who supported the League of Nations and other international entanglements. Later, the university's International Relations Club came under attack from another band of local vigilants, the American Legion.

Wells himself, having received his A.M. from IU in 1927, joined the university's full-time teaching staff in 1930 and in 1935 he moved up to be Dean of the School of Business. At that time, he recalls, there was some talk in the school about international business, but it was not until after he was made acting president in 1937—fourteen years after his own graduation—and had made a trip around South America that he began to think in terms of the university's possible international dimension. "At that time," recalls Mr. Wells, "we simply began to encourage anybody who had interest in expanding the curriculum or the horizons of the university into the wider world."

During the early years of World War II, IU became very active in intensive language training courses for the U.S. Armed Services, and one of the law school faculty members, Frank Horack, made a formal proposal that the university after the war build upon this specialized training an academic competence about a single area. "We had the beginnings of the area studies idea, but we did nothing about it," said Mr. Wells. "We flubbed it."

In the immediate postwar years, IU's President moved rapidly back and forth between the educational and the public service limelight. In addition to his work at Indiana, he was named cultural adviser to the military governor of the U.S. Occupied Zone in Germany. He represented American universities at the SEATO Conference on Higher Education. He held ministerial rank when he helped supervise the first postwar Greek elections, and in 1957 President Eisenhower named him among the five U.S. delegates to the UN General Assembly. In 1958 Dr. Wells was one of the American educators who surveyed Soviet higher education, and their report —which praised Soviet achievements—led to a serious reevaluation of American methods in colleges and universities.

On campus during these years a few forceful personalities, in the Indiana University tradition, were magnetizing clusters of fellow professors and students in their specialized fields, and these became the bases for the university's expansion into international education. One such was Professor Stith Thompson, a distinguished folklore specialist who had established a worldwide reputation prior to World War II. Folklore, like mathematics, is universal and cross-cultural, and Professor Thompson began to gather around him at IU specialists from all over the world in the related fields of anthropology and linguistics. Other universities tried repeatedly to hire Thompson—now retired—away from Indiana: President Wells's successful countermove was a standing offer to give Thompson $1,000 above the best rival offer.

During the war years two other influential specialists joined the IU faculty. One was Charles F. Voegelin, an anthropologist and now the chairman of the department, who came to Bloomington in 1941. The other was Thomas A. Sebeok, a linguistics specialist from Princeton, who joined the IU faculty in 1943. Because of its growing strength in linguistics, Indiana University was awarded a wartime contract for the crash training of linguists in the Altaic languages, a scholarly designation—derived from the name of the Altai mountain range—for a number of languages which roughly includes the Turkic, Mongol, and (Manchu-) Tunguz languages. This led Indiana University to import a number of Turks as language "informants"—and provided the university with a sizable group of Turkish alumni—but it also provided a postwar base for a strong program in these esoteric tongues.

Another strong international enclave formed around the department of government during the decade following 1945. Professor Hershey died in 1932, but two years later Edward H. Buehrig, who had studied international law and international relations with Professor Harold Lasswell at the University of Chicago, came to Bloomington as an instructor. Somewhat to his discomfiture, he was looked upon as a successor to Hershey, but in a few years he had evolved his own courses, built up a strong following on campus, and begun to establish an international reputation. The government department began to branch out, to expand its faculty, to bring in more comparative scholars and to attract to the campus distinguished international visitors. Professor Buehrig served with the State Department during World War II and at the San Francisco conference which established the United Nations. During 1957-58 Buehrig served as a visiting professor at the American University of Beirut, a period which included the civil war in Lebanon and the intervention of U.S. troops—"I was a political scientist in the middle of a unique laboratory," says Buehrig —and he returned to Indiana more than ever convinced of the value of field research abroad.

The Growth of International Activities

At the end of 1954 IU had entered into its first technical assistance contract, an ICA project to assist with educational development at Prasarnmitr (College of Education) in Bangkok. Indiana University's interest in Thailand had been aroused some years earlier when the Thai Minister of Education called at Bloomington, and it was brought to a head when Whack Wright, then Vice President of the University and Dean of the School of Education and a tireless worker in pushing out the frontiers of the university, went to Bangkok in mid-1954 and refined a proposal to assist the Thai college.

In the meantime another senior member of the department of government joined the faculty and played a key role in moving the university deeper into international waters. This was Walter H. C. Laves, chairman of the department since 1954. Laves, like Buehrig a University of Chicago product, had a wealth of governmental and international experience before coming to IU. From 1947 to 1950 he was deputy director general of UNESCO and in 1951-52 he served in the U.S. foreign aid agencies ECA and MSA. In 1952 he went back to international work as a member of the UN Technical Assistance Board and in 1953-54 served as an adviser to the secretary general, UN Technical Assistance Administration, and the Economic Commission for Asia and the Far East during a conference in Rangoon.

As a result of Laves' contacts and interests in Southeast Asia, discussions began on a second IU technical assistance contract for Thailand, and in May, 1955, the university signed an agreement with the U.S. foreign aid agency to provide assistance to Thammasat University in Thailand in the development of an Institute of Public Administration.

In the autumn of 1955 President Wells asked Laves to be chairman of an International Committee of faculty and administration to advise on certain international projects—such as membership in the American Universities Field Staff—which were coming up for decision. Within a year or two, international activities followed each other in rapid succession.

In 1954 IU had joined with fifteen other Indiana universities and colleges to set up a summer study program in Mexico, a modest study-abroad project which enables students of Spanish or students in any field with a competence in Spanish to earn credit by studying in Mexico at the University of Americas for six weeks.

The same year a tentative effort was made at IU to establish the beginnings of an area program in Latin American Studies. In 1946 the policy committee of the faculty of the College of Arts and Sciences had gone on record as opposed to the concept of area studies, but with the passage of years—and the evidence of burgeoning area studies centers at other campuses—resistance to the idea began to dwindle and in 1958 Professor Joseph Sutton, a government department faculty member who had just returned from three years as Chief of Party for the public administration project in Thailand, persuaded the deans to support a program in Asian Studies, of which Sutton became the chairman.

The fact that there are about one million people of Slavic background in the state of Indiana made it logical for IU to concentrate on Slavic languages and literature. Slavic languages have been taught at the university since 1944, and in 1947 a department of Slavic Studies was established. In 1958 a department of Slavic Languages and Literature was established, and in 1959 the university was awarded an NDEA grant. Courses are offered in Russian and in Bulgarian, Czech and Slovak, Polish, and Serbo-Croatian in order to give students a fluent knowledge of the languages, an introduction to the Slavic peoples, and an acquaintance with the major works of nineteenth- and twentieth-century Russian literature. In addition, since 1950, under an Office of Education contract, the university has provided a summer program, the Slavic Workshop, which offers intensive language training for NDEA students in Russian, Polish, and Serbo-Croatian. An NDEA program for secondary school teachers is part of the workshop.

This equity in the languages of Russia and Eastern Europe led naturally to a desire to build up political competence in the area. The cold war confrontation between the United States and the Soviet Union added to the case for assembling academic strengths in studies of the Soviet and satellite nations of Eastern Europe. The first efforts in this direction at Indiana came to nothing, but in 1956 a Soviet affairs expert, Professor Robert F. Byrnes, who had spent a fruitful period from 1953 to 1956 directing the Mid-European Studies Center for the Free Europe Committee in New York, joined the IU history department. Soon after his arrival in Bloomington he was made chairman of a review committee on the Soviet-East European area, and—on the strength of the committee's outspoken report—fundamental changes were made.

William B. Edgerton, a Slavic language specialist from Columbia University, was brought in in 1958 to establish the department of Slavic Languages and Literature, and the same year a Russian and East European Institute was established, with Byrnes as director, to prepare students as specialists on the Soviet Union and on Eastern Europe for jobs in teaching, government, and similar fields. In addition, the Institute was to engage in research.

The Gospel Preached Gently

At some point—and most faculty observers agree that it was within the years 1955 to 1960—Indiana University changed from an institution at which a few high points of international interest, isolated and disconnected departmental projects, showed above the surface to a university in which the international dimension, visible and solid, ran like a high ridge through many departments, divisions, and schools.

The area studies programs, for instance, began as acts of faith on the part of a few dedicated individuals, but in a matter of a year or so two of them—the Asian Studies Program and the Russian and East European Institute—had grown to be campus power centers which had the backing of the administration and had attracted faculty support from several different disciplines. Unlike some major universities, Indiana did not wait for foundation support before moving into the area studies field: Indiana University funds were used to launch both the Asian Studies Program and the Russian and East European Institute. It was not until 1961 that the Ford Foundation, which in the meantime had been impressed with what IU had achieved, made a grant of $2,300,000 to the university to provide ten-year support to the area programs, five-year support to a new area program for Africa, and assistance to a variety of other international activities.

The experience of the department of government offers another example of the rapid-spread influence of internationalization. In 1954 the offerings of the comparative government courses were provincial, or at least Western oriented—the usual courses on the United States, Britain, and Western Europe. "The single most important impact on our department," explains Professor Laves, "was its entry into the contract field when it was made responsible for an Indiana University program in Thailand." Faculty members were suddenly thrown up against the problems of public administration overseas; they began to investigate the mechanics of government in Thailand; they went on to acquire an interest in the peoples and cultures of Southeast Asia; and they brought back to the Bloomington campus a new awareness of non-Western areas. Fifty percent of the present department members have overseas experience.

John W. Ashton, who had been at IU since 1946—most recently as Vice President for Graduate Development and Dean of the Graduate School—and is now on leave to serve with the U.S. Office of Education for a second time, attributes the university's surge of internationalism to the role of Wells.

"Far and away the most important element in bringing the international dimension to Indiana University was the power and personality of Herman Wells," remarked Dean Ashton.

Chancellor Wells, who is a master in blending cajolery with control, apparent permissiveness with concealed direction, modestly describes his role during this period as "preaching the gospel gently." There was no deliberate attempt to internationalize the university: rather, on the basis that the more universal the knowledge, the better it is in the modern world, there was a steady stress on the broad view essential to a university. The approach, summed up the Chancellor, was one of "never attempting any academic project just because it was international, but never turning one down just because it was."

"Administratively," explained Mr. Wells, "Indiana University has always been something of a loosely organized university, and we have always believed in letting the individual faculty member find his own way. Through this, we have tried to make IU an exciting place. My predecessor started this, and I just tried to continue the policy.

"We felt that we couldn't at that time centralize too much without stifling initiative," Mr. Wells went on, "but on the positive side, if a faculty member came in with what we thought was a good idea in the international field, we got behind him and tried to make it work. The word soon went out that the administration was really interested. The basic idea was to spot the man in advance, and then when the man and the idea came together, to give them both a push. For those already interested in the international field, quiet support was all that was necessary. For the harder cases, there were effective ways to help—exposing them to field experience through encouraging foreign travel, or supporting their requests for books and resources which would serve our international interests."

One visible international impact on campus was the presence of foreign faculty members, initially recruited abroad. In hiring outstanding specialists abroad, the administration always made it clear to its faculty that the university was not out to recruit faculty members from abroad simply to boast of foreign faculty, but that its policy was to seek good faculty members wherever they were available. IU faculty appreciated this qualitative approach to recruitment, and welcomed rather than resented foreign faculty members at Bloomington. Today, several department chairmen are from among those faculty members originally recruited abroad.

One technique used to bring an international flavor to the campus was a simple mechanism to spot foreign visitors to the United States who might be attracted to speak at Bloomington or at least pass through on their cross-country journeys. This chore was handled by Peter Fraenkel, now with the Ford Foundation, who served as assistant to the President of IU and who enlisted the help of prominent faculty members to entertain the visitors. "That is about all the international organization we had in those days," recalls Chancellor Wells.

More important than the moral support in backing international ventures on the part of the faculty was what one dean has called "some imaginative methods of financing." In contrast to some other major universities, which have salted away grants and endowments and use only the interest to provide faculty chairs, Indiana University has followed a policy of moving a foundation-financed faculty member onto the regular university budget as soon as possible. At IU this is generally done within two years, in comparison to five years at some other institutions. Similarly, Indiana University has been willing to take the financial risk of adding faculty members, particularly in the international areas, and depending on the state legislature to provide the funds in the next biennial budget, a gamble which private universities cannot always afford to take.

Perhaps most imaginative of all university funding efforts has been the Indiana University Foundation, a nonprofit corporation chartered in 1936 to receive and administer grants, contracts, patents, gifts, and bequests for the benefit of the university. Its early purpose was to provide a channel for alumni gifts to IU, an objective which has continued to be an important activity, but over the years the Foundation's attention has increasingly been given to the sponsorship of research programs of members of the faculty. Because of their diversity and numbers, these projects require specialized attention over and beyond the university's regular academic procedures, and so the Trustees of IU assigned coordination and general supervision of research programs to the Foundation. This has enabled the Foundation to play a key role in the internationalization of the university by providing what one dean calls "jump money," the initial grants to enable faculty members and departments to launch certain programs which otherwise could not have been undertaken with regular university funds.

The University and the Community

During these years of transition, 1955 to 1960, Wells and his administrators operated on the principle that the campus of the university ran to the boundaries of the state. There were many ways of relating the university to the community which it serves, but one of the most colorful was the unique exhibit of Thai art which was brought to Bloomington and displayed in 1960. The exhibit, consisting of priceless pieces which had never been out of Thailand before, was assembled by the Thais and offered for showing abroad. Because of its contract involvement in the country, as well as the enthusiasm of Professor Theodore Bowie, an IU professor of fine arts, Indiana University convinced the Thais to ship the exhibit to Bloomington. Because of the security arrangements necessary, it took two years of complicated negotiations and eventually a U.S. battleship to get it to the United States. Indiana University billed the display as a "Salute to Thailand," and the resulting publicity was such that the exhibit was eventually shown in New York and Boston and then in Europe and, finally, in Japan. Eventually the Thai people, who had never seen this collection of their indigenous art, demanded that it be displayed at home.

The university then—and now—utilized every opportunity to show the relationship of its work in its broadest aspects to the lives and interests of the people of the state in which it is located. Thus the state's widening international interests were closely tied to efforts to broaden the curriculum to expose Indiana students to international course material. In its industrial revival of the 1930's, the state of Indiana had gone heavily into international trade, shipping its products all over the world. International know-how, it was argued, would help prepare Indiana University graduates to distribute Indiana products the world over. And when the university moved into the technical assistance field, the appeal was not only to the patriotic motive but that service abroad would better equip the sons and daughters of Hoosiers to cope with the world beyond the state boundaries.

III

Except for the earlier courses in foreign languages, government, history, linguistics, and folklore, most of the international dimension at Indiana University has been firmed up over the past decade. Just how substantial it had become became apparent to the administration in the summer of 1964, when it compiled a census of the programs, activities, and committees with major international interests or components. Not counting departments or courses in which the international interest is to some extent traditional, Indiana University discovered that it had more than 100 international programs, activities, or committees in operation or in the advanced planning state.

The more important of these will be capsuled in the section that follows. However, as the 1964 survey conceded, "neither lists nor statistics, words nor charts, can adequately portray the maze of processes at work in the university's international programs—the interlocking, interrelating, mutual support. Vigorously encouraged by the university's central administration, international activities have generally been accommodated within the regular administrative and academic structure as natural facets of conventional programs, but the university has readily made special arrangements whenever they were required to benefit a new undertaking. An atmosphere of freedom, opportunity and cooperation, carefully nurtured by administration and faculty alike, has fostered the growth of a rather hospitable jungle of informal relationships—both interpersonal and institutional."

International Course Offerings

At IU teaching is still recognized as the first function of a university. Basically, every faculty member teaches at least one course restricted to undergraduates, one combined course open to undergraduates and graduate students alike, and one course for specialists. This is not a university policy, but it seems to be the general practice at Bloomington.

Apart from the traditional language and literature courses, students at IU—unlike those at some large universities—have a profusion of course offerings of international content to choose from. In the history department, for instance, there are some 135 courses, of which fifty-five deal totally in non-Western areas. Of the history courses, nine are restricted to undergraduates (and of these, six relate to non-Western areas), sixteen are restricted to graduate students, and 110 are open to both. The government department, which offers strong comparative government courses, in 1964-65 had more than four hundred undergraduate majors, second only to the English department. This is an enrollment increase proportionately larger than in the university as a whole, a phenomenon which is occurring on other campuses as well as at IU.

A profusion of course offerings does not necessarily expose undergraduates to the international dimension, and in some departments at IU an effort has been made to infuse international content by modifying or adapting existing courses as the result of faculty experience abroad. For example, the basic course in American government, taken by many underclassmen, has been converted from a course dealing with local, state, and national government developments into a two-semester course, one of which deals with the U.S. government and the other with American foreign policy. Other courses which have been given a high international content include half a dozen in history and one in economics.

In one area, teaching nonlanguage courses in foreign languages, Indiana University is far out in front, mainly due to the remarkable results obtained in its program of raising the level of secondary school language competence in the state. In 1964-65 an experimental course in Latin American economics was taught entirely in Spanish, using a translation of a standard American textbook. In addition, a section of Latin American history was also given in Spanish. French was used to teach a history of Western civilization class during the first semester, and a fine arts course in the same language was taught the second semester. A section of the Soviet government and politics course was taught in Russian.

Despite these experimental efforts, some of the international-minded faculty members contend that IU has not yet made sufficient progress in revision of its undergraduate curriculum. The graduate curriculum, they contend, has its own built-in impetus for improvement—if Indiana University graduate students do not meet the hiring standards of the best American universities it is immediately possible to determine where improvement is needed. Improvement in undergraduate education can be brought about by the graduate schools making greater demands upon the undergraduates, or by pressure from the central administration. In the opinion of the internationalists on the IU faculty, neither has happened to a sufficient degree. The tendency has been to settle for "a good liberal education" for undergraduates, without defining what a good liberal arts education really is. A Committee on International Aspects of Undergraduate Education has existed for some years, under the chairmanship of Samuel E. Braden, Vice President and Dean for Undergraduate Development, but for some time it was moribund and has only lately shown signs of revival.

The Non-Western Project

In the opinion of Ray L. Heffner, Vice President and Dean of the Faculties, "Indiana University may have been more influential in helping other Indiana colleges and universities change their undergraduate curriculum than in altering its own courses."

What Dean Heffner had in mind is the success of the cooperative project involving IU and about three-fourths of the thirty-odd institutions of higher education in the state to encourage the study of the non-Western world in undergraduate education. Among the states, Indiana was the first to engage in a statewide effort to strengthen the study of foreign areas. New York some years later initiated a similar effort, and a few more states—Vermont, Virginia, Pennsylvania, and California—have now made beginnings, ranging from modest to ambitious, to strengthen opportunities in their educational institutions for the study of foreign areas.

The Indiana program came about on the initiative of IU. During the spring of 1958 Professor Robert Byrnes conducted a survey of the state of non-Western studies in undergraduate education in Indiana. Not surprisingly, it revealed that approximately 90 percent of the state's A.B.'s graduated without having learned anything about any non-Western society. Almost two-thirds learned little, if anything, about international affairs in general. As a result of a conference held at IU in the autumn of 1958, with the assistance of the American Council of Learned Societies, the Byrnes findings were translated into a proposal for a cooperative effort among all the colleges in the state, drawing upon the resources of IU, to encourage more study of the non-Western world. A proposal was submitted to the Ford Foundation—under the resounding title of The Project for Extending the Study of Foreign Areas in Indiana Undergraduate Education—and a three-year grant was made in 1959. The project became familiarly known as the Non-Western Project, and the name has stuck.

The program has two objectives: first, to arouse interest in the problem and to stimulate, encourage, and assist local campus action; second, to share and extend the resources in the state for undergraduate study of non-Western areas. These have been achieved in a number of ways: centrally administered by a part-time director from the IU faculty, the project has stimulated on-campus conferences and seminars, awarded summer faculty fellowships for faculty development and training, circulated traveling exhibits and arranged for special lectures and consultations among the Indiana colleges, and—in 1959 and 1960—sponsored an experimental semester TV course on Soviet history, which was utilized for credit by seven colleges. Under the IU wing, several Indiana colleges participate in joint membership in the American Universities Field Staff, bringing them visits from A.U.F.S. specialists and the 60 to 70 reports on foreign affairs which the organization issues annually.

By the time the project came up for renewal of its grant in 1962 the

results were measurable. Of the thirty-four institutions of higher education
in Indiana, representing all sizes and kinds of universities and colleges,
twenty-seven had been involved in one or more activities of the project
while at least a dozen had participated in almost all programs sponsored by
the project. By 1962 several participating colleges and universities had
broadened their undergraduate curriculum to include non-Western studies.
Hanover College had instituted a required five-hour course in the junior
year for all students, the first semester a study of East Asian civilization,
the second a genuine world literature course. De Pauw University had
organized a faculty seminar on Africa as the first step toward introducing a
multidisciplinary introductory course on Africa. Wabash was beginning to
develop a minor in Far Eastern studies. Manchester and St. Mary's had
greatly broadened their non-Western offerings in the history departments.
In addition, some ten colleges had shown serious interest and taken at least
preliminary steps in offering instruction in non-Western areas.

On the strength of these beginnings, the Ford Foundation grant was
renewed through 1967, and it is the belief of those in charge of the project
that by 1968 non-Western studies will have become an integral part of the
educational program in several Indiana colleges and will be in the process
of becoming so in a number of others.

A number of less ambitious intercollegiate study programs have been
worked out by IU. One is the summer study program in Mexico, begun in
1954, and now participated in by sixteen Indiana colleges and universities.
Another is the Indiana Inter-collegiate Study Project in England, in which
students from sixteen Indiana institutions spend six weeks on a summer
program, preferably within their major fields, of study projects in Britain.

Statewide Language Improvement

As head of the state school system, IU has special responsibility for
Indiana's secondary schools and a good many of its programs are designed
especially to strengthen the course offerings of the state's high schools and
improve the competence of their teachers.

The improvement achieved in language teaching has been as marked as
in any state of the Union. In fact, Indiana may soon be the leading state in
four-year sequences in languages. In 1957 the state stood in thirty-sixth
place, with fewer than 25 percent of its public high schools offering a
modern foreign language. By 1964 the figure had climbed to approximately
66 percent, and enrollment figures for 1964-65 showed nearly one-third of
the total high school population studying a foreign language. The demand
for foreign languages created, of course, its own problems. The most obvious was a basic shortage of foreign language teachers, and the second was
the need for the retraining of those teachers who had fallen behind in their
competence.

As a means of giving greater support to the high schools, IU in 1959 appointed a Coordinator of Foreign Languages, a full-time faculty member with a joint appointment in the College of Arts and Sciences and the School of Education, whose primary responsibilities are to represent the university's foreign language programs in the schools and to represent the cause of secondary school foreign language programs in the university.

The first major statewide program undertaken was the Indiana University Honors Program in Foreign Languages for High School Students, which began in 1962 with a three-year grant from the Carnegie Corporation, although it hoped to be self-supporting within a period of five years. The purposes are to bring about substantial improvement in the teaching of foreign languages in public and parochial secondary schools in terms of longer teaching sequences, increased enrollments, and new emphasis on spoken languages, and to increase the number and quality of high school seniors entering college as teacher trainees in foreign languages and provide university language departments with freshmen more advanced in language work. The program offers to selected students of advanced French, German, and Spanish, from schools teaching these languages in sequences of three years or more, a reward for their classroom achievement in the form of intensive summer study abroad, with scholarships given as needed. A total of 138 students were involved in the first two years of the program, and in the summer of 1964 no fewer than ninety Indiana high school students studied for nine-week periods at centers in France, Germany, and Mexico.

Developing out of these experiences, Indiana University made an appeal to the Ford Foundation to support a ten-year plan called the Indiana Language Program. In 1962, on the strength of a $650,000 Ford Foundation grant to support the first five years of the plan, the program was launched. The objects are to provide in-service training of high school language teachers, to improve the preparation of future teachers, to experiment with the learning process, and to stimulate enthusiastic interest among students and within communities for the competent use of modern European languages. The program uses fellowships, scholarships, institutes, special conferences, and other devices such as foreign travel scholarships.

The impact of the Indiana language efforts is apparent at several levels of instruction. More than 50 percent of the state's high school French teachers and 65 percent of the Spanish language teachers have found ways to travel and study abroad since the program began. As of the 1965-66 school year, the state education authorities have ruled that every commissioned high school in Indiana will be required to offer at least two years of a foreign language, and that every high school with a first-class commission or a special first-class commission will be required to offer at least two years of both a classical and a modern foreign language and at least three years of one of these languages. Inasmuch as in 1963, seventy-three public secondary schools offered no foreign language at all and 208 offered no modern foreign language, this requirement represents a radical shift in language emphasis.

At Indiana University itself, the result of better language teaching at the high school level has led the College of Arts and Sciences to eliminate college credit for the first year of a foreign language if it is the student's *first* foreign language.

Apart from its statewide language programs, IU is involved in a number of less ambitious projects to upgrade secondary standards. Since 1959 the Department of Slavic Languages and Literature has carried on an NDEA program in which twenty-five high school teachers of other subjects are selected annually for a year of intensive Russian study so that they can teach the language on return to their own schools. A series of intensive Russian language courses makes it possible for these teachers, as well as other students, to acquire the equivalent of four years of college Russian in two summers and the intervening academic year.

Duplicating its efforts to improve statewide language teaching, IU has also appointed a Coordinator of Social Studies, whose duty it is to establish close relations between the university and the secondary schools in order to improve and enrich social studies (including world affairs). As with languages, teacher seminars, lectures, and institutes have been utilized, as well as consultation. Similar concern may in time center on the teaching of history in Indiana, as the result of a three-year survey of the teaching of American history in the high schools of the state, conducted by three IU history professors and published in 1964. Their findings: 66 percent of the state's teachers of American history in the high schools had earned their bachelor's degree in fields other than history: 30 percent had taken no graduate work in history; over half had read no book on American history during the past year.

Area Studies

The Latin American Studies Program, established in 1954, is the oldest of the area programs at Indiana University. It is also the least substantial. Until early 1963 the committee which administered Latin American Studies was drawn strictly from the College of Arts and Sciences, and had a strong language bias, but in May, 1963, when Professor Robert Quirk of the history department assumed the chairmanship of the committee, it was reconstituted to include representatives of several disciplines and schools.

The undergraduate program in Latin American Studies provides for a general cultural knowledge with a regional focus, rather than the traditional specialization in one academic discipline. It embraces courses which deal with the races, geographic conditions, historical evolution, social problems, folklore, and literatures of the respective Latin American nations.

IU's Latin American specialists are aware of the program's limitations.

Not having a full range of professional schools, the program must be oriented toward the disciplines represented, and it therefore cannot match the wide-ranging Latin American programs at some other universities. However, Bloomington would like to become a chief center for the study of Latin American history and—banking on its strengths in the government and history departments—concentrate on Latin American-U.S. relations and intrahemispheric diplomacy.

A Rockefeller Foundation grant in 1961 (which runs through 1967) helps Indiana University support the Latin American Music Center, which provides an extensive collection of scores, recordings, and tapes of Latin American music, promotes the study and research of Latin American music, offers courses and seminars and encourages the performance of Latin American music in the United States and abroad. Headed by an outstanding Latin American musician, Juan Orrego-Salas, the program has brought prominent Latin American composers to Bloomington and sponsored a series of concerts, including an elaborate Latin American music festival in April, 1965, which attracted a large number of musicians and other Latin American specialists from both North and South America.

IU's Asian Studies Program, launched in 1958, is not as firmly established as its seven-year history would indicate. It has developed unevenly, in part because of differing views held by leading professors. It provides undergraduate and graduate work in most of the social science fields in both the Near East and the Far East and is able to grant doctoral degrees in Chinese, Japanese, and Korean. The newly established Near Eastern Languages and Literature department is being built up: Arabic, Hebrew, and Persian are already being taught. However, despite the fact that Indiana University has been engaged in technical assistance programs in Thailand, Indonesia, and Pakistan for at least the past ten years, literally nothing has been carried over from this involvement into an area studies program. IU's head librarian, who served as a consultant in Indonesia for a year, has made it a personal interest to collect materials from Indonesia in the belief that the university will someday wish to specialize in Southeast Asia.

IU's Asian Studies includes the Far East, the Near East, Southeast Asia, and South Asia, but in fact the last two of these major areas are almost ignored. The reason for this goes back to a faculty committee decision of almost ten years ago. At that time the argument was made that area studies should rest on language mastery, and that as IU could not hope to offer courses in the many languages of South and Southeast Asia, it should concentrate on Chinese, Japanese, and, later, Korean and Arabic. "We decided to back our strengths," said a faculty member.

The decision led to the building up of a small but strong department of East Asian Languages and Literature, under Professor Wu-chi Liu. The department was organized in 1962, as a result of the expansion of the Asian Studies Program. It provides courses both for undergraduate majors in the East Asian Languages and Literatures and for students in other disciplines who desire a working knowledge of Chinese, Japanese, or Korean for area studies.

Following the same pattern, the department of Near Eastern Languages and Literature was established in 1965, offering language and literature courses in Arabic, Hebrew, Turkish, and Uzbek.

Not part of the Asian Studies Program, but impinging on both the East Asian and the Near Eastern areas is Indiana University's unique program in Uralic and Altaic Studies.

More than one hundred million people—dispersed over a vast area stretching from the Atlantic to the Pacific oceans and from the Arctic to the Mediterranean—speak Uralic and Altaic languages. Some are completely westernized, such as the Finns or the Hungarians; others, such as the Koreans, belong to the cultural area of the Far East; still others, like the Turks, numbering about 58,000,000, can be found from the Balkans, through the Middle East, and far into Siberia. The study of this heterogeneous group can be best achieved through knowledge of at least one of the major Uralic and Altaic languages. A full range of these is offered at IU. Hungarian, Finnish, Mongolian, Turkish, and Korean are given each year in a cycle lasting three years. Accelerated courses are being introduced in both Estonian and Uzbek. Among other Uralic and Altaic languages currently offered and taught from a linguistic point of view are Cheremis, Mordvin, Azerbaijani, Chuvash, Old Turkish, Takur, and Manchu. In addition, various background subjects are currently taught, such as the history of Hungary, Hungarian literature, and the history of the Turks and the Mongols.

Indiana University's involvement in this esoteric field grew out of its earlier involvement with folklore studies and Slavic languages, and its wartime work with the Altaic languages. In the postwar years, only Columbia University in the United States specialized in the Uralic-Altaic tongues, but in 1962 IU recruited from Britain a linguist and Hungarian history specialist, Denis Sinor, who had taught at Cambridge. At the same time the National Defense Education Act provided for the establishment at IU of a Uralic and Altaic Language and Area Center, and Sinor was installed as director.

In the spring of 1965, underscoring the close link between Asian Studies and Uralic and Altaic, Professor Sinor—who prefers to style himself "an Orientalist of a classic pattern, rather than a linguist"—was appointed acting chairman of the Asian Studies Program, replacing Joseph Sutton, who had meantime been designated Dean-elect of the College of Arts and Sciences.

IU's Russian and East European Institute has existed in its present form since 1959, but work by faculty and students on the Slavic and East European area antedates the present Institute by a number of years. At the end of World War II the university began teaching the Russian language, and in a few years expanded the curriculum to include a general course in Russian studies under the department of Slavic Studies. In 1953 an Institute for the study of East Europe was formed, drawing on the faculty of several departments, but it failed to find its place on campus and in 1959, under the directorship of Professor Byrnes, the Russian studies and East European programs were combined to form the Russian and East European Institute. At that time, it was set up to offer a certificate in an area and a degree in a discipline. The Institute offers no undergraduate majors, but a minor in Russian and East European studies is accepted by a number of departments.

From its founding, the Institute has grown in size and reputation, and it is now one of the two or three leading centers for Slavic studies in the United States. Enrollment has steadily mounted, from twenty-seven students the first year to 123 in 1964-65. The faculty now numbers thirty-seven scholars on Russia and Eastern Europe. Professor Byrnes resigned as director in 1962, although remaining on the IU faculty, and was succeeded by Professor Robert W. Campbell, the Institute's present director.

The program in African Studies at IU, the latest of the area programs to be established, began in 1961 as a result of the grant which the university received from the Ford Foundation to stimulate international studies. When the program began there were only four courses dealing with Africa: during 1964-65 the program offered thirty-three courses in the departments of anthropology, fine arts, geography, government, history, journalism, and linguistics. The focus is on Africa south of the Sahara, especially West and French-speaking Africa, but in recent years—with the addition to the faculty of Alan P. Merriam, a specialist on African music, Roy Sieber, a fine arts specialist, and John Messenger, an anthropologist—the IU program has become one of the strongest in the United States in the field of the arts of Africa.

The program is planned for both graduate and undergraduate students. Students receive their degrees in their respective departments. In 1964-65 there were ninety-nine graduate students, and each year the number is expected to increase.

Instruction in the major African languages still presents a problem. Instruction in Arabic is, of course, given as part of the Near Eastern Languages and Literature department, and in 1964 IU was able to offer a course in Swahili. However, even when funds are available to provide for African linguists these specialists are not easily found—which raises the question whether it would be more prudent for the major universities offering African studies to specialize in one particular area, such as languages, geographic areas, and the African humanities, instead of trying to offer an inadequate program attempting to cover the whole field.

In one other area Indiana University's African Studies program finds itself operating under something of a handicap. Unlike the case with the university centers in the East, no steady flow of Africans passes through Bloomington. To some extent, this is compensated for by a graduate seminar on contemporary Africa, which brings together the faculty in African Studies and most of the students, and provides a forum for distinguished visitors and Africanists visiting IU. A single theme is used for continuing discussions. In 1964 it was the arts of Africa, and in the autumn-winter of 1964-65 it was organized around the problems of urbanization in sub-Saharan Africa.

African students at IU have associated themselves with the activities of the area studies program, and, reciprocally, members of the faculty and student body have participated in the affairs of the African Students Association, with about ninety African members. In the past year or so the Association has put on an African Night on campus, held a student exhibit of African art, commemorated the independence of many of the African states, and staged a Nigerian play, "The Song of a Goat."

Library Resources

Since 1961 special library programs have been launched at Indiana University in the areas of Asian, African, and Slavic studies and International Business Administration in order to support the academic programs with appropriate materials and services. The university library has also become the depository for Near Eastern publications obtained with Public Law 480 funds. In addition to the international materials in its main library, IU also has its Lilly Library of rare books and manuscripts, included in which is the Mendel collection (named for Bernardo Mendel, a European collector, who has long lived in South America), part of which specializes in Latin Americana from the seventeenth through the nineteenth centuries, with particular attention to Mexican history.

Like most universities which have ventured into area studies, IU has found that a most severe burden, in terms of personnel and procurement, has fallen on its library. Since 1950, according to Dr. Cecil K. Byrd, associate director of libraries, IU has had to add some fifty persons to its library staff because of the demands of area studies, and it is still understaffed. Most area programs, he explains, begin on a "low key" approach and request only general area materials suitable for undergraduate needs, but in short order there is a demand for the more specialized, hard-to-find materials for graduate training. Competition among universities for these materials forces up prices: in Dr. Byrd's experience, prices of some African library materials have tripled within the past four years, and Slavic materials have undergone a 1000 percent increase since 1950, so fierce has been the competition for them. "Universities are like baseball managers," he reflects, "—competitive." The only solution, as he sees it, is that the major universities in the area fields should collaborate and agree on areas of specialization and cease competing across the board.

Centers and Institutes

Indiana Uni /ersity's International Development Research Center, established in November, 1962, came into being as a result of faculty interest and initiative in having an all-university mechanism that would encourage and facilitate interdisciplinary cooperation. Its origins go back to the winter of 1961-62, when the university made its submission for a substantial Ford Foundation grant to assist with international studies. As the plans for the foundation presentation developed, Professor Laves and Professor Fred W. Riggs, also in the government department, drew together a group of faculty who agreed that they shared a sufficiently common interest to justify including in the presentation a proposal to aid faculty and graduate student studies of the problems of the developing nations, problems which interested a hard core of IU faculty members. Conceived originally as a research seminar, once the foundation grant became available it was decided to create a somewhat autonomous research center. Riggs had meanwhile departed for a study in Thailand, but another member of the IU faculty, John P. Lewis, a business economist with much overseas experience, had just returned from a Brookings Institution study in India and was prevailed upon to take direction of the new center. Almost before it could be established, Lewis was called away to serve on the President's Council of Economic Advisers in Washington and later to head the AID mission in India, and Riggs, on his return from Asia, was named acting director.

To a great extent, the IDRC, as it is known at IU, is the personal creation of Riggs, who remained acting director until he took leave in July, 1965, to undertake an assignment at Massachusetts Institute of Technology. The announced objective of the Center is to promote faculty study of economic, political, and social change in the newly developing nations by encouraging the preparation of research projects and sponsoring study groups designed to stimulate basic planning and thinking in the field of development. The Center also took on the function of advising and helping IU faculty and graduate students obtain grants and contracts from foundations and other agencies to support study both on the campus and elsewhere. In addition, the Center provided a number of supportive services—including reference materials, secretarial support, and information on potential sources for contracts and grants related to international development. In the absence of any other mechanism, the Center also took on some university responsibilities in Peace Corps training, in scheduling some foreign scholars visiting IU, as well as the administration of periodic A.U.F.S. staff visits. The Center in 1964 began issuing a newsletter, aimed at not only the score or more faculty members who were listed as fellows of the Center, but also to some three hundred faculty members with overseas interest and experience, thus helping to fill an information gap which existed at the university. In cooperation with the office of the Dean of Faculties, the Center also prepared and issued a register of faculty with overseas experience and interests.

Because most of the participating fellows are research-oriented, the main activity of the IDRC has revolved around several faculty committees or study groups, each of which has taken responsibility for specific development problems and has sought to focus attention on them by means of seminars, discussion papers, guest lecturers, and research projects. One such group focused its attention on problems of urbanization in the developing lands; a second looked into the problems of minority entrepreneur groups in the developing countries, such as the Chinese in Thailand and the Indians in East Africa; a third group has been concerned with the problems of communication in nation building; while a fourth study group was to deal with demography and development.

The IDRC has played a useful role in providing seed money for research projects, modest subventions to individual faculty members to enable them to explore larger research possibilities or to prepare major submissions to foundations for research funds, but for all its efforts the Center fell short of what Riggs felt was its potential. On several occasions, it explored the possibilities of entering into contracts with AID for overseas technical assistance, but without result—mainly because the Center itself was not equipped to undertake the staffing of a contract and lacked the authority or the influence to commit other elements at Indiana University. From the outset, the Center's precise relation to other parts of the university was never spelled out. Professor Riggs, who had a clear conception of the desirability of enlisting all parts of the university in the triple functions of teaching, research, and service in any contracts involving the underdeveloped world, carried neither the weight nor the mandate to engage other disciplines in the projects he proposed.

A related program directed by Professor Riggs, and one which resulted in reciprocal cooperation with the IDRC, was the Faculty Seminar on Political and Administrative Development, which was carried out at Bloomington from 1962 to 1965 on the strength of a grant from the Carnegie Corporation. The seminar was open to faculty members and graduate students from all departments, and its purpose was to focus attention on the political requisites for effective administration—the structure and functioning of local government (both rural and urban), the role of violence and military groups in governmental processes, the development of political parties, and so on. As another outgrowth of both the Faculty Seminar and the presence of the IDRC on campus, IU has been able to enroll no fewer than sixty-seven local members of the Society for International Development, one of the largest local chapters in this international organization.

Indiana University is believed to have now the largest and most active group of folklore students and scholars ever gathered together: both students and faculty come from around the world. Its first Ph.D. degree in folklore was awarded in 1953. Today there are as many as half a hundred Ph.D. candidates in the program.

The growth of the program encouraged its institutionalization, and in late 1963 IU transformed its interdepartmental program into a Folklore Institute, which has its own faculty attached—mostly on joint appointments with related departments—and which provides its own archives, field work, library, journals, and monographs as well as the instruction and research program.

In the 1963-64 academic year, the Folklore Institute undertook the sponsorship of two new journals. The *Journal of the Folklore Institute,* published in Holland, was conceived as an international journal in English representing the worldwide theoretical scholarship of folklore. A second journal, *Asian Folklore Studies,* is actually published in Tokyo, but bears the seal of IU on its cover. It is the official organ of the Society for Asian Folklore, which was organized by folklore faculty and students from Asian countries meeting in Bloomington in 1963. In addition, a series of books— *Folktales of the World*—is being edited from the Folklore Institute. A summer Folklore Institute is held at Bloomington quadrennially.

In addition to the Folklore Institute, IU also mounts a Research Center in Anthropology, Folklore, and Linguistics, under the chairmanship of Thomas A. Sebeok, who is professor of Uralic and Altaic Studies and linguistics and played an important role in building IU's language instruction programs during and after World War II.

The Center includes five major divisions. One is the Languages of the World File, a compilation of essential data on some 3,000 languages, a comprehensive overview of human languages obtained by tape recordings, field analyses, and informants on the campus. A project first developed by the Office of Education in Washington in 1959, it is under the direction of two IU anthropologists, Charles and Florence M. Voegelin. A second branch of the Center is the Archives of Traditional Music, which collects recordings and musical instruments and publishes albums of folk music and the journal, *The Folklore and Folk Music Archivist.*

Also part of the Research Center in Anthropology, Folklore, and Linguistics is the Human Relations Area Files. IU is one of twenty-one member institutions entitled to a full set of Human Relations Area Files— background information of an interdisciplinary nature gathered from a wide variety of sources—for use by faculty and students. The Center is also engaged in a sizable publishing program, and since 1955 it has published thirty-five volumes in the *Uralic and Altaic Series* and thirty-one volumes in the *Publications of the Research Center in Anthropology, Folklore and Linguistics.*

Based on its wartime experiences, IU has continued to stress its competence in linguistics. Under an NDEA program, the department of linguistics offers an interdepartmental program to introduce students to methods of analysis in the comparison of languages and to acquaint them with some of the results achieved by the application of these methods. In addition to introductory, descriptive, and methodological courses, linguistic study of the following specific languages and language subfamilies is offered: Albanian, Arabic, Hungarian, Finnish, Greek, Rumanian, Uzbek, Estonian, Turkish, Hebrew, Chinese, Japanese, Korean, English, French, Russian, Mongolian, Krio, Bambara, and Swahili.

IU's Intensive Language Training Center originated in 1959 as the U.S. Air Force Language Program, but took on its broader name in 1962-63 when the Air Force began to reduce its program and IU determined to broaden the scope of the Center beyond its Air Force contract. In 1964-65 the Center was teaching Air Force students only in Russian, having dropped along the years its programs in Albanian, Hungarian, Chinese, and Egyptian-Arabic. The Center, which uses the audio-lingual approach and emphasizes oral comprehension, transcribing, speaking, and reading in that order, has also provided concentrated training programs for IU's School of Business and for the Peace Corps.

Neither an institute nor a center is the virtually one-man project being carried out by IU faculty member Nicholas DeWitt, a Harvard-trained specialist in comparative and Soviet education. He is engaged in a three-year survey of the role of education in the development of nations, a study of the elements which make up human resource development particularly in the emerging nations of the world. Assisted by an initial grant from the IDRC at Indiana University, Professor DeWitt—who is styled principal investigator on the project—is backed by a grant from the Carnegie Corporation.

Administered from Indiana University is the Inter-University Committee on Travel Grants, a joint venture of forty-six U.S. institutions of higher learning with an interest in Russian and East European studies or in academic exchanges with these countries in other fields. Funded by grants from the Ford Foundation and the State Department, among other sources, the program was originally based in 1955 at Columbia University. In 1960 it was moved to the Indiana University campus. The program seeks to strengthen American education through the support of research-related travel in exchange with the Soviet Union and countries of East Central Europe—Bulgaria, Hungary, and Czechoslovakia. Arrangements are made by the committee for the exchanges of graduate students and young faculty members either for a semester or year, teachers of Russian and English during the summer months, and professors and instructors for research and lecturing.

A similar program, but on a much less ambitious scale, is the American-Yugoslav Exchange Program, a Department of State–Ford Foundation-financed project which has been administered from IU since 1961. Its aim is to encourage and promote the exchange of scholars and ideas between the two countries by means of seminars on topics of mutual interest held both in Yugoslavia and the United States, by the exchange of faculty members and graduate students, and by year-long lecture programs given by American professors at various Yugoslav universities.

Contract Operations

Like most American universities engaged in overseas contract operations, Indiana University to date has largely responded to pleas for help from AID, the Department of State, or the foundations. Thus, while its overseas ventures have been closely related to its competence, they are widely scattered around the world and do not reinforce each other in the field and seldom on campus. The result is, as some faculty members candidly admit, that the overseas programs have lost some of their luster among those who have participated in them.

One of the pioneer contract ventures at IU was undertaken by the government department beginning in 1955 and continued until 1964. This was the contract, funded by AID in its final years and AID's predecessor agencies earlier, to develop a Public Administration Training Program in Thailand. This included, over the years, strengthening Thammasat University's academic program in public administration, developing in-service programs for Thai government officials, and occasional consultation and advice on Thai administrative problems.

On the strength of the Thai experience, the department of government undertook a similar program, also under an AID contract, in Indonesia. Beginning in 1959 and carrying on up to the autumn of 1963, IU provided technical assistance and training in public administration to the government of Indonesia through the facilities of the Indonesian National Institute of Administration.

In 1963, as the government department contract came to an end, IU's School of Business embarked on a Ford Foundation-sponsored project in Indonesia. This involved the establishment of a center for education in office administration as a semiautonomous agency of the National Institute of Administration in Djakarta. The center's mission was to raise the efficiency of operations in Indonesian government offices and the offices of state-controlled enterprises, through training, the preparation of teachers, supervisors, and administrators, and a demonstration center.

IU's School of Business, paced by some of its international-minded faculty members, now leads the university in willingness to involve itself in overseas projects. It has its own International Projects Committee, headed by Professor Stefan H. Robock, Chairman of the Department of International Business Administration, to review proposals for international contract activities arising from overseas institutions or governments, as well as those planned by the School of Business itself. Special international training programs in management and marketing have been held on the Bloomington campus, and in December, 1963, the School of Business mustered more than one hundred deans and professors from more than seventy universities for a conference on international business programs. The International Business Administration department of the school has discussed with AID the establishment of training centers in Latin America, and has worked out an exchange program with the faculty of Yugoslavia's Ljubljana University.

The School of Medicine's major overseas involvement is its contract, initiated by ICA and continued under AID, to supply technical assistance to Pakistan's Basic Medical Sciences Institute, which is a national center for postgraduate training of medical college teachers. This program, begun in 1957, is due to run to 1965. In addition, under the auspices of the U.S. Public Health Service and the World Health Organization, IU's Medical School since 1957 has provided short-term environmental health programs for small groups of health inspectors and laboratory personnel from around the world.

In 1961 the chemistry department of IU's College of Arts and Sciences was asked by the Rockefeller Foundation to cooperate with Brazilian chemists at the University of Brasilia to establish an Institute of Chemistry. IU's contributions up to 1964-65 have been limited to consultation by IU faculty members in Brazil and instruction on the Bloomington campus.

The university's School of Law has been relatively untouched by the move into the international field, but in 1962 it established a comparative law program, which provides courses, seminars, and public speakers in the field of international and comparative law.

The School of Education has been in the overseas assistance field even longer than the department of government, but the impact on the school itself has been minimal by comparison. Except for the few individuals involved in contract operations and the campus coordinators at Bloomington, the experience gained overseas has not yet been translated into broader-horizoned courses or comparative studies of education in other lands.

The first IU overseas contract venture was the School of Education's assignment, undertaken in 1954, to provide assistance to Thailand's Prasarnmitr (College of Education) to raise the level of Thai teacher education. The School's second overseas engagement, beginning in 1956, was an ICA and later an AID contract to train elementary school principals, supervisors, and normal school faculty members for the Belo Horizonte school in Minas Gerais, Brazil, and various other research centers, laboratory schools, and state departments of education. This contract ended in early 1964. In the meantime the School of Education had embarked on a second AID project in 1959, extending to 1970, in which IU is to provide assistance and guidance in the establishment of an institute of education and research in Pakistan. The institute is to prepare teachers and specialists for teacher training colleges and primary teacher training institutions, to prepare instructional materials, and to provide short courses for teachers and administrators.

Under a third AID contract the School of Education in 1963 began to provide assistance to the Universidad Del Trabajo in Uruguay to upgrade its mechanical and electronic engineering divisions by installing new equipment, planning new layouts, and assisting its faculty in rewriting course syllabi. This contract is due to run through 1966.

In many ways the IU division that has perhaps made the greatest international impact on the campus and the community is the Division of Educational Media and the Audio-Visual Center. The Division of Educational Media is under the School of Education and the A-V Center operates under the Division of University Extension, with faculty members holding appointments in both. Departmental walls have never been high at IU, and there is a long tradition of joint appointments.

Indiana University's audio-visual program is world-renowned, and currently graduates perhaps the majority of those acquiring Ph.D. degrees in the field today in the United States. Its reputation was established by Professor Lawrence C. Larson, a veteran in the audio-visual areas, who is now associate dean of the Division of University Extension, director of the Audio-Visual Center, and professor of visual education in the School of Education. Larson, who came to IU from the University of Minnesota in 1940, began by collecting a film library, an assignment he continued after service with the U.S. Navy's Audio-Visual program, and today it is reputed to be the second largest educational film library in the world (the largest being in London). The A-V Center today ships some 3,000 films daily to subscribers.

The A-V Center's interest in overseas work goes back to 1953, when the U.S. Office of Education sent a small group of Filipino students to IU for training. Their presence aroused interest on the part of the Center's staff, and in 1955, when Syracuse University indicated it was unable to provide audio-visual training for a few ICA participants from Iran, the IU A-V Center took over the contract. In 1956 this was expanded into a full-scale program in which the Bloomington Center undertook to provide training for various foreign nationals, nominated by ICA and then by AID, in the field of communications, including educational and communications media leadership, education texts materials, and educational broadcasting. By 1964-65, with the program in its ninth year, more than three hundred foreign participants from fifty-four countries had passed through the training program, most of them for a one-year period. Some of these students come for an M.A. degree, but the majority of them are adult specialists seeking American techniques and skills in the field. The contract is an open-ended one, and it is expected that the training will continue. This is unique in the United States.

IU's A-V Center, drawing an analogy from the university's Medical School, was set up as a learning laboratory, and in its work with the foreign participants it has devised an ingenious method of involving both the participants and the communities of the state in common problems, in line with the university's audio-visual experts' belief that A-V techniques, to be effective, must go beyond the *visual* and produce participation on a citizen level if they are to produce change. The Center's answer has been to use what it calls "campaigns," projects worked out by the A-V students in common with community groups or statewide organizations, in which all the newfound skills of the students, as well as technical aids such as mobile film vans, brochures, posters, wall charts, and radio and TV programs, are enlisted to put across to the public matters of civic concern. As many as four "campaigns" have been put on in a single year, and they include such subjects as a county-wide drive for immunization, a campaign for good farm workshops on behalf of the Indiana Statewide Rural Electrification Cooperative, a drive for better breakfasts among Indiana school children, and an exhibit on the practical and peaceful uses of atomic energy. Foreign students—sometimes in full national regalia—put on the campaigns, which take them into remote rural communities (a sort of Point IV program in reverse) and give them an insight into the American way of life not usually seen from a university campus.

The impact of this participant training program has been felt throughout the A-V Center, according to Professor Warren D. Stevens, who supervises production planning. Courses have been modified because of the experiences with foreign students, and many of the Center's faculty of some forty teachers (out of a total staff of some two hundred) have had their interest aroused in service abroad.

Work with the participants encouraged the A-V Center in 1959 to enter into another AID contract to assist in developing administrative structures, training personnel, and establishing the physical facilities for communications media in a number of ministries throughout Nigeria. Professor Stevens went to Nigeria for a year to establish the program, and in 1964-65 the A-V Center had a staff of five in the country. Up to that time, about fifty Nigerian audio-visual experts had been trained on the job in Nigeria, and twenty-seven Nigerians had been trained at Indiana University. The AID contract is due to end in 1966, at which time IU hopes to have established in Nigeria seven new A-V Centers and to have expanded three that were already in existence.

A similar but smaller communications media project was carried out by the IU Center in Sierra Leone from 1961 to 1964. Under an ICA-AID contract, Indiana University's audio-visual experts assisted the government of the soon-to-be-independent nation to set up an audio-visual center in the capital city of Freetown and to train personnel, especially in the ministries of education and agriculture.

IU's Extension Division, through its Bureau of Industrial and Labor Services, undertook an AID contract in 1962 and 1963 to train trade union leaders from overseas in union organization and administration, education, and collective bargaining methods, and in comparative studies of labor conditions in various countries. The 1964 program, scheduled for

Cyprus, was canceled because of the civil war there, but the possibility is being explored of extending this type of training program to Latin American trade unionists.

Another training program which centers on Indiana University is the Foreign Journalist Project, a Department of State program which annually brings to the United States some thirty foreign journalists, most of them on the second-echelon level in their own countries, who are then given an overview of the American way of life and the operation of a free press in a democratic society. The program was originally located in 1950 at Northwestern University, where it was in the charge of Professor Floyd G. Arpan of the journalism faculty, and when he transferred to IU in 1960 he brought the project with him. Each group of foreign journalists spends up to six weeks on the IU campus in seminars, two three-week periods on professional work assignments with newspapers, magazines, radio and TV stations, advertising agencies, and public relations firms throughout the United States, one week each in seminars in Washington, D.C., and at the United Nations and approximately a month on individual travel within the United States. Their impact on the IU campus is minimal. They mix with the university's journalism students, and experience a mutual rub-off of ideas and cultures, but—mainly because they are guests intent on going their own ways—no attempt is made to use them as resource persons in visits to communities or in classes.

Three groups of Peace Corps volunteers have been trained on the IU campus since the program began in 1962, one bound for Thailand, a second for Tunisia. In the summer of 1964 and again in 1965 the university's African Studies faculty helped train a P.C. group bound for Sierra Leone. In addition, the Midwest Universities Consortium is supporting a research project for evaluation and training of Sierra Leone P.C. members, to which four IU faculty members have contributed.

A small but significant overseas contract involves Indiana University's administration. This is a three-year contract which IU has with the Ford Foundation to help upgrade the administrative procedures of the University of San Marcos in Lima. Undertaken in 1964, the effort is being carried out under the supervision of Indiana University's Vice President and Treasurer.

One program centered on IU is now being copied in other states. This is the program, supported by the U.S. Department of Health, Education, and Welfare, the Indiana State Department of Public Instruction, and the Indiana Language Program, to train Cuban refugees, professionals or high school teachers of Spanish, and then place them in teaching positions. Indiana State University and IU cooperate in this program, and have so done since 1963.

Study Abroad

Indiana University has not gone in for wholesale study-abroad programs. The university offers undergraduate study-abroad programs in Mexico, Peru, Germany, France, Spain, and Italy and graduate study abroad in Eastern Europe, Japan, and elsewhere, but they are modest ventures, with limited scholarships and fellowships, and do not involve more than a handful of students at each location. In addition, of course, many departments have long had provision for credit work abroad.

The summer study-in-Mexico program, a joint effort of sixteen Indiana colleges and universities, has been noted earlier. Another joint venture is the Junior Year in Peru, a Department of State project which provides for students at IU and other colleges and universities—provided they possess a competence in Spanish and an interest in Latin America—an opportunity to spend an academic year (February to December) at the University of San Marcos, in Lima, Peru. About fifteen IU students participate every year.

An interdepartmental Advisory Committee on Study Abroad has existed at IU since 1959 to assist in the supervision and coordination of study-abroad opportunities for IU students. In 1964 the committee completed plans to establish jointly with Purdue University a modest junior-year-abroad program. Arrangements were made for the academic year 1965-66 for some fifteen to twenty IU or Purdue juniors (although others are eligible) to enroll for the year at one of three locations, Hamburg, Strasbourg, or Madrid. IU later set up a relationship with the University of Bologna, Italy. Students will enroll mostly in regular classes at the selected institutions, and most are expected to live in private homes while abroad. In time, the program hopes to expand to an eventual maximum of about forty students a year per installation and to open admission to qualified students from other Indiana colleges and universities. A high degree of language competence is a prerequisite, and it is planned to supplement language capabilities by intensive summer programs prior to departure abroad.

Foreign Students

Indiana University has welcomed foreign students to its campus for some decades, and so easily have they fitted into the pattern of university life that they were hardly thought of as foreign. In more recent years, however, IU—in common with most American universities and colleges—has been confronted with a much higher rate of foreign student applications, a rising percentage of admissions and, in consequence, concern with what is loosely called "the foreign student problem."

During 1963 and 1964, for instance, IU's Office of Records and Admissions received and answered inquiries from approximately 7,600 different foreign applicants, and analyzed and circulated and reported action on

2,865, involving altogether 19,871 pieces of incoming mail. Applications and inquiries for 1964 rose about 50 percent over 1963.

As of 1964-65, foreign students at Indiana University—graduate and undergraduate—numbered 1,234: IU ranked sixteenth among American educational institutions in the number of foreign students enrolled. The impact of foreign students at IU is especially strong in certain departments. For instance, at the graduate level, foreign students made up 42 percent of those in linguistics, 40 percent in government, 30 percent in economics and folklore, 20 percent in physics, chemistry, mathematics, and education.

The Division of Student Personnel, through the Associate Dean of Students and the Counselor for Foreign Students, provides a variety of services for foreign students, including visa assistance, personal, social, and cultural counseling, operation of a speakers bureau, and liaison with a hospitality program with community contacts throughout Indiana. The linguistics department provides courses designed, through drills, dialogues, and exercises, to improve understanding of spoken English for entering foreign students.

An Advisory Committee on Foreign Students was set up in 1963 to study "the foreign student problem," but its recommendations to date concern themselves mainly with the maintenance of IU's academic standards. Apart from a program operated at the university on behalf of the Institute of International Education—a summer orientation program for foreign students recently arrived in the United States, few of whom remain on the IU campus—there is no substantial orientation effort made by IU for its foreign students. Fortunately, the university's active student organizations have moved into this breach and have taken on the responsibility for helping newly arrived foreign students. The International Affairs Commission is a student government agency which for the past two years has provided special services by American students to foreign students, both on an initial orientation basis and on a continuing basis throughout the school year. Each autumn about forty American undergraduates return to campus early to meet arriving foreign students, help them find housing, and show them around the campus and town during the early weeks of the semester. Usually there are twice as many applications as there are openings for these "brother" and "sister" assignments. Through the year the Commission's coordinating committee helps relate the foreign student work of such campus groups as the YMCA, YWCA, and various national student clubs.

Another informal organization which brings foreign and American students together on campus is the Cosmopolitan Club, which meets weekly at the International Center. For some years the club has also put on annual International Dinners, which feature cuisine, exhibits, and entertainment representing the many nations making up the IU student body.

A large number of foreign graduate students—three hundred to four hundred in recent years—reside in the Graduate Residence Center on campus, along with six hundred or so American graduate students. The Center has its own Foreign Student Committee which sponsors its own programs, assists in all-campus foreign student activities, and helps coordinate the activities of the various national groups within the Center.

Campus Constituency

The nine regional campuses of the University Extension Division provide convenient colonies through which the international dimension can be extended to the boundaries of Indiana. They are not being adequately utilized for this purpose as yet. Occasional seminars, lectures, and special programs on international subjects are held at certain of the regional campuses, but much of the organizing initiative must come from Bloomington, and few faculty members volunteer for extra work in the provinces. Similarly, the regional campuses are not systematically used by foreign undergraduate students, although foreign students would make a greater relative impact on the regional communities than they do at Bloomington.

However, in other ways the Extension Division effectively reaches into every corner of the state. The Division's Bureau of Public Discussion, directed by Robert W. Hattery, has the responsibility of helping the adult citizens of Indiana arrive at a better understanding of contemporary public issues, and through special classes on international subjects, conferences, and seminars it attempts to offer information on alternative courses of action.

One of its services is unique. This is its Public Affairs Reference Service, the new name for the old-time "package library" which used to be an adult education service in many mid-West states and which now survives apparently only in Indiana. A non-book library, it consists of special collections of reading materials, newspaper clips, brochures, and so on, carefully filed and catalogued under subject headings, which are sent out in packages in response to requests for information on specific subjects. The Service, according to Professor Hattery, now receives about 4,000 requests per year for materials, and about one-third of these deal with international subjects.

The Bureau of Public Discussion also collaborates with another unit of the Extension Division, the Labor Education and Research Center, in arranging seminars and discussion sessions for trade union members.

In early 1964 Indiana University became a member of the Mid-West Seminar on United States Foreign Policy, an annual, invitation-only conference of business, civic, professional, and academic opinion leaders which has been jointly sponsored, prepared, and presented by the universities of Illinois, Michigan, Minnesota, and Wisconsin since 1954. These regional conferences were patterned after the national seminars on U.S.

he University Looks Abroad

foreign policy which the Brookings Institution initiated in 1947. Each seminar in the mid-West series is limited to an audience of about eighty and centers on a single issue.

Campus communication facilities at IU devote a respectable amount of coverage to international matters. *The Indiana Daily Student,* published by the department of journalism as a laboratory newspaper for its students, looks more like a metropolitan daily than a student paper, is a member of the Associated Press, and carries a high column count of world news. The campus radio station, FM only, uses certain Broadcasting Foundation of American programs, many of which have a high international content. The university's TV station, WTTV, an educational station affiliated with National Educational Television, until 1964 enjoyed an additional outlet of half an hour daily on an Indianapolis commercial TV channel, which it frequently used for international programming.

Foreign Alumni

At the urging of Chancellor Wells, IU's Alumni Office in 1964 prepared a special program for maintaining contact with the university's 2,500 foreign alumni. A special questionnaire was sent to all foreign alumni as the first step in establishing a new foreign alumni program. A director of the Foreign Alumni Program has been designated within the Alumni Office, and the incoming files as a result of the questionnaires are being used to enable IU faculty and administration representatives to make contact with alumni in the course of their international travels. Consideration is being given to the possibility of using IU's foreign alumni to assist in the advance screening of new foreign student applicants.

IV

"Some of the past difficulties in university programs in world affairs, at home and abroad, have arisen from the fact that many programs have been sporadic, *ad hoc,* and inadequately related to one another," said the 1960 report of the Committee on the University and World Affairs (the Morrill report). "What may often be needed is a long-range, university-wide approach, under the highest auspices, to the total complex of substantive activities and administrative arrangements in the international field."

By early 1964 there was an emerging consensus at Indiana University that the committee's observation could be applied to the university, that the time had come when some institutional framework had to be devised to link the teaching, research, and service components of IU's international involvements in order to obtain increased educational fallout from them.

To outside observers, even the formal organization of the university seemed like a highly complex structure, and the apparatus for dealing with international activities seemed to involve widely separated and sometimes unrelated procedures. Under an eight-member Board of Trustees, the President and four vice presidents constitute IU's central administration. On the academic side, nine colleges and schools, the Division of University Extension, the library and the units in military science all process their budgets, appointments, curricula, and so on, through the Vice President and Dean of the Faculties. Certain programs, such as the university press, the radio and TV stations, museums, and research centers, operate under the Vice President for Research and Advanced Studies. The Office of Records and Admissions, all the activities under the Dean of Students, and cooperative educational relations with secondary schools, colleges, and universities elsewhere in Indiana operate under the Vice President and Dean for Undergraduate Development. These three vice presidents meet informally as a Committee for Academic Development. On the business side, all operations of the plant and fiscal matters in general are under the supervision of the Vice President and Treasurer. The President and all the vice presidents, along with the staff members in their offices, constitute the Administrative Committee, which meets regularly to discuss general policy matters and prepare the agenda for the monthly meetings of the Board of Trustees.

As a natural response to the informal and decentralized pattern of operations that had long characterized IU, the university created committee after committee to aid the faculty and administration in conducting business. In time, there were no fewer than seven all-university bodies concerned with aspects of international activities. Some were quite informal, called together to serve a special or long-range purpose. Some became powerful campus centers, others remained moribund, but by their very existence they acted to postpone the consideration of an overall institutional mechanism to coordinate the university's international academic development, research programs, and overseas operations.

There was the Advisory Committee on Study Abroad, formed in 1959 to supervise and coordinate study abroad opportunities by students from IU and other Indiana colleges and universities; the Committee on International Aspects of the Undergraduate Curriculum, which has long been quiescent; the Advisory Committee on International Studies, headed by Professor Buehrig and formed in 1961 to administer the $2,300,000 Ford Foundation grant; the Advisory Committee on Foreign Students, formed in 1963 and representing all graduate divisions of the university and each department with more than twenty foreign students; the Committee of Coordinators, an informal committee of campus coordinators of overseas contract programs, who came together for the first time in 1964; and the Advisory Committee on International Activities, which was constituted in 1964 to supervise and coordinate Indiana University's participation in the Mid-West Universities Consortium for International Activities, Inc. (MUCIA).

Institutionalizing the International Dimension

Within a year after assuming office, President Stahr expressed concern publicly at a campus meeting about the university's organization for participation in international affairs, and a short time later, in making his annual appointments to committees, he asked Chancellor Wells to assume chairmanship of what was then known as the International Relations Committee. The committee was asked to give special attention to the question of a more adequate organization for international affairs, one that would still preserve wide scope for the centers of individual initiative traditional to IU.

Almost from the outset of its meetings, the committee—renamed the University Committee on International Affairs, but known on campus as the Wells Committee—established that the existing machinery for providing coherence to IU's many and varied international activities left much to be desired and it moved in the direction of establishing an international focus in the central administration. Many-sided discussions within the committee brought out the need to provide the international activities with authoritative advice and support within the university, and assistance and liaison outside the university, to achieve the necessary degree of communication within IU and to represent the university clearly and unequivocally in dealing with external agencies. Not all faculty members were in agreement. There were those who felt that the genius of IU has been its ability to maintain a wide variety of autonomous activities and who hankered for the old permissiveness which enabled department chairmen to make themselves into the real centers of power on campus.

In the autumn of 1963 President Stahr asked the committee to come up with proposals which would improve the coordination of the university's expanding international programs while preserving the broad centers of initiative on campus. The committee's first step was to familiarize itself with how other major universities had set about institutionalizing their international activites. The next step was to embark on a campuswide survey of the programs, activities, and committees which made up the IU international dimension, an inventory which surprised even the administration and the faculty by revealing that the university had mounted or had ongoing well over one hundred projects or programs with international implications. The survey, issued in June, 1964, brought out the need for better information about IU's many international activities, and underscored the case for an adequate institutional mechanism for their coordination.

A few months after the survey's appearance, a subcommittee was appointed to consider what additional university procedures or mechanisms were required to achieve the leadership and coordination desired. Professor Byrnes, who had pioneered in the university's Non-Western Project and gained national stature as a Soviet scholar and former director of the Russian and East European Institute, was named chairman of the subcommittee. By the spring of 1965 Byrnes and his colleagues on the sub-committee had produced a proposal for the establishment at IU of a central organization for international affairs. By May it had been approved by the University Committee on International Affairs and accepted by the president, and its implementation had begun. Chosen to head the new structure—inaugurated in September, 1965—was Professor Byrnes.

The International Affairs Center

The structure proposed for IU's international affairs builds on the existing components, and incorporates them into a rational relationship to each other.

At the core of the new structure is an International Affairs Center (ICA), headed by Professor Byrnes as its director, or principal officer. The director will report primarily to the Vice President for Research and Advanced Studies, but he will also maintain close relations with the Vice President and Dean of Faculties and with the Vice President and Dean for Undergraduate Development.

The ICA will advise the administration on the main lines of policy in the international dimension of the university. It will also coordinate the university's activities and provide the imagination, leadership, and initiative to make certain that IU in its long-term development achieves its maximum goals in international education. At the same time, the director of the IAC will serve as the principal spokesman of the university in questions relating to instruction, research, and graduate training in the international field. In addition, under the general direction of the Vice President for Research and Advanced Studies, the center will represent IU in the international field in its relations with foundations and with other private and government agencies. Specifically, the new IAC will take on the responsibility for preparing and negotiating, in close cooperation with every segment of the university, the request to the Ford Foundation for a second, long-term grant to IU in the autumn of 1966. The IAC will also have principal responsibility for seeking and making recommendations concerning the use of foundation and government grants intended to support international studies at IU as a whole. In this, it will assume the operational responsibilities formerly exercised by the Advisory Committee on International Studies and the Advisory Committee on International Activities for the Mid-West Consortium, which may remain in being or in modified form as advisory committees.

The Center's director, who will serve as the principal university official for all of its work in the international field, will advise the president, vice presidents, and the administration and faculty concerning every aspect of university programs affecting instruction, research, and public service in this field, with particular attention to major policy problems and IU's long-term strategy.

It is anticipated that the work of the Center will have three principal foci or divisions, headed by assistant directors—International Studies, International Development Research, and International Activities. Each division is intended to have an advisory council of faculty members closely involved with its respective functions. In addition, the Center will have an administrative assistant—Professor Richard F. Crabbs, a younger member of the department of government who served for two years as executive secretary of the University Committee on International Affairs—who will have the title of special assistant for international affairs and will be responsible for many of the information and logistical activities formerly shouldered by the committee and the IDRC. These would include maintaining a continuing index of university activities and resources in the international field, a register of faculty with overseas experience, and a directory of IU international programs and activities; informing the faculty of research opportunities; publishing a newsletter; and keeping a calendar of foreign visitors and administrative and faculty travel abroad.

The International Studies section will have a coordinating and review function over all the foreign area centers and other programs for graduate and undergraduate training in international fields, as well as responsibility for the sustained and efficient growth of these programs. It will also have responsibility for increasing the international component in every school and department in the university. The existing programs over which the section will have a coordinating and review function include: the African Studies Program, Archives of Traditional Music, Archives of Languages of the World, Asian Studies Program (which may be divided into an East Asia and a Middle East Program, with encouragement to launch a Southeast Asian Program in short order), Uralic and Altaic Studies, Folklore Institute, Foreign Study programs, honors program in High School Languages, Latin American Studies Program, the Non-Western Project, Research Center for Anthropology, Folklore, and Linguistics, Russian and East European Institute and West European Studies. Professor John M. Thompson, a history professor who had been associated with Byrnes in the Russian and East European Institute and in conducting a survey of non-Western studies in Indiana, will be in charge of the International Studies section of the IAC.

The section for International Development Research is intended to inherit the research-related activities of the IDRC, to promote further research on international development and to be responsible for ensuring that the university obtains the maximum advantage or feedback from its overseas activities. With a personnel change at the top of the IDRC, however, the future shape and contribution of IU's development research center is uncertain.

The division of International Activities assumes responsibility for the general direction of all IU overseas contracts and programs, with departments and schools retaining operational authority. The head of the section will advise the chief administrative officers of the university concerning overseas contracts and programs under consideration, will act as entrepreneur, will serve as the central—but not exclusive—point for contract negotiations with agencies of government, will assist in the preparation and negotiation of programs, and on occasion will administer or coordinate programs involving several departments or schools. This section would also provide advice and assistance throughout the university for those exploring or involved in international activities, in the United States as well as overseas, coordinate procurement and purchasing, and also facilitate travel arrangements. A major concern of this section would be to assist in ensuring that foreign students, undergraduates, graduate students, or postgraduates, obtain the maximum benefits from their study at IU and that the university and its programs serve its best interests in working with these students, from the time of their first expression of interest, application, or nomination, until their return to their native lands. Thus, the director of the Foreign Student Office—now the Office of International Services—would be a member of the advisory council for International Activities, and the Advisory Committee on Foreign Students would assist the head of the section in dealing with foreign students.

Professor Byrnes, who has carefully retained his scholar status throughout his years at IU, insists that those who occupy the new positions in and under the IAC should remain active teacher-scholars, devoting up to one-half of their time to research and instruction, so that they not only maintain their academic standing with their colleagues but also continue to reflect an academic rather than a bureaucratic viewpoint. However, Byrnes has also carefully made sure that his and the Center's new relationship to the central administration is clear and reinforced daily: a suite of offices adjacent to the Office of the Vice President for Research and Dean of Advanced Studies is being made ready for occupancy by the Center.

One consequence of the IAC's emergence should be a transformation of some of the operating committees into advisory bodies. The Advisory Committee on International Studies may remain in existence with a purely advisory function. Byrnes has recommended that the functions of the Advisory Committee on International Activities, concerning IU participation in the Mid-West Universities Consortium, should be assumed by the IAC, and that a Committee on Research Grants should be named to advise him on the allocation of funds for faculty research and travel in the international fields.

It is the intention at Bloomington that the University Committee on International Affairs continue in existence, exercising its role as the broadly based, policy-planning committee with university-wide concern for all research and instruction concerning foreign areas and for the international activities of the university. It also provides a forum for the discussion of ideas and concepts from all parts of the university, as well as the informal consideration of experiences and proposals from beyond the university family.

As the capstone of its new structure Indiana University will create an advisory council of public men—drawn from Indiana, from other parts of the United States, and from other countries, particularly those with which IU has had close connections—who are interested in international affairs and equipped to assist the university as a whole and the new Center in particular in defining its goals and setting its priorities. The advisory council is intended to meet once every two or three years, although individual members can be called upon more frequently for advice.

A Look Ahead

Freed of its preoccupation with organizational matters, the University Committee on International Affairs can now concentrate on issues and problems which have been accumulating for some time in the international realm. It has enough on its agenda to occupy it for at least a year or two. The issues and problems have already been identified. They include: reorganizing and perhaps reshaping the university's area programs away from the conventional geographic concentration in favor of comparative and international studies, a shift favored by the major foundations; determining guidelines for the university's overseas operations to make sure that they satisfy more adequately important IU desires as well as overseas needs; investigating foreign student issues at IU—the potentials of transcultural learning, the adequacy of the training given as against the requirements of other cultures, and so on; overcoming apathy on the part of some schools, departments, and individual faculty members who are not yet convinced of the values of internationalizing the university's offerings and learning opportunities; devising an orientation and language instruction program to help prepare faculty members for service overseas; strengthening the regional campuses so that the international dimension becomes an integral part of the off-campus and extension services of the university—in other words, constantly improving the lines of communication to the Birdseyes of Indiana and between the Birdseyes and the wider world.

The outlook that will infuse the new International Affairs Center was put down on paper as long ago as 1959, when Professor Byrnes—in a farsighted attempt to set forth the goals which Indiana University should seek to achieve by 1970 as far as research and instruction in foreign areas are concerned—ventured to look ten years ahead.

"By 1970," he wrote, in an interdepartmental memo, "research and instruction on foreign areas should be an integral part of the university, and any foreign area programs we have should be just as much an assumed part of university life as any established department. We should seek to change the entire atmosphere of the university. Interest in and knowledge of foreign areas should pervade the entire institution. . . .

"We should establish a first-class foreign area center, the best in the country on some areas, highly qualified in every foreign area in which we work, and the best in the United States so far as foreign areas in general are considered," the memo continued.

"In everything we do, we should keep in mind the state, the nation, and the world. We should try to make the impact of our work felt in a series of circles. To begin with, we should try to improve education so far as the foreign areas are concerned in the high schools and other colleges and universities of this state and should try to raise the general level of informed understanding on the part of the citizenry of the state. Indiana University cannot progress in the long run in an intellectual desert. We should uplift instruction in the high schools and raise our entrance requirements. We should press for improved and expanded foreign language instruction within the university, so that by 1970 every graduate of the university would be able to understand, speak, read, and write at least one foreign language. Just as we seek to change the atmosphere of the university, so should we do the same for the state.

"We should keep in mind national resources and national needs, so far as they can be defined, and we should try to make our contribution to understanding other peoples and cultures unique and distinctive. . . . Thirdly, we should strengthen our ties with universities abroad, those in Western Europe and Latin America as well as those in the specifically non-Western areas. We should attract foreign scholars and foreign students here, we should enable our staff and students to study and travel abroad, and we should always keep in mind that a university is by nature universal."

*   *   *   *   *

The fact that a state university in the heart of middle America has become a leading international institution is attributable to the interplay of three elements: (1) the individual enthusiasm on the part of faculty members; (2) the backing of the administration, especially the internationalizing influence of Chancellor Wells; (3) the resulting climate on campus, which helped stimulate more and more international involvement.

Much of what IU has achieved in the international field is remarkable. Not a land-grant university and therefore not having the full range of professional schools, it has nonetheless shouldered a number of technical assistance programs overseas, a role in which the land-grant institutions have predominated. Especially commendable is the leadership it has provided for cooperative efforts with the high schools and other higher educational institutions of its state, by which it has influenced the internationalization of education in the entire state of Indiana.

Offsetting these accomplishments, a survey of the university's present international involvements pinpoints several critical areas to which IU has not yet given sufficient attention. There is need for greater coordination among its overseas contract programs, a need for greater faculty participation in them and for systematic feedback from them to the campus. IU's contract operations to date have been largely departmental programs, not university programs. With few exceptions, they have not made as much lasting impact on the campus as those at Michigan State. They have been carried out autonomously by departments and schools, with insufficient attention to the university's international program or to general university priorities.

Much more needs to be done to increase the international content of undergraduate education. The state of Indiana's high school language program, which owes much to IU's leadership, brings to the university some freshmen with a high level of language competence. IU has yet to devise a program that would bring these students into area study programs and overseas activities, so as to make effective use of their language skills.

Until its new International Affairs Center became operational, Indiana University did not have an adequate means of exchanging information about projects in the planning stage. Hardly any institutional attention was given to the desires of individual faculty members or graduate students to gain additional overseas experience, and foreign faculty members and IU faculty returned from overseas were perhaps underutilized as international campus resources.

IU has always been by choice a loosely organized institution, and the organizational framework recently devised to coordinate its international activities, the International Affairs Center, reflects this preference. It is intended to provide leadership and coordination for the university's international dimension, while at the same time retaining the opportunity for faculty initiative at every stage, continuing the university's internal procedures and maintaining the spirit and atmosphere which has characterized IU and its approach to international affairs. At another university, these intentions might cancel each other out: at Indiana University they are not necessarily contradictive.

THE
UNIVERSITY
IN
WORLD
AFFAIRS:

QUESTIONS
AND ISSUES

In the two decades since the end of the Second World War, when the consequences of victory swept them into the mainstream of international life, the universities of the United States have been profoundly changed. Many of the changes directly result from their approaches to world affairs.

American universities have a strong tradition of social responsibility, and many of them were quick to respond to the challenges of the world's developing areas. The long tradition by which government agencies and land-grant colleges and universities work together in the service of the community—in itself a distinctive characteristic of American higher education—has been continued in collaborative arrangements to bring the skills and talents of our higher educational institutions into the service of the emerging nations. As regards the more academic centers, the talent and institutional resources that served the national need during the Second World War continue to be called on by a range of government agencies and foundations.

In response to many post-war challenges, abroad and on campus, the very character of universities has altered. Specialized area centers and institutes for geographic and subject matter study have mushroomed alongside and compete with the traditional disciplines and departments, demanding new teaching resources and international library facilities. Faculty members are dispersed to the ends of the earth on assignments to share their personal competence in assisting educational and public institutions in the underdeveloped lands, or in pursuit of their own research interests. At some American institutions students—often ahead of their faculty and administration—agitate for study opportunities abroad and international course content that will help prepare them for today's world. Meanwhile, eager foreign students, in an uncontrolled flow, crowd the campuses and compete for scarce student places. The fiscal base of the internationally involved university has been changed by frequent transfusions—on which some schools have come to depend—of government and foundation funds.

These postwar changes have in turn fostered some important issues and problems—of both substance and procedure—for universities with international interests. Some have been met squarely: others have been avoided, postponed or turned over to a faculty committee.

The purpose of this concluding chapter in EWA's case studies of six American universities is to identify some of these issues and problems, and to examine them either from the experience of these universities or on the basis of general findings made during the survey.

Deliberately this chapter is not a balanced account of university accomplishments and shortcomings in the international field since the war. The universities' achievement is evident from the wide range of international activities at the six institutions covered in this survey. The intention here is not to focus on past performance but rather to raise issues that are both relevant and open for discussion—issues that in the main the universities themselves must confront and to which they must respond.

Nor is this a full catalog: rather, issues and problems have been singled out to help other universities and colleges, less involved internationally, benefit from the experience of the international activities of the more experienced. Not all the issues or problems are new—some have been raised repeatedly—but they are included in the hope that a new focus may bring them closer to solution.

Some of the problems and issues are phrased as questions. This is not only an admission that those of us who participated in this survey are not sure of the answers. It is also an acknowledgement that in our increasingly pluralistic system of higher education each institution tends to be unique in its background, traditions, geographic location, resources and objectives, so that no one answer, formula or plan is applicable to all, to most, or to many. Each institution must arrive at its own objectives, its own commitments, its own policies, its own depth of immersion in the international field, its own organizational arrangements to achieve order in its international activities. Institutional experiences accumulated at other universities may be relevant, but only the individual institution can decide this, from its own evolution and its own idiom.

Leadership

The international dimension of an educational institution, if it is to be meaningful, requires long-range planning and assessment and reassessment of the institution's goals and objectives. It also requires time, decisions and money—along with many other things. In fact, some aspects of internationalization, like specialized area centers, siphon off a good deal more money than most universities realize when they enter upon the commitment, because of the ever-widening nature of the activity.

The international demands therefore make leadership—a least from president, trustees, deans and key faculty—both central and critical to an effective program. The role of the leadership is to make it continually clear—inward to the university community, outward to the public—that the international dimension is a permanent, integral part of the university's total educational mission.

The format of this book, focusing as it has on the purely international activities of six universities long involved in the field, may contribute to the impression that an educational institution's "international" dimension is a separate function, apart from the rest of the university. We cannot stress too strongly that international activities, to be successful, must be integrated into the total university. The cliches of international education are nonetheless to the point: the world *is* the proper university classroom; all literature *is* its library; international as well as domestic problems *are* its laboratories; and scholarship increasingly knows no national or cultural boundaries.

Therefore, although international studies, activities, and overseas operations all have aspects that justify special organization and attention within a university institution, their successful development requires wide support within the whole university community, which in turn is enriched by the total experience. To confine international concern to anything less than the total university environment is to deprive both the international aspects and the university itself of full benefits.

Given total university involvement, coordination, and direction of the international dimension then become major administrative responsibilities. How to achieve this, however, is less important than the atmosphere: the creation of a favorable climate of opinion is essential on any campus if the international dimension is to take hold and flourish. The best mechanics devised can seldom produce a proper atmosphere in a hostile environment.

Some central administrative concern for international activities seems essential. Over the past eight years—and increasingly in the past year or so—more than twenty-five universities have found it desirable to create a central administrative organization or at the very least to designate an individual to coordinate their international activities. All but one of the six universities visited by EWA teams on this study have incorporated into their administration a top-level body responsible for international activities. These organizations range from Michigan State's highly structured (and greatly staffed) central program office, with responsibility for all the university's overseas programs, to Stanford's prestigious coordinating committee of faculty members involved in international studies or programs, headed part-time by a scholar-teacher who achieves a measure of coordination by persuasion and quiet precedent.

What key considerations should a university consider in institutionalizing its international activities? Where should an international coordinating body fit into the hierarchy of university administration?

The fact that such a body or office is labeled "international" tends to set it apart on campus, rather than helping integrate it with all other campus activities.

The location and function of these coordinating offices within the university vary slightly from institution to institution, but in all universities visited where the office exists it is near the top of the administrative hierarchy. This seems necessary for the successful functioning of such an office. To be most effective, it should be under the immediate supervision of the president, chancellor, presidency (when the president and vice presidents function as parts of a whole), provost or vice president for academic affairs, in close and direct contact with those responsible for the institution's overall as well as international policies. Furthermore, it should be clear to the faculty, students, and outside world that it has direct access to the top administration to publicize the institution's continuing commitment to internationalism.

In other words, if the goal is university-wide awareness and response to internationalizing education, a high-level location is as important for access *down* as for access *up*.

Broadly considered, a university may coordinate its international activities in two ways. One—typified here by Michigan State—is the institution-wide approach by which the administration, preferably with faculty participation, works to an overall plan and a deliberate strategy to extend the international dimension throughout the institution. The second approach—exemplified by Stanford and Indiana—is the slower, selective method of identifying and encouraging individuals, disciplines, schools, and colleges within the institution where the international dimension has already become rooted and providing the atmosphere by which they can hopefully interact.

Between these two approaches there is great diversity in the institutional mechanisms that have been developed. This is as it should be, for each campus must reflect its own character as it administers its international aspects. The great danger, as one prominent educator puts it, is that we will allow "institutional emulation to homogenize our higher educational system."

Commitment

In 1964 and 1965, sixty-seven American universities were carrying out technical assistance tasks in forty-one countries under 101 separate contracts with the U.S. Agency for International Development. More than $170 million was involved in these contracts. In addition, university personnel were busy all over the world performing similar but fewer technical assistance assignments for U.S. foundations. To take one specialized branch of assistance—the aid provided only by U.S. land-grant universities and colleges to help develop institutions for agricultural education and research in the lesser-developed countries—over the past fifteen years no fewer than thirty-five U.S. land-grant colleges and universities have assisted more than fifty such foreign institutions in some thirty countries.

Senator Frank Church has asked whether the United States is not suffering from "an excess of interventionism" (our troops are in thirty countries; we are pledged to defend forty-two; and we are extending aid, in one form or another, to nearly 100). Without espousing isolationism, are our universities overextending themselves in their international activities—or, as some contend, could they do a great deal more than they are doing now?

The president of one of the institutions visited during this study, President J. E. Wallace Sterling of Stanford, asserts that we are spreading our available higher education resources too thin in view of U.S. requirements. Despite the fact that in 1964 our universities awarded a record number of

Ph.D. degrees—14,500—we simply cannot cope with the demands we are making on the college and university community, says Sterling, and therefore we keep diluting our supply to take on more and more overseas commitments. Further, the relative number of Ph.D. holders going into academic work has been steadily declining.

For perhaps the next two decades we will face critical manpower shortages in our higher educational establishments. The demand for university personnel in the public service will not lessen. To meet the demand, every institution must reassess continuously its priorities, must be willing to explore new ideas. Modified personnel procedures might permit better use of the available specialist manpower jointly by universities and the government. One such policy might be the decision to overstaff faculty to release an estimated percentage each year for overseas assignments. Another might be a decision to restrict the absence from the campus of more than an approved percentage of faculty members. Universities might also try using government personnel, foreign service officers and government specialists on home leave, or journalists, foundation experts and businessmen with international experience who could be given short-term teaching assignments to offset the loan of faculty members for government tours of duty.

Have our universities—either singly or through their national associations—fully explored the possibilities of using graduate and postdoctoral students in overseas positions to ease the demand on experienced faculty? Do we really know the requirements of all the new nations—which can make the best use of senior teachers, which could utilize—and would accept—the less experienced? In one year of experience in helping staff overseas educational institutions in the developing countries, Overseas Educational Service* has found that sometimes teaching applicants with an M.A. are acceptable, provided agreed-upon academic standards are met. Can anything be done to alter the attitude of those new nations that insist on "prestige" teachers? Could we consider sending teams of American teachers, led by senior professors but including younger teachers?

The expansion of intercultural courses has alone contributed to severe faculty shortages and competition for scarce specialists. For instance, during the 1964-65 academic year President John A. Hannah of Michigan State reported that his university had 300 tenure vacancies it could not fill; during the same period the University of Massachusetts was seeking some 200 faculty members, and said it would consider itself lucky to find fifty of them. By no means all of these vacancies, of course, are due to intercul-

---

* Overseas Educational Service, an affiliate of EWA, was established in 1963 to help bring together overseas vacancies in education and well-qualified persons in the American academic community. Operating under the general authority of EWA, its sponsors, in addition to EWA, are the American Council on Education and the National Academy of Sciences, in cooperation with the American Council of Learned Societies, the Social Science Research Council and the Institute of International Education.

tural expansion. Ten years ago only fifty American colleges and universities offered intercultural courses, other than languages. Today more than 700 colleges and universities offer some such courses. The growth in language teaching can be illustrated by what has happened at one expanding institution. Five years ago Michigan State offered instruction in ten languages: today it offers about twenty. Five years ago the university had some 500 language students; today it has more than 4,500.

Over-commitment is sometimes evident on the campus. In their eagerness to get into area specialization, to follow the leaders in establishing multidisciplinary centers to focus on particular regions of the world, universities in general have overlooked the resulting strain on their libraries.

Development of the specialized library collections needed to support area studies is far more complex than universities initially assume— because of the nature of area studies, if nothing else. This has been the experience of all six universities covered in this study. Most such area specializations require different kinds of library service and different types of publications from those normally provided by a university library, creating problems of language, subject specialization, staff, and procurement. Even a modest undergraduate program in a specialized area requires special publications—some in the vernacular—usually not obtainable through regular domestic booksellers and dealers. Graduate and faculty research needs go well beyond this and require masses of primary sources as well as backfiles in Western and non-Western languages.

Servicing area programs confronts a university with serious budgetary and financial problems: obviously these should be considered before any new program is begun. There are few shortcuts: it takes time and money to build a library collection adequate to a first-class area program. And, as some of the universities included in this survey have learned, the basic library costs for the support of a relatively limited area program—at least at the graduate level—are about the same as for a major program.

Library procurement is a problem that requires more extensive institutional collaboration than universities have so far achieved. Regional variants of the Farmington Plan, by which college and university libraries in a given area would collaborate on purchases and share resources, and the extensive use of faculty members on overseas assignments to find and buy library materials abroad, are possibilities that should be more thoroughly explored.

Allocating greater resources to new and strategically important world areas has led to some neglect of old and strategically important areas, like Western Europe and Canada. At least three of the six universities visited by EWA teams are trying to readjust the emphasis with renewed attention to these areas, but for some time to come the areas that pushed to the fore in university studies over the past decade or so—Soviet, Asian, Latin American, and African—will continue to take the major share of university support.

Then there is the problem of individual overcommitment, resulting in the "jet set professor" (described as "one who is on so many panels, has so many consultancies and administers so many contracts that a student can only talk to him on the way to the airport"). Are these itinerant faculty members—what one critic calls "a new kind of *condottieri*, mercenaries of science and scholarship hooded with doctorates and ready for hire on studies done to contract specifications"—impoverishing the teaching function? Unquestionably this off-campus involvement feeds broad advantages back to the campus, at least in enriched faculty experience; offsetting this, the constant turnover of academic personnel, the rotation of top people to and from the campus, and the resulting strain on the remaining teachers who pick up the burdens of their absent colleagues dilute college and university teaching.

Feedback

In the universities visited for this study, few systematic efforts are being made to achieve feedback, the shorthand description of the process by which institutions analyze their overseas experiences, evaluate the results, particuarly the impact on teaching and research on the home campus, and draw lessons from both.

As regards building into an overseas assignment a research component for faculty members or graduate students or both, two approaches mentioned in this study should be singled out for their deliberate effort to influence the home campus.

One is the technical assistance contract Michigan State's Institute for International Studies in Education signed with AID in 1964 to improve educational planning in Thailand. Similarly, in two of its newest undertakings with AID—in Brazil and Nigeria—the University of Wisconsin has tried to build into the contracts provisions for on-site research for credit by the university's graduate students.

A visit to any university campus will confirm the observation that it is easier to put the feedback process into words than it is to bring it about. In a sense, to lament the absence of feedback is merely another way of noting that a major university is large and complex.

One major obstacle to feedback is that the faculty at work on the university's behalf abroad and the faculty concerned with teaching students and doing research in the international field on the home campus are generally from diverse parts of the university. Much of the overseas technical assistance work is in the hands of the professional schools, whereas much of the international work on campus is the province of language specialists, humanists, and social scientists, working through area centers, international affairs programs, and essentially the colleges of arts and sciences and the general graduate schools of the institutions. In the nature of the university the faculty of the professional schools on the one hand and the faculty of the arts and sciences colleges on the other do not have much in common, seldom talk much to each other, often do not know each other and only rarely work together on common projects.

Bridging this campus gap is thus the first step toward achieving feedback from international activities. Some progress is being made on the job, as the "production" scientists from the professional schools and the social scientists find themselves working together overseas and discovering in the process that technical problems frequently respond to nontechnical solutions and the reverse. However, consciously to explore all the ways institutional feedback can be drawn from overseas activities and then to put them into action in the mainstream of the learning processes on the home campus requires both a mechanism and a strategy.

Of the universities surveyed here, Michigan State has made the most significant attempt to solve the problem of feedback, not merely by establishing its Office of International Programs, but by employing it consciously and deliberately to link the diverse parts of the university.

One frequently overlooked feedback is in students who return to the home campus after months or even years of study abroad, and foreign students or visiting foreign research scholars. On few campuses are either systematically used as an educational resource. Few universities seem to have systematically or purposefully studied the impact of their study programs abroad on courses and degrees—for instance, how many returning students change their majors because of exposure abroad, or continue into graduate work, or enter international service careers? Stanford proposes to undertake such a survey of its own students, and Tulane is evaluating its Junior Year Abroad program with some of these considerations in mind.

Nationally, there is need for an overall feedback in which all university technical assistance programs abroad—the unsuccessful as well as the successful—are systematically studied and evaluated. The foreign aid files in Washington and at the key universities are bulging with field reports, end-of-project surveys, and other materials brought back from projects abroad. The time is long past for a thorough analysis and assessment of what the university contract system has and has *not* accomplished, both toward overseas development goals and toward the academic development of American institutions.

Resistance

Resistance to embarking on or furthering a university's world role takes many forms, and no two of the campuses visited by EWA teams had had quite the same experience in countering or overcoming opposition within the institution, whether from faculty or administration.

Can we therefore generalize about resistance? Is it a generational phenomenon? Is it found more in certain disciplines than in others? Is it geographic, or sectional—is it easier to introduce the international dimension at educational institutions on the East and West coasts than in the South and midwest?

Sweeping generalizations merely obscure the complex picture. Although the social sciences—anthropology, history, and political science in particular—were relatively quick to adapt to the postwar concept of area studies, there have been exceptions, and, within disciplines, there are differences from university to university. Thus while economists have gained a reputation for being notoriously resistant to such special techniques as area studies, on certain campuses the economists have led their universities into international and human resource development work. On some campuses the most entrenched opposition to further internationalization comes from the humanities, particularly the conservative language departments.

Often what is often construed as resistance on the part of a department or faculty member toward internationalizing the curriculum or the staff is in essence an honest difference of opinion or at least a different view of priorities.

How much of what is taken as resistance to international involvement on some campuses is merely what John W. Gardner, Secretary of Health, Education, and Welfare, calls "the deep-seated aversion of many faculty members to extensive innovation within the institution"? Says Gardner: "Most faculty members are enthusiastic proponents of innovation in the abstract, but the slogan carved over the mantlepiece at the faculty club reads 'Innovate Away From Home.' If you must innovate, try West Pakistan!"

Internationalizing the Curriculum

Despite some advances in internationalizing the curriculum over the past twenty years, the gap is widening between the demands and needs of the United States in a world society and the ability of American education to meet them. The international dimension in the college and university curriculum is more visible than ever before, yet the influence on the students seems discouragingly slight.

A 1962 inquiry sent to 683 liberal arts colleges then members of the Association of American Colleges revealed that 282, or 41 percent, offered varying options to learn about non-Western cultures; however, most of these courses were electives taken by fewer than 5 to 10 percent of the students. Continued parochialism emerged in a similar 1964 survey, which indicated that fewer than 10 percent of the students in liberal arts and other four-year colleges offering courses on the non-Western world actually took such courses. Fewer than 1 percent studied a non-Western language—this despite the fact that 70 percent of the liberal arts colleges and roughly 50 percent of the other four-year institutions offered at least one and usually several such courses. However, most of these courses were upper-class electives not required of majors or for graduation.

Fewer than two dozen of our 1,500 universities or four-year colleges seem to require all candidates for the baccalaureate to take even a single course dealing primarily with the non-Western areas. For most of these students these few courses are terminal as well as introductory. And if these courses are limited to liberal arts students, the parochialism is increased: at any given moment about half our undergraduates are taking their four baccalaureate years in a professional school, where exposure to international course content is generally even more restricted.

How to make intercultural materials and the study of international affairs part of a liberal education for all college graduates still concerns only a minority of faculty and administration. The pressure to find adequate remedies will continue to mount, but the need will not be met until more educational leaders become committed to its importance and devise effective ways to meet it.

The most obvious way to attack is to include appropriate international materials in the introductory, general education courses in history, the social sciences, and the humanities. These are the principal traffic courses in the undergraduate curriculum.

Drawing on the six universities surveyed here, the integrated social science course revised to take in a substantial international component that is required of all undergraduates at Michigan State's University College offers a model for the inclusion of appropriate international content in heavy traffic courses. However, at all the universities visited—which are in the front rank in international curriculum—many approaches are used to strengthen the international dimension in undergraduate education. Among these are the development of new intercultural courses; the addition of specialized area or comparative courses on the history, politics, social organization, and literature of non-Western areas; the establishment of multidisciplinary area studies, primarily at the graduate level but open on some campuses to undergraduates; the expansion and strengthening of foreign language study, particularly of non-Western languages; and programs of undergraduate study abroad.

Students and World Affairs

Undergraduate study abroad arouses mixed emotions on most campuses. At the six visited by EWA teams the viewpoints ranged from those of observers who see study-abroad programs, provided they are organized and directed, as an integral part of undergraduate education, to those who judge overseas study programs as primarily touristic experiences.

Can the universities themselves do anything to curb the uncontrolled, uncoordinated, ill-prepared spread of undergraduate study-abroad programs? Until 1950 only half a dozen such programs existed, mostly of the Junior Year Abroad type. By 1965 they had grown in scope and number until they now cover approximately 30,000 students each year.

The alarming proliferation, the duplication of effort, and—in certain areas—the academic illegitimacy of study abroad "threatens to become a national educational scandal," according to Stephen A. Freeman, who did a study for the Consultative Service on U.S. Undergraduate Study Abroad. And, apart from the problems of lack of coordination in overseas offerings and impositions on foreign universities—to mention only two of the major problems involved in study abroad—are any universities addressing themselves to the larger question: how is the foreign experience obtained merged into the mainstream of education on the home campus?

Even when there are on-campus stimuli for worldwide interests—Peace Corps, Operation Crossroads Africa, international student exchanges, study abroad programs, and the like—the problem arises of how to direct this general student interest into a specific academic program. In general, students seem to have trouble identifying courses with international content, from most college and university catalogs, which often describe these courses inadequately. One solution is to group these courses in a separate, supplemental international course catalog, so that a student with an international bent can design a program to meet both his interests and his discipline requirements. Cornell now prepares and issues biennially a special catalog, titled *International Studies at Cornell University: Courses of Instruction*. Stanford is preparing a similar supplement.

Foreign Students

Foreign students are no longer a novelty on most American campuses, but few institutions where they are present in fair numbers seem to have given much thought to the fundamental issues of what is loosely called "the foreign student problem." Too, foreign students present more than an educational problem: their concerns—and concern for them—extend well beyond the academic.

Merely including foreign nationals in the student body does not relieve the admitting institution of further responsibility. The presence of foreign students on campus should be the result of a carefully thought out rationale, and their academic program should be an integral part of the institution's educational strategy.

There were about 85,000 foreign students in the United States in 1965. Of these probably only 15 to 20 percent had really planned an effective sponsorship, and many were either chronically hard-pressed financially or were just barely meeting their annual expenses. The prediction is that foreign students at American institutions will increase to 100,000 or even

150,000 over the next five years, with no ceiling in sight. This growth is expected at a time when an ever-greater number of American students will be seeking higher education.

That the entire foreign student problem in the United States requires national attention and study as well as individual institutional planning was the main finding of a 1964 report by EWA, *The Foreign Student: Whom Shall We Welcome?*

None of the universities included in this survey seem to have very coherent plans for relating their interests to foreign student needs or competences. In some, foreign students appear to be admitted in a haphazard, unplanned manner from among those who happen to apply in one way or another for admission. At most of the universities surveyed, foreign graduate students are admitted by decision of the colleges and departments concerned: there is no all-university coordination and therefore no control over numbers admitted, or over the desired mix between graduate and undergraduate applicants.

Some universities apparently have quietly imposed a quota on foreign students—sometimes in response to or in anticipation of criticism from constituents, state legislatures, the press, alumni, and so on over the admission of out-of-state and foreign students at a time when facilities for American students are in short supply. None of the six universities covered in this survey have instituted a fixed quota, although two or three use a rule of thumb to limit their proportion of foreign students to not more than 10 percent of total enrollment.

The questions growing from concern with the foreign student problem have repeatedly been pinpointed.

Are foreign student applicants being properly selected and screened in their home countries? Are our institutions maintaining reasonably high admission standards in admitting those who come here? Are foreign students coming to the United States at the proper level of their educational development? Are they being placed in the appropriate schools when they get here? Are they sufficiently oriented in advance to our educational system, customs, institutions, and values, and is their command of English sufficient to enable them to hold their own with American students under competitive conditions?

Many of our services and activities need improvement badly. Perhaps equally important, foreign students must be better selected before they leave their home countries. The educational and manpower needs of the students' home countries also deserve careful consideration. The lack of adequate overseas facilities for proper screening is one of the greatest weaknesses of the present loose arrangement. With this in mind EWA has sponsored a study of the feasibility of establishing overseas field offices to serve the various needs of American colleges and universities. The functions to be performed by such offices might include screening and selection services for foreign students wishing to study in the United States, services for visiting American scholars and students, and information to American colleges and universities about the local educational scene.

Once in the United States, how much assistance should foreign students receive from their host institutions? What special services should a university reasonably provide?

Many extra duties have been undertaken by foreign student advisers' offices: with increasing numbers of foreign students and mounting costs, these should be continually reexamined to determine their real legitimacy. Virtually every step in the educational process—from the initial contact, to screening, to enrollment, through academic counseling, to reentry and effective employment in the home country and the continuation of alumni relations—requires special treatment and modification to match the needs of individual students from abroad. Yet in some colleges and universities the mere designation of a foreign student adviser—a procedure followed by some 600 institutions—often seems to relieve the rest of the institution of any further responsibility for its foreign students.

Are universities ever justified in adjusting their academic standards to meet the needs of their foreign students? Do some institutions in fact operate a double standard without admitting it? At one major university with a high percentage of foreign students, a survey over a two-year period revealed that 28 percent of the foreign graduate students were failing, a rate twice that of the all-university average for failing students. A follow-up survey revealed that in the second quarter of the year just over half the foreign students who were below satisfactory performance in the first quarter were still in school and that many had dropped further in their grade point average. As for undergraduates, the study found that students performing just below or barely at a satisfactory academic level may be having their greatest difficulty in their declared major. The study suggests that universities tend to treat foreign students the same as American students in certain areas of university administration where their "foreignness" demands different treatment, and that in the more academic areas they tend to treat the foreign student differently—and usually more generously—when more equal treatment might be in the better interest of both student and university.

This in turn raises the question whether the academic programs prescribed for foreign students will in fact prepare them for their roles back in their home culture. We must examine these products of our educational system back in their home countries to learn more about the applicability of American education to the rest of the world, particularly its developing areas. And there is a further question: do foreign students in fact return to their home countries at the completion of their studies? Do some nations have a higher rate of "nonreturnees" than others, and if so, why? Are undergraduate foreign students more likely to remain in the United States than graduate students? Among possible alternatives, should we or the home countries consider some form of "return scholarships" as inducements to persuade American-trained foreign students to return and contribute their newly acquired skills to the development of their own nations?

What are the pros and cons of a university's utilizing its alumni in foreign lands to assist in screening and selecting student applicants? On occasion Wisconsin's graduate school and various departments do tap alumni for this assistance; Indiana is considering mobilizing its foreign alumni more systematically than it has in the past; and Tulane is considering calling on its graduates in Latin America to do preliminary screening of prospective applicants.

Can foreign students be used while in America as educational resources, either in intercultural studies or through extracurricular programs? Are there any instructive instances of the imaginative use of the resources of foreign students or scholars? Disappointingly, although our educational institutions have played host to foreign students for decades—even on a small scale in the years between the wars—no systematic study has been made of the contribution foreign students make toward international understanding on the part of American students. Nor, for that matter, does there appear to have been a nationwide study of the contribution to international understanding foreign students make to foreign students of a different nation on the same campus, or to students of their own nation.

Competence

Few if any of our universities can claim to have *all* the resources and competences for all the complex technical assistance programs they have been invited to undertake either by the United States government or by the foundations. The real problem for a major university is not only to determine what it can and should do overseas, but to decide what it cannot and should not do. If a university undertakes to do abroad all that is asked of it, it may end by destroying itself. As one dean at Stanford has put it: "In the long run other institutions can be created to perform that part of the economic- and social-development function that is not congenial to universities, but . . . there are not and cannot be other institutions that perform the functions of the university."

The capabilities of American universities abroad have on occasion been severely stretched even when faculty members engaged in activities they knew best: the universities' effectiveness is made more problematic when these same professors are expected to engage in direct managerial operations that are only vaguely and remotely related to teaching and research.

There is also a tendency, perhaps stemming back to the between-wars provincialism of the average American campus, to assume that American principles and operating experiences can be transferred overseas wholesale. Too often we seem to bring a "made-in-America" solution to problems that simply do not respond to this approach. Put another way, the technical aid we offer is often too sophisticated for the recipient country's economy.

For instance, simply importing American technology and educational methods will not solve the subtle problems of life in Africa's rural areas, where most of the continent's people live. Similarly, advance techniques of educational development often overlook the basic need to communicate with and to change the minds and mores of the people undergoing development. Teaching literacy, for instance, is not enough: these who are being taught to read must have the basic reading materials on which to practice their new skills.

University competence in the international field is not evenly distributed. The present development of language and area centers, a notable achievement in itself, nonetheless provides uneven coverage of important non-Western countries and regions, and in some cases there is scarcely any systematic coverage. First-class regional study centers are needed to cover such areas and countries as North Africa, Pakistan, Afghanistan, Soviet Asia, the Philippines, Vietnam, and Korea. Also, there is no effective division of labor among our universities covering African and Latin American studies. Latin American studies are now offered at more than thirty universities, but only about a dozen afford the quality of scholarship common among other non-Western area centers, and of the dozen that have become major centers in the past few years perhaps six can be classed as first-rank.

What can universities do among themselves (with or without foundation finance) to fill the gaps, spread the coverage, and share the responsibilities?

Individual faculty competence should not be overlooked. Although the knowledge explosion has not hit international affairs with the same intensity as it has the sciences, rethinking international subject matter is necessary from time to time, especially as half a hundred new nations have appeared in the world society over the past few years.

Arrangements are made on many campuses for professionals and business men to return occasionally for updating and retraining. Can we afford to do less for faculty members? Faculty members' competence in the international field can be extended by such means as faculty seminars, visiting scholars or interinstitutional cooperation combined with study abroad. It may be a matter of reorienting the interest of a faculty member, or rediscovering some rusty skills, or stretching the boundaries of his discipline, or developing a new competence altogether.

Overseas Contract Operations

Is too much reliance being placed on the university as the "chosen instrument" in handling technical aid overseas? During this study a clear impression persisted that the AID-university contract relationship runs on bureaucratic momentum and is a convenience to both parties. Foreign aid administrators admit that no government agency can equal the university in the mobilization and skilled use of academic personnel, in bringing resources and talent to bear on problems. In general, the university contract has been successful beyond expectations. But there are also problems inherent in the contract system.

For one, AID contracts seem to have a homing instinct, resulting in extremely uneven participation in overseas educational activities among the 1,500 or so four-year American colleges and universities. Over and over, those responsible for placing overseas contracts seem to turn to the same major universities, even to the same professional and graduate schools within them. This not only places an impossible burden on the few institutions involved, but also overlooks the possible contributions of many other institutions. At present, for instance, it is not easy for the individual faculty member of a small liberal arts institution, highly qualified and motivated though he may be, to enter overseas service. An instrumentality through which the resources of the small institution can be channeled into overseas assistance was needed, and it was in part to meet this need that Overseas Educational Service was established.

The very convenience of the AID-university contract relationship may discourage the agency from thoroughly exploring and considering the use of nonuniversity contract groups to carry out as many of the technical assistance programs as possible and so preserve scarce university resources.

In his report *AID and the Universities* (a study mounted and staffed by EWA) John Gardner, then President of the Carnegie Corporation of New York, recommended that the government examine the possibilities of recruiting in nonuniversity areas—industrial laboratories, museums, research institutions of various sorts. Also, the United States government has never adequately explored the possibility of tapping the reservoir of 2,300,000 federal employees, or examined the possibilities and legal complications of calling on state and local employees for service overseas.

State governments and education departments have also tended to neglect the international dimensions of education at home, as well as the potentially rich academic benefits that might accrue to their systems from state department of education staff members or teachers returning from overseas teaching, research, and service activities under overseas contract or other auspices. New York State—with its pioneer Office of Foreign Area Studies—California, Florida, Indiana, and Pennsylvania exemplify others that have taken notable steps to infuse the international dimension into their systems. Far more needs to be done in these fields, however.

Is there a role for universities in identifying and making known to the government talents and competencies from nonuniversity sources that could be mobilized for overseas operations? Could universities do more to marshal talent from colleges or even public schools in their areas for assignments overseas? In some areas of expertise—for instance, the applied use of educational television, programmed learning and advanced teaching techniques—some American public school bodies are ahead of some universities and at the same time are closer to the real educational needs of the emerging countries. In communications, it should not be necessary to turn again and again to the same few universities for aid in establishing radio networks, educational television programs, or indigenous publishing ventures. The efforts of Franklin Book Programs to stimulate better indigenous publishing may offer a model for comparable enterprises in allied fields.

In academic assistance overseas, should we try to upgrade whole foreign educational institutions instead of working piecemeal in a department-to-department, school-to-school relationship? In other words, is not an attempt to improve the quality of one department or college of a foreign university doomed from the beginning if the other units of the same institution are not improved at the same time and to the same degree?

What are the possibilities of using a semiuniversity or even nonuniversity organization to carry out most of the housekeeping details of a university's overseas contract, thus freeing the university personnel to pursue basic research or teaching assignments? Stanford is experimenting on a small scale along these lines with the Stanford Research Institute. The results will be scrutinized both in Washington and throughout the university community.

Orientation

Two decades have passed since the first crash program threw university personnel into overseas assignments without adequate predeparture preparation and orientation, yet during that time surprisingly little attention has been given to preparing university personnel to live and work abroad.

Not one of the universities visited in this survey operates a systematic program of orientation for educational service abroad. Michigan State, which has been as aware of the problem as any university in the United States and has tried several approaches to orientation, relies at present on a fairly informal indoctrination of faculty members and their families going abroad on contract work. Wisconsin tried out an intensive briefing session for its faculty members going to Nigeria in 1965, and intends to follow up with a study of results.

There is no consensus on what makes up the necessary predeparture orientation, or on whether a follow-up briefing in the country of assignment is essential. Extremes range all the way from a brief exposure to guidebook literature—the Temple Fielding approach—to the total immersion of nine long months that missionaries heading overseas for some years undergo at the Missionary Orientation Center at Stony Point, New York. The need for something in-between in training and preparation seems to be recognized year after year by many university bodies.

The 1962-63 annual report of the Committee on Institutional Cooperation (CIC) noted that exploratory discussions had been held among its members universities—the Big Ten universities plus the University of Chicago—on possible joint action in training professors for overseas assignments. Little resulted from these talks. In their November, 1963, draft, proposal to the Ford Foundation for funds, the Midwest Universities Consortium (MUCIA) recommended establishing a cooperative orientation and training program to include intensive language training and instruction in the history, economics, and culture of the country to which the faculty member is being assigned. As the months passed, Michigan State finally took the lead in developing a proposal for a MUCIA orientation and training program, a step it hopes to get approved in 1965 or 1966.

Despite continuing indications of real need, there seems to be little response from much of the university community, in ideas or action, beyond the classic solution to an unwelcome chore: propose, dispose, repose.

Institutional Collaboration

Universities and colleges are discovering that self-sufficiency is no longer the unqualified academic virtue it once was. Increasingly, institutions are turning to cooperative ventures, student and faculty exchanges, and joint efforts covering every activity from study abroad to fund raising. At the outset of 1965 the Association of American Colleges listed 360 institutions involved in forty-seven different kinds of academic cooperation—and admitted that the list was already out of date.

Two of the best-known interinstitutional arrangements have been referred to frequently in this study. One is the Committee on Institutional Cooperation, launched in 1958 with support from the Carnegie Corporation, to provide for voluntary cooperative arrangements among eleven Midwestern universities. The other is the Midwest Universities Consortium for International Activities, Inc., financed by a grant from the Ford Foundation, in which four Midwestern universities—Illinois, Wisconsin, Indiana, and Michigan State—agreed to pool their resources to undertake certain international activities too large for any one of them. A similar consortium, an old idea newly applied to college and university associations, is being considered for Stanford and the University of California, Berkeley, and possibly other California institutions.

Relentless financial pressures make administrations receptive to collaboration with other institutions. The biggest obstacle seems to be faculty resistance. Departmental pride or the sovereignty of the school or college involved are reefs on which many a proposal for academic partnership has been wrecked.

One dean of a member-institution of the CIC complains that for all the talk at meetings about the desirability of sharing scarce resources or developing them jointly very little real collaboration emerges from their efforts, which are nullified by their own faculties. University representatives on, say, the CIC agree on the wisdom of cooperative efforts in—for example— the exotic languages, but when they return to their home institutions they find their own language departments or areas determined to add to or retain their own exotic language offerings so that they will not fall behind rival institutions.

Much more attention needs to be given to interinstitutional cooperation. Perhaps new organizational arrangements must be devised to overcome faculty resistance, to insure that there is no loss of institutional or departmental prestige or identity. In exploring the range of possible cooperative arrangements on a neighborhood, statewide, regional, national, and even overseas basis there is undoubtedly a role for the professional organizations of higher education, such as the American Council on Education, the Association for Higher Education, the Association of American Colleges, the Modern Language Association, the American Political Science Association, and Education and World Affairs.

Communications

The lines of communication in educational institutions often make orderly minds despair. The same might be said of communication within the university community.

In fact, Cornell's President, James A. Perkins, who has worked both the foundation and the university sides of the street, has said it.

"The most striking feature of a university community is its relative disinterest in the educational activities of others," he has written. "The institutional life of a university is guided not by the research or publication activities of fellow professionals, but by its own educational programs and theories. These programs seem to be most difficult to transmit from one institution to another. In fact, it might be said that the individuality of each university is so tough and leathery, and their mutual disinterests so pronounced, that they have developed a rich tradition of unsuccessful effort in transmitting to one another the results of their experiments."

The communications problem of the universities has three dimensions— internal, national, and international.

Internally, the integration of the university has been whittled away by the increased specialization of its scholars. Institutional loyalty is fast decreasing and is being replaced by outside allegiances. Scholars are inclined to communicate up through their discipline, within departments, through their professional organizations and journals, and in personal contacts with scholars in the same discipline rather than within their own institution. As Perkins has said: "Specialist has called to like-minded specialist, and together they have found their long-run interests better satisfied in larger organizations elsewhere than in the university which is their home base."

Cross-university communication can no longer be taken for granted. It must be worked at—another argument for the effective operation of some kind of central coordinating office in the field of international affairs.

Foundations tend to assume that our universities interact or somehow operate in a connected fashion, and that a foundation-financed experiment that proves successful at one institution will, by what Perkins has called "a process of academic osmosis," affect the programs of other universities. If the six universities visited by EWA are typical—and they are probably as little isolated as any in the nation—this assumption is unwarranted. Ideas simply are not transmitted from institution to institution by natural transfer: they must be moved from one to another, and for the moment they seem to rely for their movement on outside people and forces, rather than on the universities themselves.

The role of higher education in world affairs requires international collaboration among universities, but it is demonstrable today that government agencies, businesses, and nongovernmental organizations know more about their opposite numbers in other nations than do our universities and colleges. American educational institutions generally lack an intimate knowledge of their counterparts abroad, especially of the requirements and standards their diplomas and degrees represent, and at least until recently—when the U.S. Office of Education moved to make its accumulated files of comparative education materials more widely available—we could not make what knowledge we had about our neighbors available to our own higher education system.

The communication challenge must be met. We need new, improved mechanisms for communication within universities, among universities, and between the universities and the world outside. This may mean developing new organizational structures within universities and new patterns of relationship within the higher education community.

The communication gap is among the most serious of the unsolved problems encountered by EWA teams on campus visits. This study—like *Education and World Affairs* itself—was undertaken to help close the gap. Failure to bridge it will mean, at best, inability to share common experiences, and, at worst, continued institutional parochialism.

U.S. HIGHER EDUCATION AND WORLD AFFAIRS: A SELECTED BIBLIOGRAPHY

In the course of its study of six universities EWA learned that a bibliography of more than 800 items covering American higher education and world affairs had been compiled by the University Committee on International Affairs of Indiana University. EWA is grateful to Richard F. Crabbs and Frank W. Holmquist, who compiled that bibliography, for permission to extract from it many of the items cited in the following pages.

INTERNATIONAL ACTIVITY (GENERAL)

American Council on Education. *Education Without Boundaries.* Washington, D. C.: American Council on Education, 1959.

Bowles, Frank. "American Responsibilities in International Education," *Educational Record,* 45:19-26, Winter, 1964.

The Committee on the University and World Affairs, J. L. Morrill, chairman. *The University and World Affairs.* New York: The Ford Foundation, 1960.

Frankel, Charles (ed.). *Issues in University Education.* New York: Harper and Row, 1959.

—————. *The Neglected Aspect of Foreign Affairs: American Educational and Cultural Policy Abroad.* To be published by The Brookings Institution in November, 1965.

Henry, David D. "The American University Looks Abroad: View from the President's Office." Paper delivered at the regional conference of Education and World Affairs, East Lansing, Michigan, October 11, 1963.

International Programs of American Universities. Prepared by the Institute for Advanced Projects, the East-West Center, University of Hawaii. To be published by Michigan State University Press in late 1965.

Reed, Howard A. "Intercultural or Non-Western Studies in General Education," in *General Education: Current Ideas and Concerns,* edited by James G. Rice. Washington, D.C.: Association for Higher Education, National Education Association, 1964, 51-60.

—————. "Universalizing the Disciplines: Intercultural or Non-Western Studies in General Education," *AHE College & University Bulletin,* 17: 2, 5-6, October 15, 1964.

Taylor, Harold. "The Idea of a World College," *Saturday Review,* 47:29-32, November 14, 1964.

Weidner, Edward. *The World Role of Universities.* New York: McGraw-Hill, 1962.

Wilson, Howard E. and Florence H. Wilson. *American Higher Education and World Affairs.* Washington, D.C.: American Council on Education, 1963.

CURRICULA

The International Content of Undergraduate Curricula

American Association of Colleges for Teacher Education. *AACTE Handbook of International Education Programs.* Washington, D.C.: American Association of Colleges for Teacher Education, 1963.

Bidwell, Percy W. "Foreign Affairs in the Colleges," *Journal of Higher Education,* 35:426-33, November, 1964.

————. *Undergraduate Education in Foreign Affairs.* New York: King's Crown, 1962.

Buehrig, Edward H. "Implications for the Undergraduate Curriculum of the Growing Importance of International Affairs and the Mounting Need to Understand World Cultures," in *Current Issues in Higher Education, 1961.* Washington, D.C.: Association for Higher Education, National Education Association, 1961.

The Challenge of a Revolutionary World: Progress Report, 1964. Albany, New York: State Education Department, 1964.

The Committee on the College and World Affairs, John W. Nason, chairman. *The College and World Affairs.* New York: The Hazen Foundation, 1964.

McClelland, Charles A. *College Teaching of International Relations: Problems of Organization and Collaboration.* San Francisco: Department of International Relations, San Francisco State College, 1962.

Parker, William Riley. *The National Interest and Foreign Languages.* Rev. ed. Washington, D.C.: U.S. National Commission for UNESCO, Department of State, 1957.

Swift, Richard N. *World Affairs and the College Curriculum.* Washington, D.C.: American Council on Education, 1959.

Teacher and Curriculum. Report of the Conference on American Education in a Revolutionary World held at Gould House, Dobbs Ferry, New York, April 22-24, 1964, under the joint sponsorship of the U.S. National Commission for UNESCO and the New York State Education Department. Washington, D.C.: U.S. National Commission for UNESCO, 1964.

Area Studies

American Universities Field Staff. *A Select Bibliography: Asia, Africa, Eastern Europe, Latin America.* New York: American Universities Field Staff, 1960. *Supplements,* 1961, 1963.

Area Studies and the Library. Proceedings of the Conference on Area Studies and the Library, May 20-22, 1965. To be published by the University of Chicago Press in January, 1966.

Association of American Colleges. Commission on International Understanding. *Non-Western Studies in the Liberal Arts College.* Washington, D.C.: Association of American Colleges, 1964.

Bennett, Wendell C. *Area Studies in American Universities.* New York: Social Science Research Council, 1951.

Bigelow, Donald N. and Lyman H. Legters (eds.). "The Non-Western World in Higher Education," *The Annals* of the American Academy of Political and Social Science, Vol. 356, November, 1964 (entire issue).

Boardman, Eugene P. (ed.). *Asian Studies in Liberal Education.* Washington, D.C.: Association of American Colleges, 1959.

Creel, H. G. (ed.). *Chinese Civilization in Liberal Education.* Chicago: University of Chicago, 1959.

de Bary, William Theodore. *A Guide to Oriental Classics.* New York: Columbia University, 1964.

————. "Education for a World Community," *Liberal Education,* 50:437-57, December, 1964.

————. and Ainslie Embree (eds.). *Approaches to Asian Civilizations.* New York: Columbia University, 1964.

Ehrman, Edith (ed.). "Guide to Asian Studies in Undergraduate Education." *Newsletter* of the Association for Asian Studies, Vol. 10, Supplement No. 1, September, 1964.

Hart, Henry C. *Campus India.* East Lansing: Michigan State University, 1961.

Legters, Lyman H. *The National Defense Education Act and Latin American Studies.* Austin: Institute of Latin American Studies, University of Texas, 1964.

Library of Congress. Africana Section. *Africa South of the Sahara: A Selected Annotated List of Writings,* edited by Helen Conover. Washington, D.C.: Library of Congress, 1964.

————. Hispanic Foundation. *Education, Spanish America: An Annotated Bibliography,* edited by Russell G. Davis. Washington, D.C.: Library of Congress, 1965. (Handbook of Latin American Studies, No. 25.)

Morehouse, Ward (ed.). *Asian Studies in Liberal Arts Colleges.* Washington, D.C.: Association of American Colleges, 1961.

———— (ed.). *Foreign Area Studies and the College Library.* New York: Foreign Area Materials Center, University of the State of New York, State Education Department, 1965. (Occasional Paper No. 1.)

Sauvaget, Jean. *Introduction to the History of the Muslim East: A Bibliographic Guide,* edited by Claude Cahen. Berkeley: University of California, 1965.

Singer, Milton. *Introducing India in Liberal Education.* Chicago: University of Chicago, 1957.

Teng, S. Y. (ed.). *Asian Studies and State Universities.* Bloomington: Indiana University, 1960.

Undergraduate Instruction in Critical Languages and Area Studies. Recommendations and report of a conference held at Princeton University, October 12-13, 1964. (Out of print.)

Ward, F. Champion. "What Did Confucious Say?: Animadversions on the Tribal Curriculum," *Journal of General Education,* 11:3-6, January, 1958.

Training U.S. Specialists for International Service

Cleveland, Harlan, Gerard J. Mangone and John Clarke Adams. *The Overseas Americans.* New York: McGraw-Hill, 1960.

Esman, Milton J. *Needed: An Education and Research Base to Support America's Expanded Commitments Overseas.* Pittsburgh: University of Pittsburgh, 1961.

Mangone, Gerard J. "How Can We Better Educate Americans to Work and to Study Abroad," in *1960: Current Issues in Higher Education.* Washington, D.C.: Association of Higher Education, National Education Association, 1960.

EDUCATIONAL EXCHANGE

General

Committee on Educational Interchange Policy. *College and University Programs of Academic Exchange.* New York: Institute of International Education, March, 1960.

Cormack, Margaret L. *An Evaluation of Research on Educational Exchange.* Washington, D.C.: Bureau of Educational and Cultural Affairs, Department of State, 1962.

————— and Edward W. Weidner. *The International Exchange of Teachers and Students.* To be published by Prentice-Hall in 1965.

Klineberg, Otto. "Research on International Exchanges in Education, Science, and Culture." Working paper prepared for an International Social Science Council meeting on the above topic, April 8-10, 1964, in Tel Aviv.

Mestenhauser, Josef A. (ed.). *Research in Programs for Foreign Students: A Report of the Waldenwoods Seminar.* New York: National Association for Foreign Student Affairs, 1961.

Porter, Robert D. (ed.). *Selected Studies in Intercultural Education.* New York: National Association for Foreign Student Affairs, 1962.

Sharp, Paul F. "International Commitments of the American College," *Liberal Education,* 50:321-27, October, 1964.

Teacher and Scholar Abroad: First-Person Reports of the U.S. Exchange Program. Washington, D.C.: Bureau of Educational and Cultural Affairs, Department of State, September, 1964.

Warmbrunn, Werner (ed.). *Research Studies in Intercultural Education: Reviews and Implications for Exchange of Persons.* New York: National Association for Foreign Student Affairs, 1960.

U.S. Nationals Abroad

Consultative Service on U.S. Undergraduate Study Abroad. *Undergraduate Study Abroad.* New York: Institute of International Education, 1964.

Garraty, John A. and Walter Adams. *From Main Street to the Left Bank.* East Lansing: Michigan State University, 1959.

Goodwin, Leonard. *American Professors in Asia: A Study of the Selection and Adaptation of Fifty American Professors Who Went to India, Pakistan and Korea Under the Fulbright-Hays Program During 1962-63.* Washington, D.C.: Bureau of Educational and Cultural Affairs, Department of State, June, 1964.

Shank, D. J. "Junior Year Abroad: A Critical Look," *Institute of International Education News Bulletin,* 36:11-19, October, 1960.

Foreign Nationals in the United States

American Association of Collegiate Registrars and Admission Officers. *Guides to the Academic Placement of Students from Foreign Countries in Educa-*

tional Institutions in the U.S. Washington, D.C.: AACRAO. The pamphlet series, edited by William H. Strain, includes: Canada (1957), Germany (1957), Korea (1958), Thailand (1959), Austria (1961), Netherlands (1961), Mexico (1961), Venezuela (1961), Caribbean (1961), Afghanistan (1961), Tanganyika (1961), Rumania (1961), Hong Kong (1961), Philippines (1962), Argentina (1962), Italy (1962), United Kingdom (1963), France (1964), India (1964), Japan (1964), Switzerland (1964), Lebanon (1964).

Barakat, Mohamed Khalifa et al. *Studies on the Role as Culture Carriers of Eastern Students Who Received Their University Education in Western Countries: Report on the United Arab Republic's Study.* Paris: UNESCO, 1964. (UNESCO/SS/COM/6).

Beals, Ralph L. and Norman D. Humphrey. *No Frontier to Learning: The Mexican Student in the United States.* Minneapolis: University of Minnesota, 1957.

Bennett, John W., Robert K. McKnight and Herbert Passin. *In Search of Identity.* Minneapolis: University of Minnesota, 1958.

Bowles, Frank. *Access to Higher Education.* Report of the international study of university admissions. New York: Columbia University, 1963.

Coelho, George V. *Changing Images of America; A Study of Indian Students' Perceptions.* Glencoe, Ill.: Free Press, 1958.

———— (ed.). "Impacts of Studying Abroad." *Journal of Social Issues,* 18:1, 1962 (entire issue).

Committee on Educational Interchange Policy. *Foreign Professors and Research Scholars at U.S. Colleges and Universities.* New York: Institute of International Education, 1963.

Committee on the Foreign Student in American Colleges and Universities. *The College, the University and the Foreign Student.* New York: National Association for Foreign Student Affairs, 1963.

Cotner, Thomas. *Evaluation of Educational Exchange Programs Now in Operation* (Report ACLS-22110). Washington, D.C.: Office of Education, Department of Health, Education and Welfare, 1963.

Davis, James M. "Some Trends in International Educational Exchange," *Comparative Education Review,* 8:48-57, June, 1964.

The Foreign Student: Whom Shall We Welcome? New York: Education and World Affairs, 1964.

Fox, Melvin J. "Foreign Students in American Colleges," *College Board Review,* Winter, 1962. Also a Ford Foundation reprint.

Harari, Maurice. "American Higher Education and the Foreign Student: Laissez-Faire Versus Planning." Speech delivered at the annual conference of the National Association for Foreign Student Affairs, Philadelphia, April 29, 1965.

Higbee, Homer. *The Status of Foreign Student Advising in United States Universities and Colleges.* East Lansing, Michigan: Institute of Research on Overseas Programs, Michigan State University, 1961.

Kuppusamy, B. *Studies on the Role as Culture Carriers of Eastern Students Who Received Their University Education in Western Countries: Report on the Indian Study.* Paris: UNESCO, 1964. (UNESCO/SS/COM/7)

Lambert, Richard D. (ed.). "America Through Foreign Eyes." *The Annals* of the American Academy of Political and Social Science, Vol. 295, September, 1954 (entire issue).

────── and Marvin Bressler. *Indian Students on an American Campus.* Minneapolis: University of Minnesota, 1956.

Lundstedt, Sven (ed.). "Human Factors in Cross-Cultural Adjustment." *Journal of Social Issues,* Vol. 19, July, 1963 (entire issue).

Raushenbush, Esther. *The Fulbright Professor Meets the American College.* New York: John Hay Whitney Foundation, 1962.

Ruedisili, Chester H. and Harry Sharp. *Survey of Foreign Students at the University of Wisconsin and Also of Foreign Alumni Who Have Returned to Their Home Countries.* Madison: University of Wisconsin, 1965.

Sanders, Irwin T. *The Professional Education of Students from Other Lands.* New York: Council on Social Work Education, 1963.

Seltiz, Claire, Stuart W. Cook and June R. Christ. *Attitudes and Social Relations of Foreign Students.* Minneapolis: University of Minnesota, 1963.

Smith, M. Brewster (ed.). "Attitudes and Adjustment on Cross-Cultural Contact: Recent Studies of Foreign Students." *Journal of Social Issues,* Vol. 12, 1956 (entire issue).

Strain, William H. "Which Foreign Students Should U.S. Institutions Admit?" *Phi Delta Kappan,* 46:332-35, March, 1965.

Thurber, Clarence E. and Edward W. Weidner. *Technical Assistance in Training Administrators: Lessons from the American Experience.* Bloomington: Institute of Training for Public Service, Department of Government, Indiana University, January, 1962. (Selected Papers on Public Administration, No. 2.)

Training for Leadership and Service: Proceedings of the National Conference on the International Training Programs of AID, June 25-26, 1962. Washington, D.C.: Agency for International Development, 1962. (Out of print.)

U.S. College and University Policies, Practices and Problems in Admitting Foreign Students. New York: Institute of International Education, 1965.

Useem, John and Ruth Hill Useem. *The Western Educated Man in India.* New York: Dryden Press, 1955.

INSTITUTIONAL RELATIONSHIPS

U.S. Government Policy in International Education

American Assembly. *Cultural Affairs and Foreign Relations,* edited by Robert Blum. Englewood Cliffs, N.J.: Prentice-Hall, 1963.

Coombs, Philip H. *The Fourth Dimension of Foreign Policy: Educational and Cultural Affairs.* New York: Harper and Row, 1964.

Cotner, Thomas E. *A Summary of the Exchange and Training Programs Administered by the Bureau of International Education, Office of Education, U.S. Department of Health, Education, and Welfare 1939-1964.* Washington, D.C.: Office of Education, 1964.

Haviland, H. Field, Jr. "Federal Programs of International Education," in *Higher Education and the Federal Government,* edited by Charles G. Dobbins. Washington, D.C.: American Council on Education, 1963.

Laves, Walter H. C. *Toward a National Effort in International and Cultural Affairs.* 87th Congress, 1st Session, House Committee on Foreign Affairs, Doc. No. 199. Also, in slightly abreviated form, a pamphlet in the International Information and Cultural Series 78, Department of State Publication 7238, 1961.

–––––– and Charles A. Thompson. *Cultural Relations and U.S. Foreign Policy.* Bloomington: Indiana University, 1963.

U.S. Advisory Commission on International Educational and Cultural Affairs. *A Beacon of Hope: The Exchange of Persons Program.* Washington, D.C.: Government Printing Office, 1963.

––––––. *A Sequel to a Beacon of Hope: The Exchange of Persons Program.* Washington, D.C.: Government Printing Office, 1964.

The U.S. Office of Education: A New International Dimension. New York: Education and World Affairs, 1964.

U.S. Higher Education and International Organizations

Laves, Walter H. C. and Charles A. Thompson. *UNESCO: Purpose, Progress, Prospects.* Bloomington: Indiana University, 1957.

Relationships of U.S. Higher Education with U.S. Government in International Education

Bell, David E. "The University Contribution to the Developing Nations." Address delivered at the regional conference of Education and World Affairs, East Lansing, Michigan, October 11, 1963.

Caldwell, Lynton K. "The Universities and International Technical Assistance," *Journal of Higher Education,* 36:266-73, May, 1965.

Department of State. External Research Staff (ed.). *The Scholar and the Policy Maker.* A series of talks given at the plenary session of the Association for Asian Studies, Mayflower Hotel, Washington, D.C., March 20, 1964. Washington, D.C.: Department of State, External Research Paper 151, 1964.

Gardner, John W. *AID and the Universities.* New York: Education and World Affairs, 1964.

Rosenzweig, Robert M. "Universities and the Foreign Assistance Program," *Journal of Higher Education,* 35:359-66, October, 1964.

Shiver, Elizabeth N. (ed.). *Education and the Modernizing of Nations.* Summary proceedings of a conference sponsored by the Commission of International Education of the American Council on Education and Wayne State University, September, 1964. Washington, D.C.: American Council on Education, 1964.

Silvert, Kalman H. "American Academic Ethics and Social Research Abroad: The Lesson of Project Camelot." *American Universities Field Staff Report,* 12:3 (entire issue). (West Coast South America Series.)

Wells, Herman B. "Widening Horizons," *Educational Record,* 38:136-40, April, 1957.

U.S. Institutions of Higher Education and International Development

Adams, Walter and John Garraty. *Is the World Our Campus?* East Lansing: Michigan State University, 1960.

Butts, R. Freeman. *American Education in International Development.* New York: Harper and Row, 1963.

Cerych, Ladislav. *Educational Aid to Developing Countries* (draft report). Bologne, France: The Atlantic Institute, 1963.

Curle, Adam. *Educational Strategy for Developing Societies.* London: Tavistock, 1963.

Enarson, Harold L. "The Universities' Stake in the Developing Nations," *Educational Record,* 45:27-32, Winter, 1964.

Harbison, Frederick. "Education for Development," *Scientific American,* 209: 140-47, September, 1963.

—————— and Charles A. Myers. *Education, Manpower and Economic Growth.* New York: McGraw-Hill, 1964.

International Rural Development. Washington, D.C.: Agency for International Development, Department of State, 1964.

Marvel, William W. "The Place of Education and Human Resource Development in Foreign Assistance." Report on a conference organized by the Carnegie Corporation and held at Williamsburg, Virginia, April 8-10, 1962.

National Planning Association. Special Policy Committee on Technical Cooperation. *The Role of Universities in Technical Cooperation.* Washington, D.C.: National Planning Association, 1955.

Robinson, Mary E. *Education for Social Change: Establishing Institutes of Public and Business Administration Abroad.* Washington, D.C.: The Brookings Institution, 1961.

Smuckler, Ralph H. "University Responsibilities and International Development Research." Presented at the American Council on Education meeting on "University Goals and Responsibilities in Foreign Operations," May 12-13, 1965.

RESOURCE MATERIALS

Handbooks, Guides and Reference Works

American Agencies Interested in International Affairs. New York: Praeger, 1964.

Department of State. External Research Staff. *Language and Area Study Programs in American Universities.* Washington, D.C.: Department of State, 1964.

——————. External Research Staff. *Research Centers on the Developing Areas.* Washington, D.C.: Bureau of Intelligence and Research, Agency for International Development, November, 1964.

Handbook on International Study: For Foreign Nationals. New York: Institute of International Education, 1965.

Handbook on International Study: For U.S. Nationals. New York: Institute of International Education, 1965.

International Institute for Educational Planning. *Educational Planning: A Directory of Training and Research Institutions.* Paris: International Institute for Educational Planning, 1964.

Open Doors, 1965. New York: Institute of International Education, 1965.

Some U.S. Government Agencies Engaged in International Activities. Washington, D.C.: Bureau of Educational and Cultural Affairs, Department of State, November, 1963.

United Nations Educational, Scientific and Cultural Organization. *UNESCO Handbook of International Exchanges.* Paris: UNESCO, 1965.

Bibliographies

Department of State. External Research Staff. *Cross-Cultural Education: A Bibliography of Government-Sponsored and Private Research on Foreign Students and Trainees in the U.S. and in Other Countries, 1946-1964.* Washington, D.C.: Bureau of Intelligence and Research, Department of State, April, 1965.

————. Policy Review and Research Staff. *International Educational and Cultural Exchange: A Selective Bibliography of Materials on Both Governmental and Private Programs.* Washington, D.C.: Bureau of Educational and Cultural Affairs, Department of State, June, 1963.

Teacher Exchange Opportunities, 1965-66, summer seminars, teacher research, study for American elementary, secondary and college teachers under the International Educational Exchange Program of the Department of State, the Office of Education, and the Department of Health, Education and Welfare. Washington, D.C.: Office of Education, Department of Health, Education and Welfare, 1964.

Teaching Abroad (annual). Paris: UNESCO.

INDEX